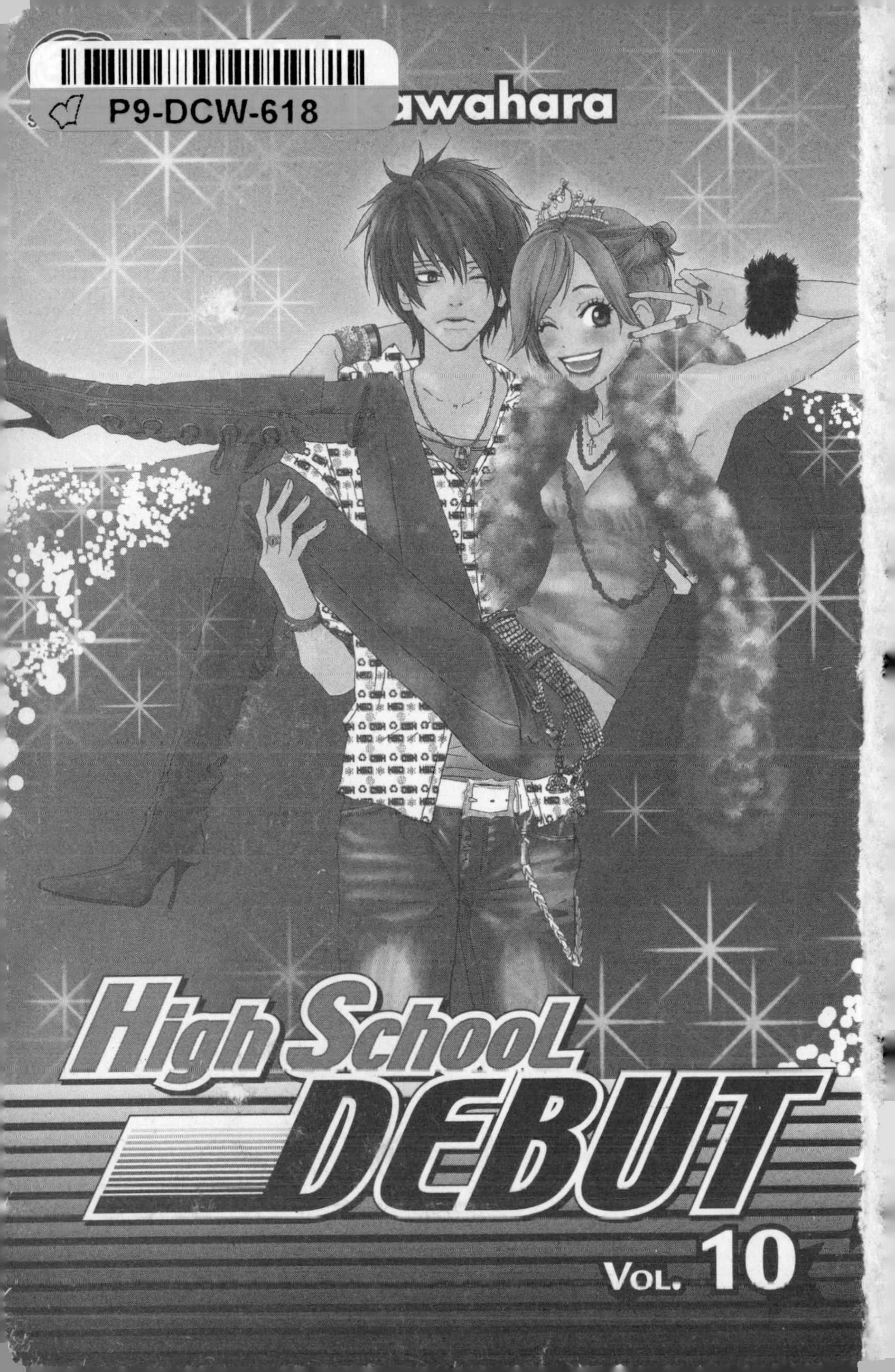
awahara
High School
DEBUT
VOL. 10

High School DEBUT

Contents

Story Thus Far...

High school student Haruna used to spend all her time playing softball in junior high, but now she wants to give her all to finding true love instead! While her "love coach" Yoh is training her on how to be popular with guys, the two of them start dating.

Now that Haruna is in her second year, it's time for the school sports festival. Yoh is elected to be a school captain for the event! He doesn't want to participate, but he tries his hardest since he feels obligated after being elected. Haruna is right there to support him, but Asaoka has been hanging around her a lot in Yoh's absence... Is Asaoka trying to seduce Haruna?!

Yoh tells Asaoka that he knows that he likes Haruna but to give her up. Asaoka, however, will only give Haruna up if Yoh does better than him at the sports festival. Now Yoh has to put in an even greater effort!

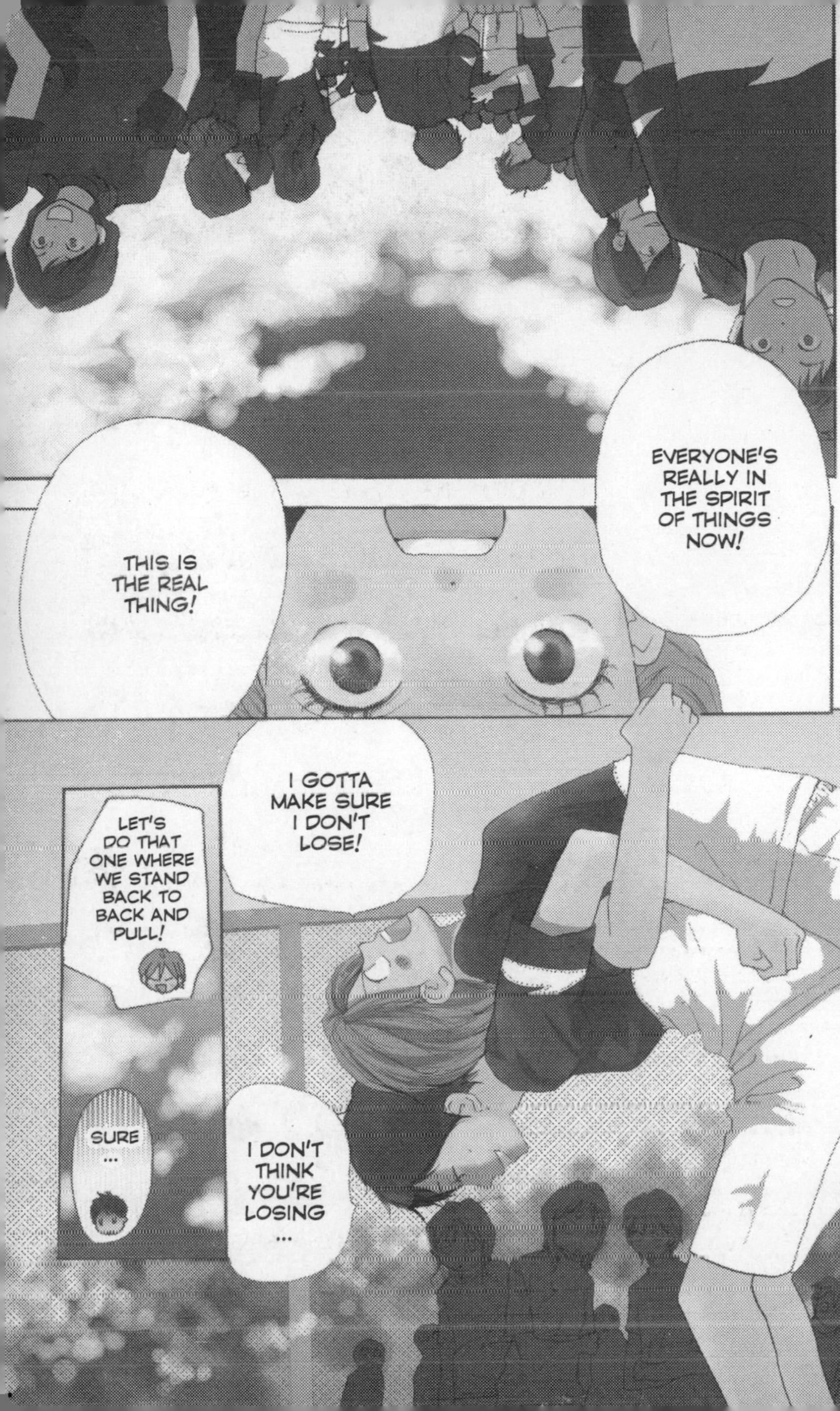

EVERYONE'S REALLY IN THE SPIRIT OF THINGS NOW!
THIS IS THE REAL THING!
I GOTTA MAKE SURE I DON'T LOSE!
I DON'T THINK YOU'RE LOSING ...
LET'S DO THAT ONE WHERE WE STAND BACK TO BACK AND PULL!
SURE ...

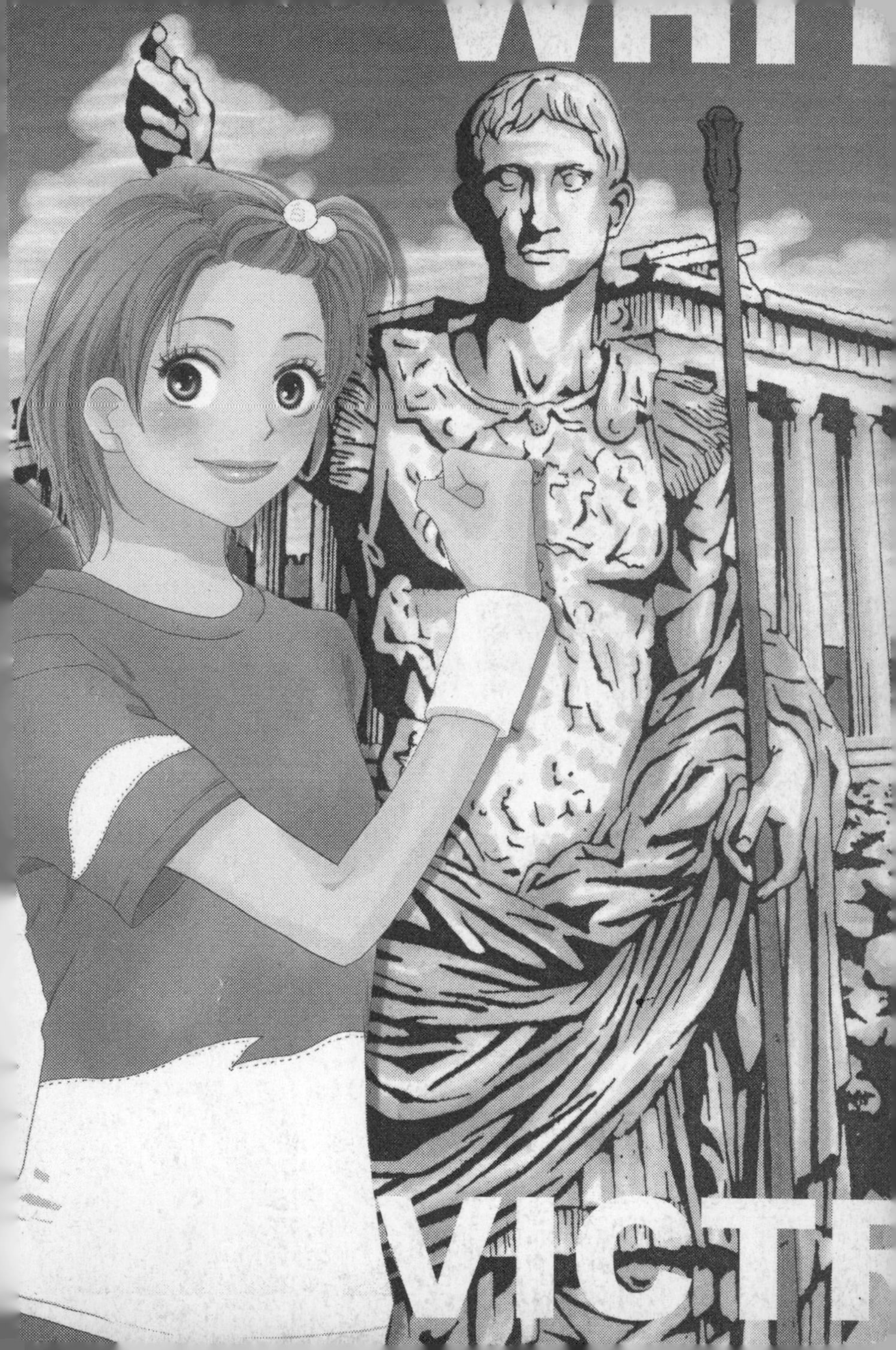
VICT

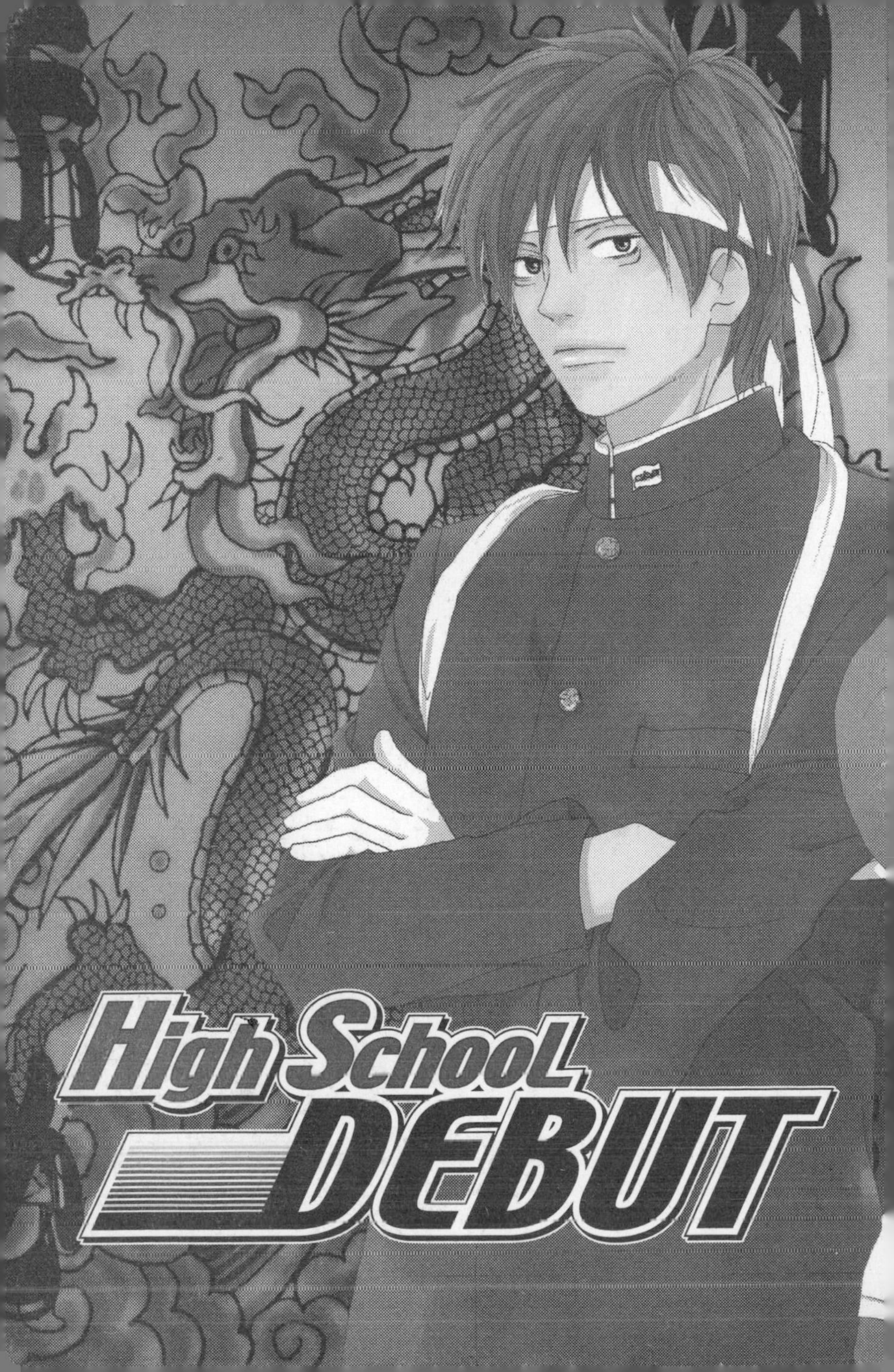
High School
DEBUT

I GIVE MY BEST
EVERY TIME!

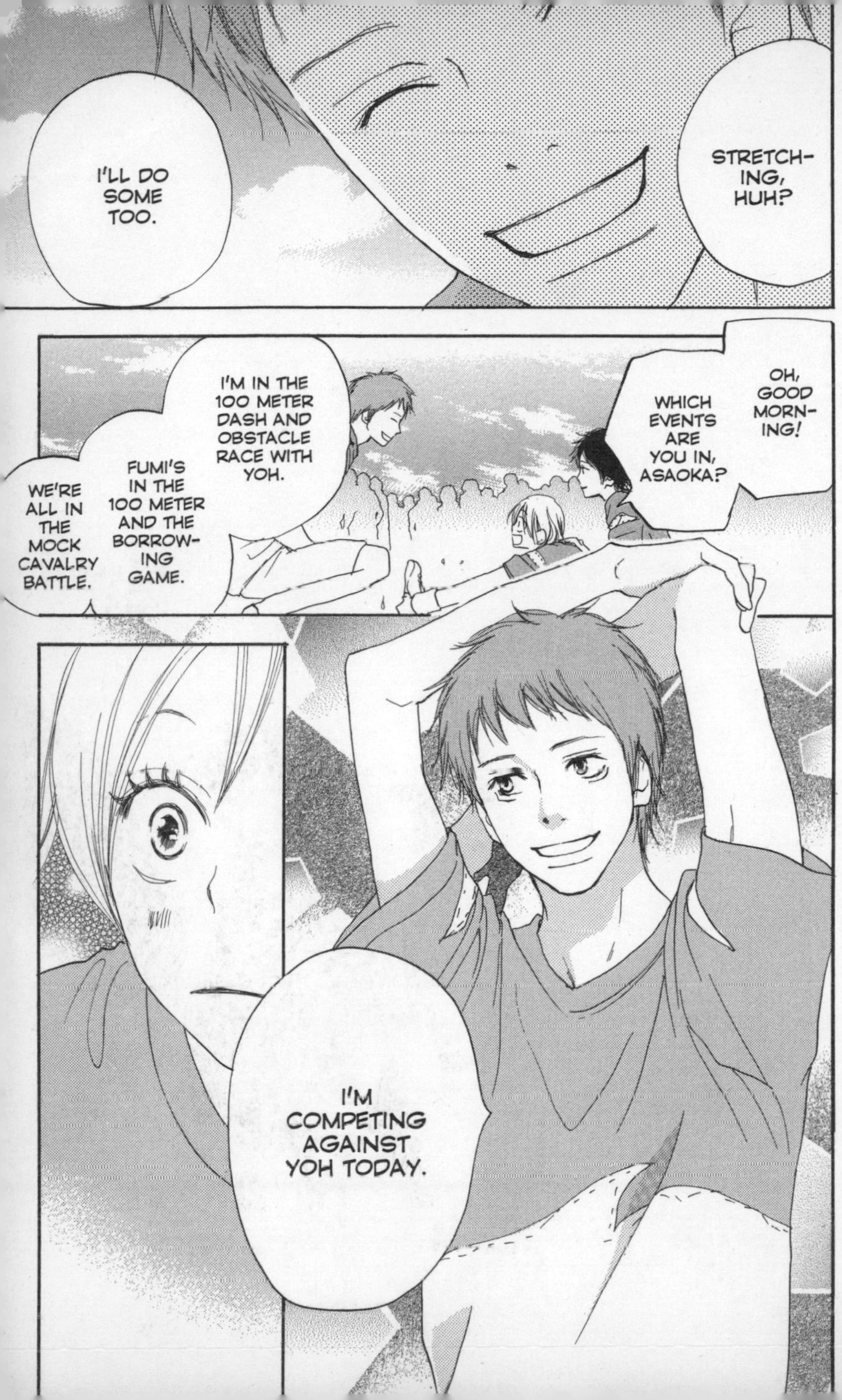
STRETCHING, HUH?
I'LL DO SOME TOO.
OH, GOOD MORNING!
WHICH EVENTS ARE YOU IN, ASAOKA?
I'M IN THE 100 METER DASH AND OBSTACLE RACE WITH YOH.
FUMI'S IN THE 100 METER AND THE BORROWING GAME.
WE'RE ALL IN THE MOCK CAVALRY BATTLE.
I'M COMPETING AGAINST YOH TODAY.

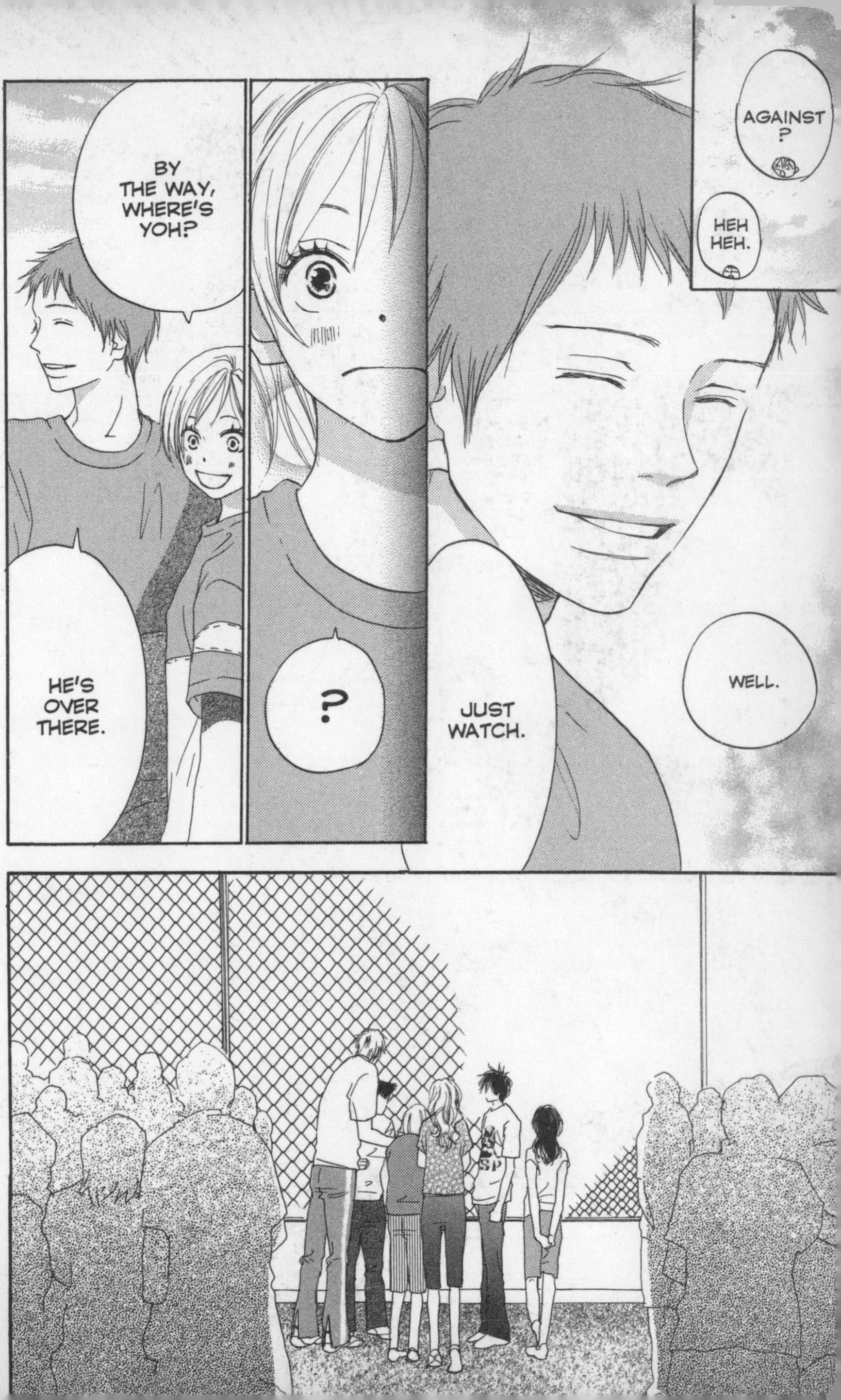
AGAINST?
HEH HEH.
WELL.
JUST WATCH.
?
BY THE WAY, WHERE'S YOH?
HE'S OVER THERE.

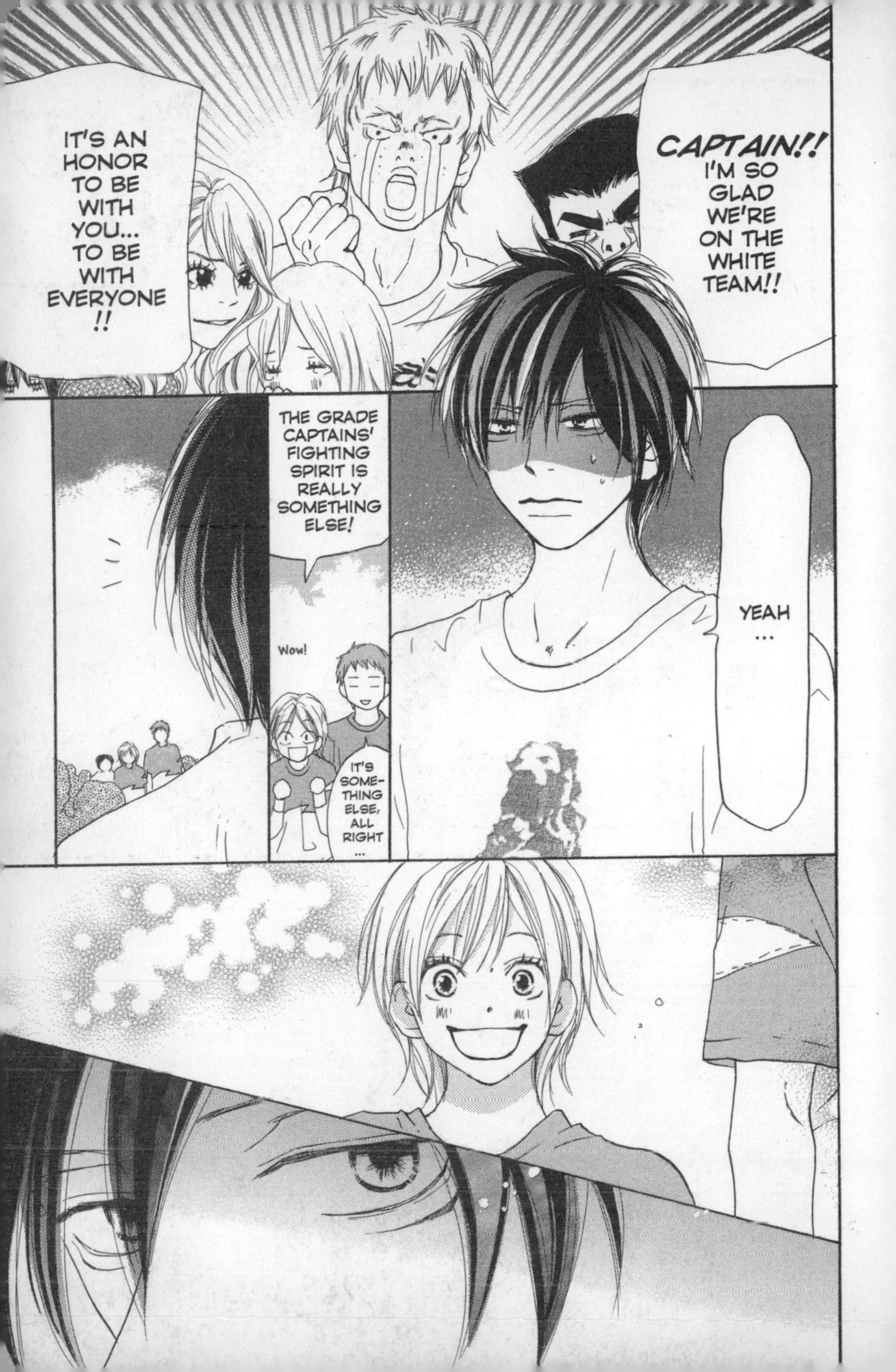
CAPTAIN!! I'M SO GLAD WE'RE ON THE WHITE TEAM!!
IT'S AN HONOR TO BE WITH YOU... TO BE WITH EVERYONE !!
YEAH ...
THE GRADE CAPTAINS' FIGHTING SPIRIT IS REALLY SOMETHING ELSE!
Wow!
IT'S SOME-THING ELSE, ALL RIGHT ...

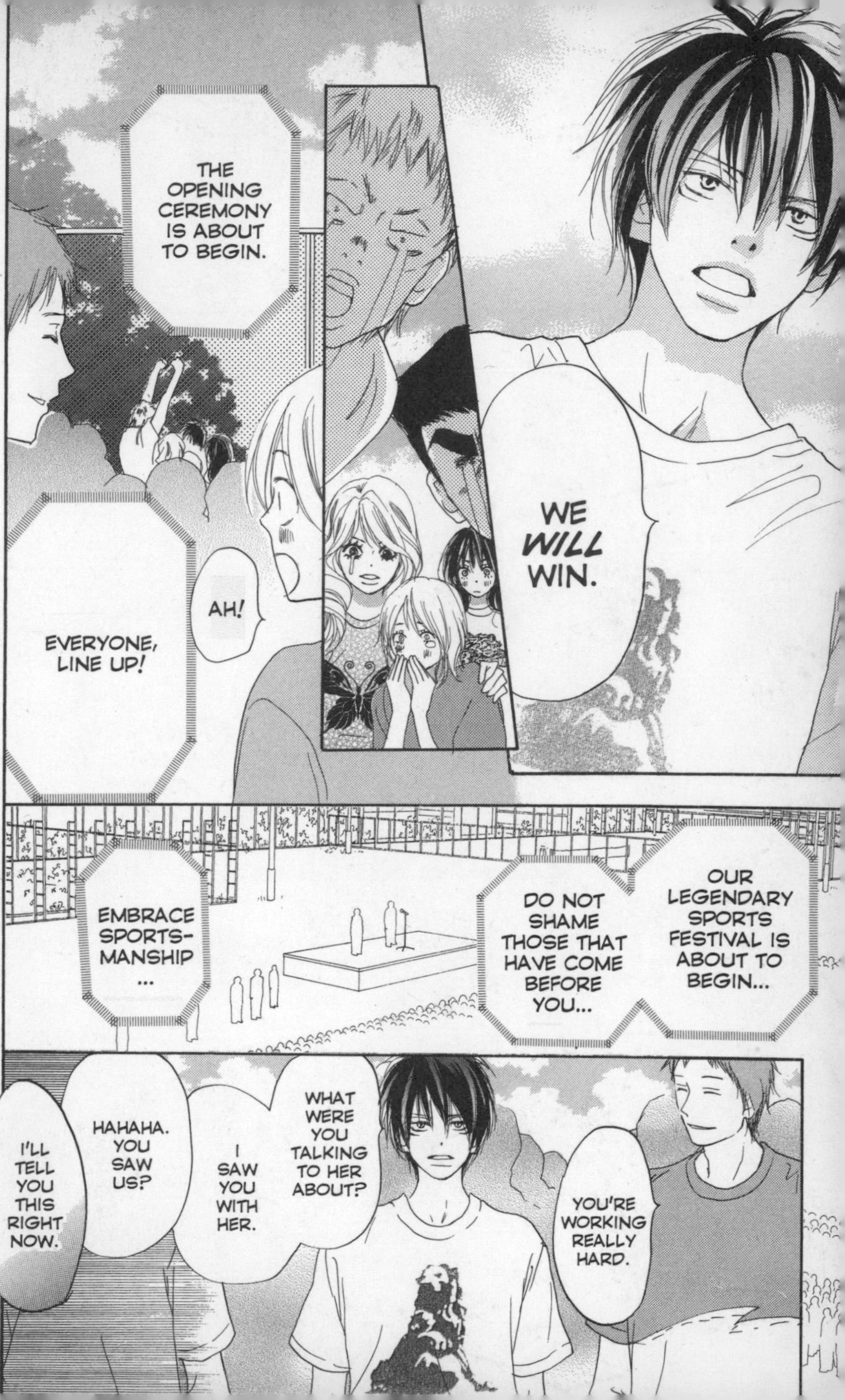
WE *WILL* WIN.
THE OPENING CEREMONY IS ABOUT TO BEGIN.
AH!
EVERYONE, LINE UP!
OUR LEGENDARY SPORTS FESTIVAL IS ABOUT TO BEGIN...
DO NOT SHAME THOSE THAT HAVE COME BEFORE YOU...
EMBRACE SPORTS-MANSHIP ...
YOU'RE WORKING REALLY HARD.
WHAT WERE YOU TALKING TO HER ABOUT?
I SAW YOU WITH HER.
HAHAHA. YOU SAW US?
I'LL TELL YOU THIS RIGHT NOW.

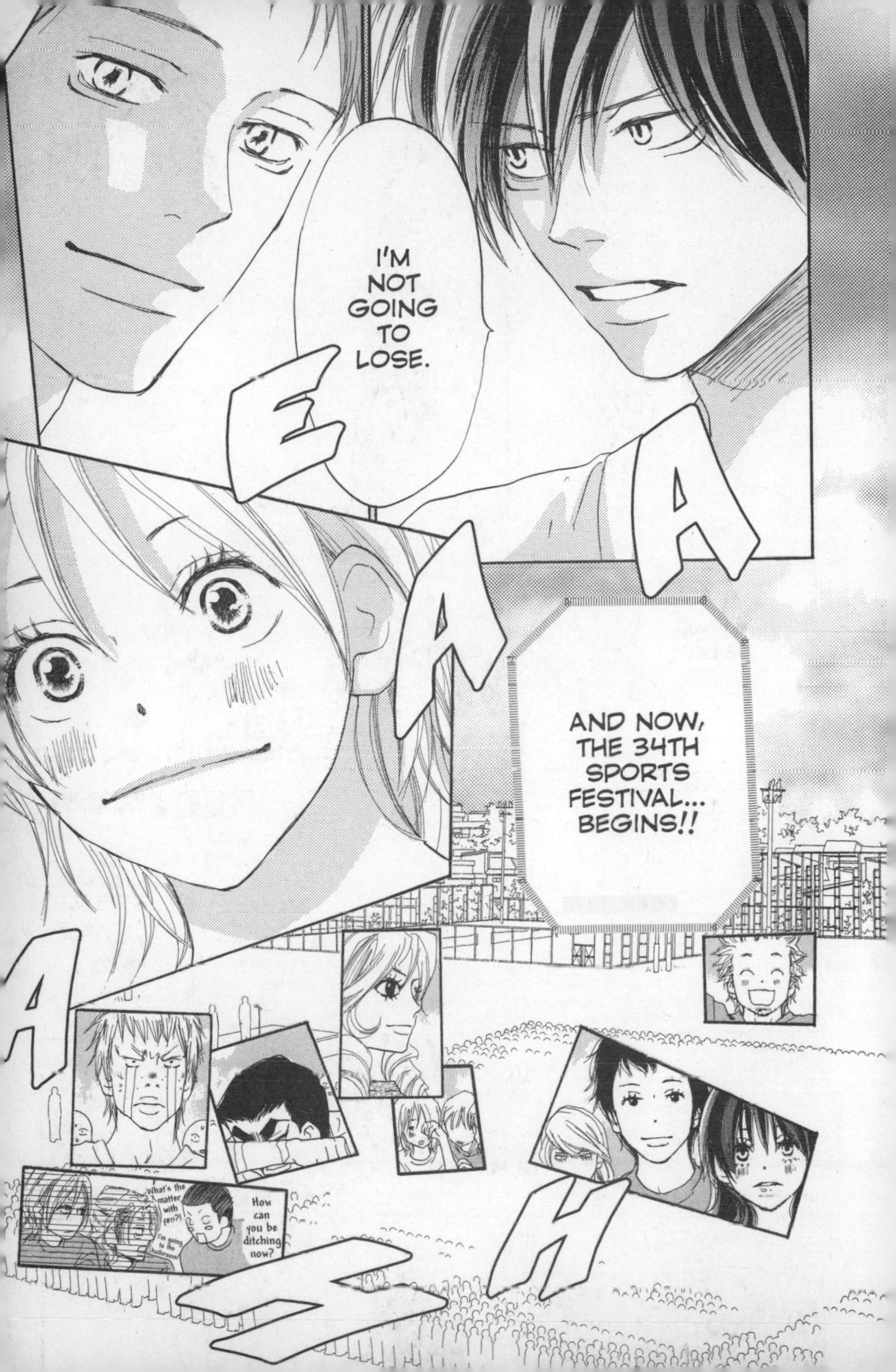
I'M NOT GOING TO LOSE.
AND NOW, THE 34TH SPORTS FESTIVAL... BEGINS!!
How can you be ditching now?
What's the matter with you?!
I'm going to the bathroom!

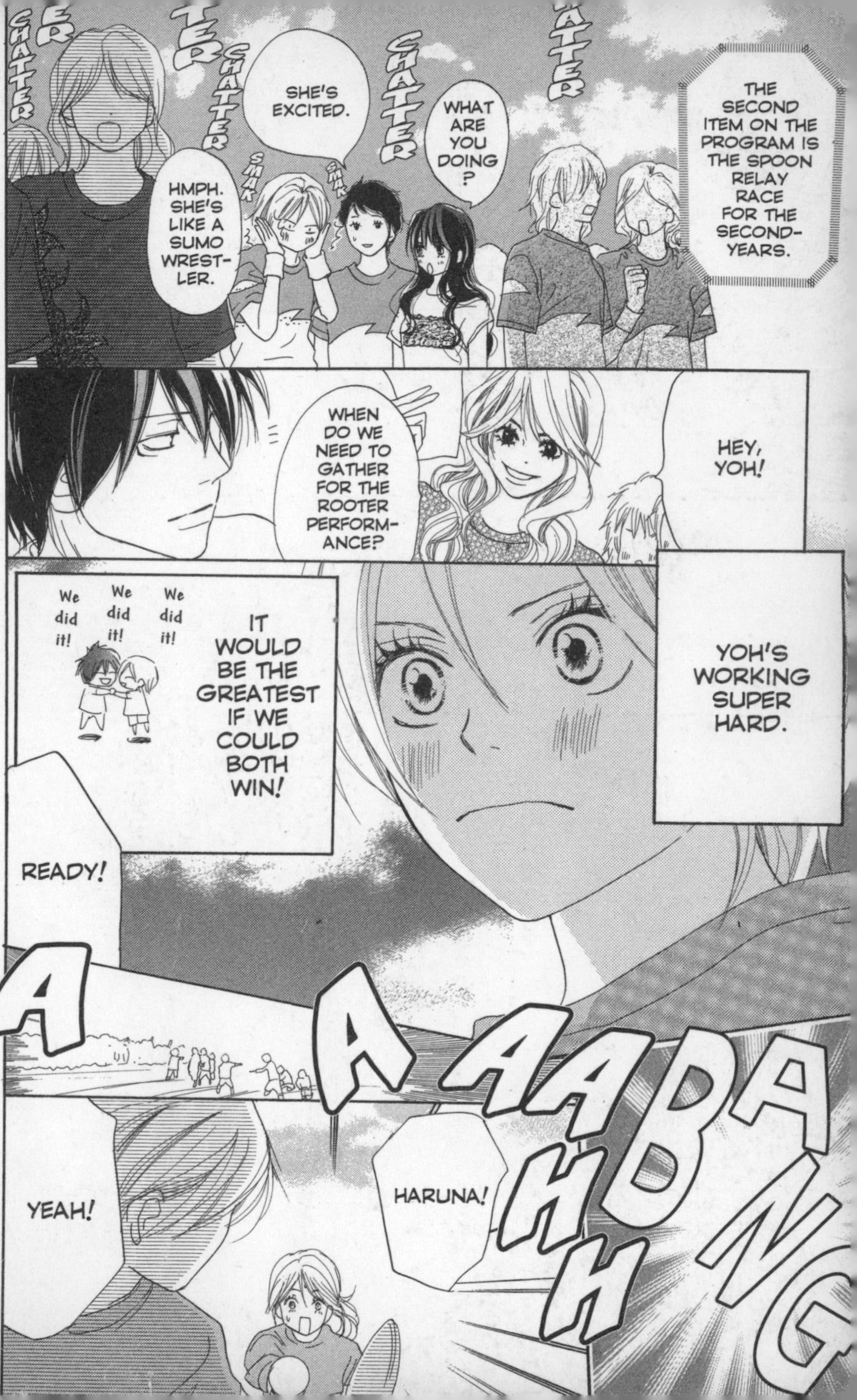
THE SECOND ITEM ON THE PROGRAM IS THE SPOON RELAY RACE FOR THE SECOND-YEARS.
CHATTER
CHATTER
WHAT ARE YOU DOING?
SHE'S EXCITED.
SMAK
SMAK
CHATTER
CHATTER
HMPH. SHE'S LIKE A SUMO WRESTLER.
HEY, YOH!
WHEN DO WE NEED TO GATHER FOR THE ROOTER PERFORMANCE?
YOH'S WORKING SUPER HARD.
IT WOULD BE THE GREATEST IF WE COULD BOTH WIN!
We did it!
We did it!
We did it!
READY!
A A AA HH H
DA B D NG
HARUNA!
YEAH!

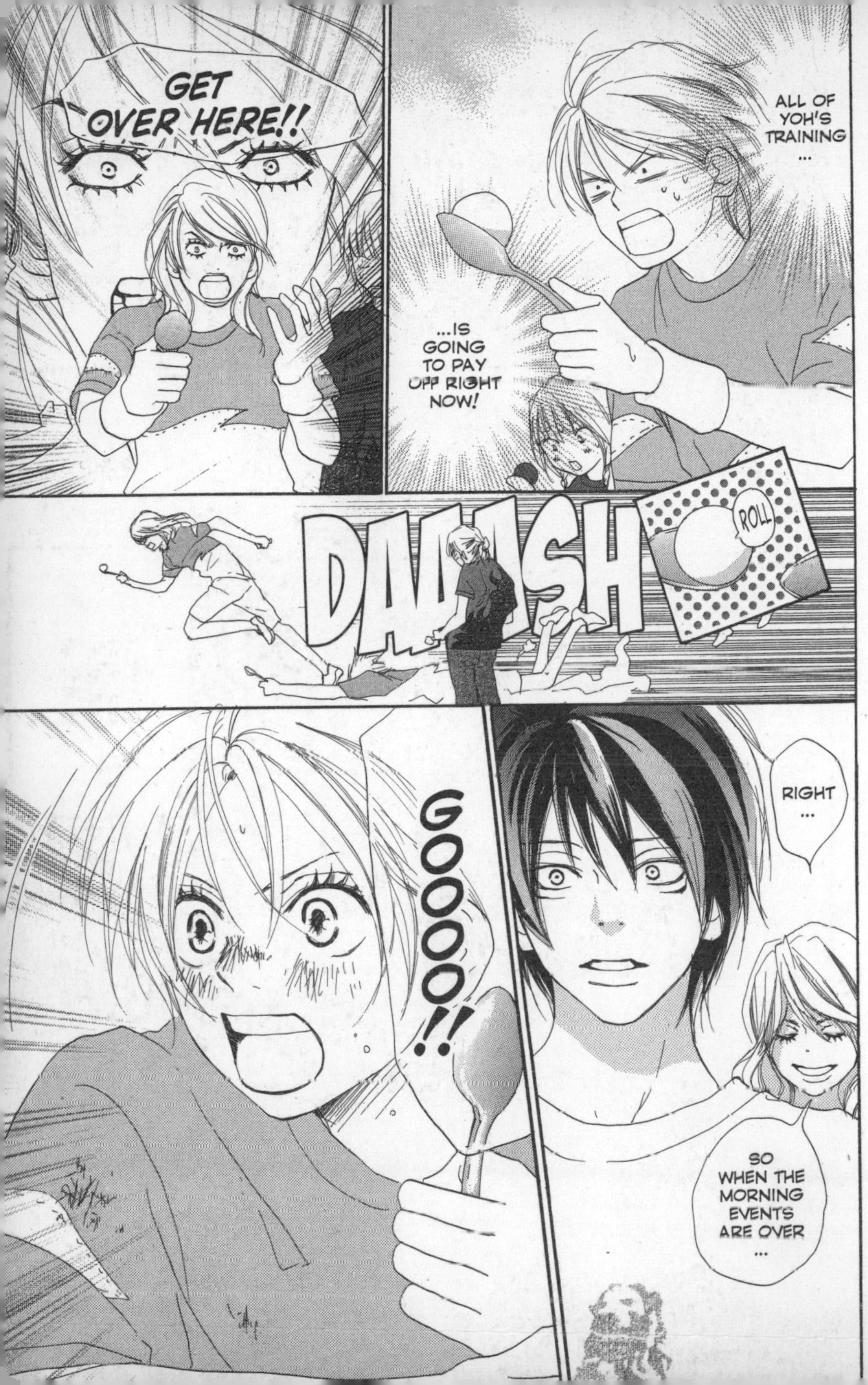
ALL OF YOH'S TRAINING ...
...IS GOING TO PAY OFF RIGHT NOW!
GET OVER HERE!!
ROLL
DASH
RIGHT ...
SO WHEN THE MORNING EVENTS ARE OVER ...
GOOOOOO!!

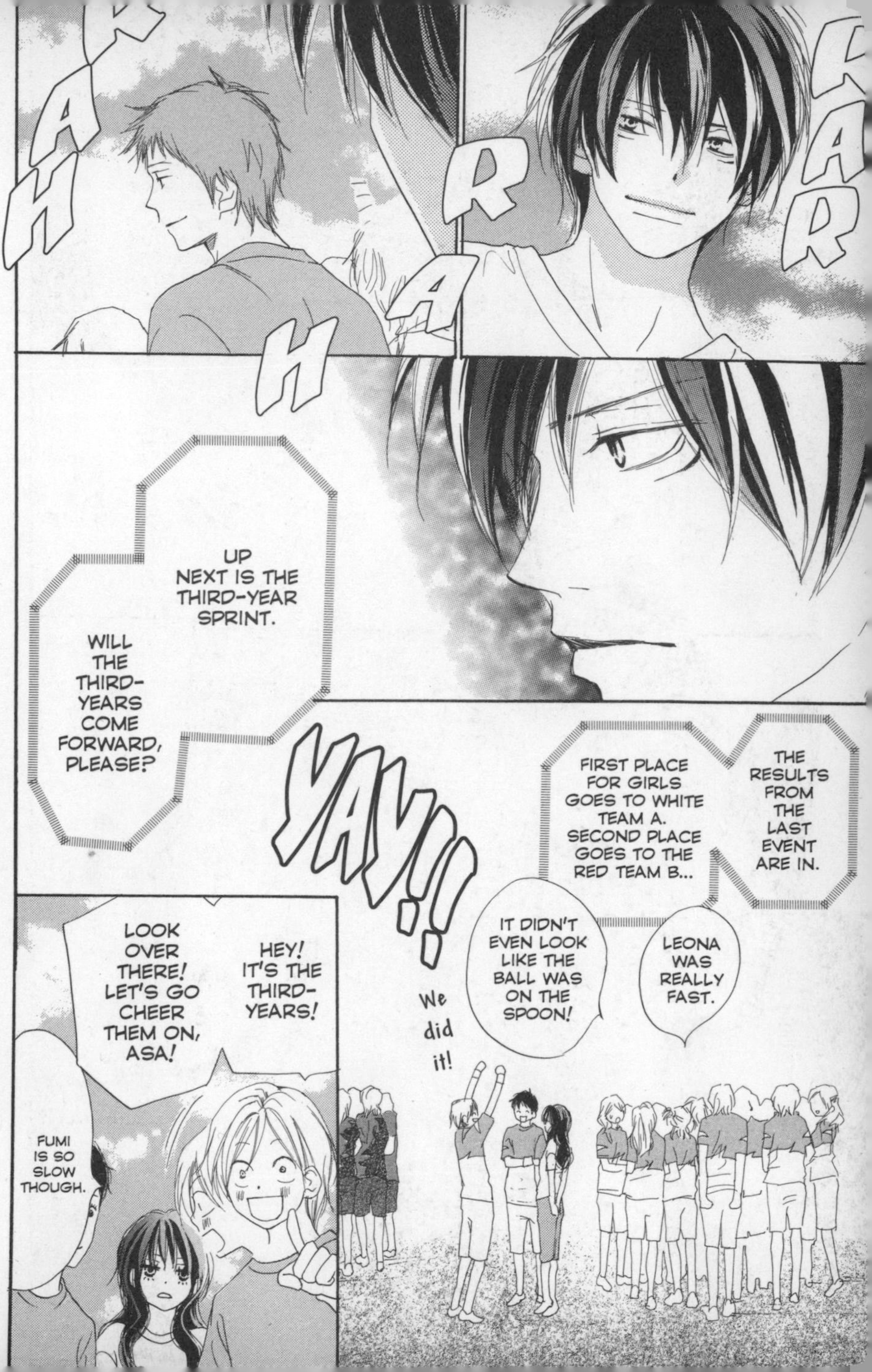
RAH
KAH
UP NEXT IS THE THIRD-YEAR SPRINT.
WILL THE THIRD-YEARS COME FORWARD, PLEASE?
THE RESULTS FROM THE LAST EVENT ARE IN.
FIRST PLACE FOR GIRLS GOES TO WHITE TEAM A. SECOND PLACE GOES TO THE RED TEAM B...
YAY!!
LEONA WAS REALLY FAST.
IT DIDN'T EVEN LOOK LIKE THE BALL WAS ON THE SPOON!
We did it!
HEY! IT'S THE THIRD-YEARS!
LOOK OVER THERE! LET'S GO CHEER THEM ON, ASA!
FUMI IS SO SLOW THOUGH.

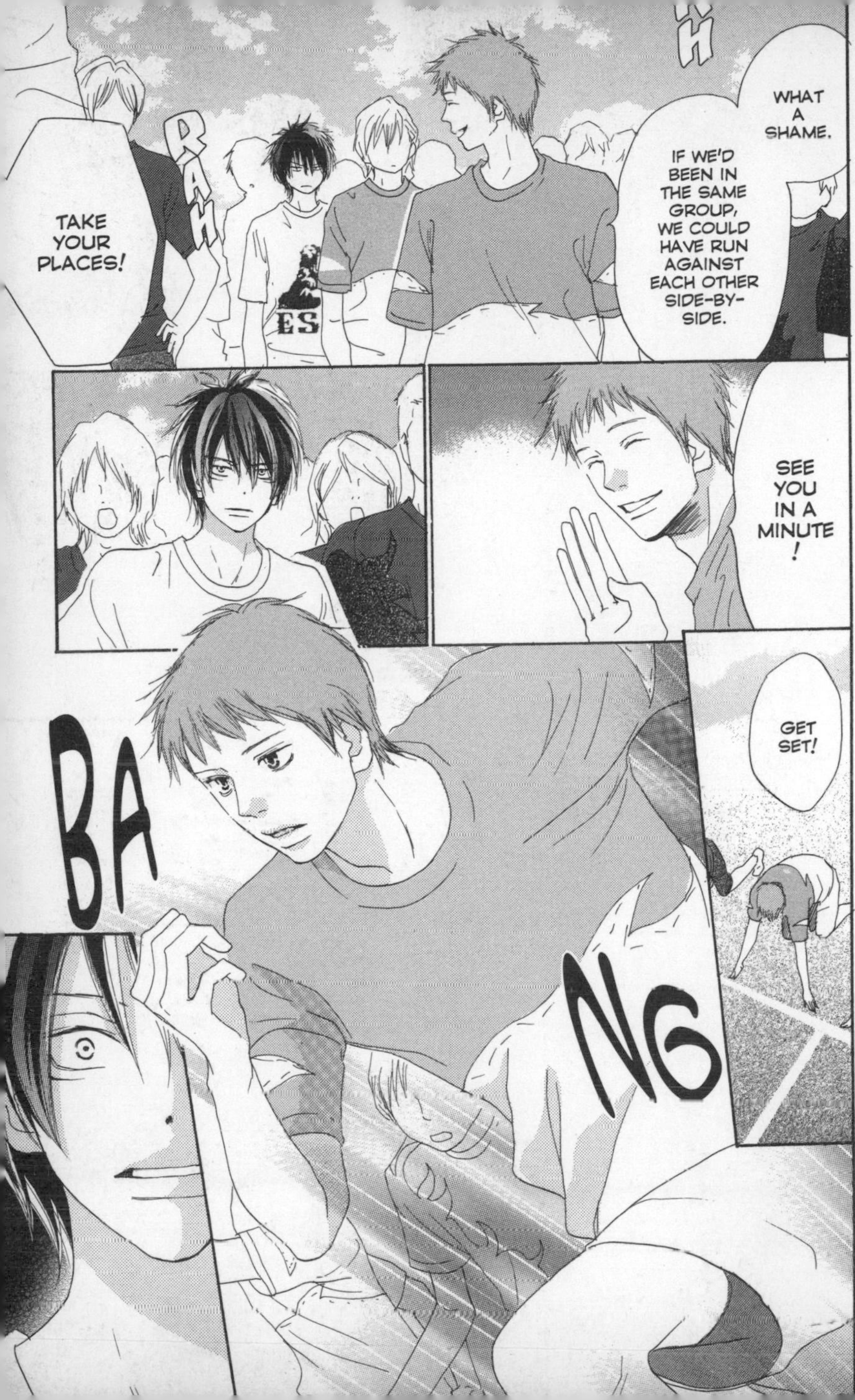
WHAT A SHAME.
IF WE'D BEEN IN THE SAME GROUP, WE COULD HAVE RUN AGAINST EACH OTHER SIDE-BY-SIDE.
RAH
TAKE YOUR PLACES!
SEE YOU IN A MINUTE!
GET SET!
BA
NG

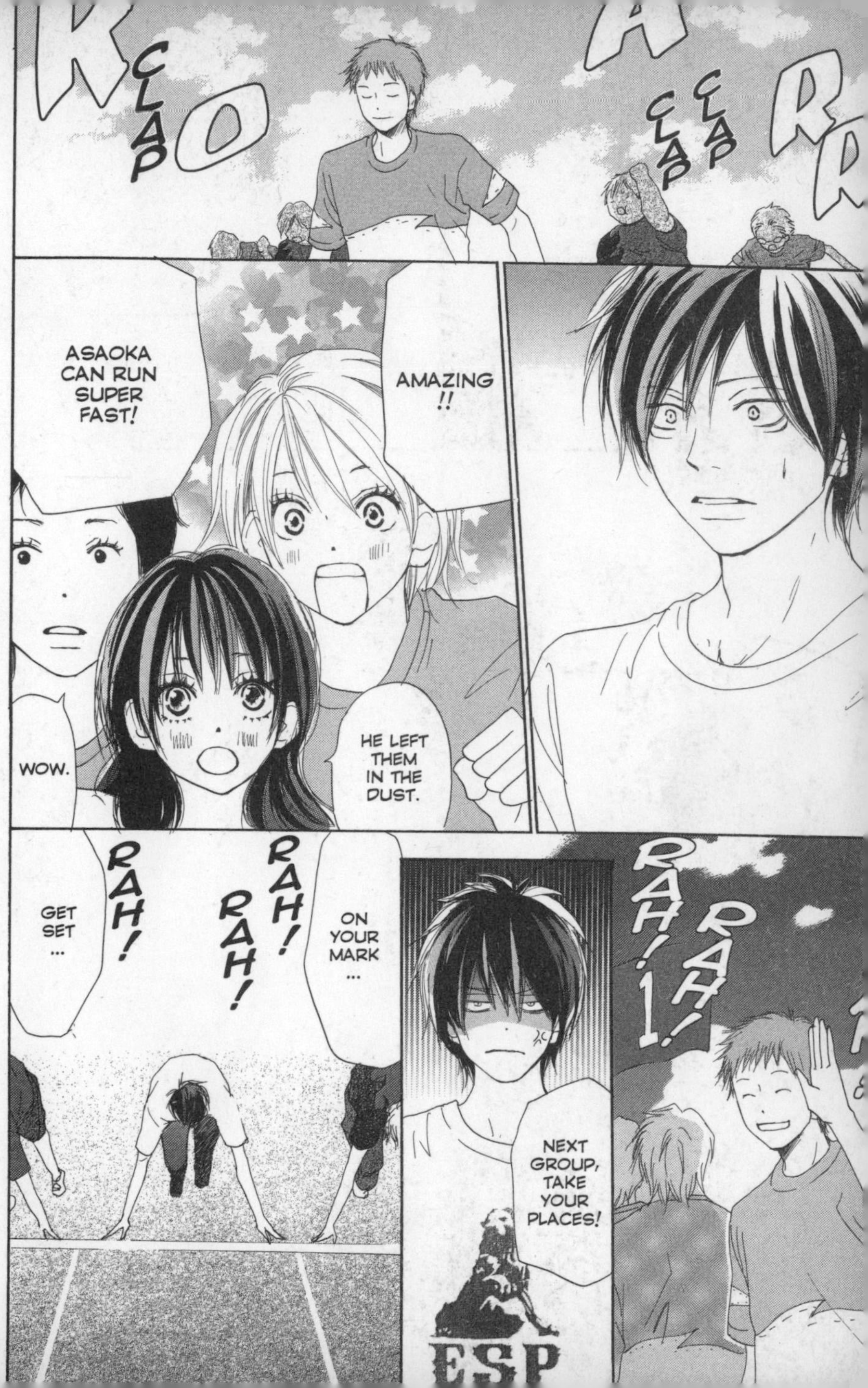

CLAP CLAP
CLAP
K O A R R
AMAZING!!
ASAOKA CAN RUN SUPER FAST!
HE LEFT THEM IN THE DUST.
WOW.
RAH! RAH!
NEXT GROUP, TAKE YOUR PLACES!
ESP
ON YOUR MARK ...
RAH! RAH!
RAH!
GET SET ...

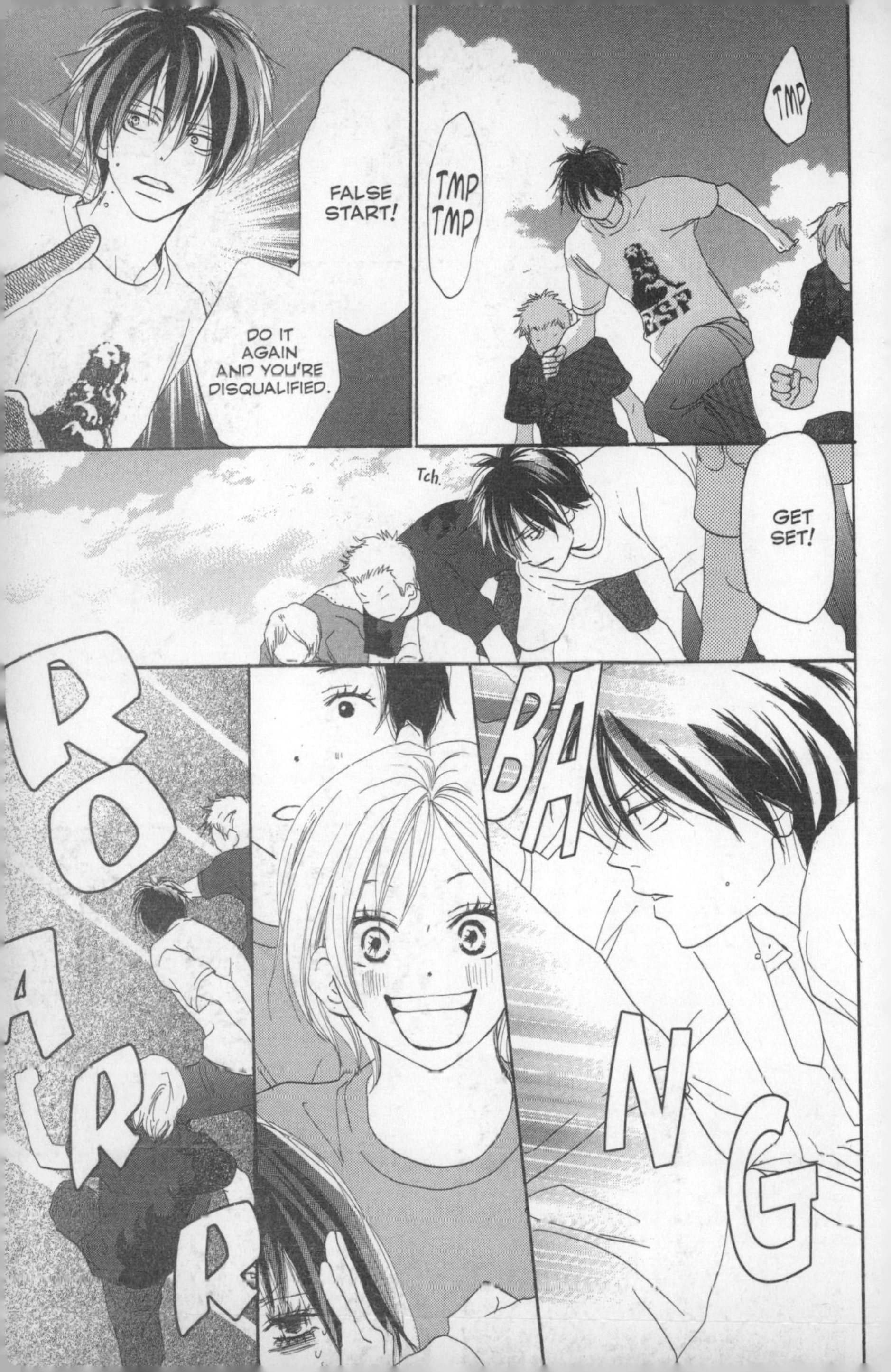
TMP
TMP TMP
FALSE START!
DO IT AGAIN AND YOU'RE DISQUALIFIED.
GET SET!
Tch.
BANG
ROARR

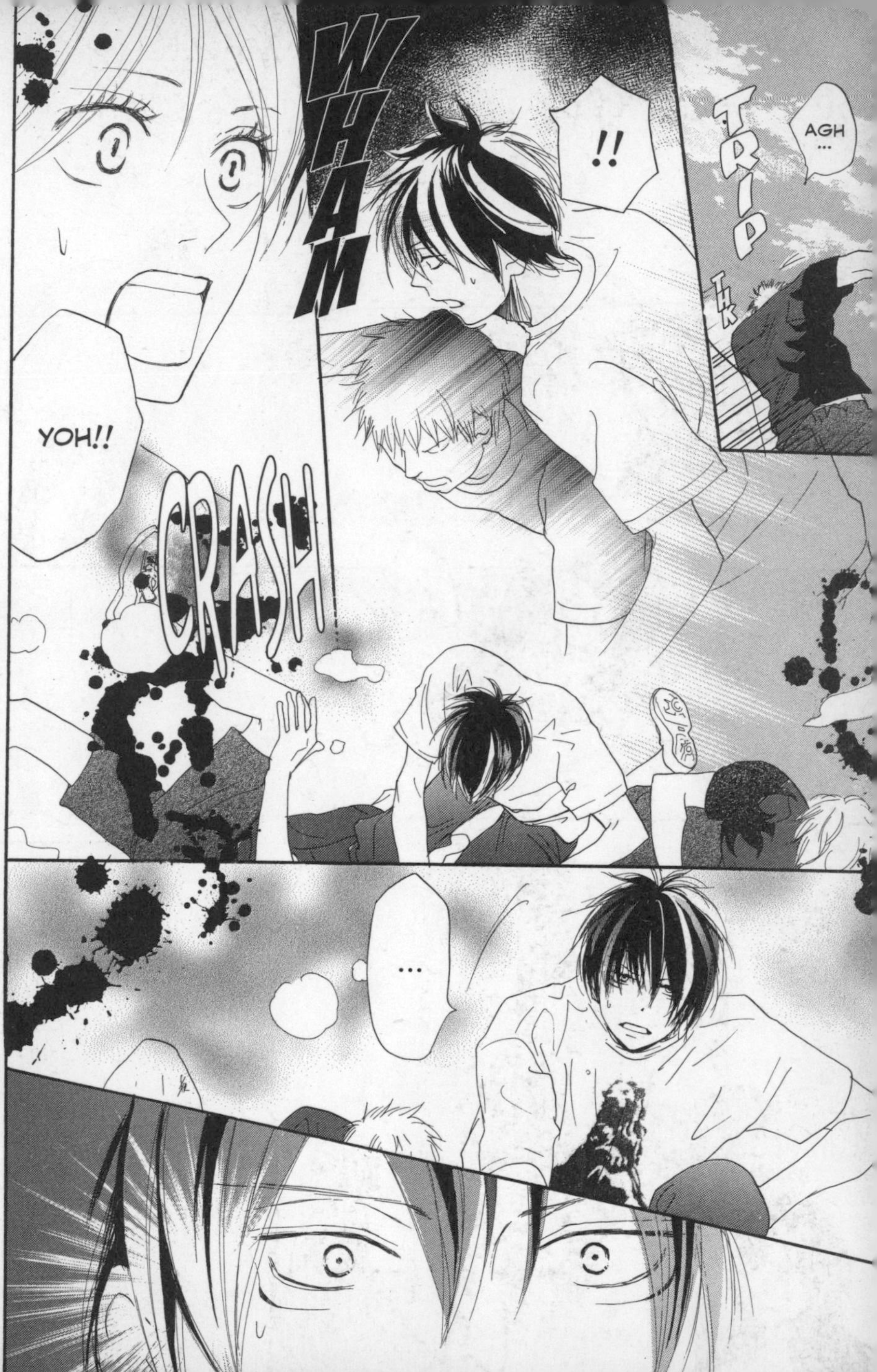
AGH...
TRIP
THK
!!
WHAM
YOH!!
CRASH
...

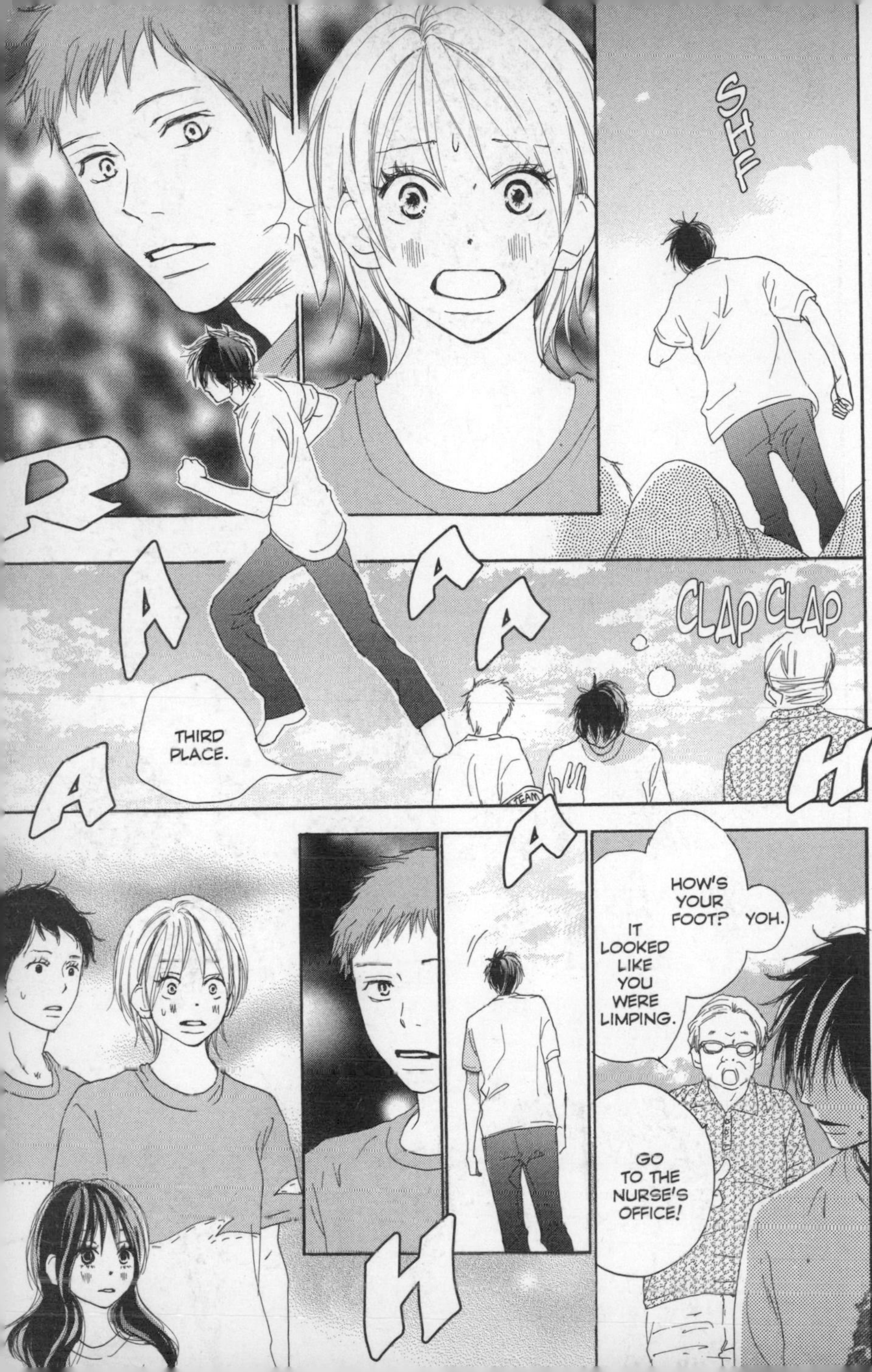
SHF
RAAAAAHH
CLAP CLAP
THIRD PLACE.
TEAM
YOH.
HOW'S YOUR FOOT? IT LOOKED LIKE YOU WERE LIMPING.
GO TO THE NURSE'S OFFICE!

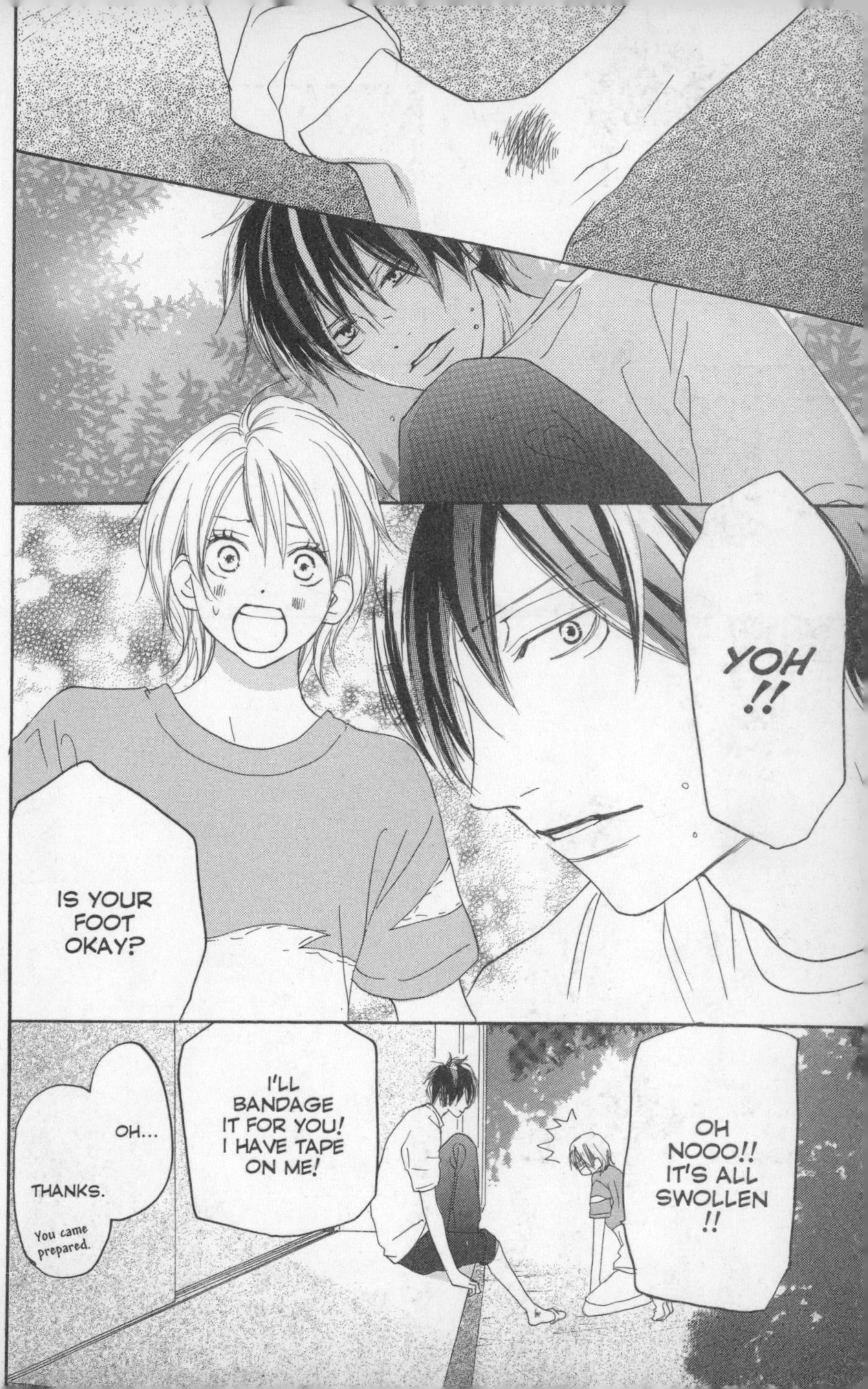
YOH!!
IS YOUR FOOT OKAY?
OH NOOO!! IT'S ALL SWOLLEN!!
I'LL BANDAGE IT FOR YOU! I HAVE TAPE ON ME!
OH... THANKS.
You came prepared.

AH, SORRY!

OW!

IT'S OKAY.

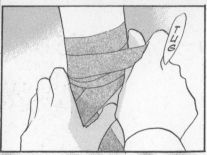

TUG

YEAH...

THE 100 METER ...

YOU DON'T HAVE TO RUN! YOU COULD WITHDRAW!

BUT I HAVE TO RUN.

I HAVE MY REASONS.

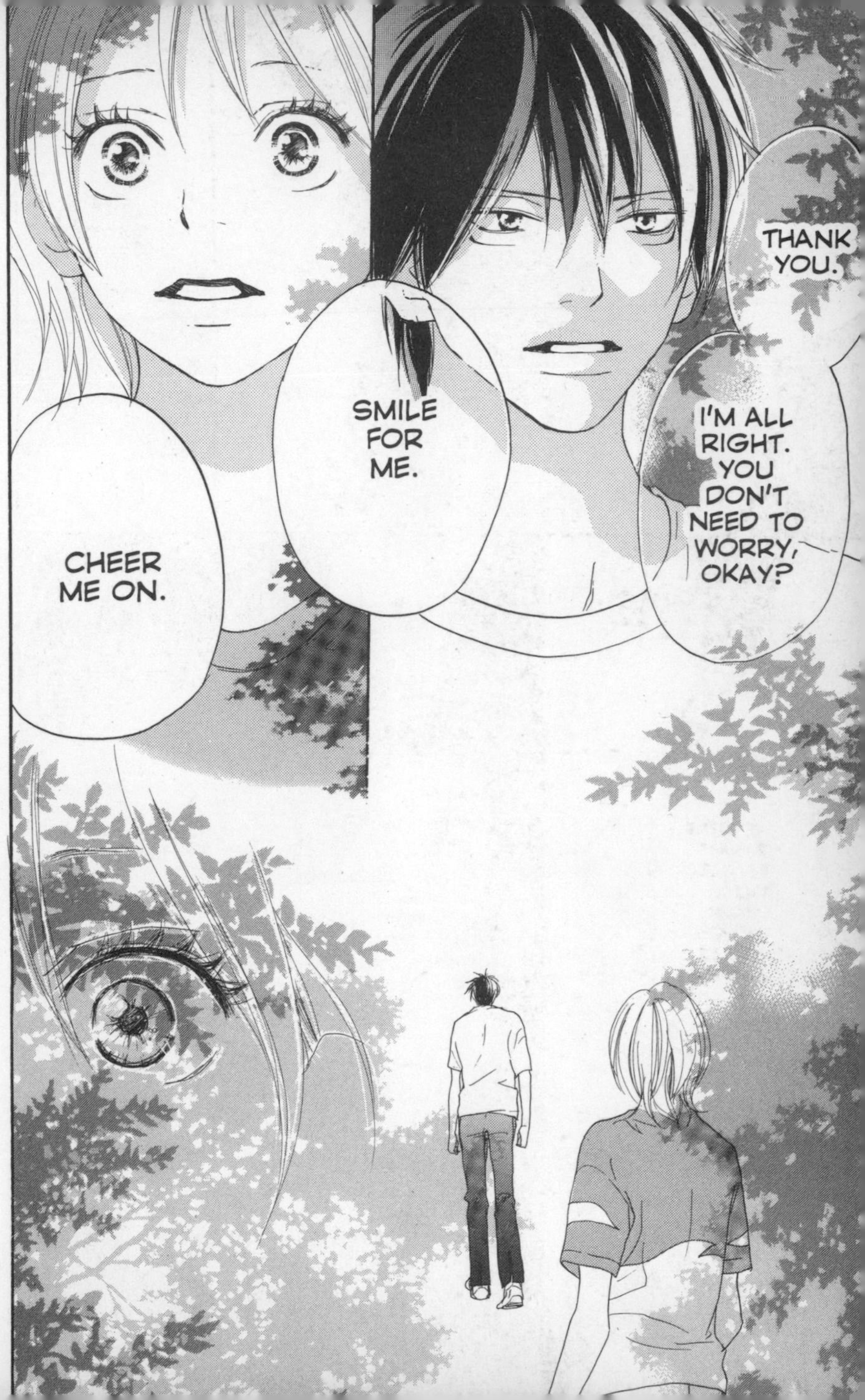
THANK YOU.
I'M ALL RIGHT. YOU DON'T NEED TO WORRY, OKAY?
SMILE FOR ME.
CHEER ME ON.

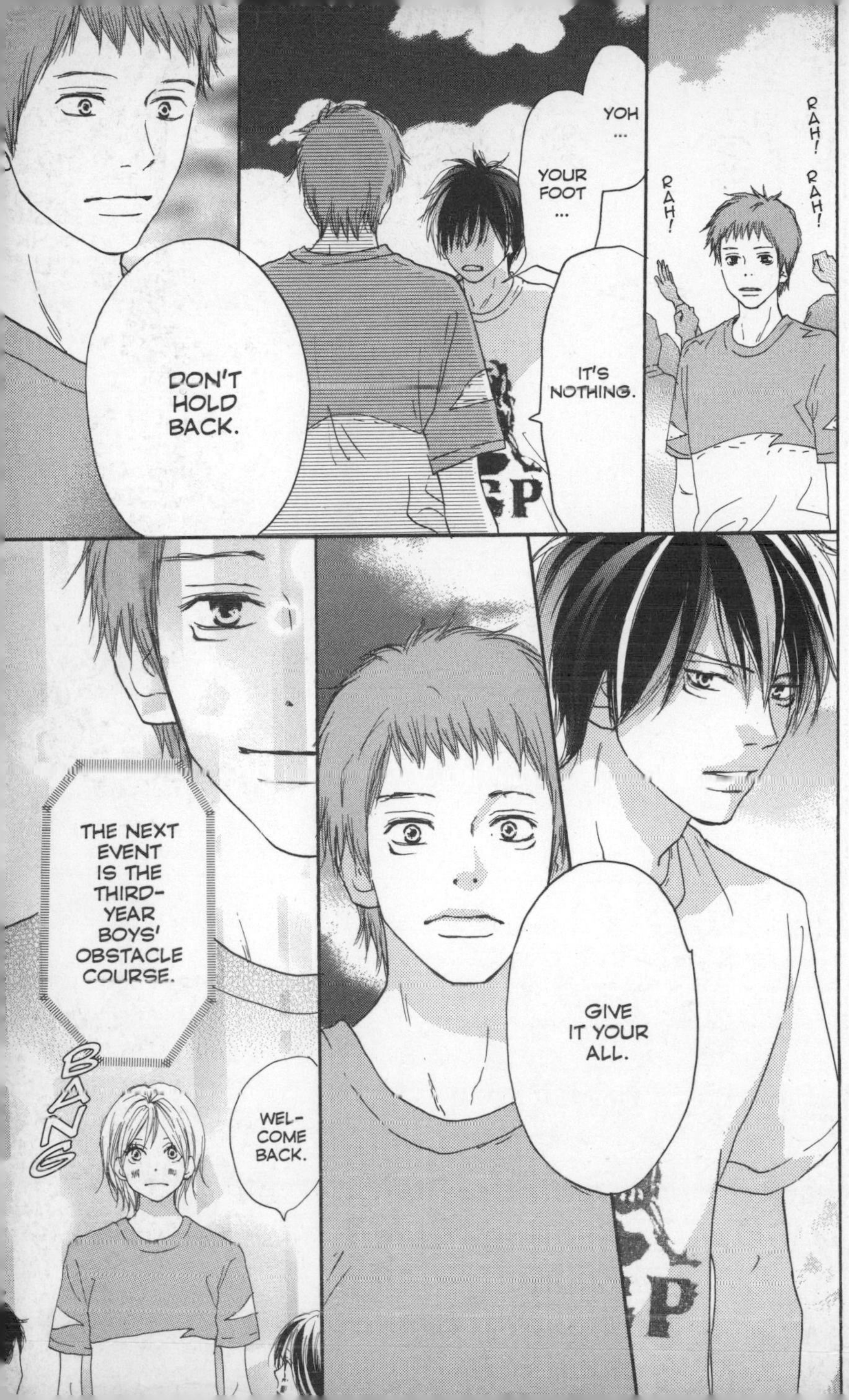
RAH! RAH!
RAH!
YOH ...
YOUR FOOT ...
IT'S NOTHING.
DON'T HOLD BACK.
GIVE IT YOUR ALL.
THE NEXT EVENT IS THE THIRD-YEAR BOYS' OBSTACLE COURSE.
BANG
WEL-COME BACK.

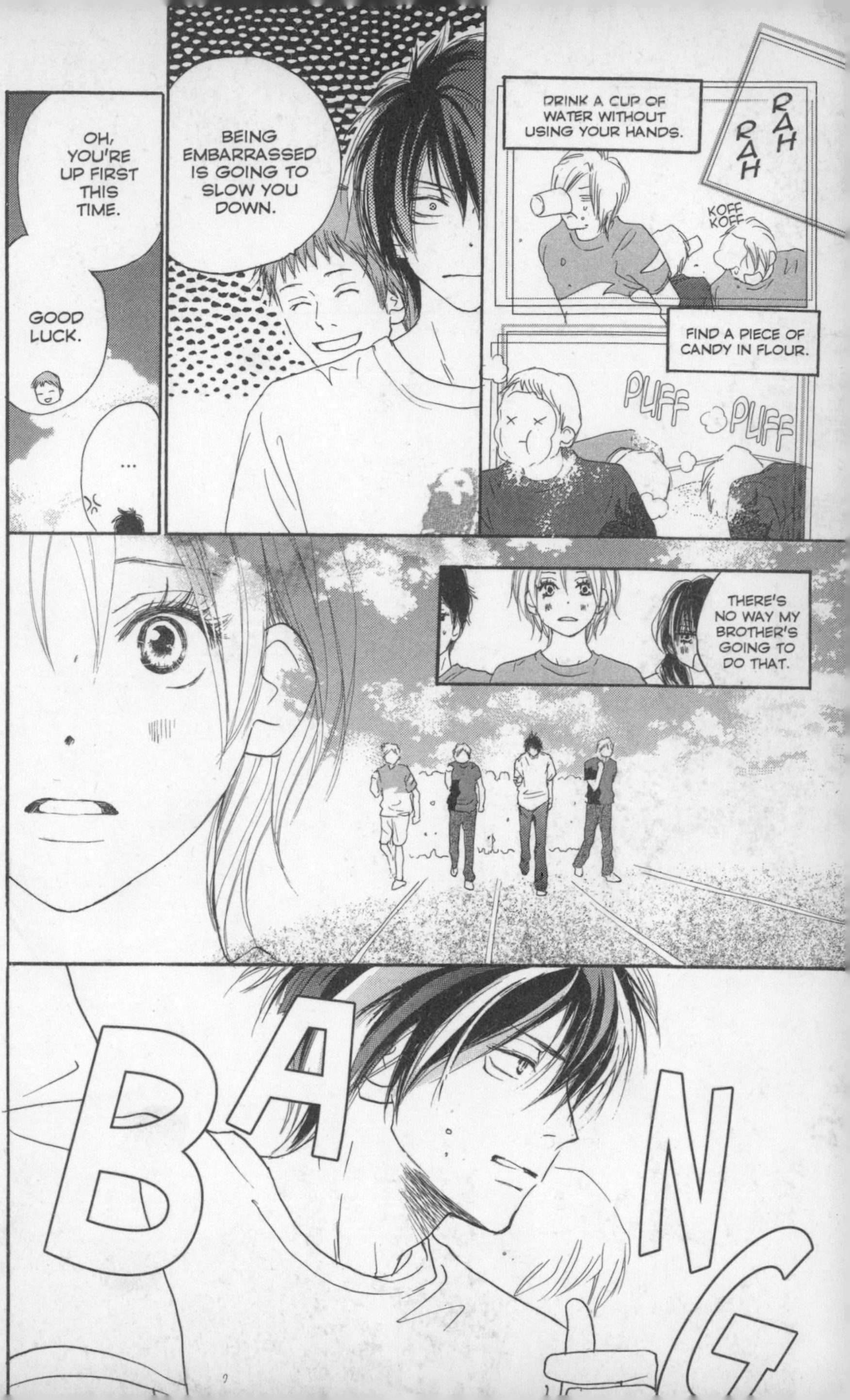
RAH
RAH
DRINK A CUP OF WATER WITHOUT USING YOUR HANDS.
KOFF
KOFF
FIND A PIECE OF CANDY IN FLOUR.
PUFF
PUFF
BEING EMBARRASSED IS GOING TO SLOW YOU DOWN.
OH, YOU'RE UP FIRST THIS TIME.
GOOD LUCK.
...
THERE'S NO WAY MY BROTHER'S GOING TO DO THAT.
BANG

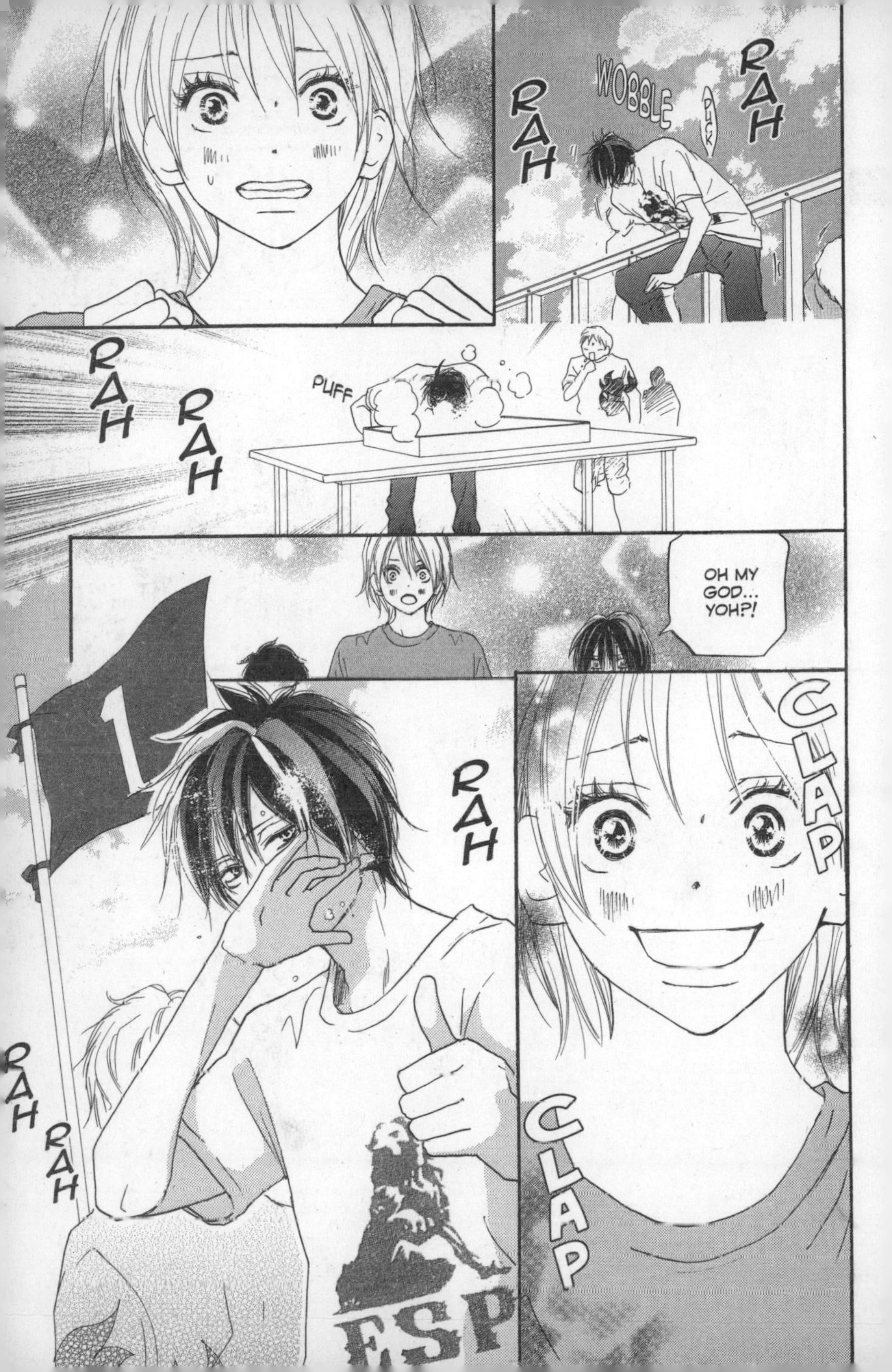
RAH
DUCK
WOBBLE
RAH
PUFF
RAH
RAH
OH MY GOD... YOH?!
CLAP
CLAP
RAH
RAH
RAH

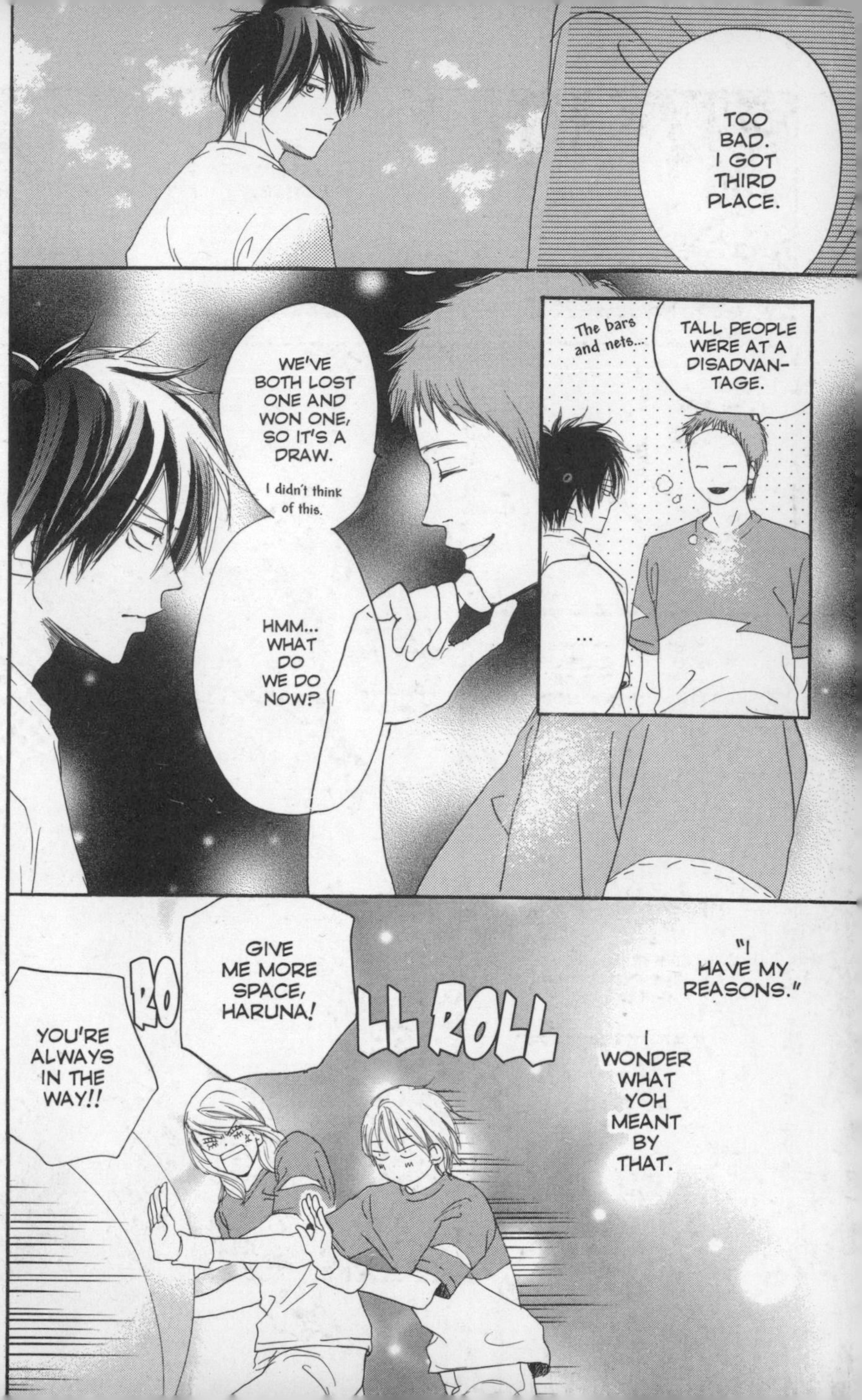
TOO BAD. I GOT THIRD PLACE.
TALL PEOPLE WERE AT A DISADVAN-TAGE.
The bars and nets...
...
WE'VE BOTH LOST ONE AND WON ONE, SO IT'S A DRAW.
I didn't think of this.
HMM... WHAT DO WE DO NOW?
"I HAVE MY REASONS."
I WONDER WHAT YOH MEANT BY THAT.
ROLL ROLL
GIVE ME MORE SPACE, HARUNA!
YOU'RE ALWAYS IN THE WAY!!

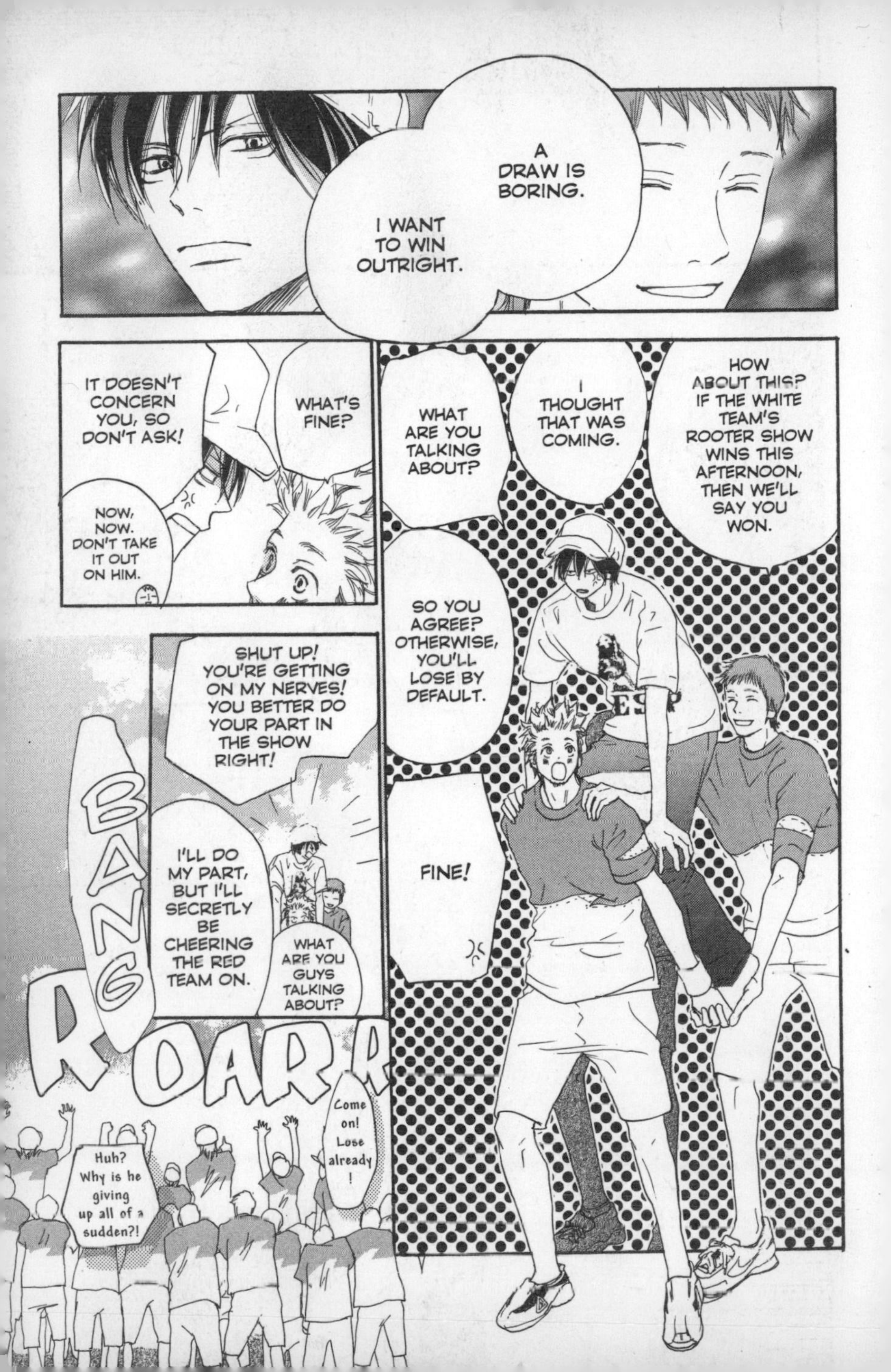
A DRAW IS BORING.
I WANT TO WIN OUTRIGHT.
HOW ABOUT THIS? IF THE WHITE TEAM'S ROOTER SHOW WINS THIS AFTERNOON, THEN WE'LL SAY YOU WON.
I THOUGHT THAT WAS COMING.
WHAT ARE YOU TALKING ABOUT?
SO YOU AGREE? OTHERWISE, YOU'LL LOSE BY DEFAULT.
FINE!
WHAT'S FINE?
IT DOESN'T CONCERN YOU, SO DON'T ASK!
NOW, NOW. DON'T TAKE IT OUT ON HIM.
SHUT UP! YOU'RE GETTING ON MY NERVES! YOU BETTER DO YOUR PART IN THE SHOW RIGHT!
I'LL DO MY PART, BUT I'LL SECRETLY BE CHEERING THE RED TEAM ON.
WHAT ARE YOU GUYS TALKING ABOUT?
BANG
ROARR
Come on! Lose already!
Huh? Why is he giving up all of a sudden?!

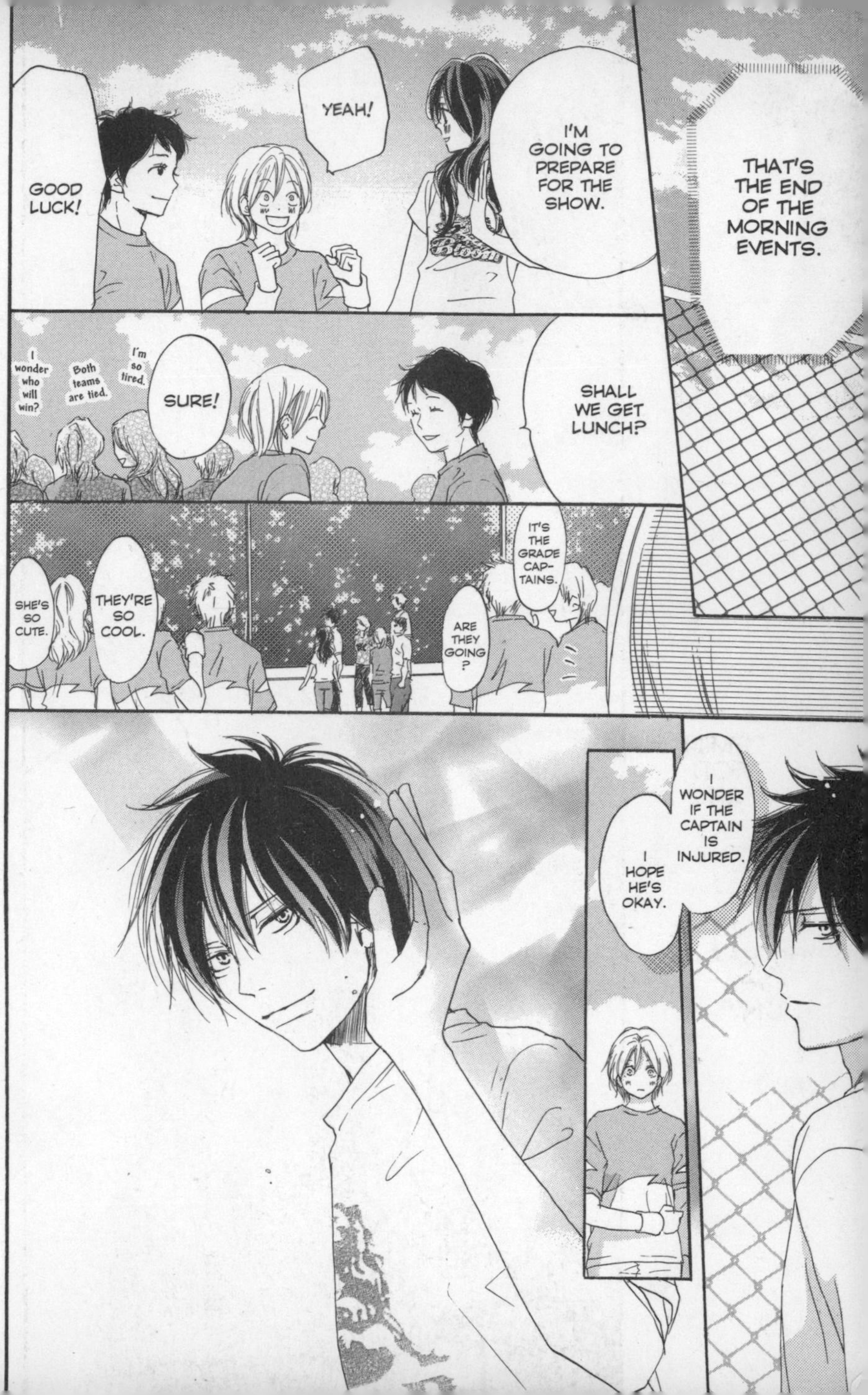
THAT'S THE END OF THE MORNING EVENTS.
I'M GOING TO PREPARE FOR THE SHOW.
YEAH!
GOOD LUCK!
SHALL WE GET LUNCH?
SURE!
I'm so tired.
Both teams are tied.
I wonder who will win?
IT'S THE GRADE CAPTAINS.
ARE THEY GOING?
THEY'RE SO COOL.
SHE'S SO CUTE.
I WONDER IF THE CAPTAIN IS INJURED.
I HOPE HE'S OKAY.

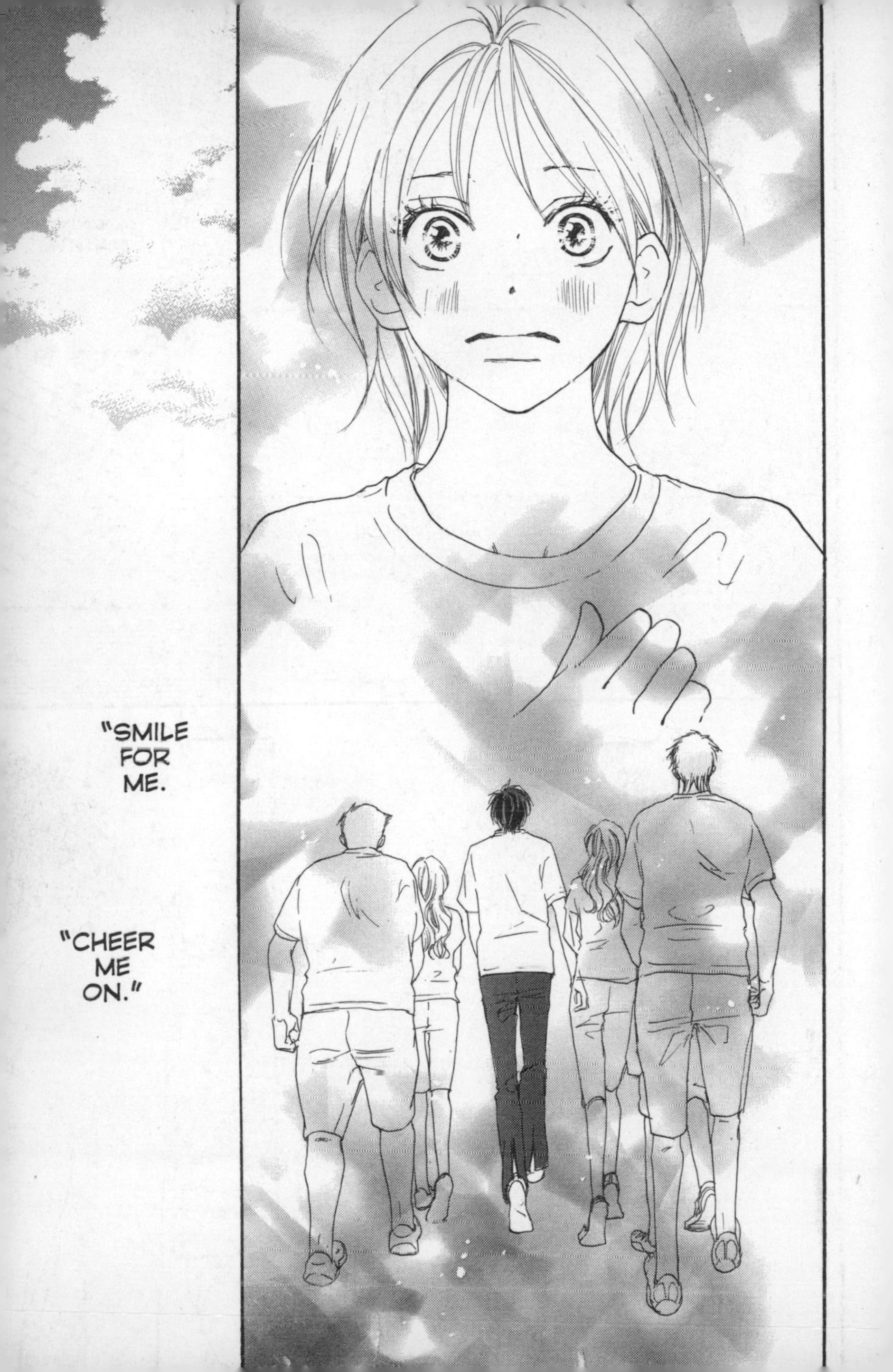
"SMILE FOR ME.
"CHEER ME ON."

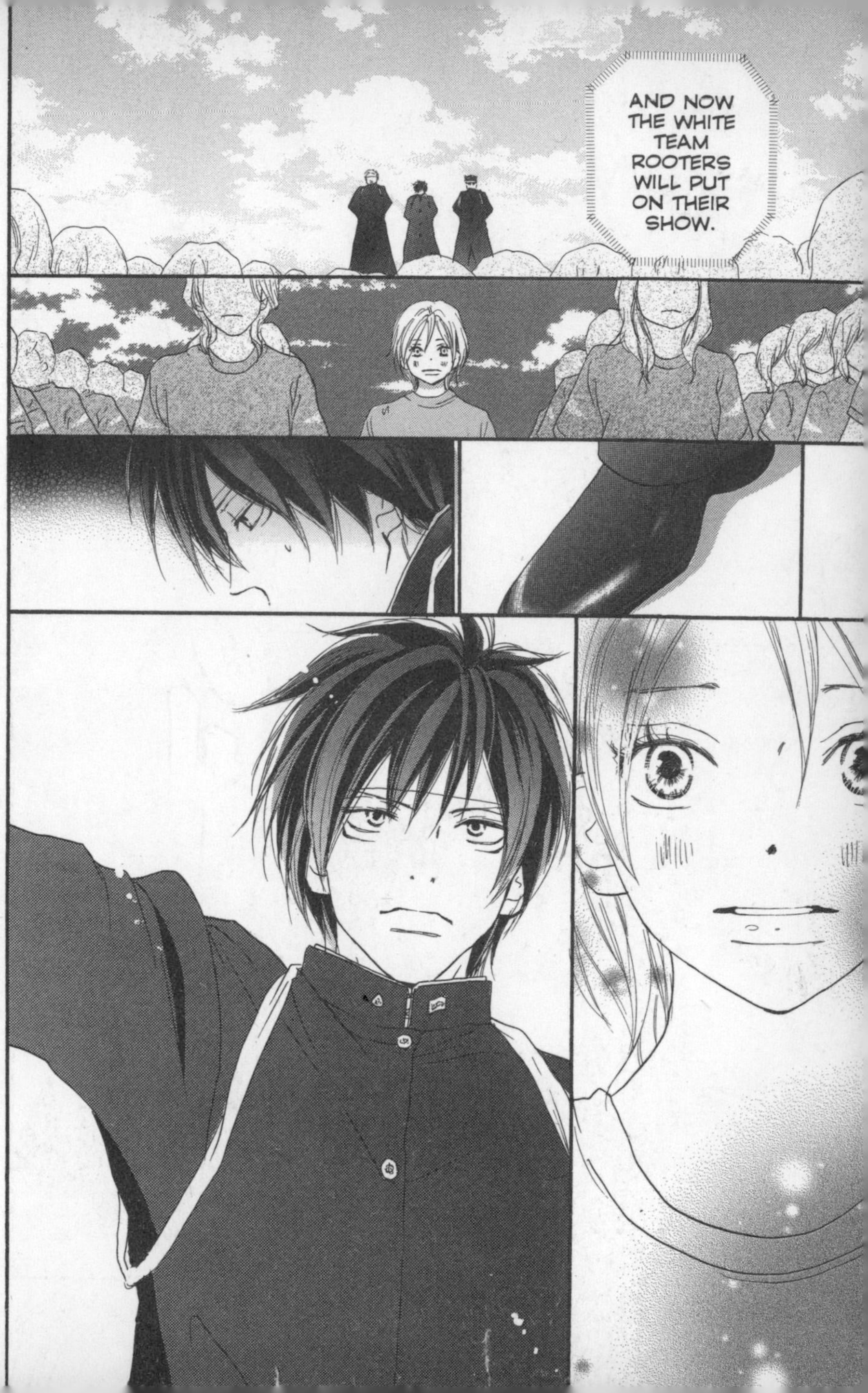
AND NOW THE WHITE TEAM ROOTERS WILL PUT ON THEIR SHOW.

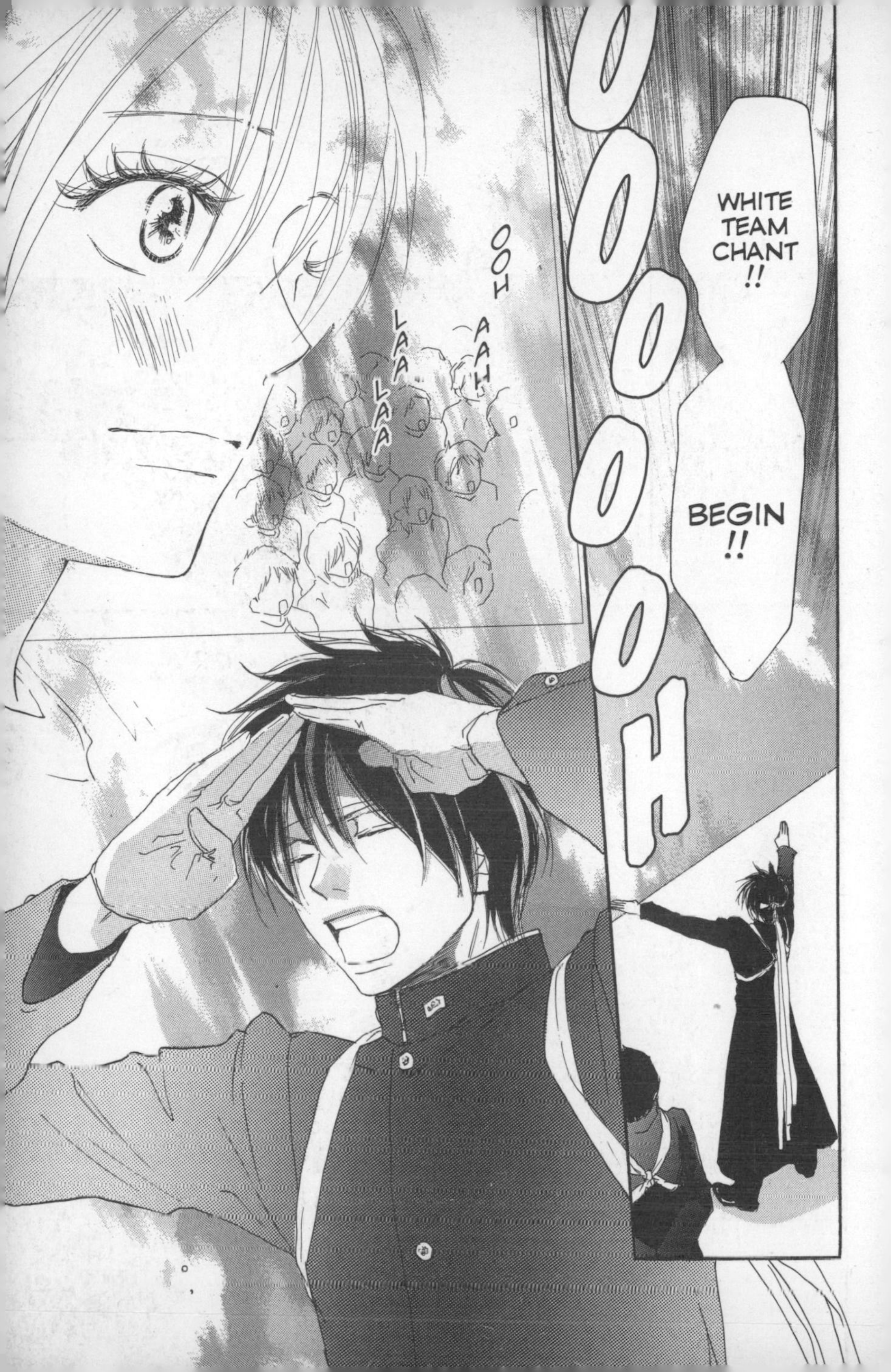
WHITE TEAM CHANT!!
BEGIN!!
OOOOOOH
OOH
AAAH
LAAA
LAAA

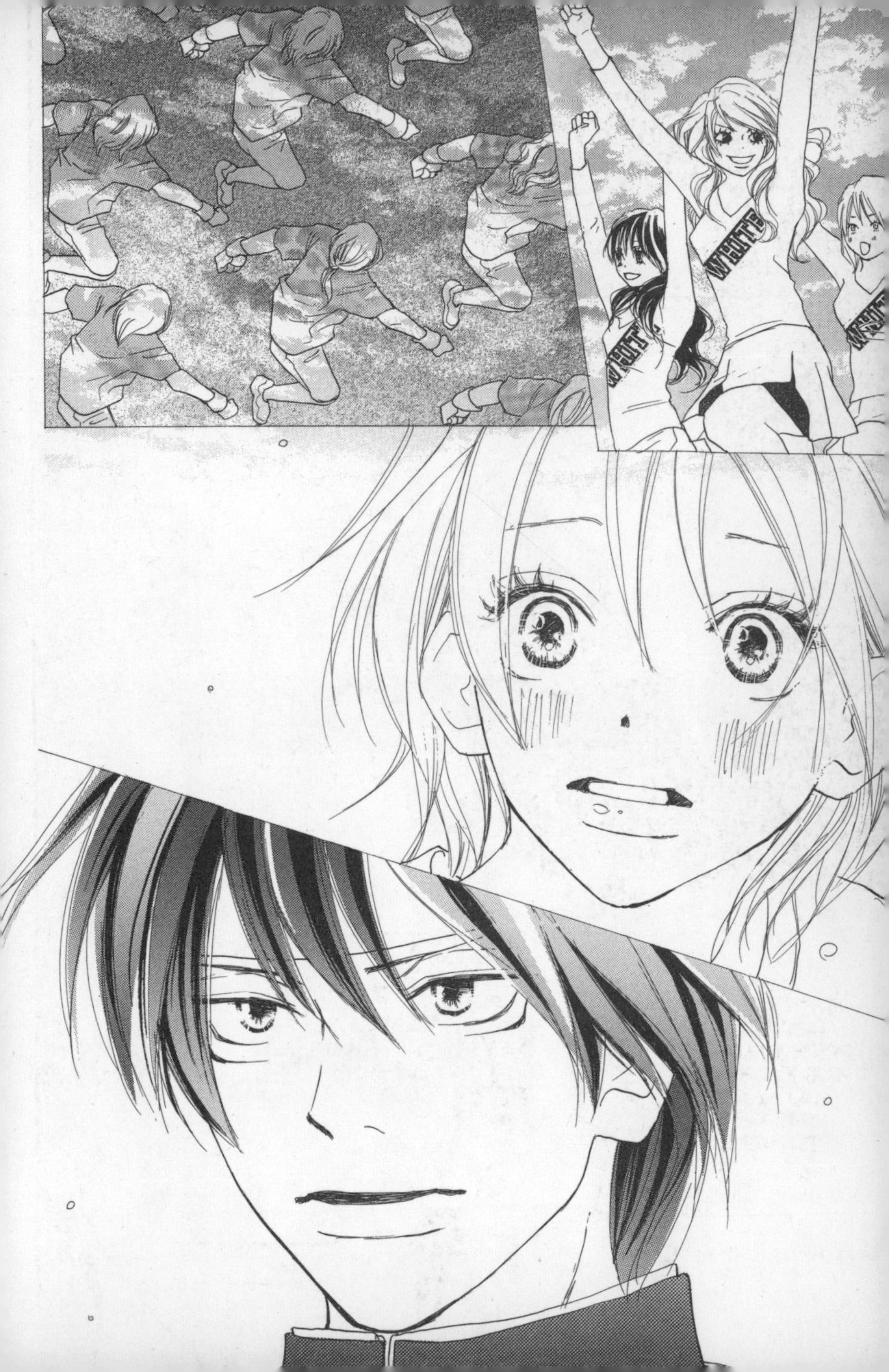

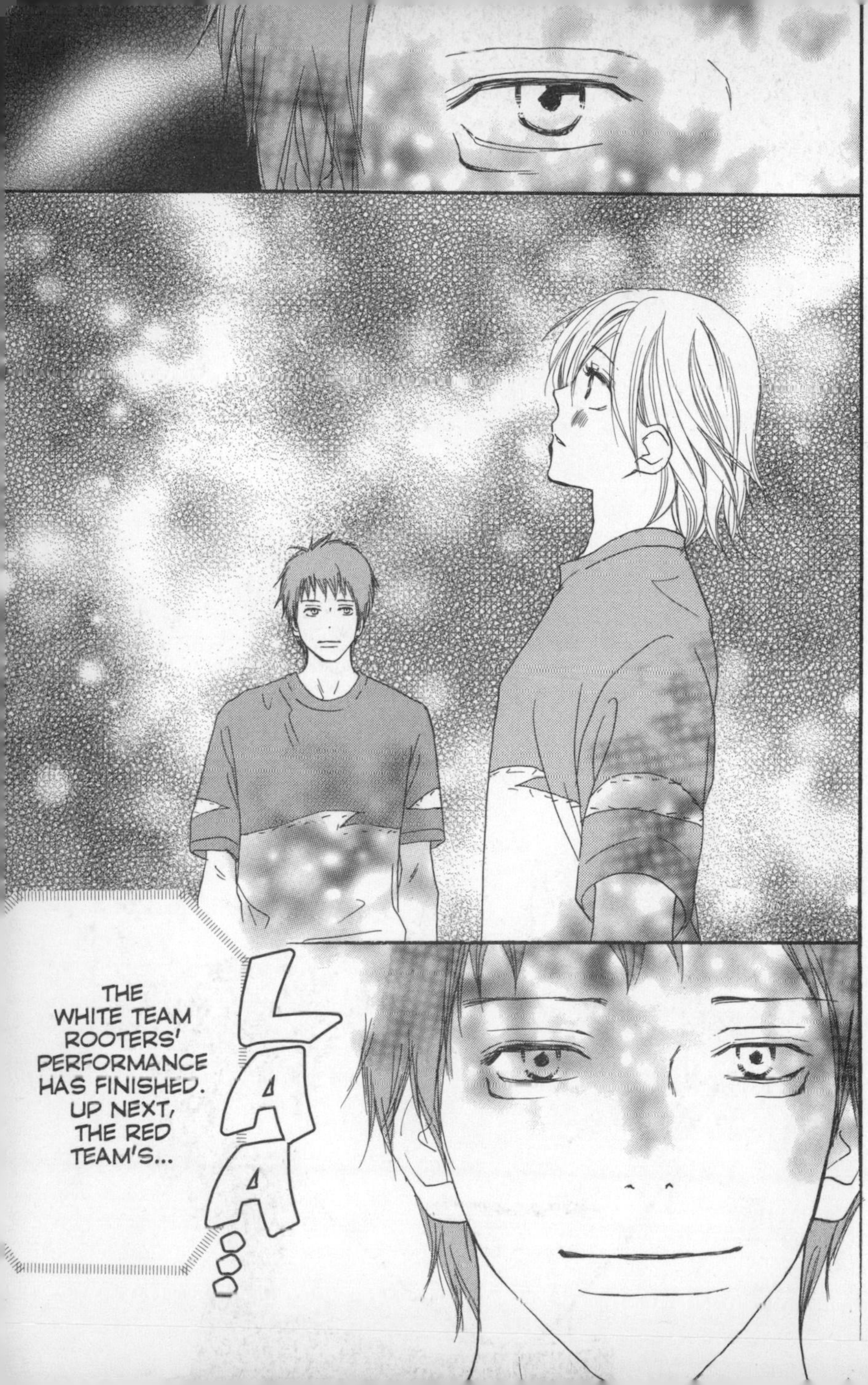
THE WHITE TEAM ROOTERS' PERFORMANCE HAS FINISHED. UP NEXT, THE RED TEAM'S...
LAA...

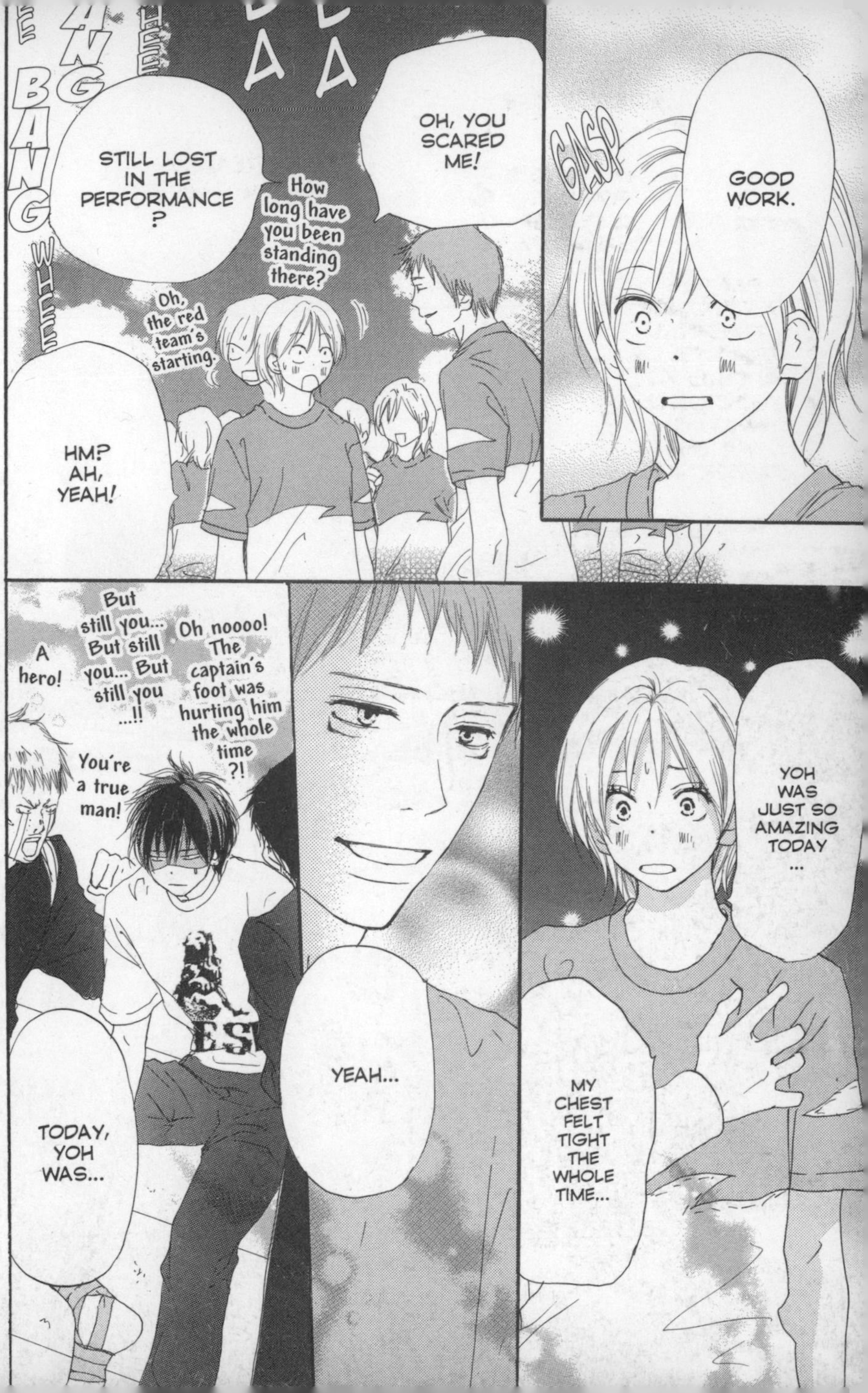
GASP
GOOD WORK.
OH, YOU SCARED ME!
How long have you been standing there?
STILL LOST IN THE PERFORMANCE?
BANG
Oh, the red team's starting.
HM? AH, YEAH!
YOH WAS JUST SO AMAZING TODAY...
MY CHEST FELT TIGHT THE WHOLE TIME...
YEAH...
Oh noooo! The captain's foot was hurting him the whole time?!
But still you... But still you... But still you...!!
A hero!
You're a true man!
TODAY, YOH WAS...

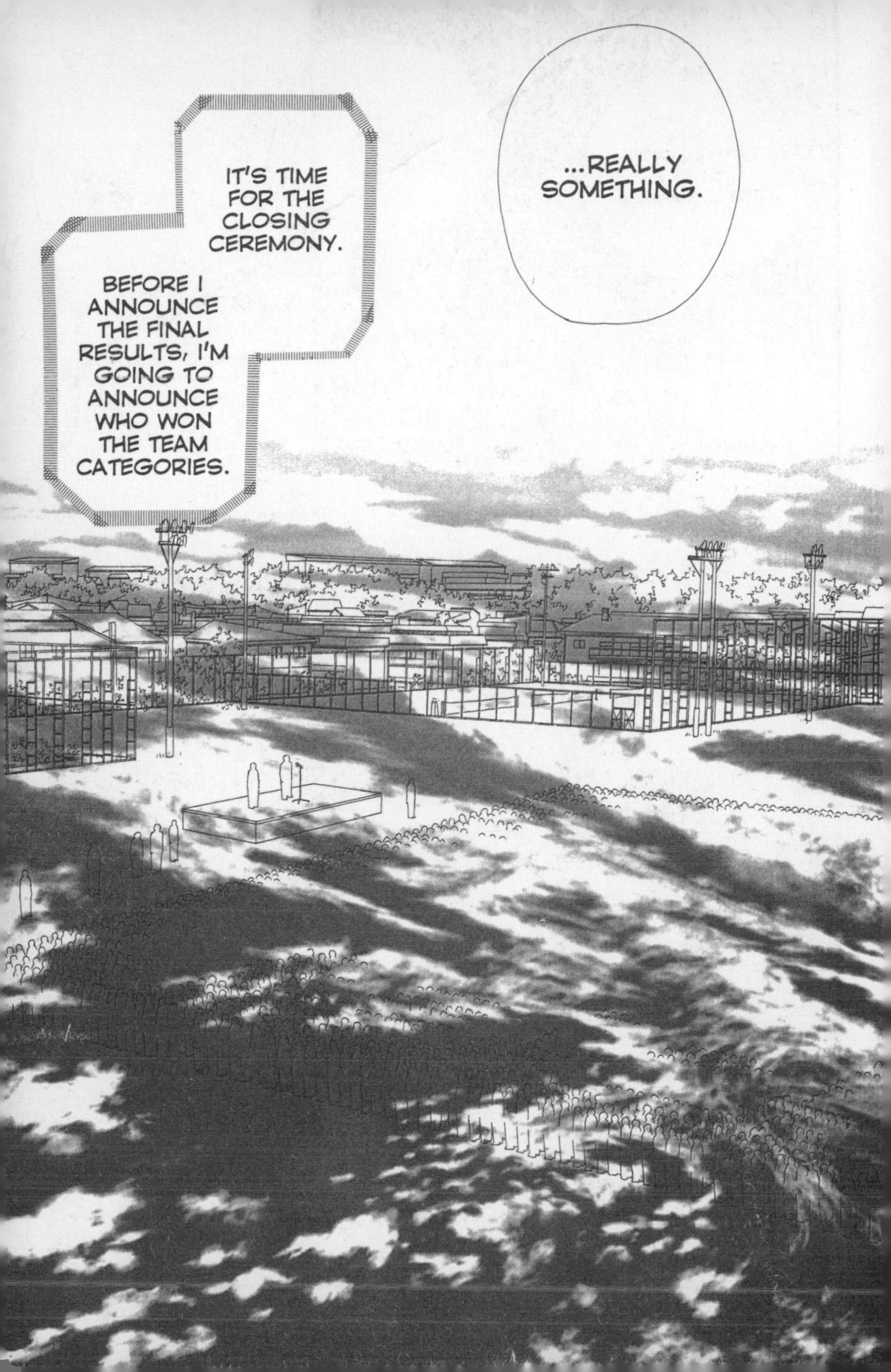
...REALLY SOMETHING.
IT'S TIME FOR THE CLOSING CEREMONY.
BEFORE I ANNOUNCE THE FINAL RESULTS, I'M GOING TO ANNOUNCE WHO WON THE TEAM CATEGORIES.

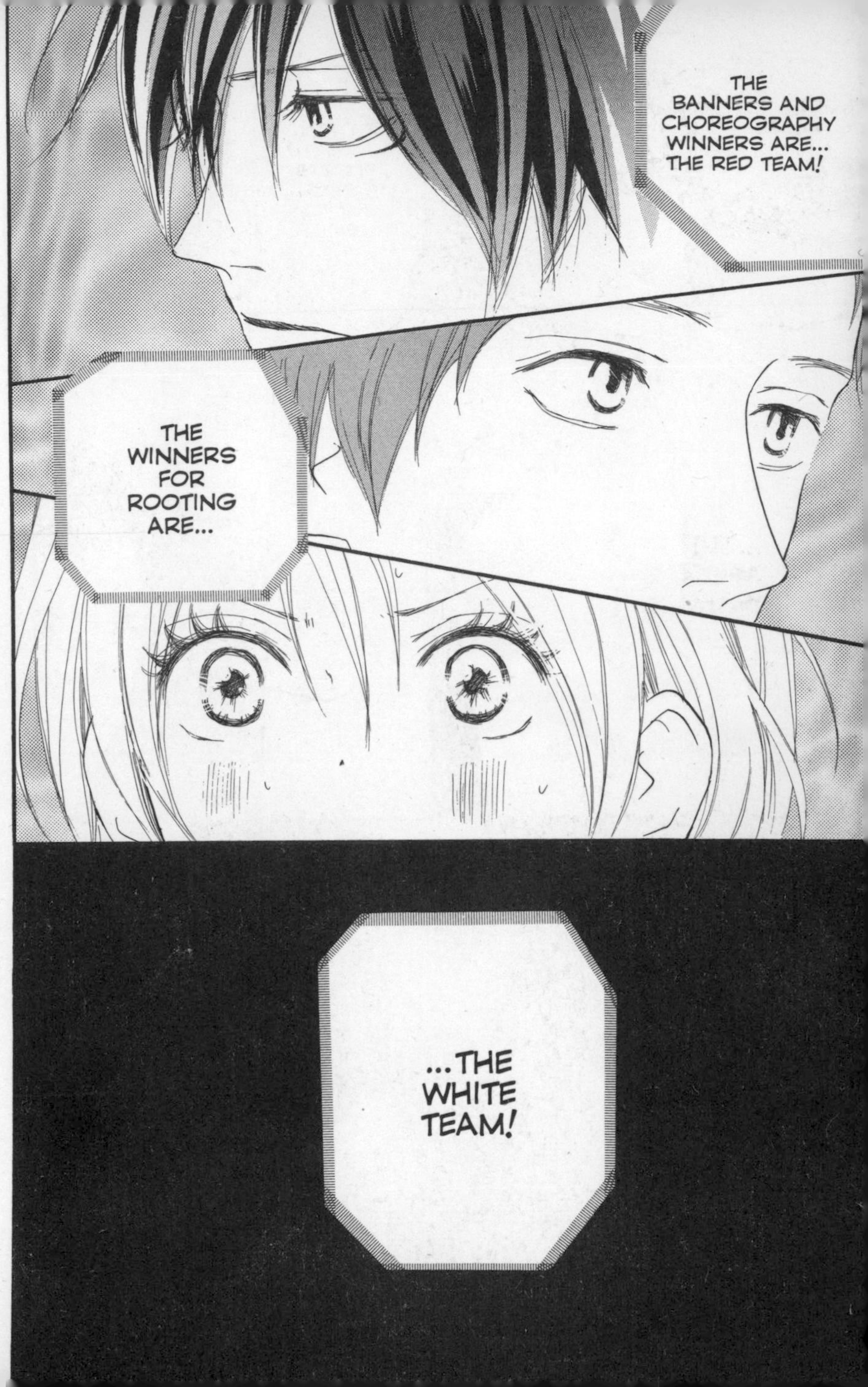
THE BANNERS AND CHOREOGRAPHY WINNERS ARE... THE RED TEAM!
THE WINNERS FOR ROOTING ARE...
...THE WHITE TEAM!

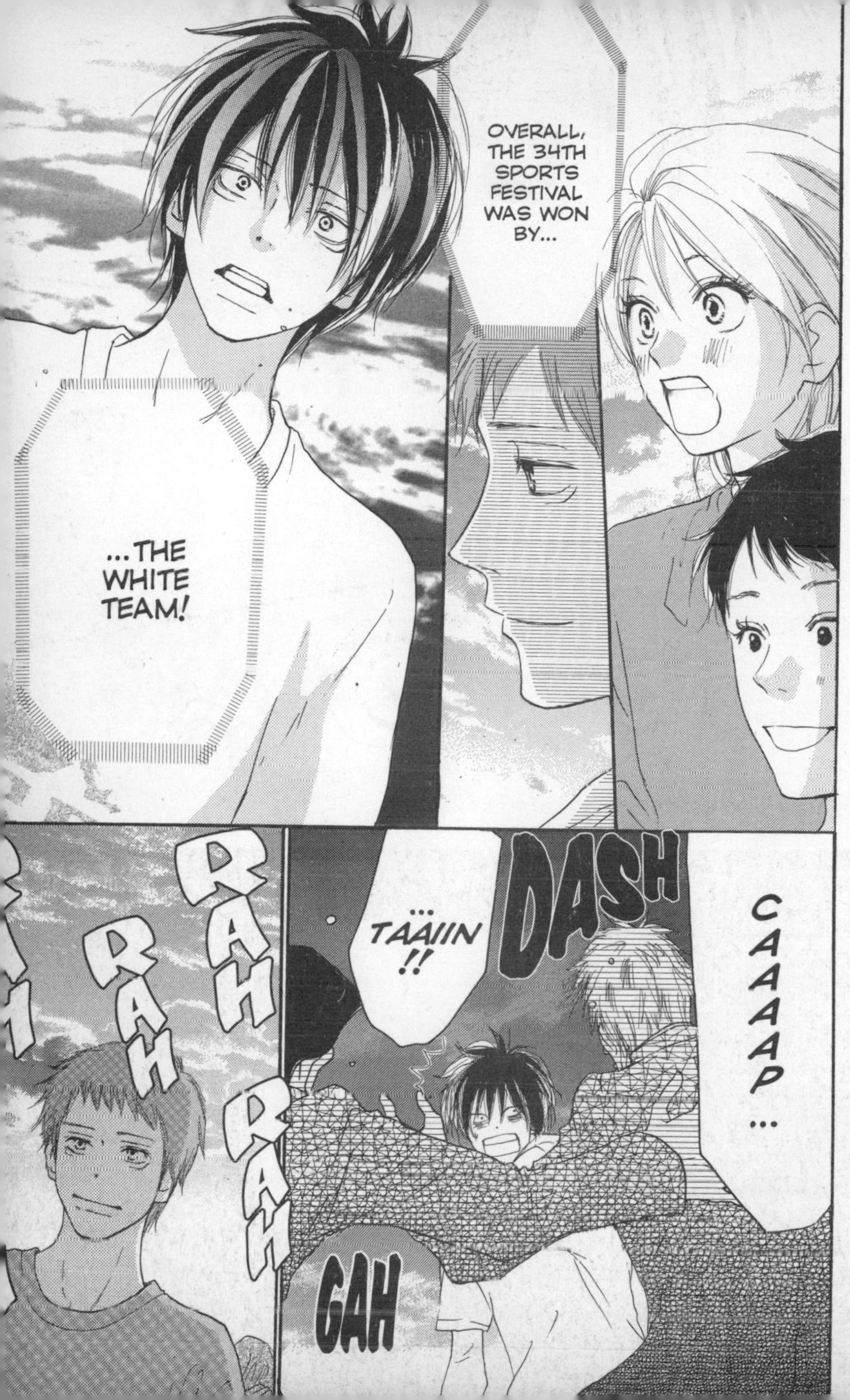
OVERALL, THE 34TH SPORTS FESTIVAL WAS WON BY...
...THE WHITE TEAM!
CAAAAP...
DASH
...TAAIIN!!
GAH
RAH
RAH
RAH

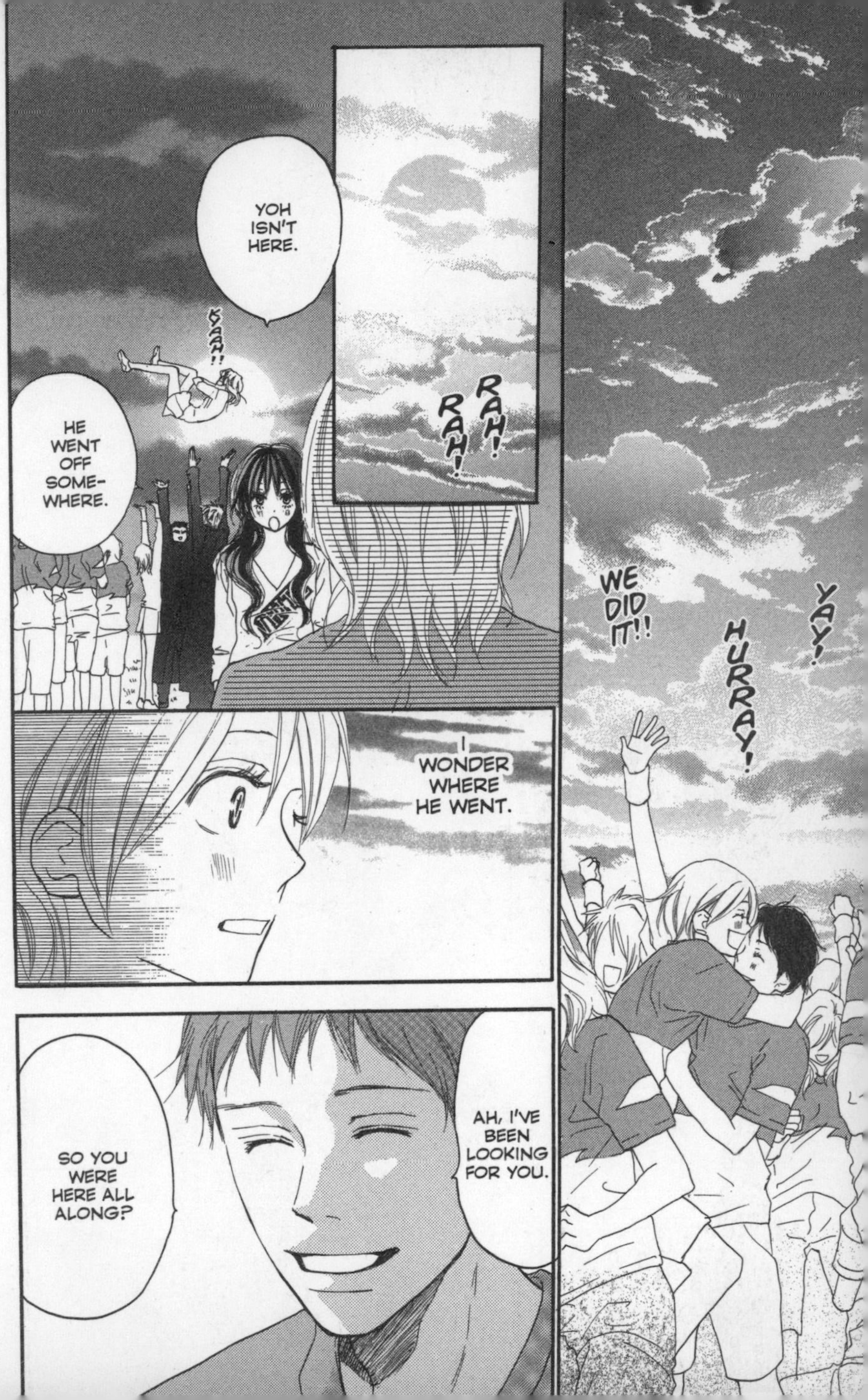
YAY!
WE DID IT!!
HURRAY!
RAH! RAH!
YOH ISN'T HERE.
KYAAH!!
HE WENT OFF SOME-WHERE.
I WONDER WHERE HE WENT.
AH, I'VE BEEN LOOKING FOR YOU.
SO YOU WERE HERE ALL ALONG?

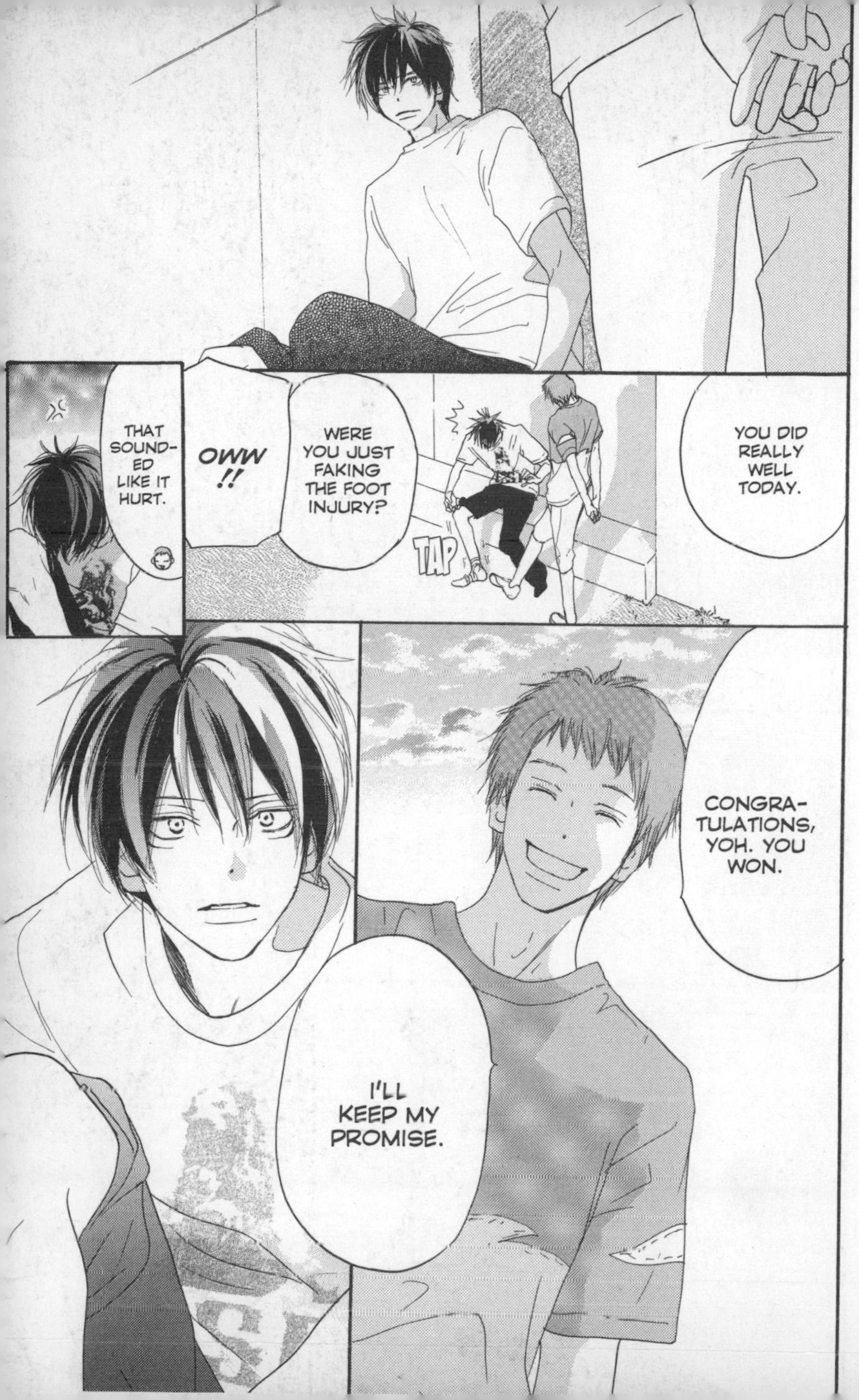
YOU DID REALLY WELL TODAY.
TAP
WERE YOU JUST FAKING THE FOOT INJURY?
OWW!!
THAT SOUND-ED LIKE IT HURT.
CONGRA-TULATIONS, YOH. YOU WON.
I'LL KEEP MY PROMISE.

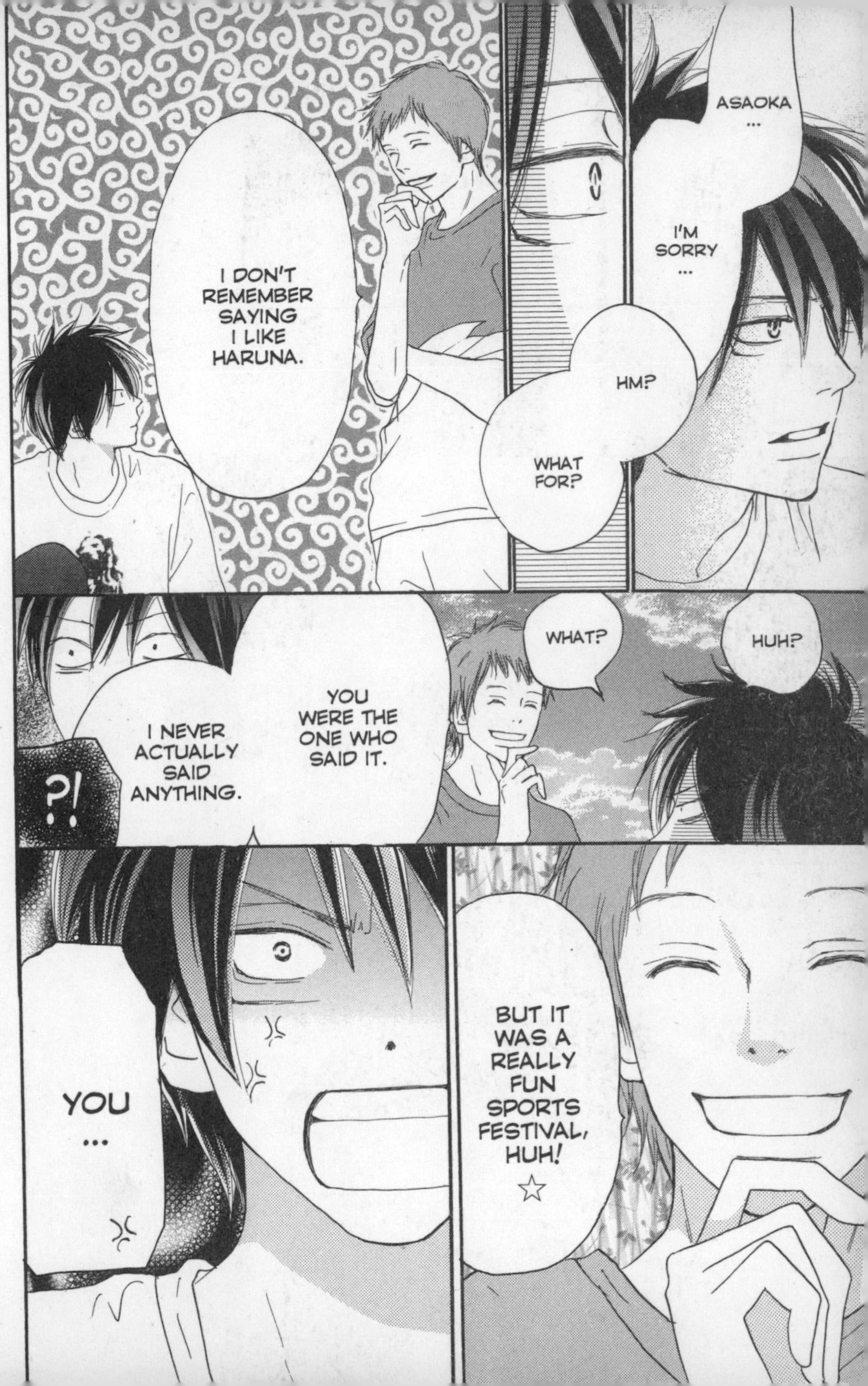
ASAOKA ...
I'M SORRY ...
HM?
WHAT FOR?
I DON'T REMEMBER SAYING I LIKE HARUNA.
HUH?
WHAT?
YOU WERE THE ONE WHO SAID IT.
I NEVER ACTUALLY SAID ANYTHING.
?!
BUT IT WAS A REALLY FUN SPORTS FESTIVAL, HUH! ☆
YOU ...

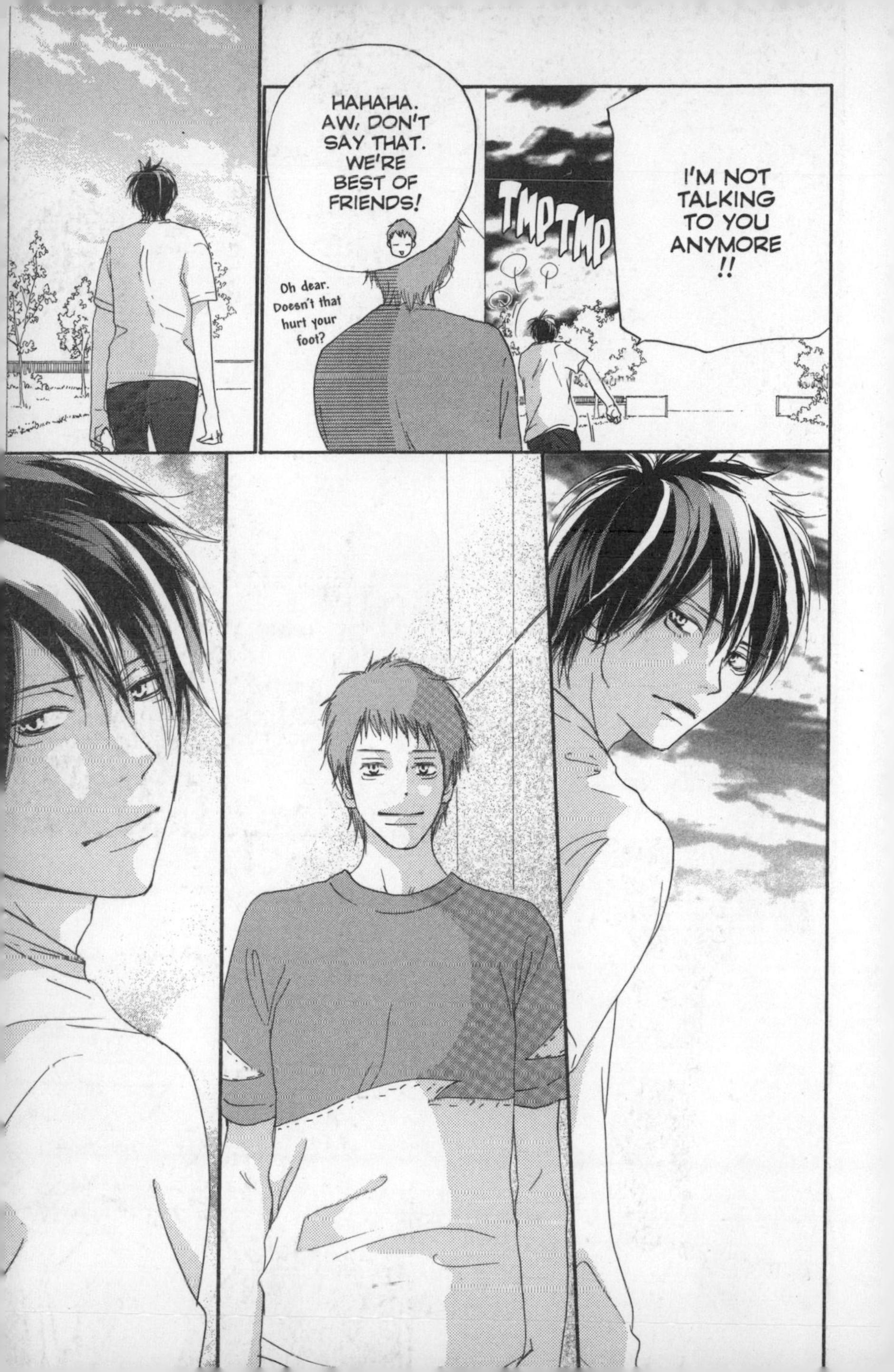
I'M NOT TALKING TO YOU ANYMORE!!
TMP TMP
HAHAHA. AW, DON'T SAY THAT. WE'RE BEST OF FRIENDS!
Oh dear. Doesn't that hurt your foot?

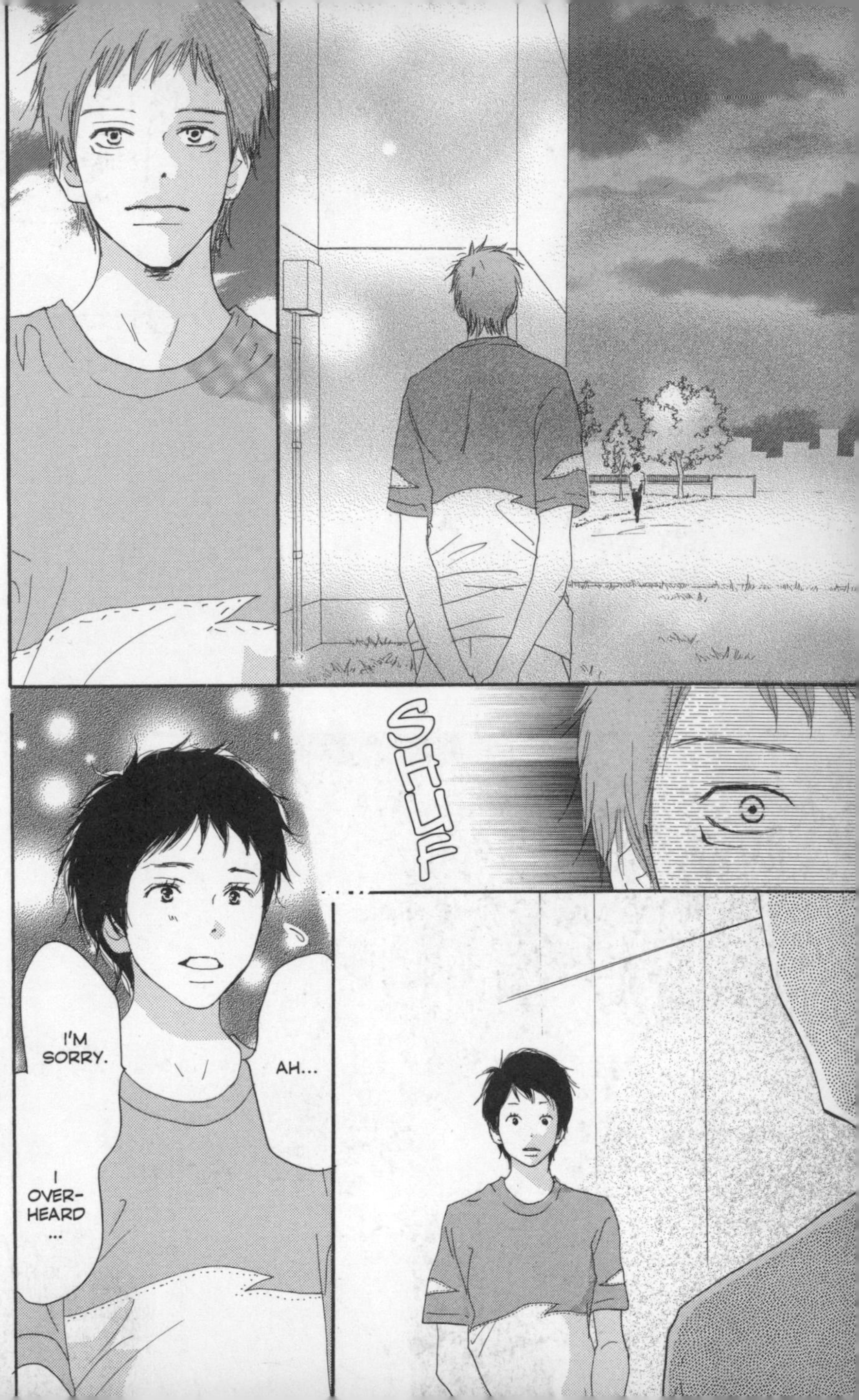
SHUF
AH...
I'M SORRY.
I OVER-HEARD ...

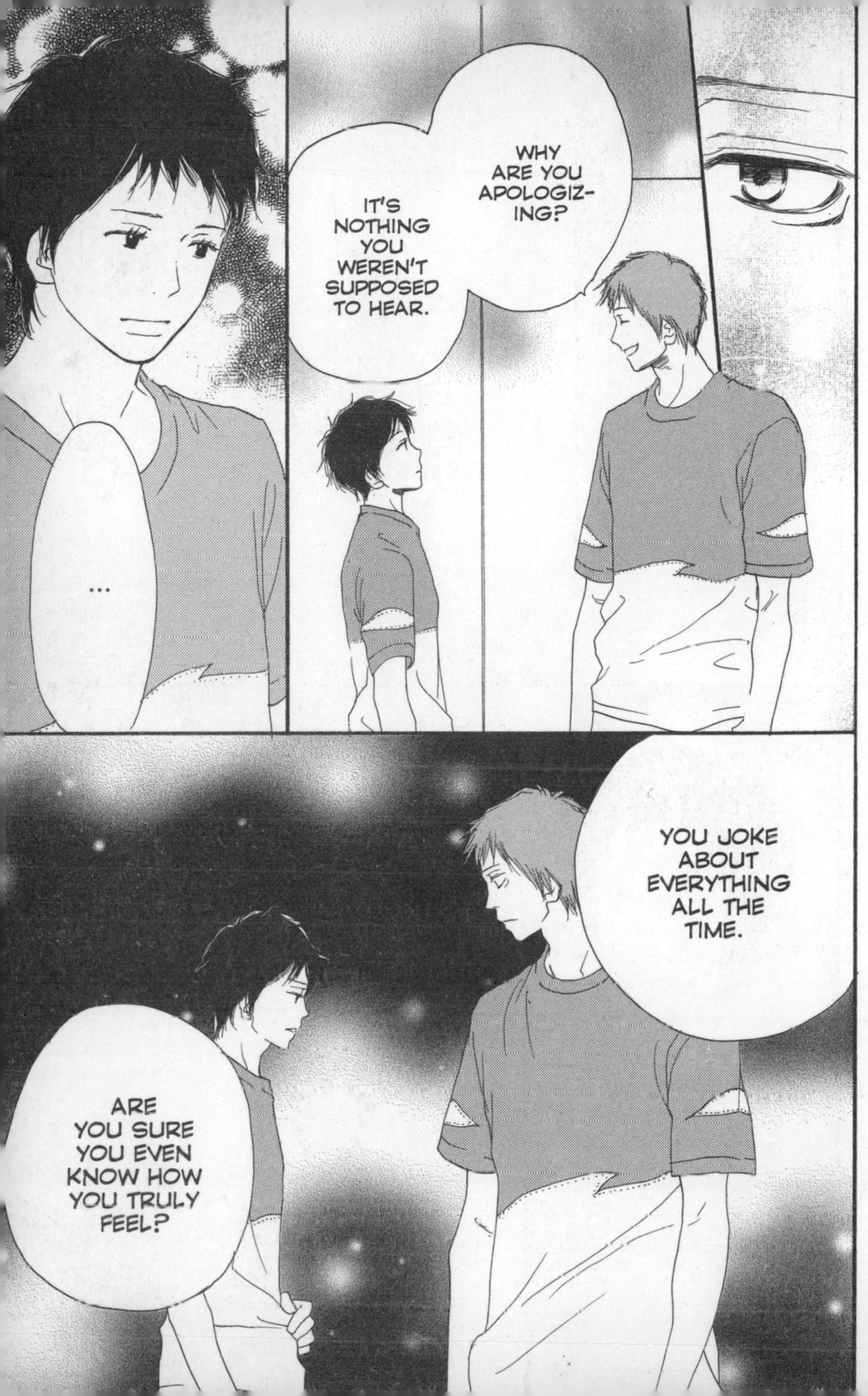
WHY ARE YOU APOLOGIZ-ING?
IT'S NOTHING YOU WEREN'T SUPPOSED TO HEAR.
...
YOU JOKE ABOUT EVERYTHING ALL THE TIME.
ARE YOU SURE YOU EVEN KNOW HOW YOU TRULY FEEL?

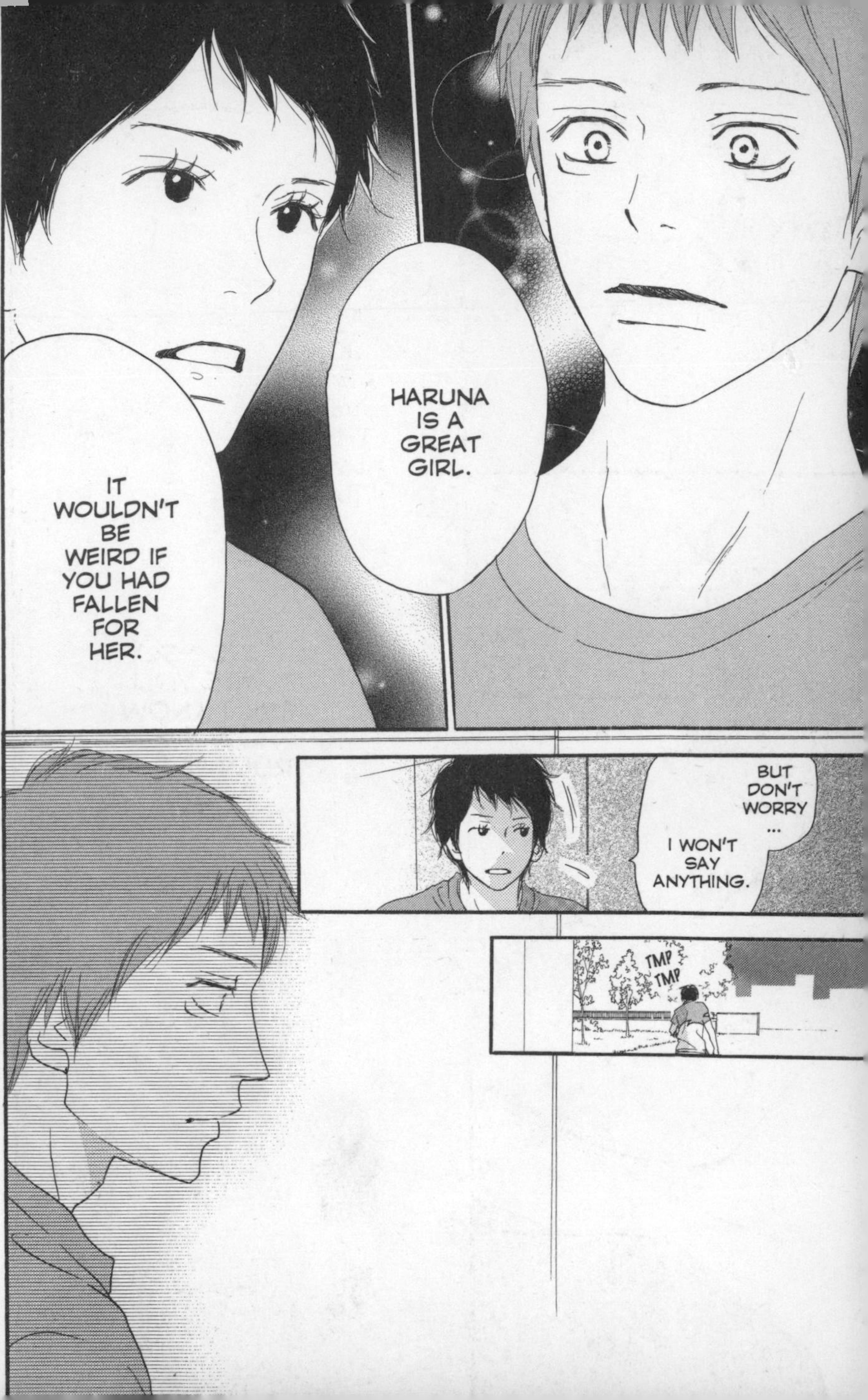
HARUNA IS A GREAT GIRL.
IT WOULDN'T BE WEIRD IF YOU HAD FALLEN FOR HER.
BUT DON'T WORRY... I WON'T SAY ANYTHING.
TMP TMP

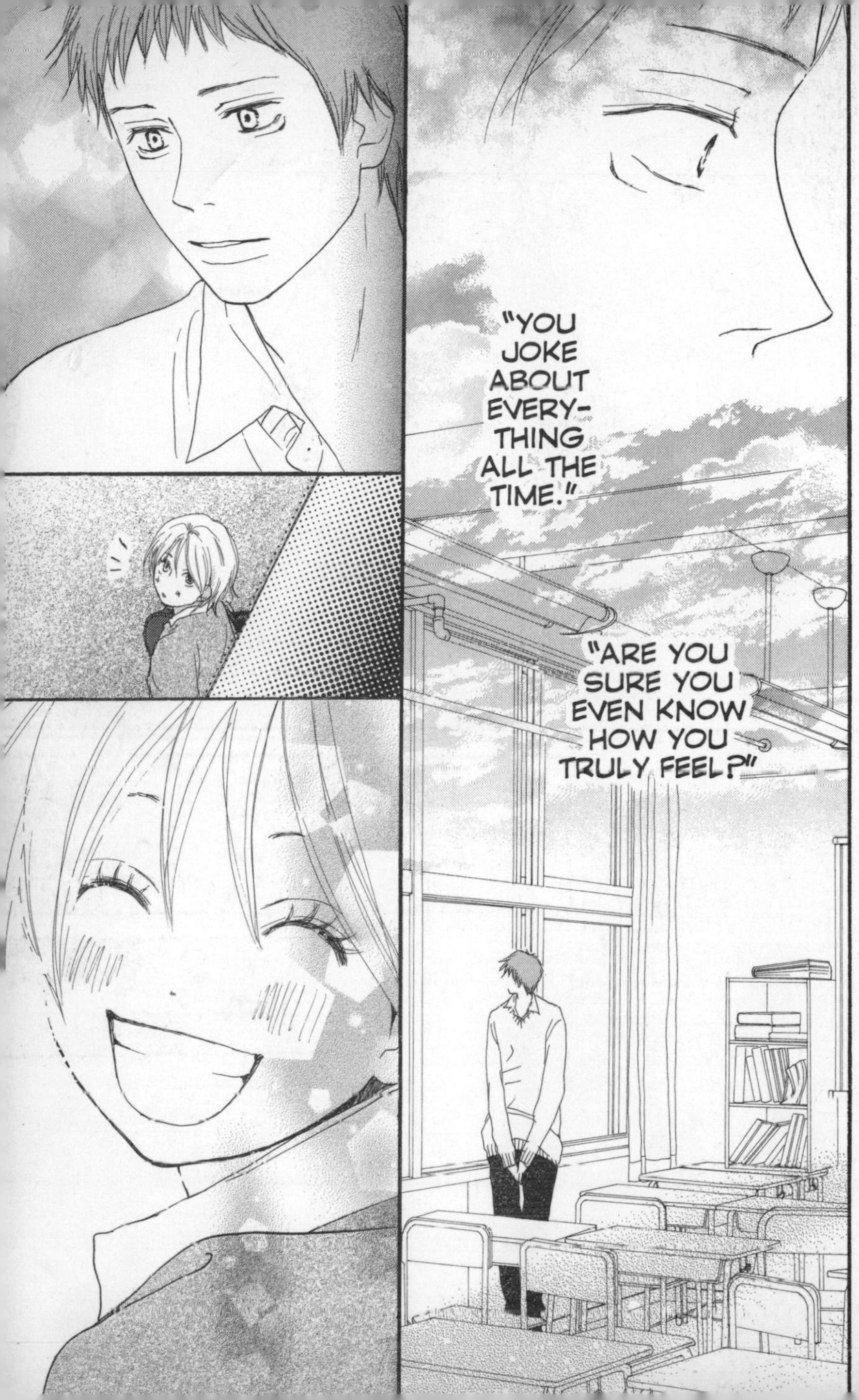
"YOU JOKE ABOUT EVERY-THING ALL THE TIME."
"ARE YOU SURE YOU EVEN KNOW HOW YOU TRULY FEEL?"

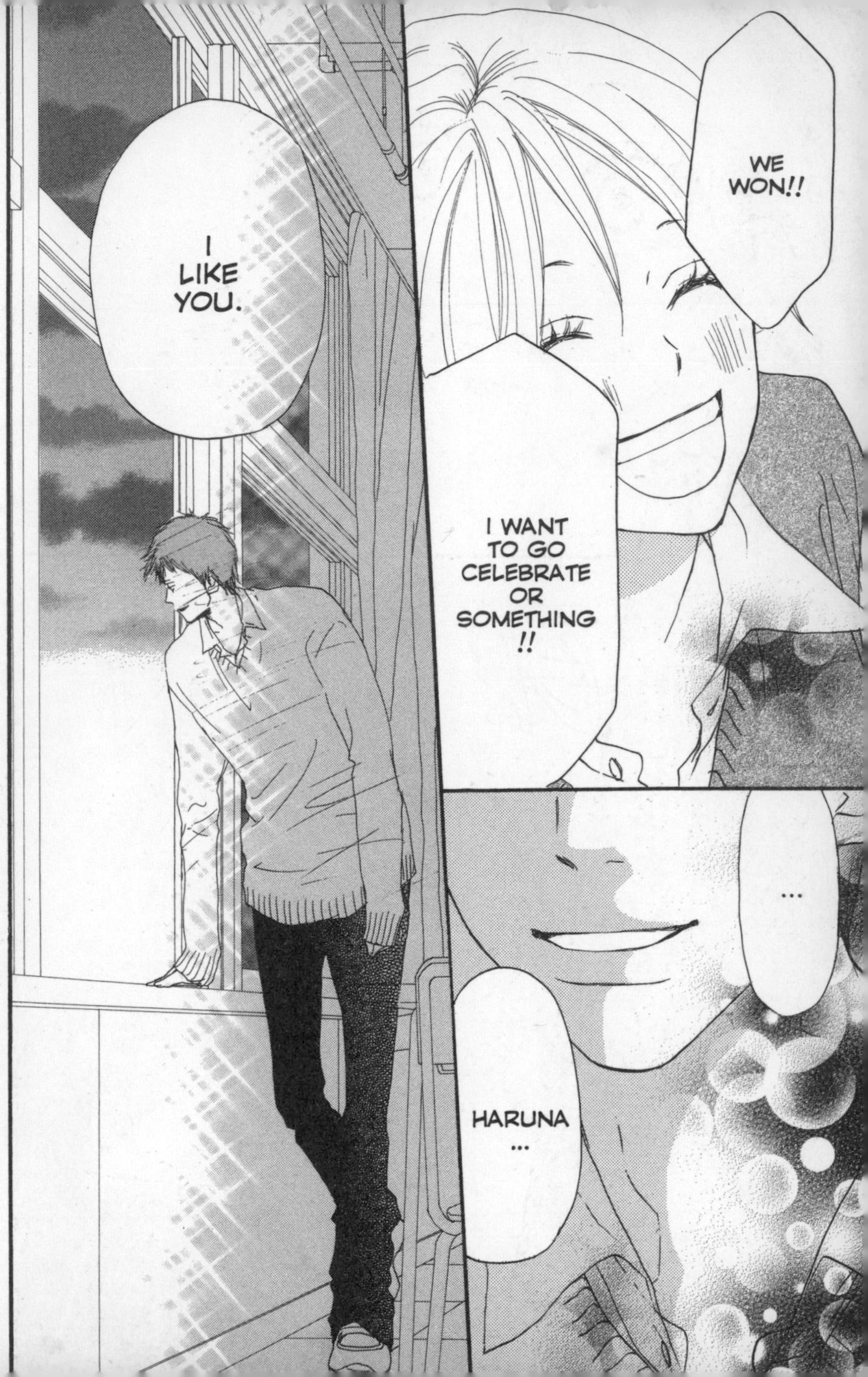
WE WON!!
I WANT TO GO CELEBRATE OR SOMETHING!!
...
HARUNA...
I LIKE YOU.

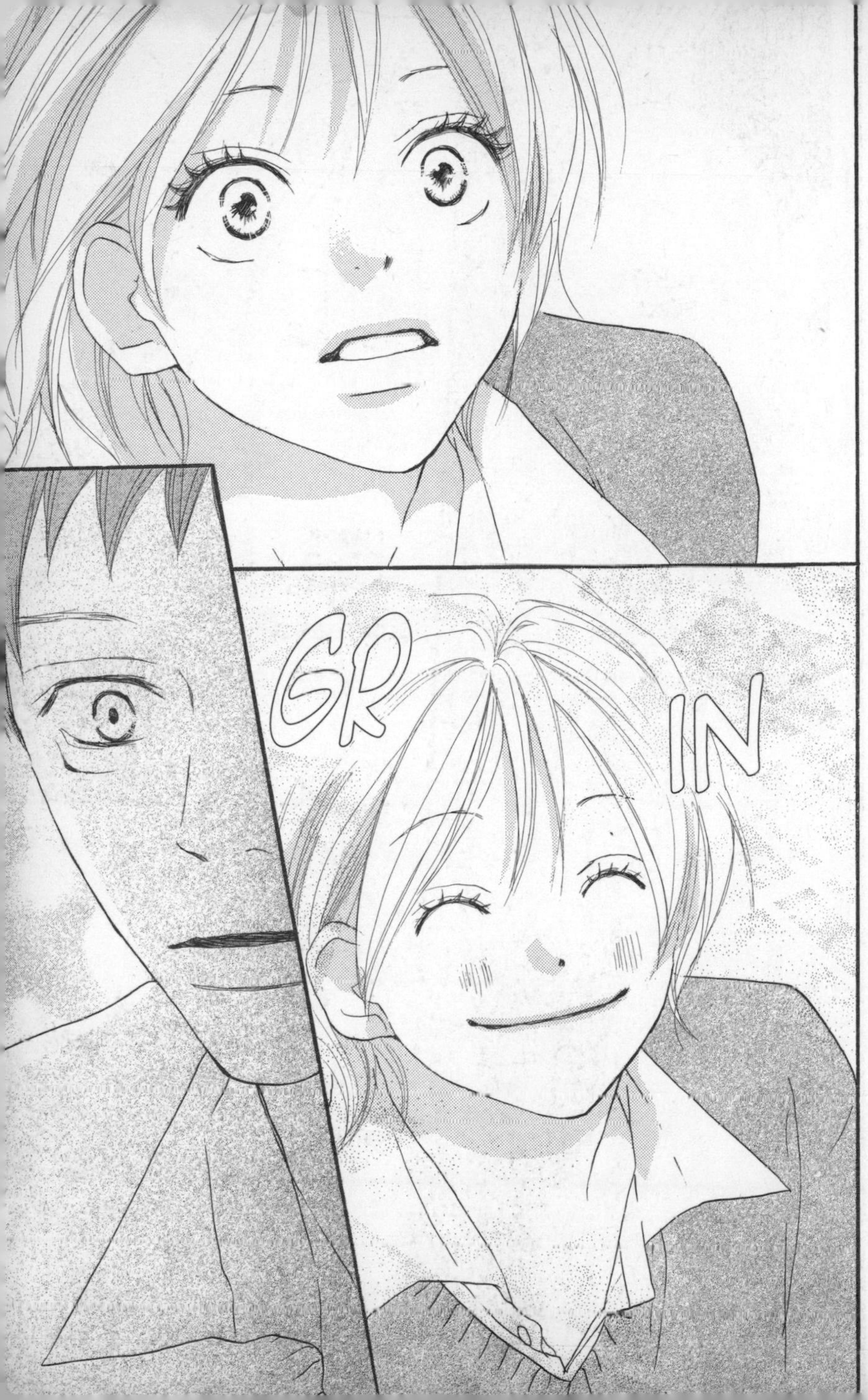
GRIN

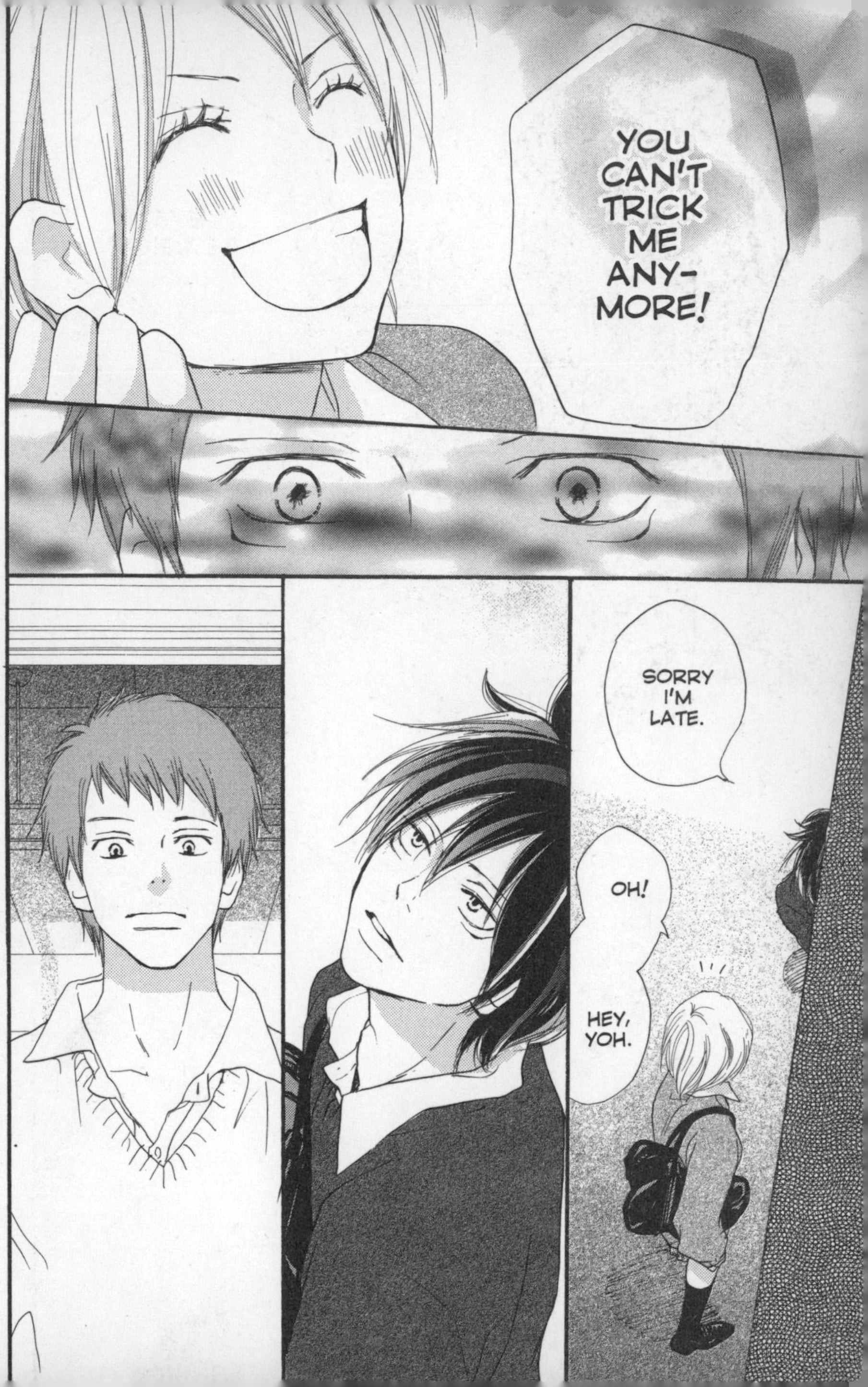
YOU CAN'T TRICK ME ANY-MORE!
SORRY I'M LATE.
OH!
HEY, YOH.

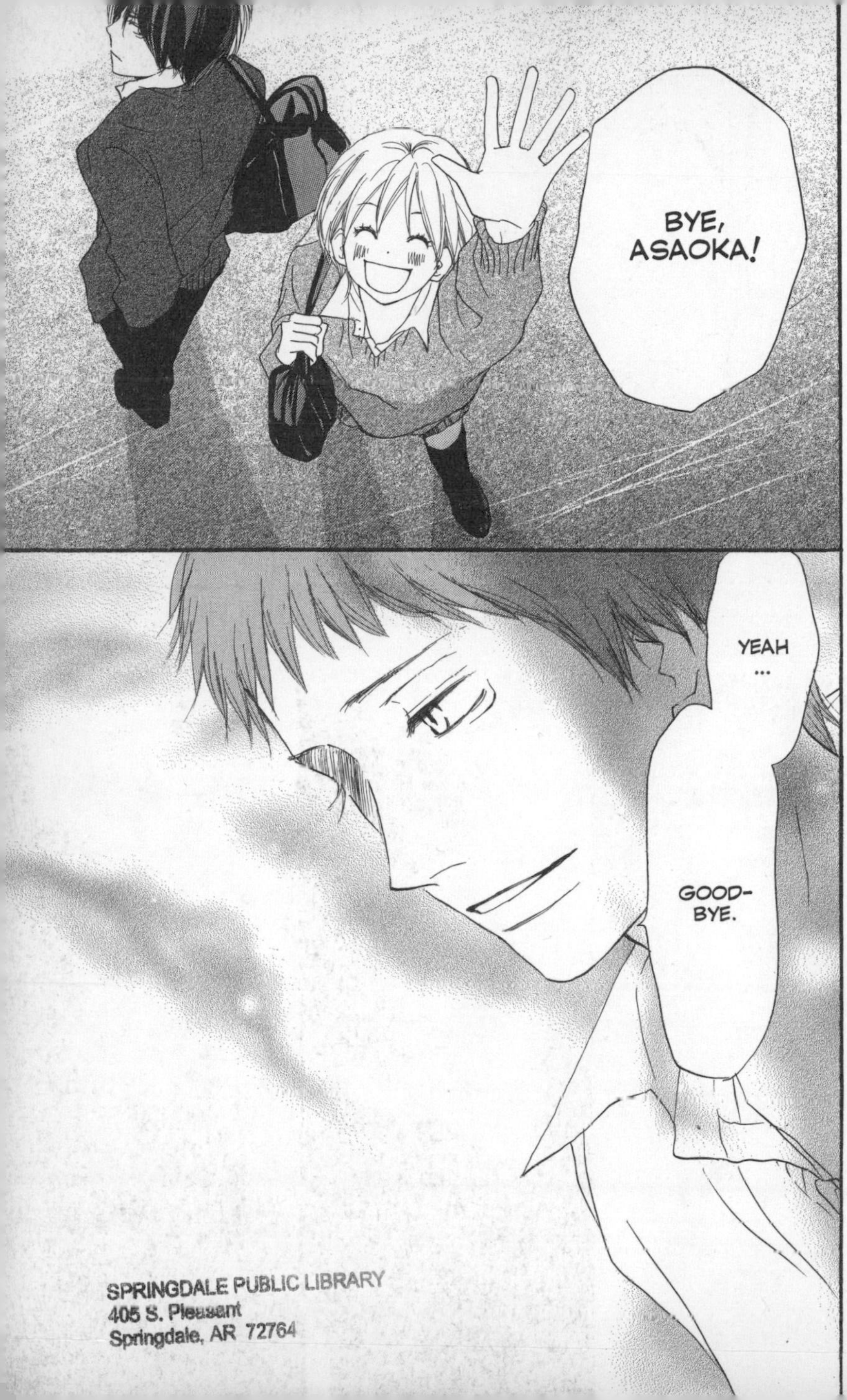
BYE, ASAOKA!
YEAH ...
GOOD-BYE.

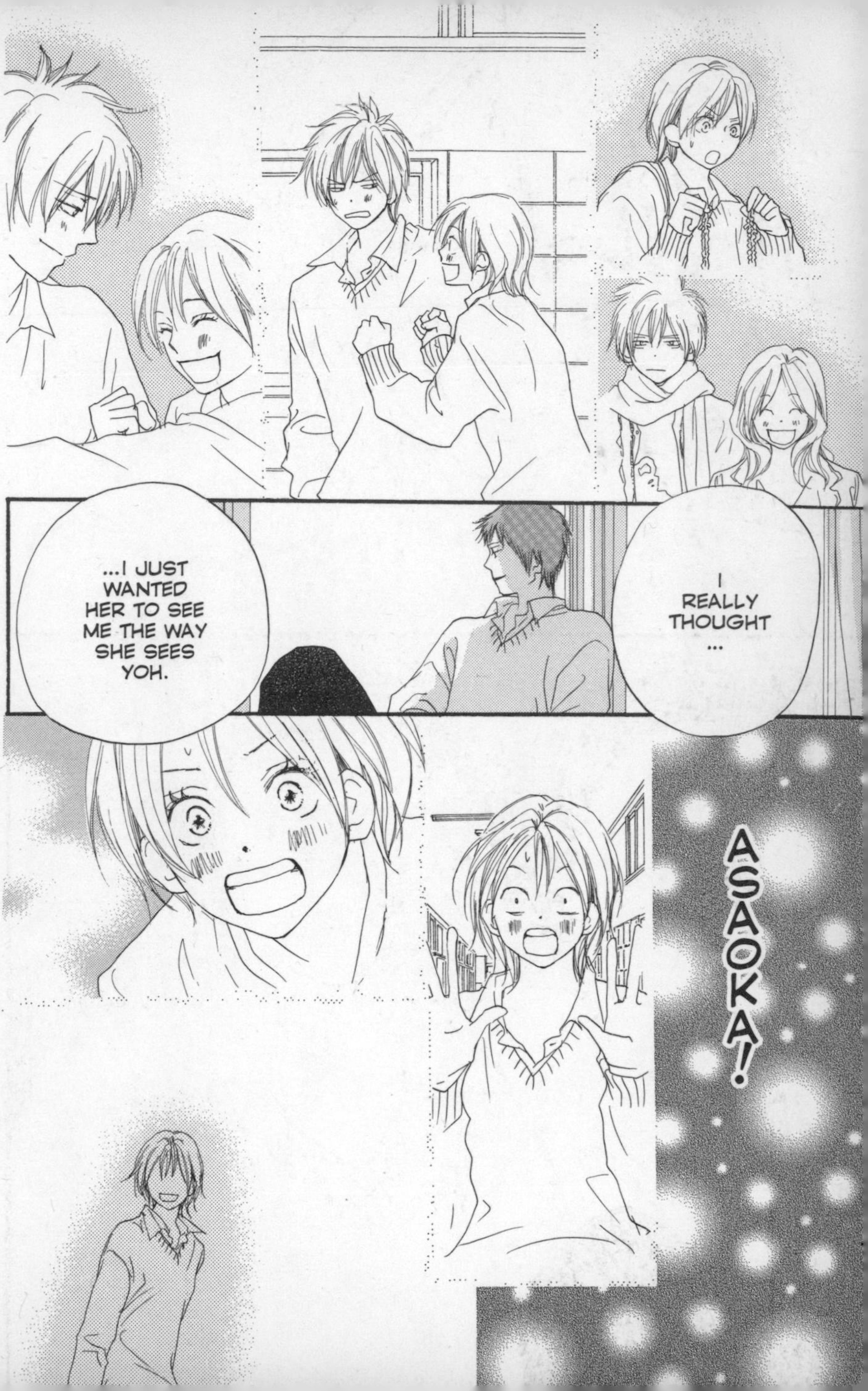

I REALLY THOUGHT ...
...I JUST WANTED HER TO SEE ME THE WAY SHE SEES YOH.
ASAOKA!

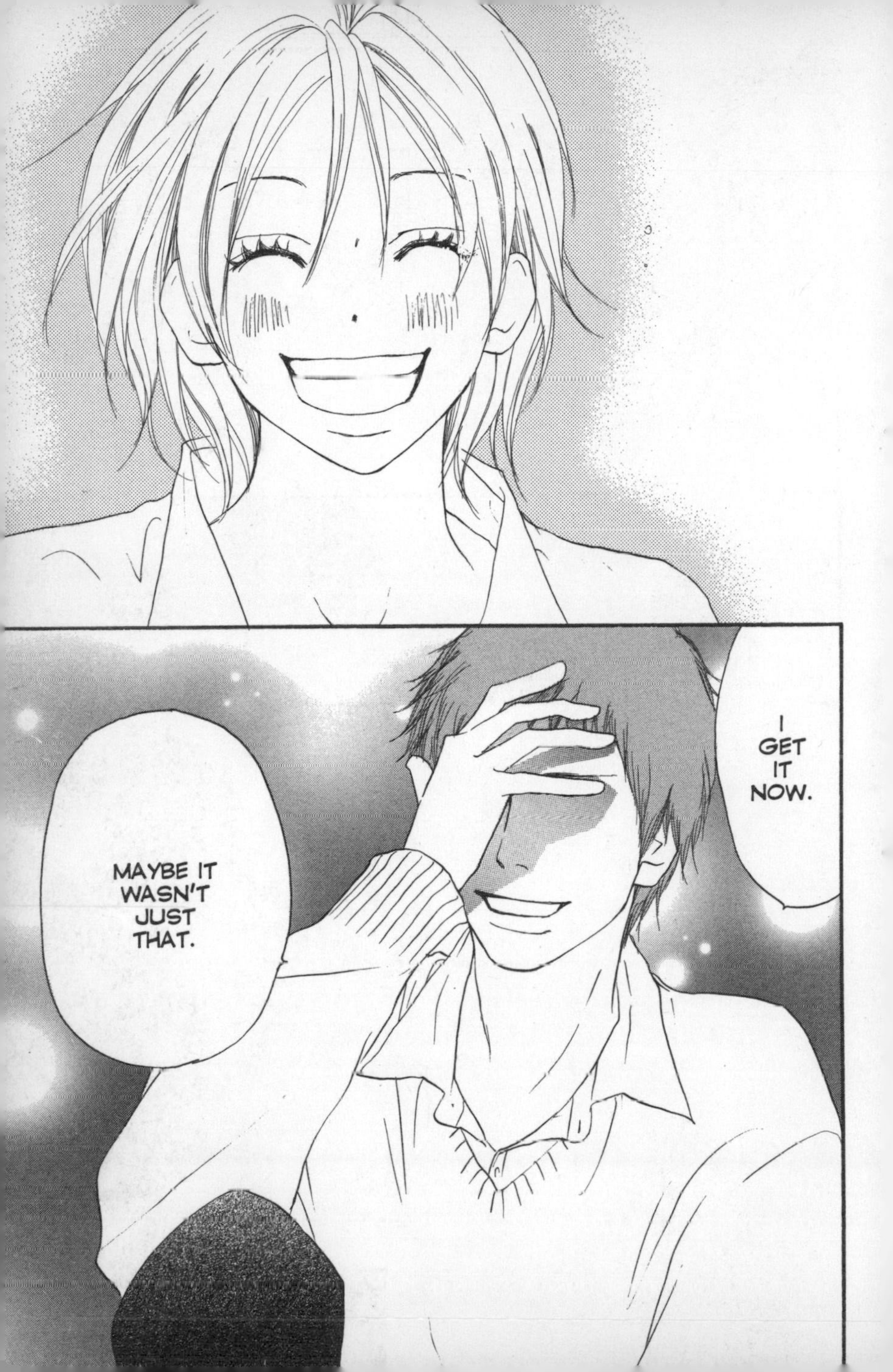
I GET IT NOW.
MAYBE IT WASN'T JUST THAT.

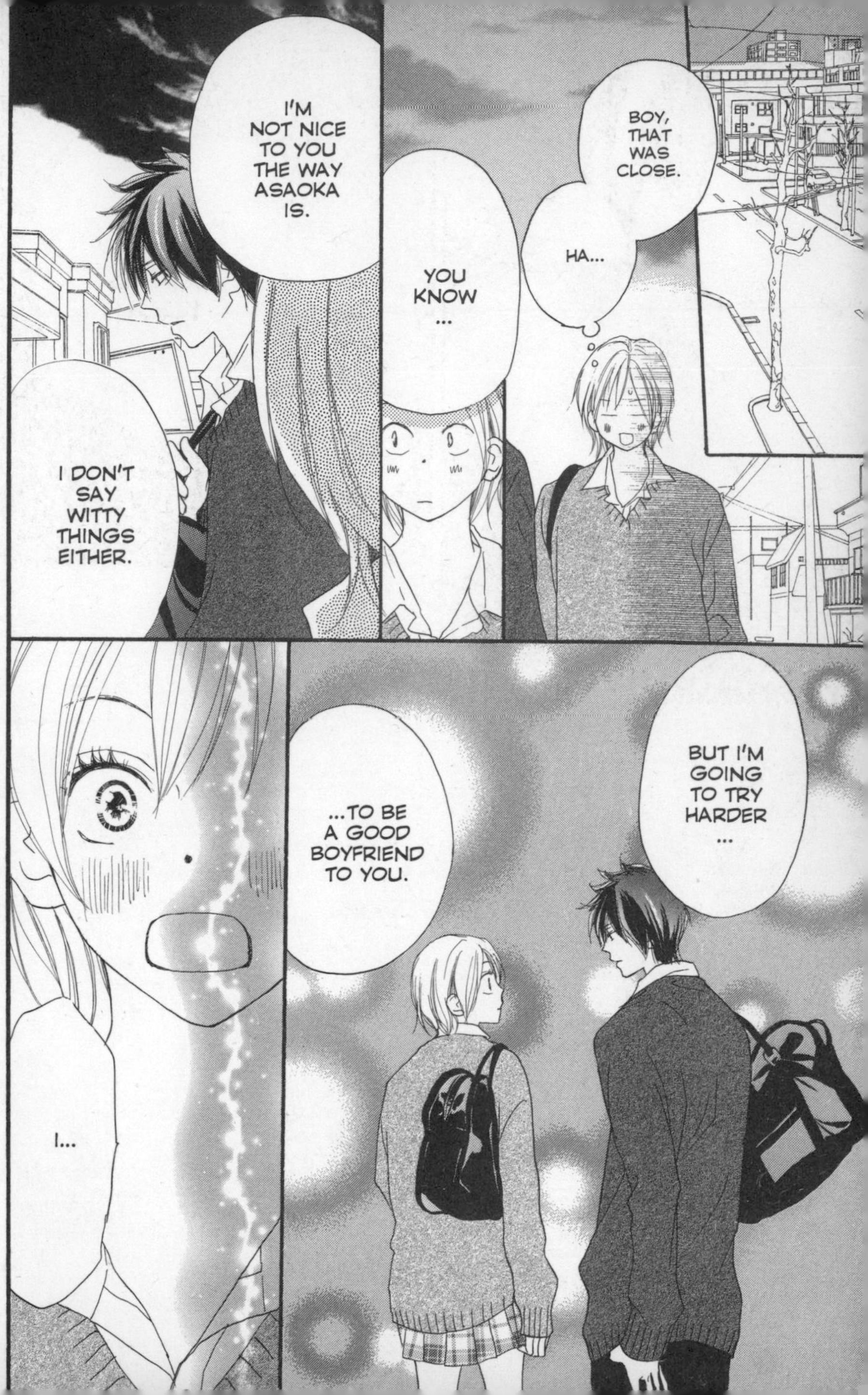
BOY, THAT WAS CLOSE.
HA...
YOU KNOW ...
I'M NOT NICE TO YOU THE WAY ASAOKA IS.
I DON'T SAY WITTY THINGS EITHER.
BUT I'M GOING TO TRY HARDER ...
...TO BE A GOOD BOYFRIEND TO YOU.
I...

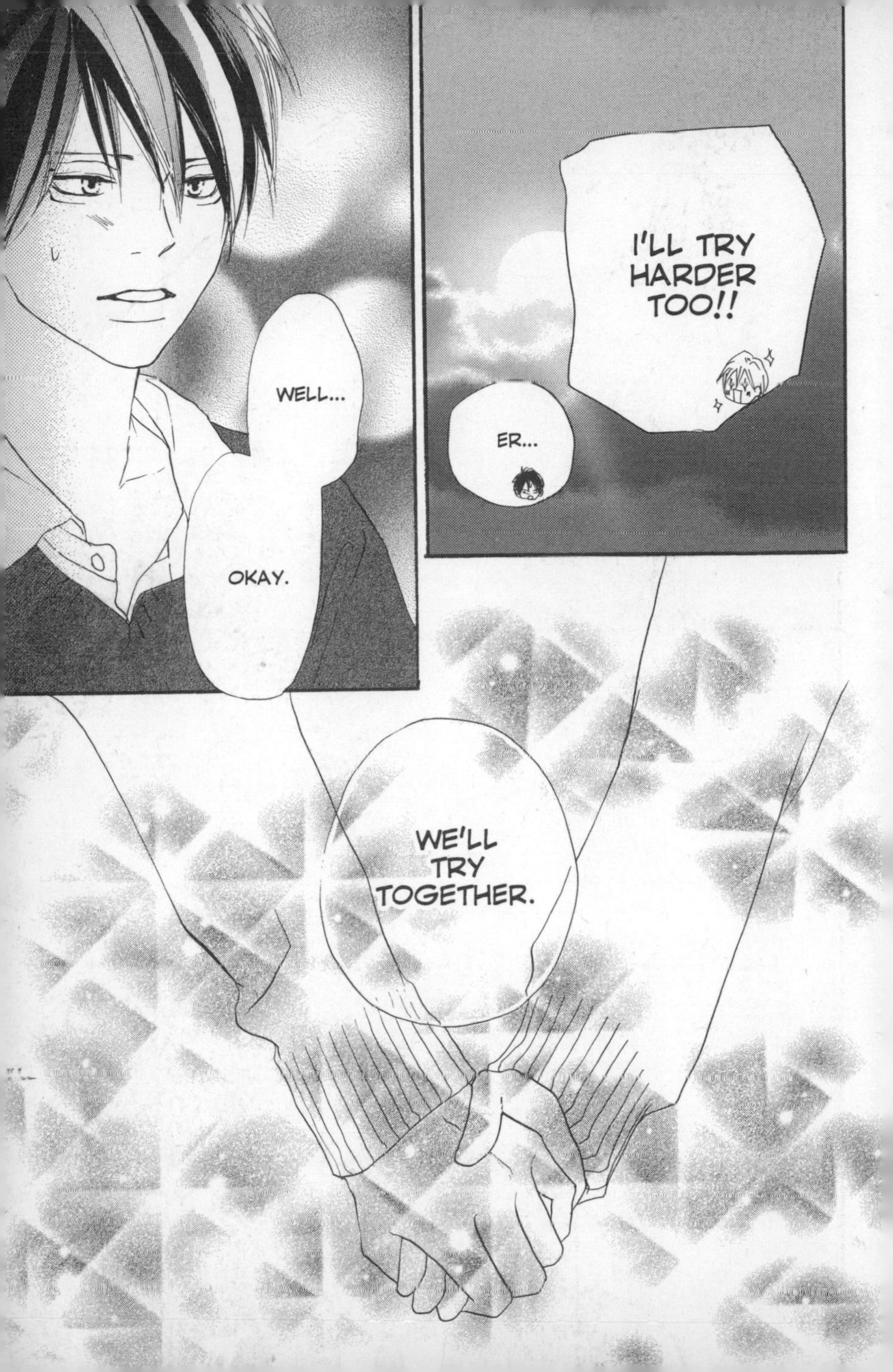
I'LL TRY HARDER TOO!!
ER...
WELL...
OKAY.
WE'LL TRY TOGETHER.

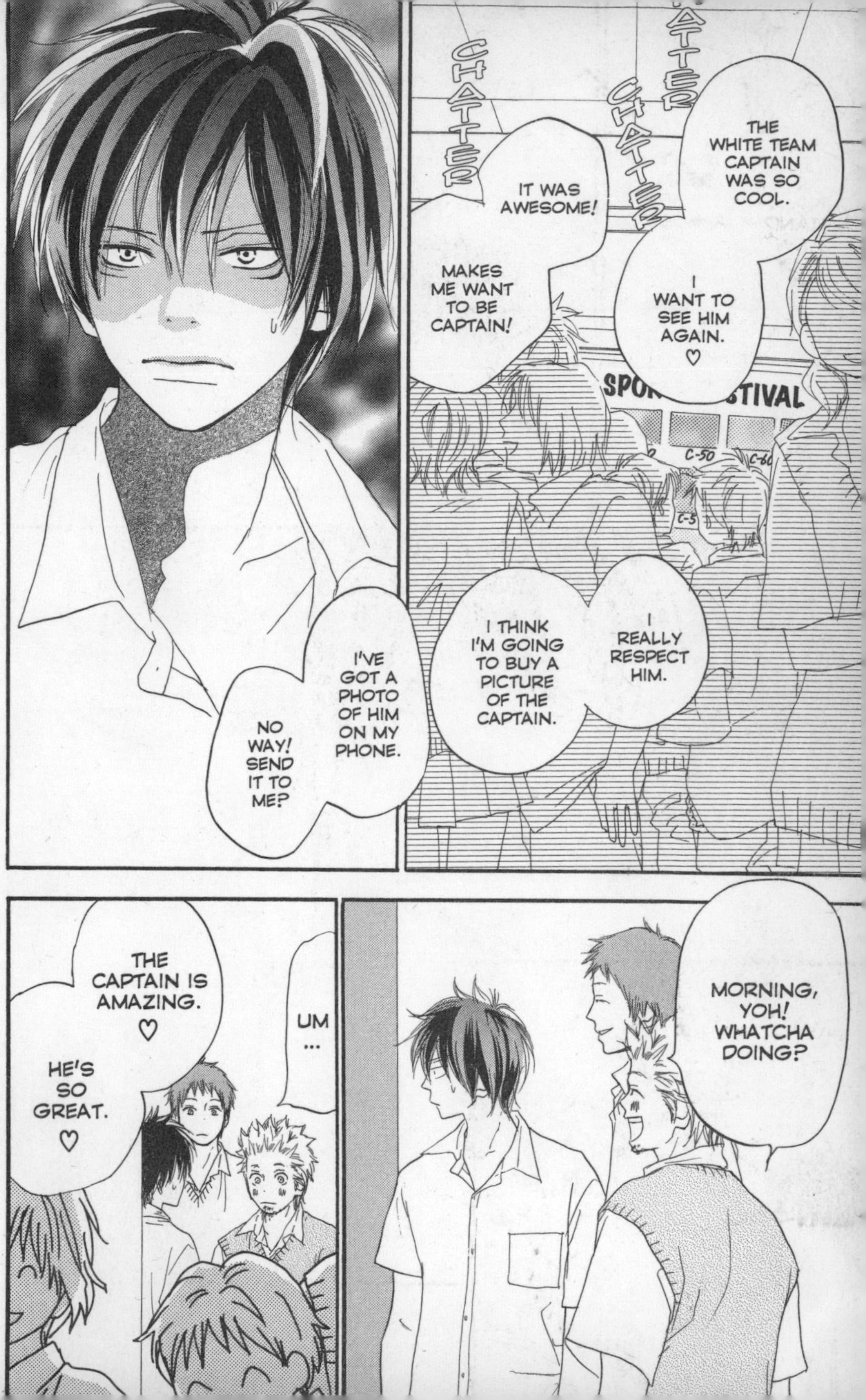
THE WHITE TEAM CAPTAIN WAS SO COOL.
CHATTER
CHATTER
CHATTER
I WANT TO SEE HIM AGAIN. ♡
IT WAS AWESOME!
MAKES ME WANT TO BE CAPTAIN!
I REALLY RESPECT HIM.
I THINK I'M GOING TO BUY A PICTURE OF THE CAPTAIN.
I'VE GOT A PHOTO OF HIM ON MY PHONE.
NO WAY! SEND IT TO ME?
MORNING, YOH! WHATCHA DOING?
UM ...
THE CAPTAIN IS AMAZING. ♡
HE'S SO GREAT. ♡

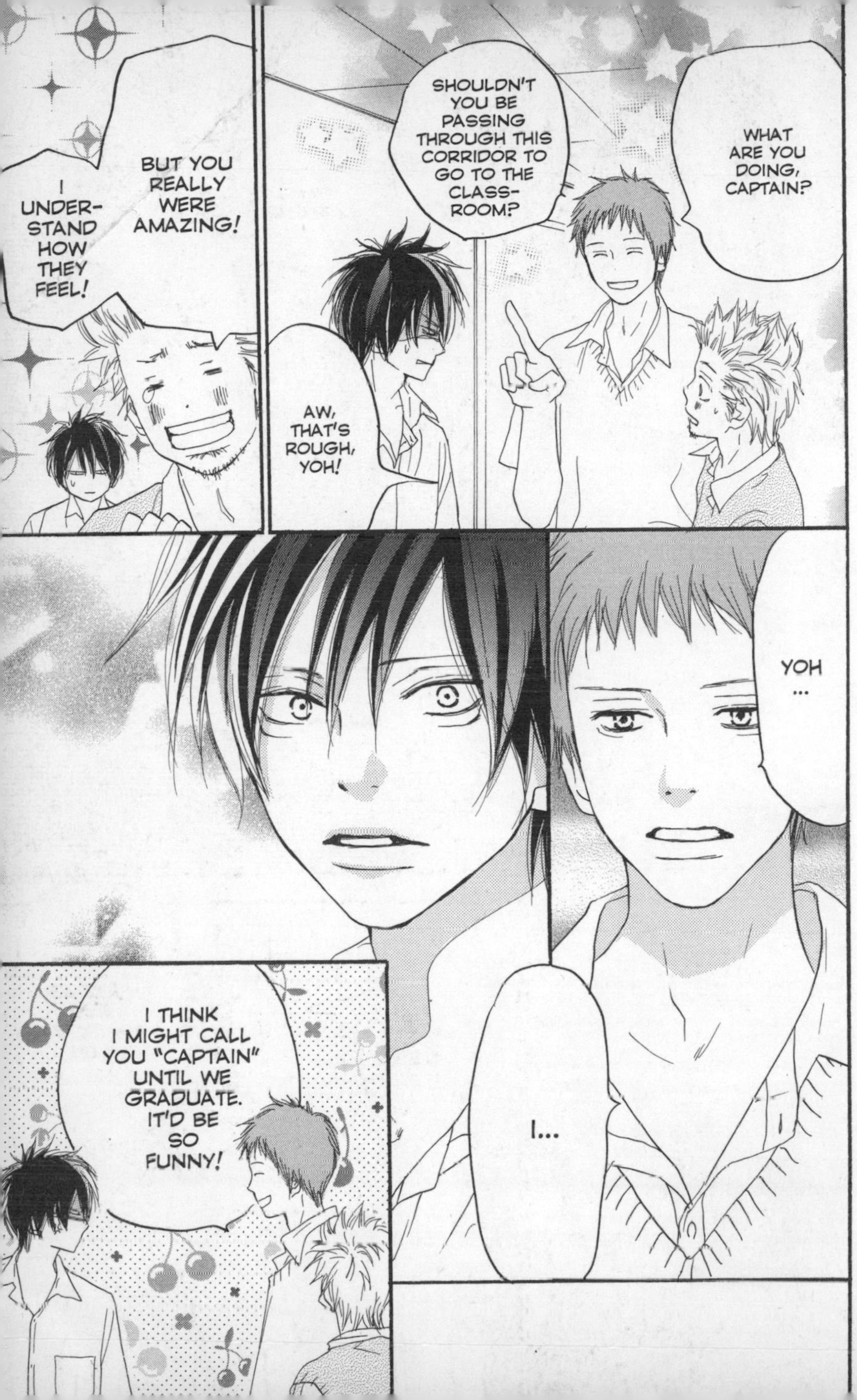
WHAT ARE YOU DOING, CAPTAIN?
SHOULDN'T YOU BE PASSING THROUGH THIS CORRIDOR TO GO TO THE CLASS-ROOM?
AW, THAT'S ROUGH, YOH!
BUT YOU REALLY WERE AMAZING!
I UNDER-STAND HOW THEY FEEL!
YOH ...
I...
I THINK I MIGHT CALL YOU "CAPTAIN" UNTIL WE GRADUATE. IT'D BE SO FUNNY!

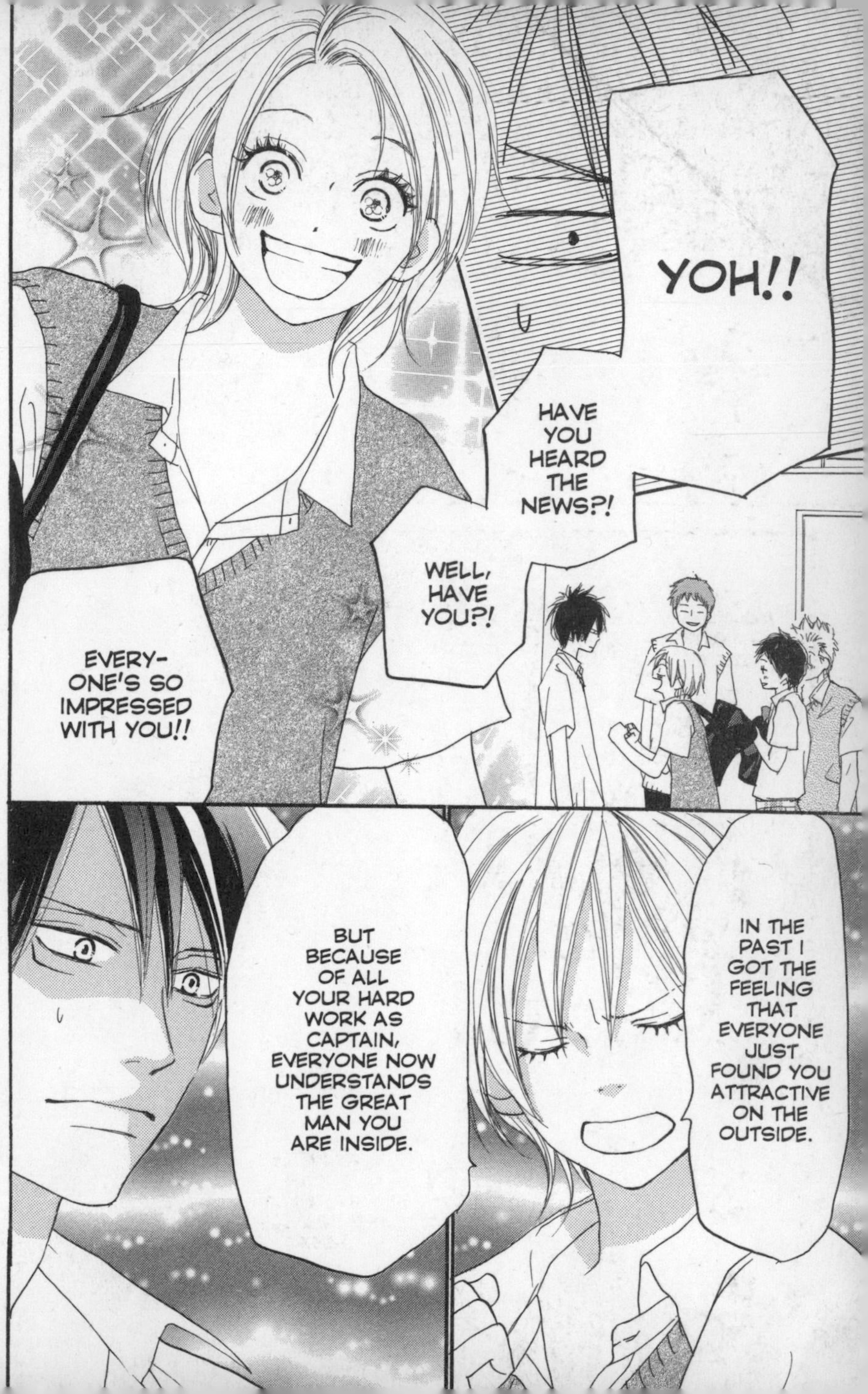
YOH!!
HAVE YOU HEARD THE NEWS?!
WELL, HAVE YOU?!
EVERY-ONE'S SO IMPRESSED WITH YOU!!
IN THE PAST I GOT THE FEELING THAT EVERYONE JUST FOUND YOU ATTRACTIVE ON THE OUTSIDE.
BUT BECAUSE OF ALL YOUR HARD WORK AS CAPTAIN, EVERYONE NOW UNDERSTANDS THE GREAT MAN YOU ARE INSIDE.

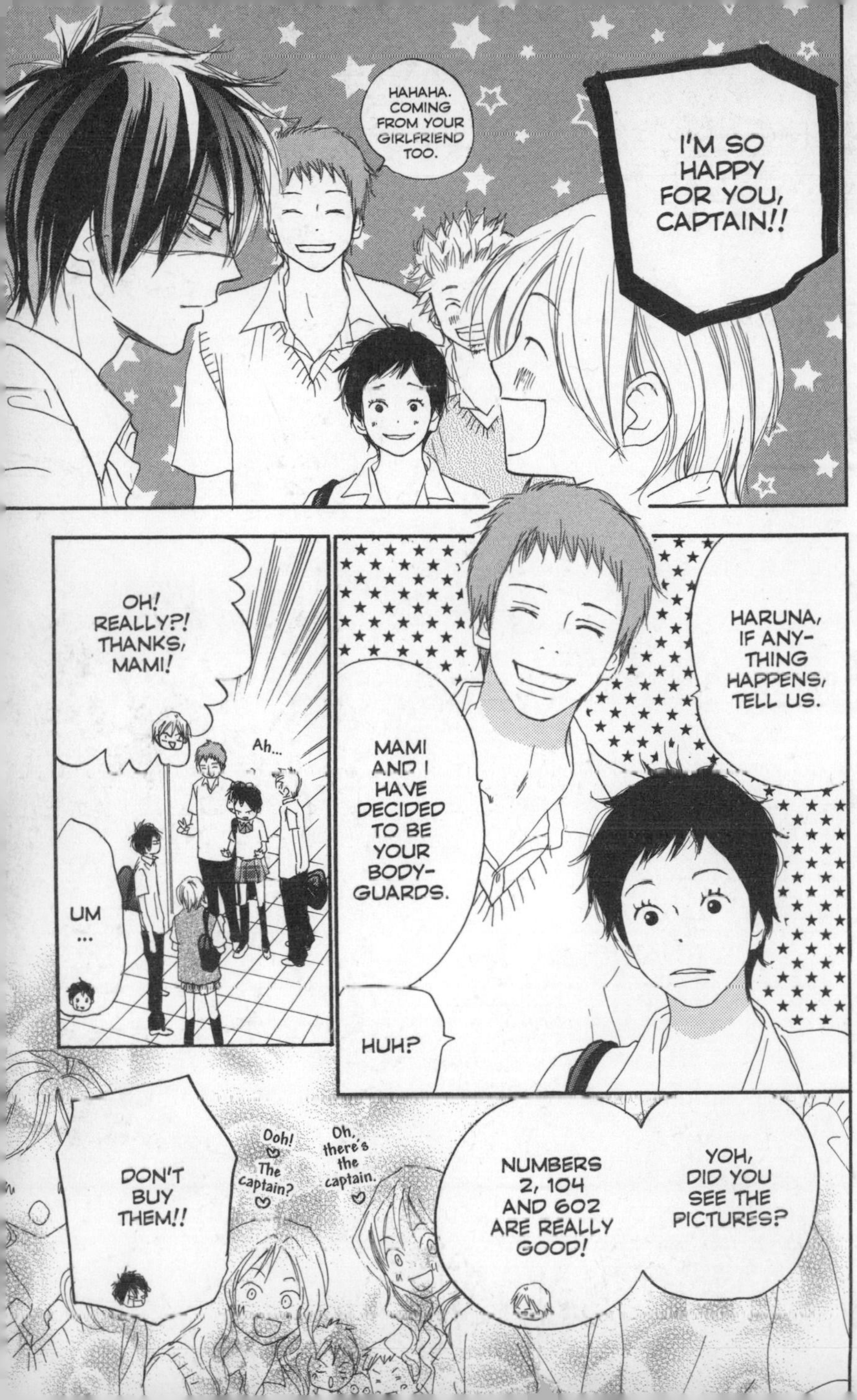
I'M SO HAPPY FOR YOU, CAPTAIN!!
HAHAHA. COMING FROM YOUR GIRLFRIEND TOO.
HARUNA, IF ANY-THING HAPPENS, TELL US.
MAMI AND I HAVE DECIDED TO BE YOUR BODY-GUARDS.
HUH?
OH! REALLY?! THANKS, MAMI!
Ah...
UM ...
YOH, DID YOU SEE THE PICTURES?
NUMBERS 2, 104 AND 602 ARE REALLY GOOD!
Oh, there's the captain.
Ooh! The captain?
DON'T BUY THEM!!

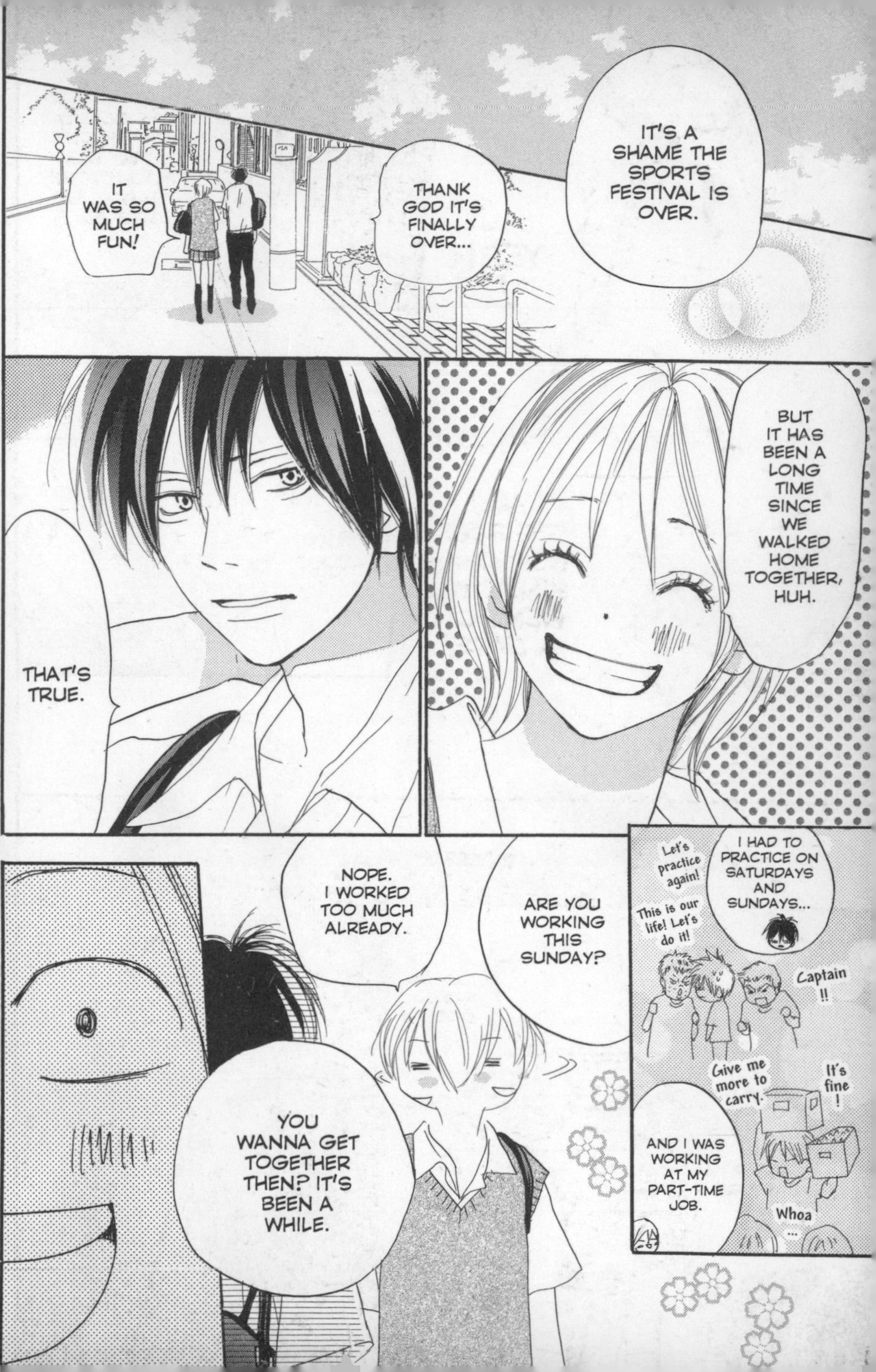
IT'S A SHAME THE SPORTS FESTIVAL IS OVER.
THANK GOD IT'S FINALLY OVER...
IT WAS SO MUCH FUN!
BUT IT HAS BEEN A LONG TIME SINCE WE WALKED HOME TOGETHER, HUH.
THAT'S TRUE.
I HAD TO PRACTICE ON SATURDAYS AND SUNDAYS...
Let's practice again!
This is our life! Let's do it!
Captain !!
It's fine !
Give me more to carry.
AND I WAS WORKING AT MY PART-TIME JOB.
Whoa ...
ARE YOU WORKING THIS SUNDAY?
NOPE. I WORKED TOO MUCH ALREADY.
YOU WANNA GET TOGETHER THEN? IT'S BEEN A WHILE.

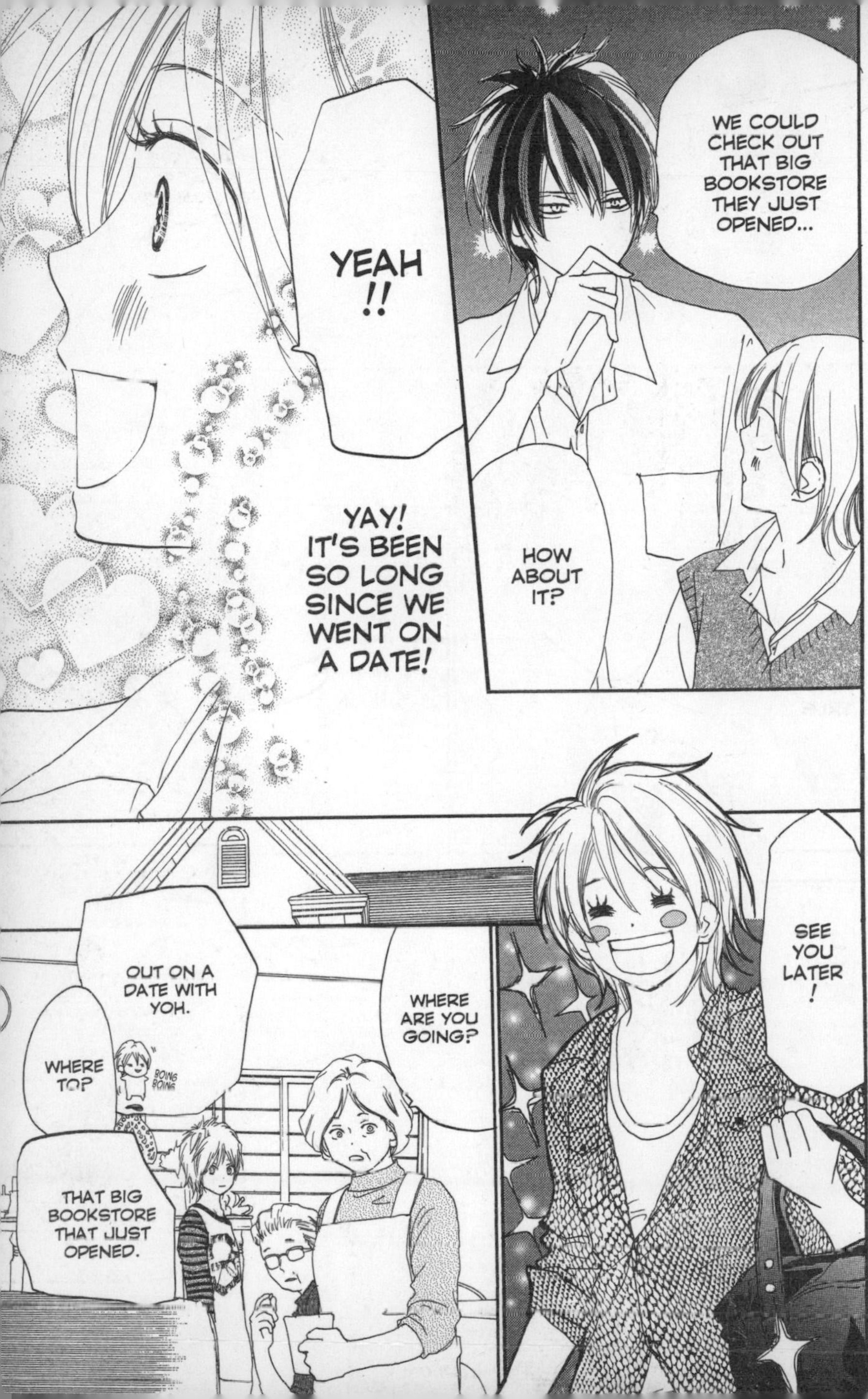
WE COULD CHECK OUT THAT BIG BOOKSTORE THEY JUST OPENED...
HOW ABOUT IT?
YEAH!!
YAY! IT'S BEEN SO LONG SINCE WE WENT ON A DATE!
SEE YOU LATER!
WHERE ARE YOU GOING?
OUT ON A DATE WITH YOH.
WHERE TO?
BOING BOING
THAT BIG BOOKSTORE THAT JUST OPENED.

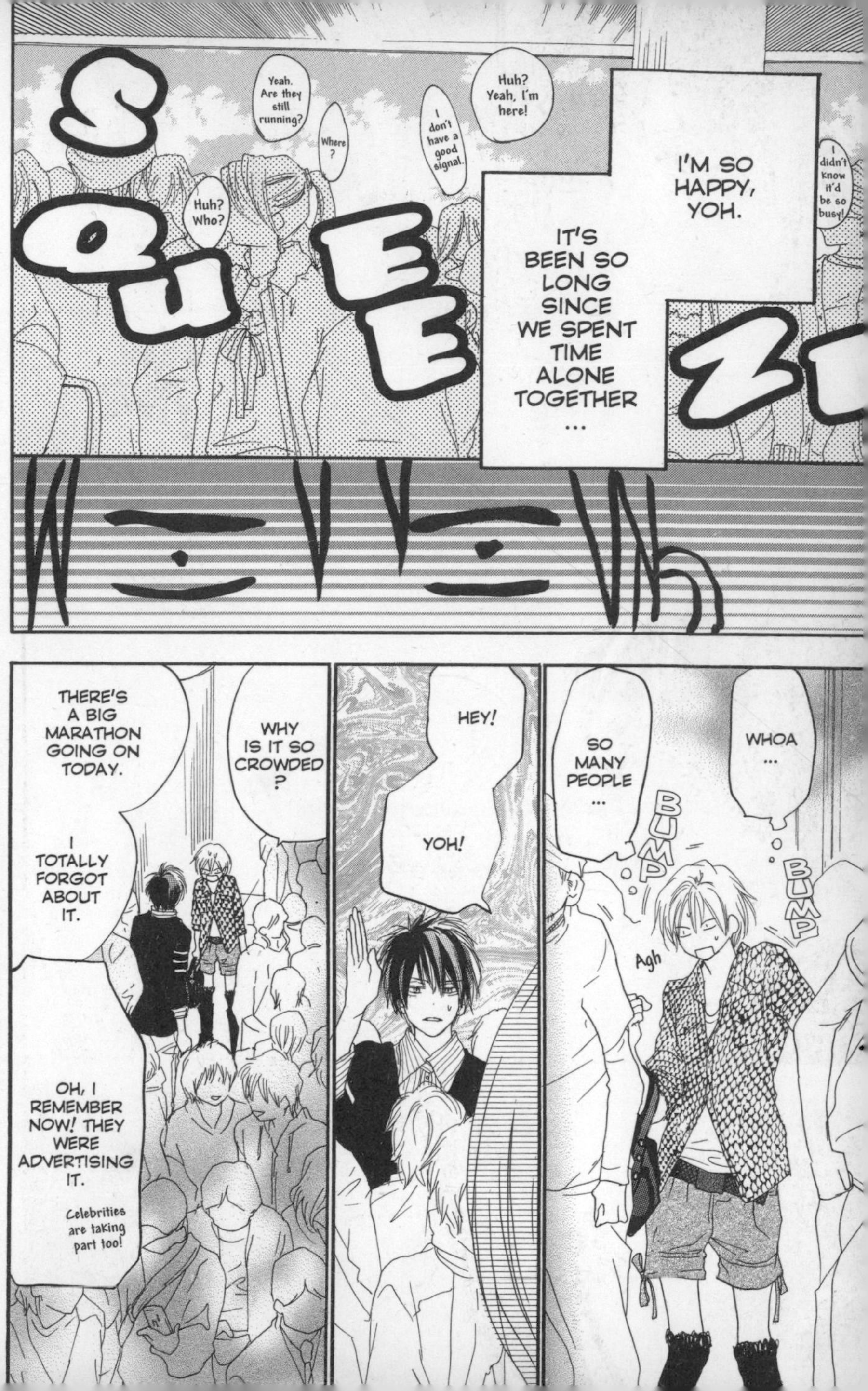
I didn't know it'd be so busy!
I'M SO HAPPY, YOH.
IT'S BEEN SO LONG SINCE WE SPENT TIME ALONE TOGETHER ...
Huh? Yeah, I'm here!
I don't have a good signal.
Yeah. Are they still running?
Where?
Huh? Who?
SQUEEZ
WHOA ...
SO MANY PEOPLE ...
BUMP
BUMP
Agh
HEY!
YOH!
WHY IS IT SO CROWDED?
THERE'S A BIG MARATHON GOING ON TODAY.
I TOTALLY FORGOT ABOUT IT.
OH, I REMEMBER NOW! THEY WERE ADVERTISING IT.
Celebrities are taking part too!

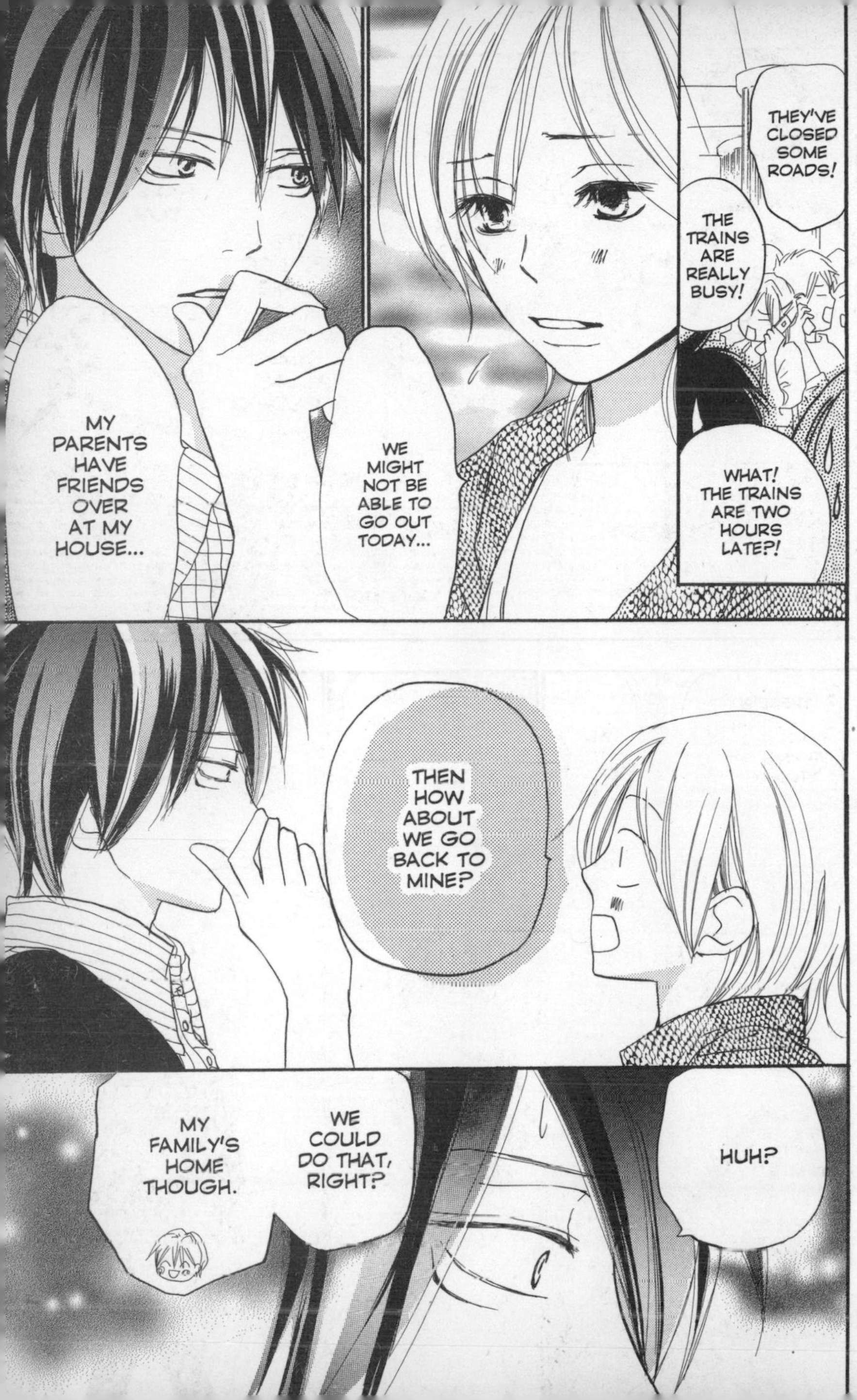

THEY'VE CLOSED SOME ROADS!
THE TRAINS ARE REALLY BUSY!
WHAT! THE TRAINS ARE TWO HOURS LATE?!
WE MIGHT NOT BE ABLE TO GO OUT TODAY...
MY PARENTS HAVE FRIENDS OVER AT MY HOUSE...
THEN HOW ABOUT WE GO BACK TO MINE?
HUH?
WE COULD DO THAT, RIGHT?
MY FAMILY'S HOME THOUGH.

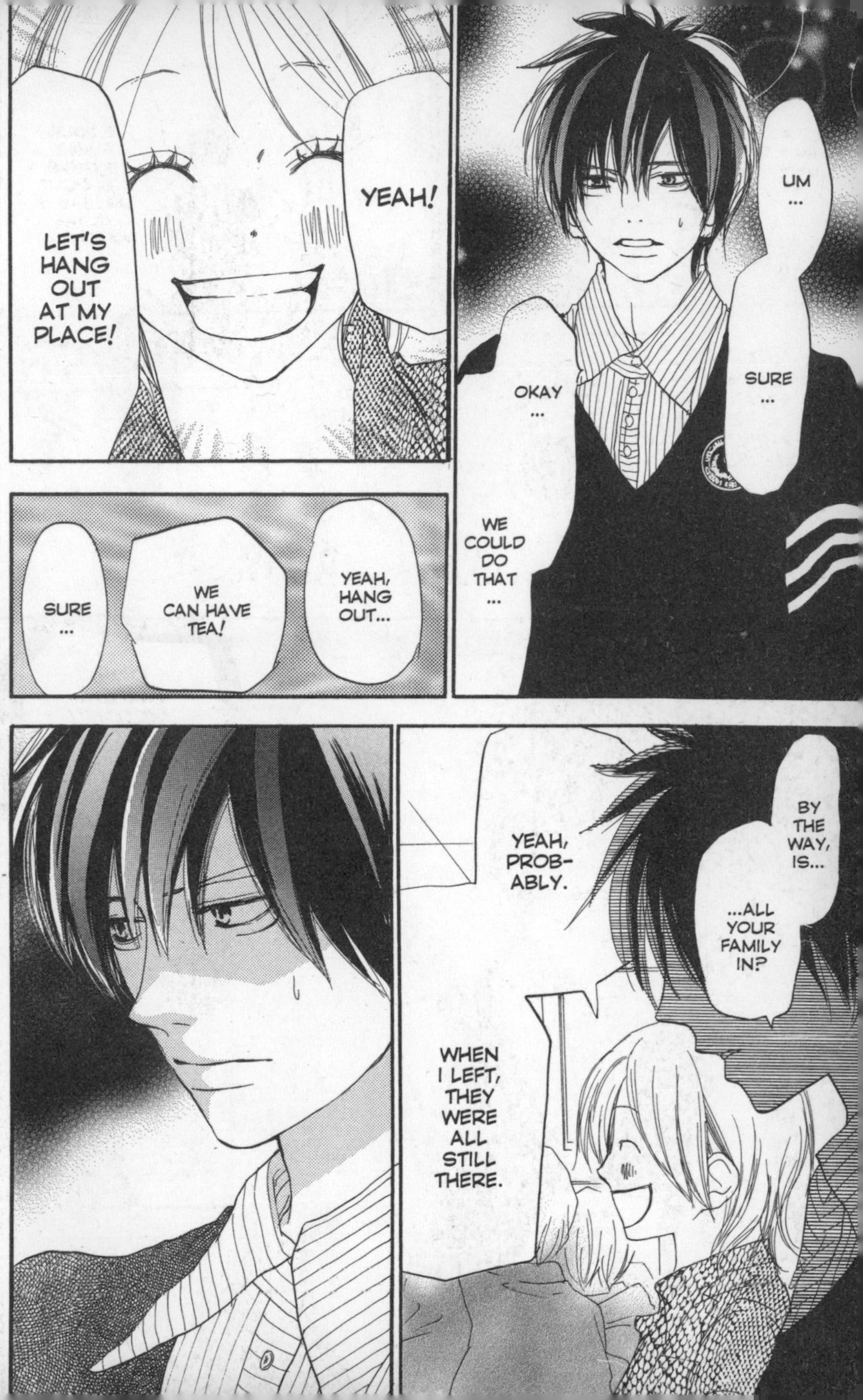
UM ...
SURE ...
OKAY ...
WE COULD DO THAT ...
YEAH!
LET'S HANG OUT AT MY PLACE!
YEAH, HANG OUT...
WE CAN HAVE TEA!
SURE ...
BY THE WAY, IS...
...ALL YOUR FAMILY IN?
YEAH, PROBABLY.
WHEN I LEFT, THEY WERE ALL STILL THERE.

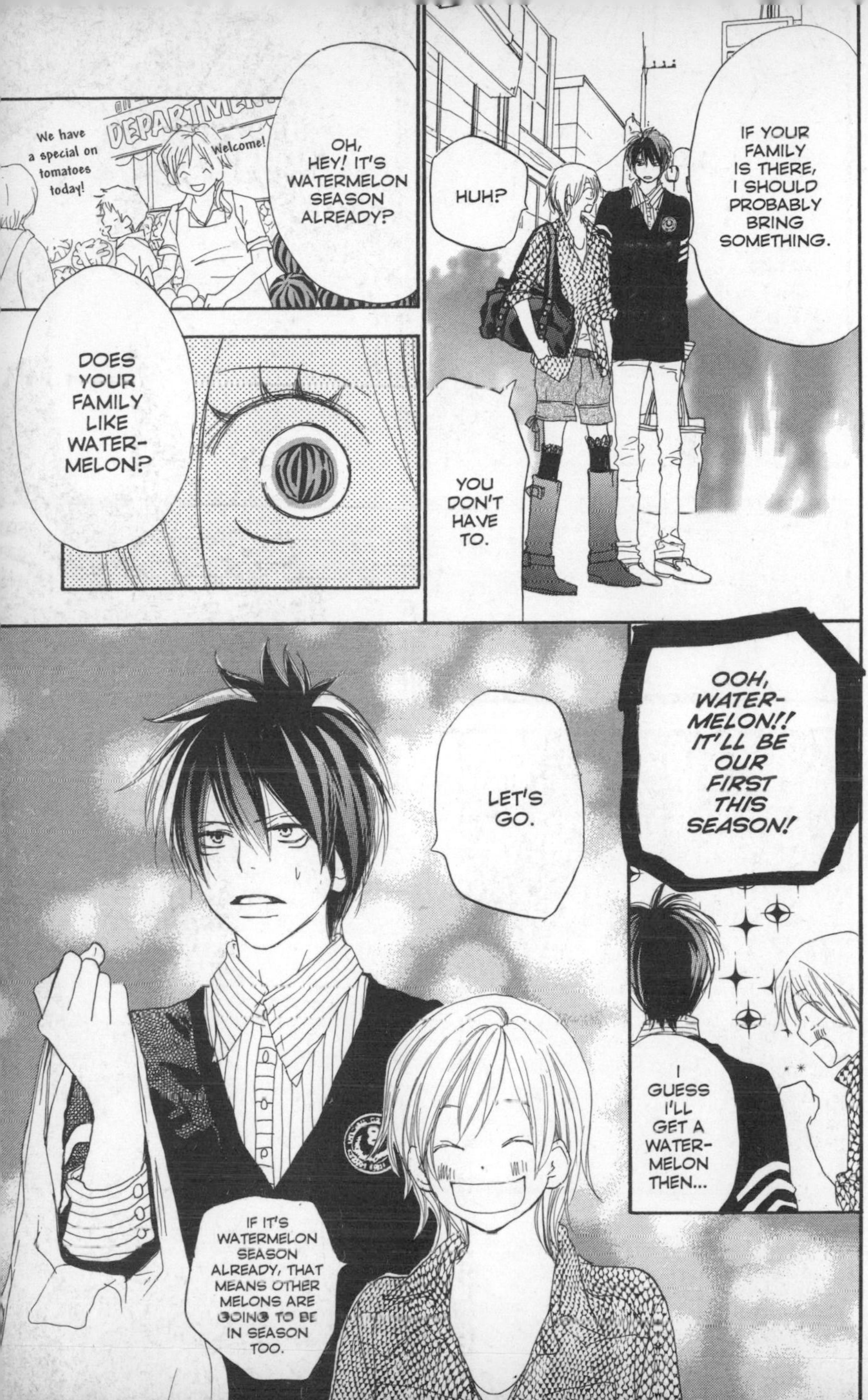
IF YOUR FAMILY IS THERE, I SHOULD PROBABLY BRING SOMETHING.
HUH?
YOU DON'T HAVE TO.
OH, HEY! IT'S WATERMELON SEASON ALREADY?
Welcome!
We have a special on tomatoes today!
DEPARTMENT
DOES YOUR FAMILY LIKE WATER-MELON?
OOH, WATER-MELON!! IT'LL BE OUR FIRST THIS SEASON!
I GUESS I'LL GET A WATER-MELON THEN...
LET'S GO.
IF IT'S WATERMELON SEASON ALREADY, THAT MEANS OTHER MELONS ARE GOING TO BE IN SEASON TOO.

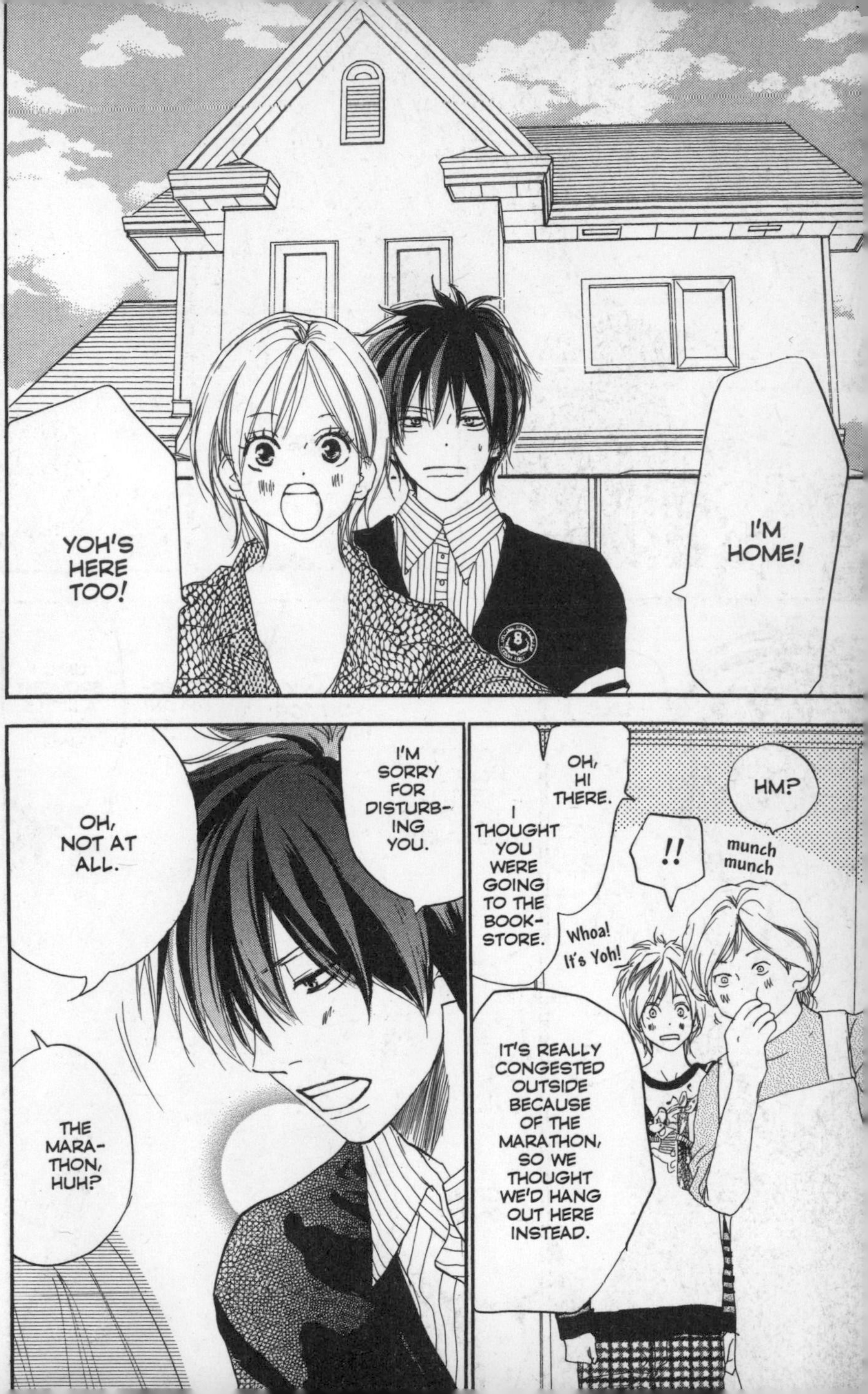
I'M HOME!
YOH'S HERE TOO!
HM?
munch munch
!!
OH, HI THERE.
I THOUGHT YOU WERE GOING TO THE BOOKSTORE.
Whoa! It's Yoh!
IT'S REALLY CONGESTED OUTSIDE BECAUSE OF THE MARATHON, SO WE THOUGHT WE'D HANG OUT HERE INSTEAD.
I'M SORRY FOR DISTURBING YOU.
OH, NOT AT ALL.
THE MARATHON, HUH?

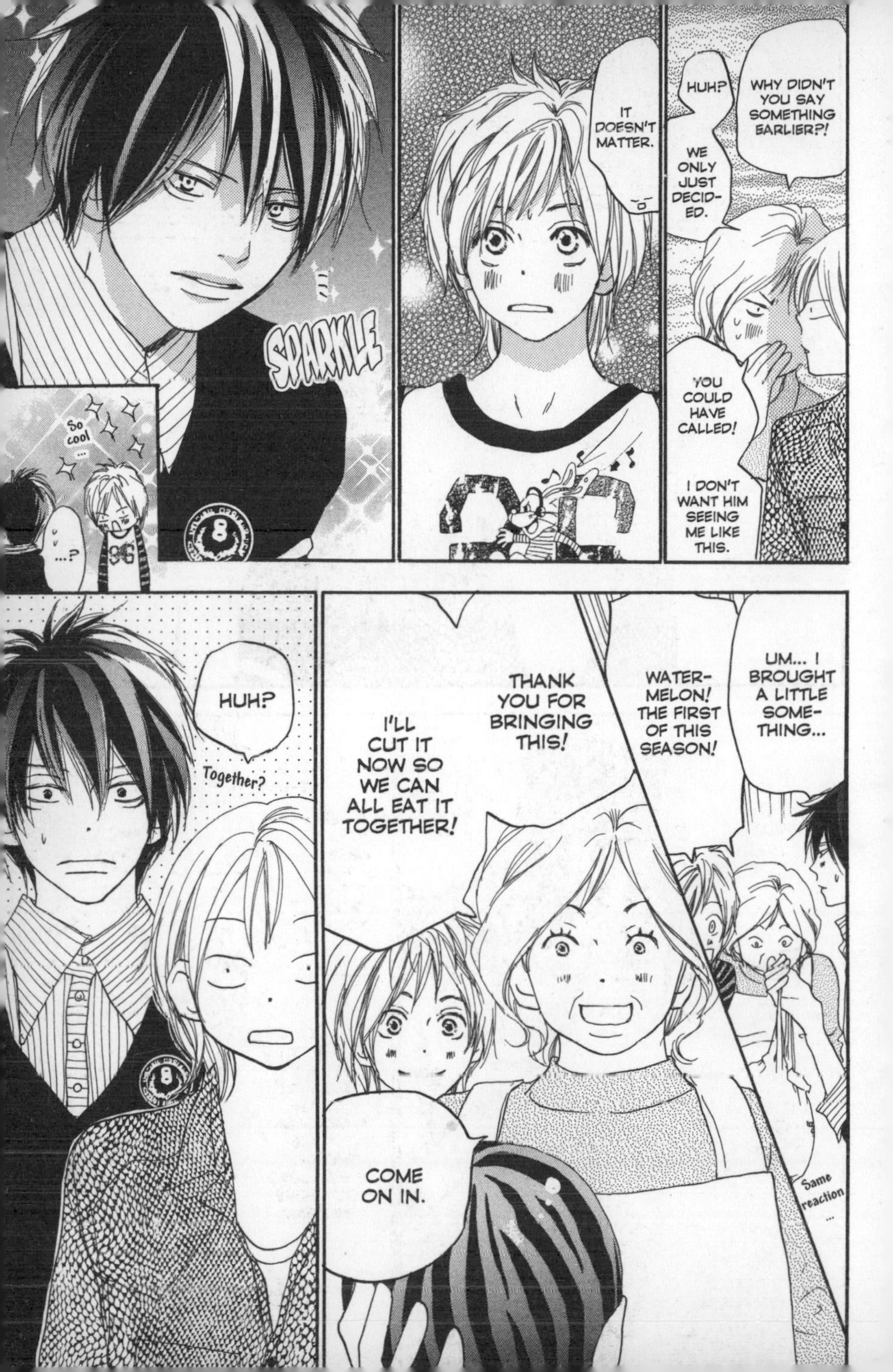
WHY DIDN'T YOU SAY SOMETHING EARLIER?!
HUH?
WE ONLY JUST DECID-ED.
YOU COULD HAVE CALLED!
I DON'T WANT HIM SEEING ME LIKE THIS.
IT DOESN'T MATTER.
SPARKLE
So cool...
...?
UM... I BROUGHT A LITTLE SOME-THING...
WATER-MELON! THE FIRST OF THIS SEASON!
Same reaction...
THANK YOU FOR BRINGING THIS!
I'LL CUT IT NOW SO WE CAN ALL EAT IT TOGETHER!
COME ON IN.
HUH?
Together?

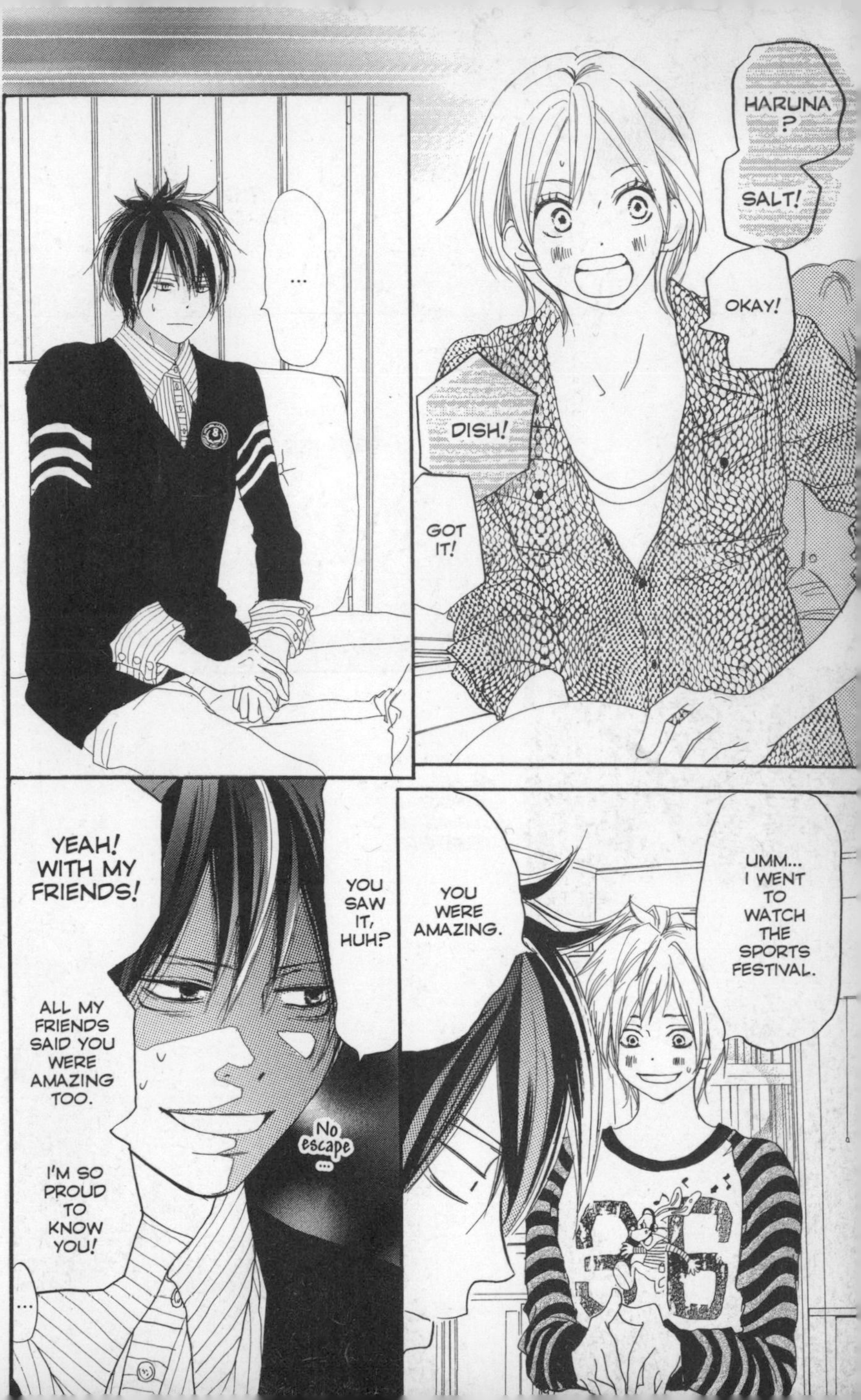
HARUNA?
SALT!
OKAY!
DISH!
GOT IT!
...
UMM... I WENT TO WATCH THE SPORTS FESTIVAL.
YOU WERE AMAZING.
YOU SAW IT, HUH?
YEAH! WITH MY FRIENDS!
ALL MY FRIENDS SAID YOU WERE AMAZING TOO.
No escape...
I'M SO PROUD TO KNOW YOU!
...

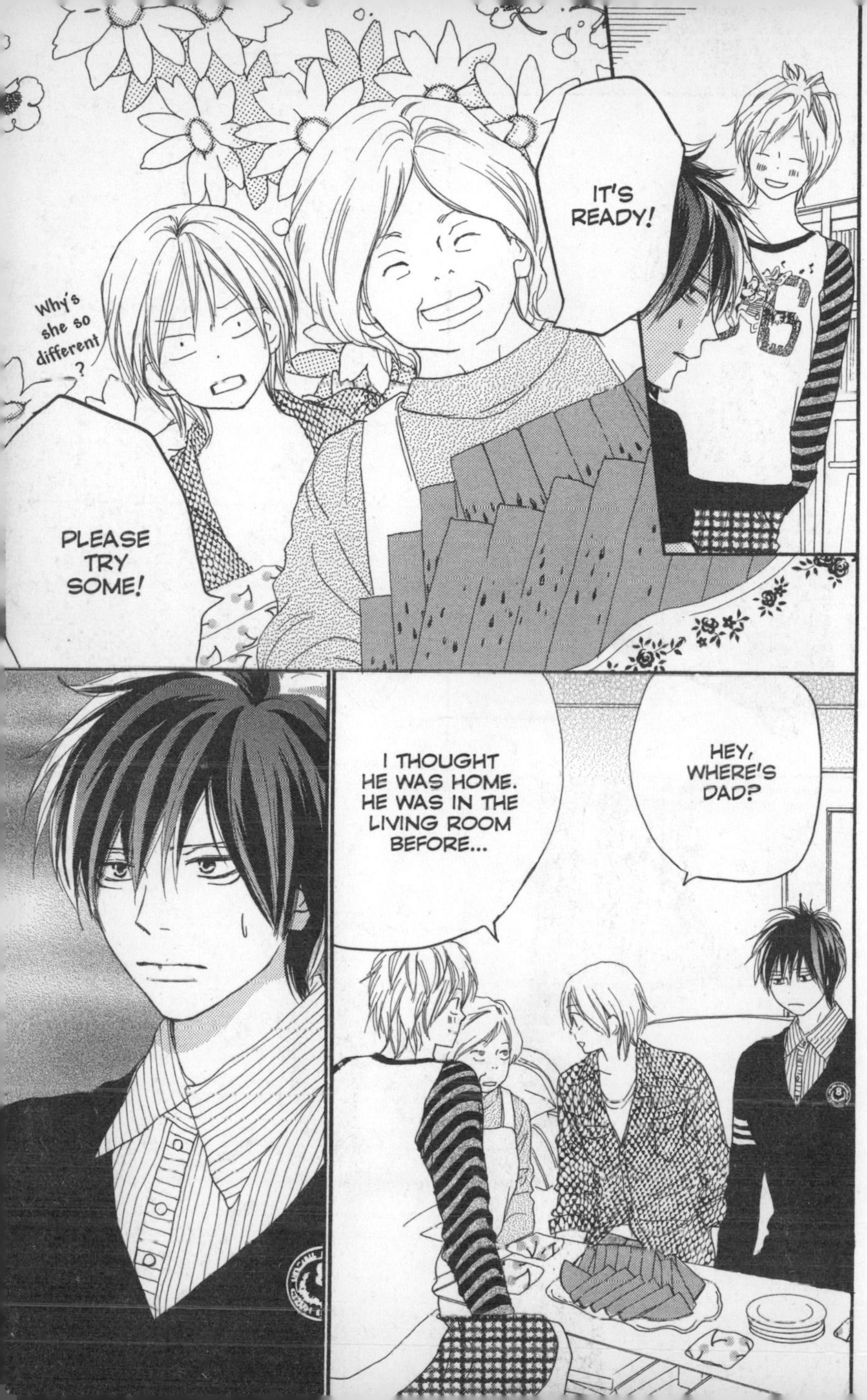
IT'S READY!
Why's she so different?
PLEASE TRY SOME!
HEY, WHERE'S DAD?
I THOUGHT HE WAS HOME. HE WAS IN THE LIVING ROOM BEFORE...

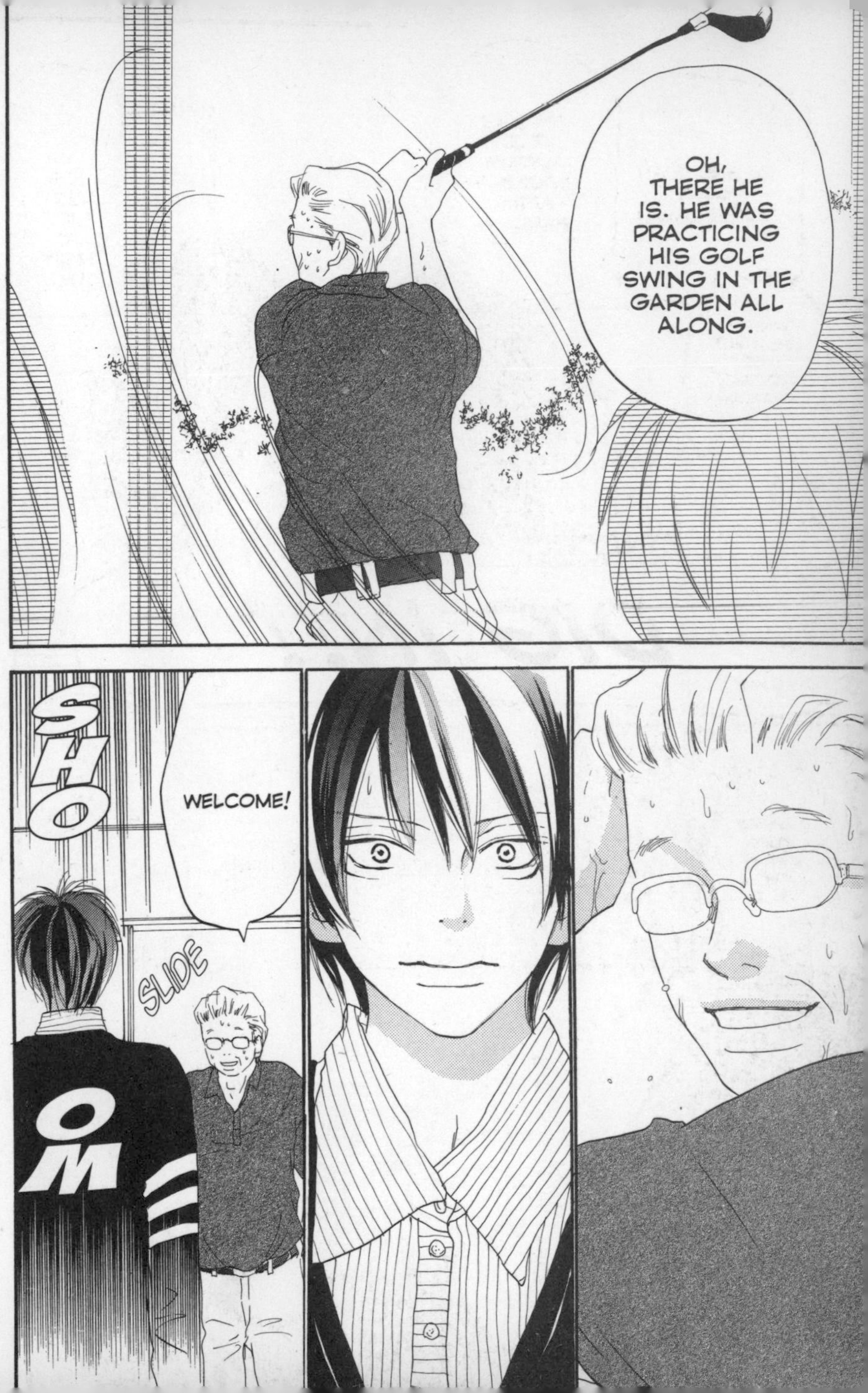
OH, THERE HE IS. HE WAS PRACTICING HIS GOLF SWING IN THE GARDEN ALL ALONG.
SHO
WELCOME!
SLIDE
OM

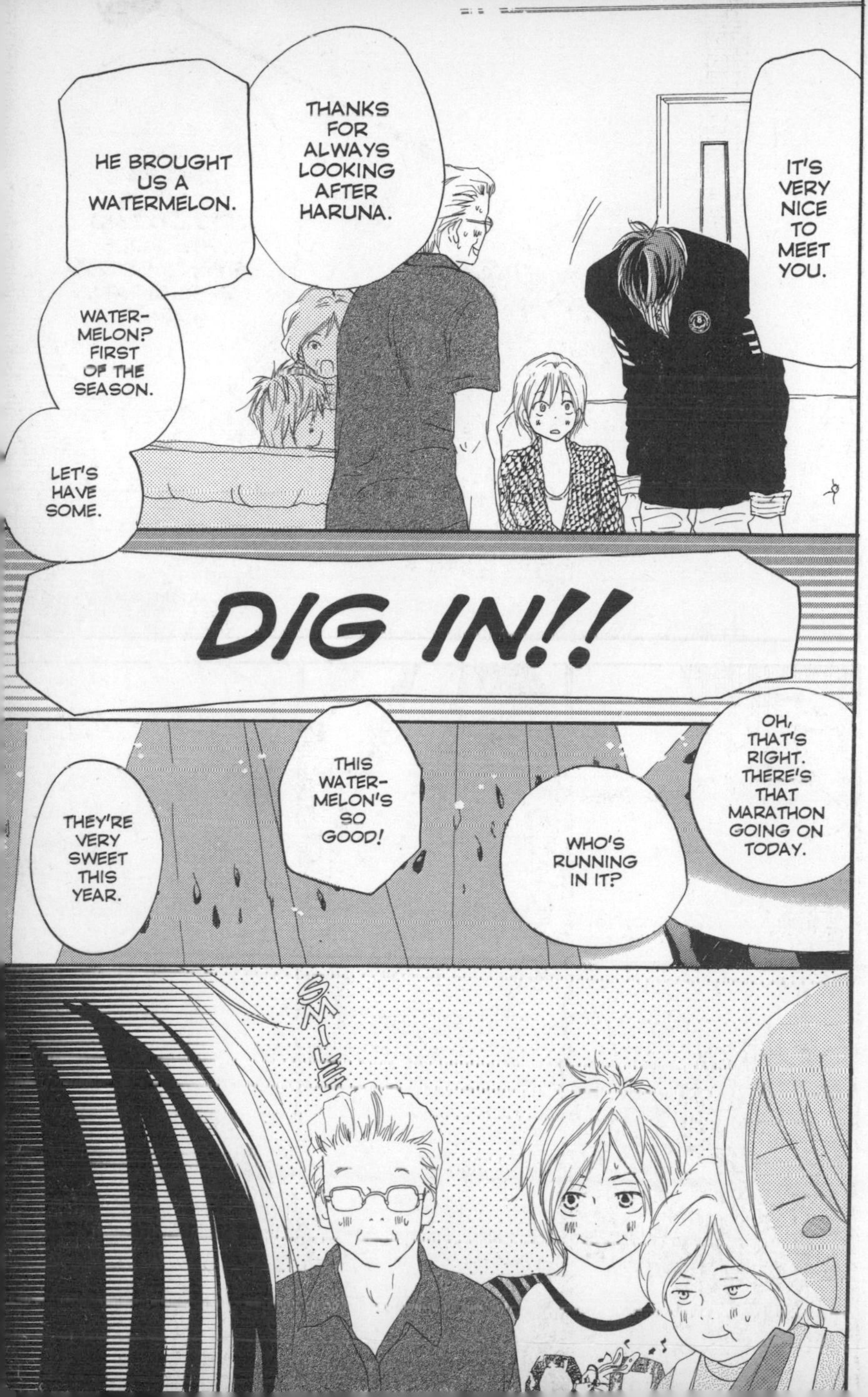
IT'S VERY NICE TO MEET YOU.
THANKS FOR ALWAYS LOOKING AFTER HARUNA.
HE BROUGHT US A WATERMELON.
WATER-MELON? FIRST OF THE SEASON.
LET'S HAVE SOME.
DIG IN!!
OH, THAT'S RIGHT. THERE'S THAT MARATHON GOING ON TODAY.
WHO'S RUNNING IN IT?
THIS WATER-MELON'S SO GOOD!
THEY'RE VERY SWEET THIS YEAR.
SMILE

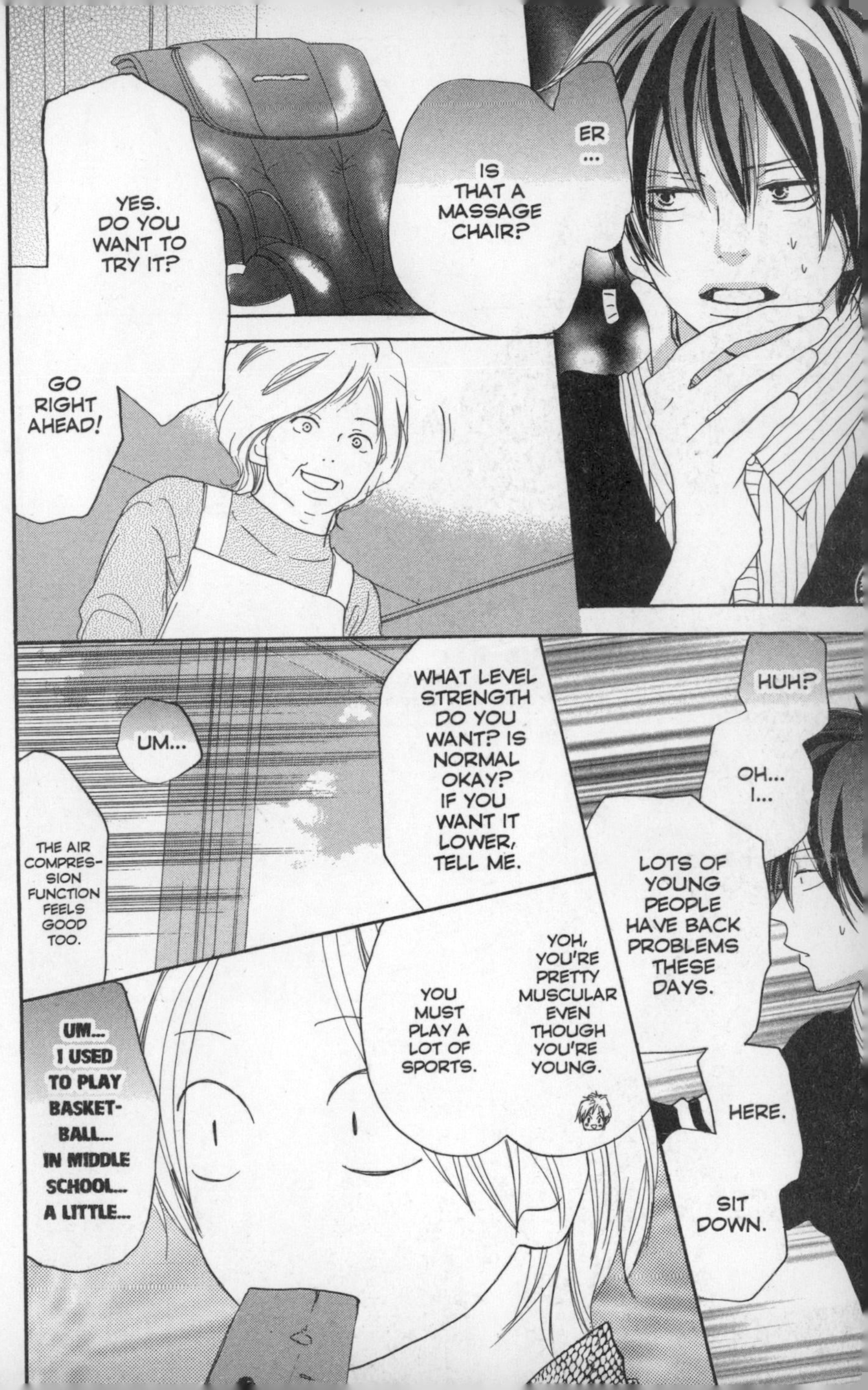

ER...
IS THAT A MASSAGE CHAIR?
YES. DO YOU WANT TO TRY IT?
GO RIGHT AHEAD!
HUH?
OH... I...
HERE.
SIT DOWN.
WHAT LEVEL STRENGTH DO YOU WANT? IS NORMAL OKAY? IF YOU WANT IT LOWER, TELL ME.
UM...
THE AIR COMPRESSION FUNCTION FEELS GOOD TOO.
LOTS OF YOUNG PEOPLE HAVE BACK PROBLEMS THESE DAYS.
YOH, YOU'RE PRETTY MUSCULAR EVEN THOUGH YOU'RE YOUNG.
YOU MUST PLAY A LOT OF SPORTS.
UM... I USED TO PLAY BASKETBALL... IN MIDDLE SCHOOL... A LITTLE...

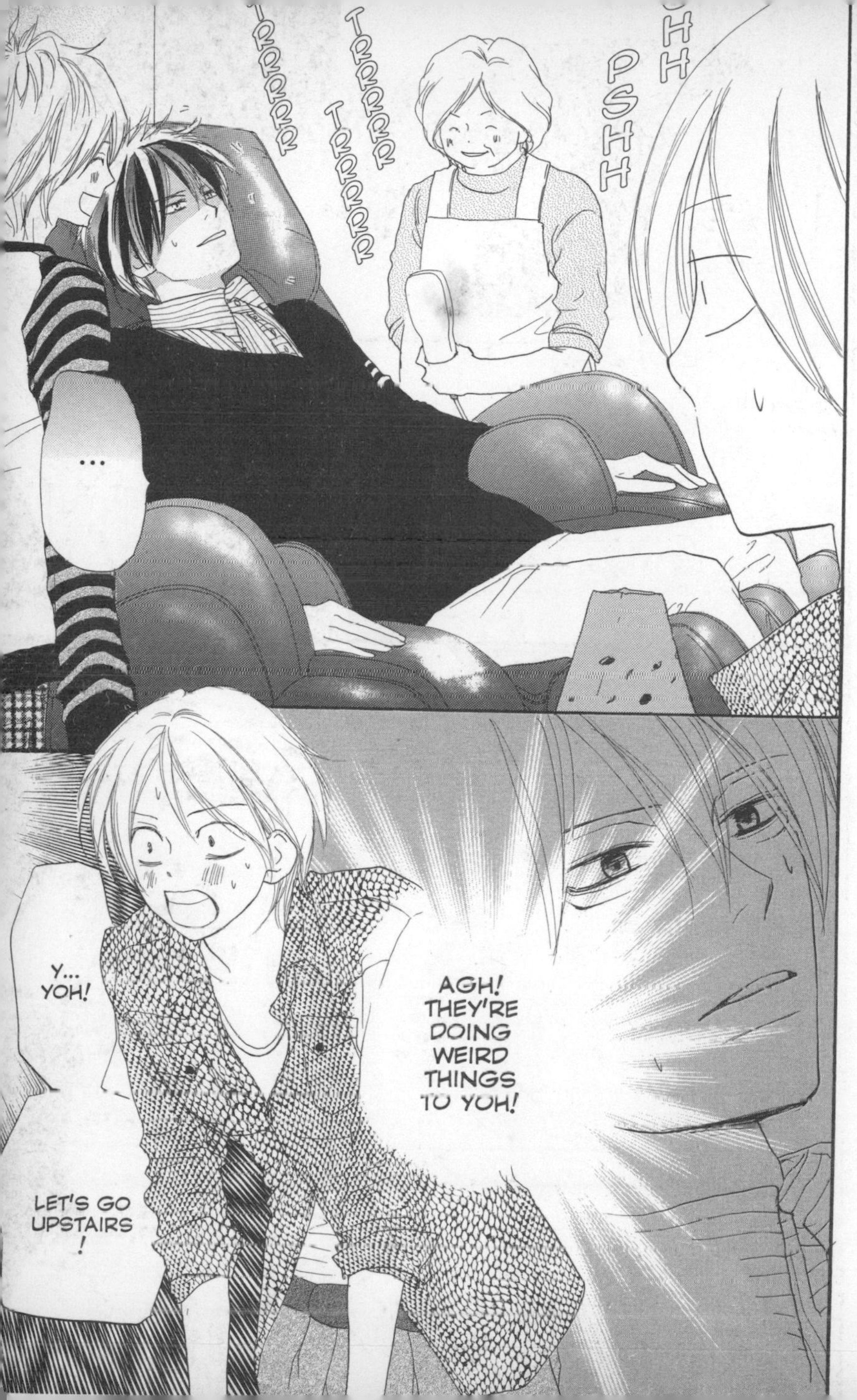
PSHH
PSHH
TRRRRR
TRRRRR
TRRRRR
...
AGH! THEY'RE DOING WEIRD THINGS TO YOH!
Y... YOH!
LET'S GO UPSTAIRS!

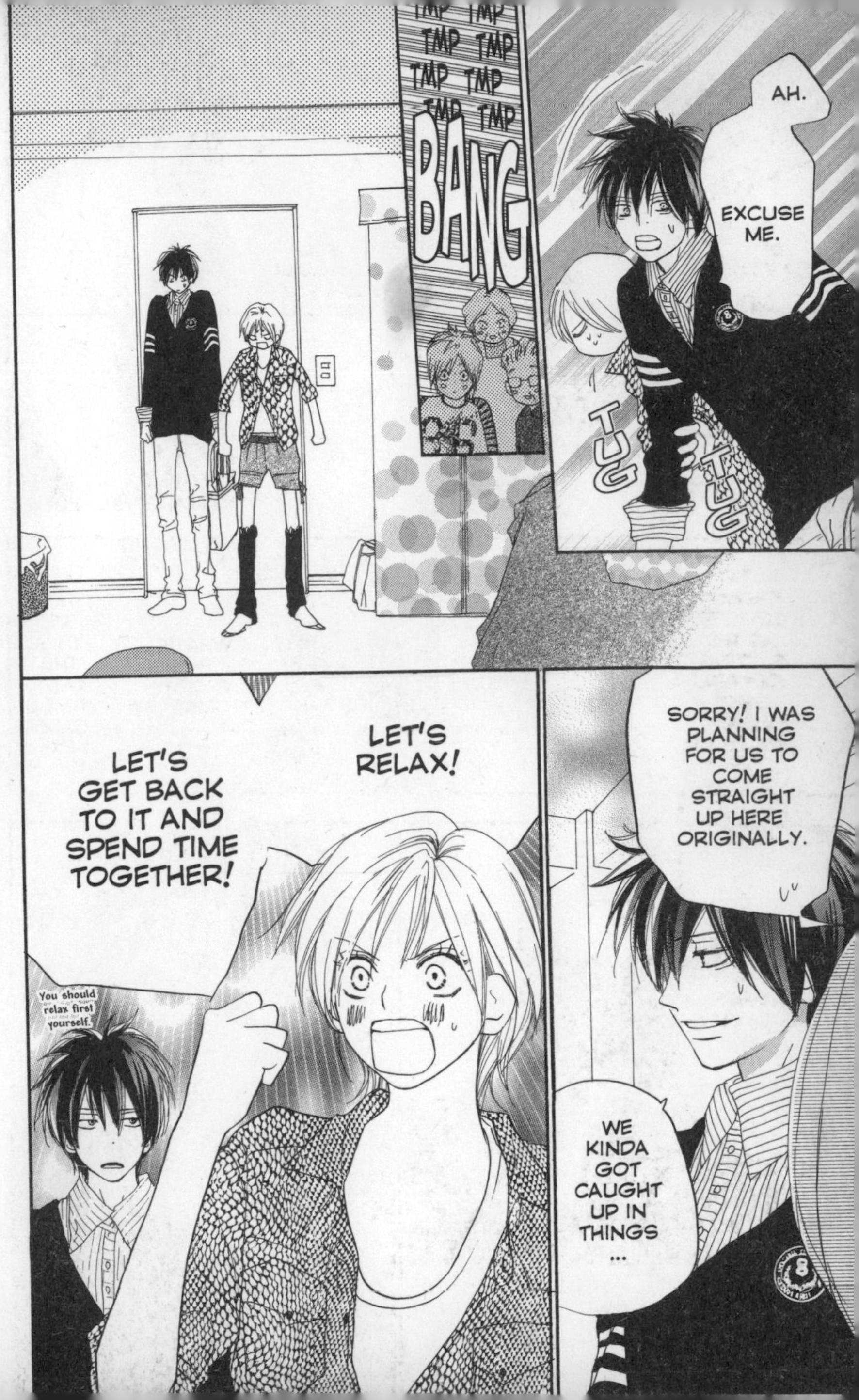
AH.
EXCUSE ME.
TUG TUG
TMP TMP TMP TMP TMP TMP TMP TMP
BANG
SORRY! I WAS PLANNING FOR US TO COME STRAIGHT UP HERE ORIGINALLY.
WE KINDA GOT CAUGHT UP IN THINGS ...
LET'S RELAX!
LET'S GET BACK TO IT AND SPEND TIME TOGETHER!
You should relax first yourself.

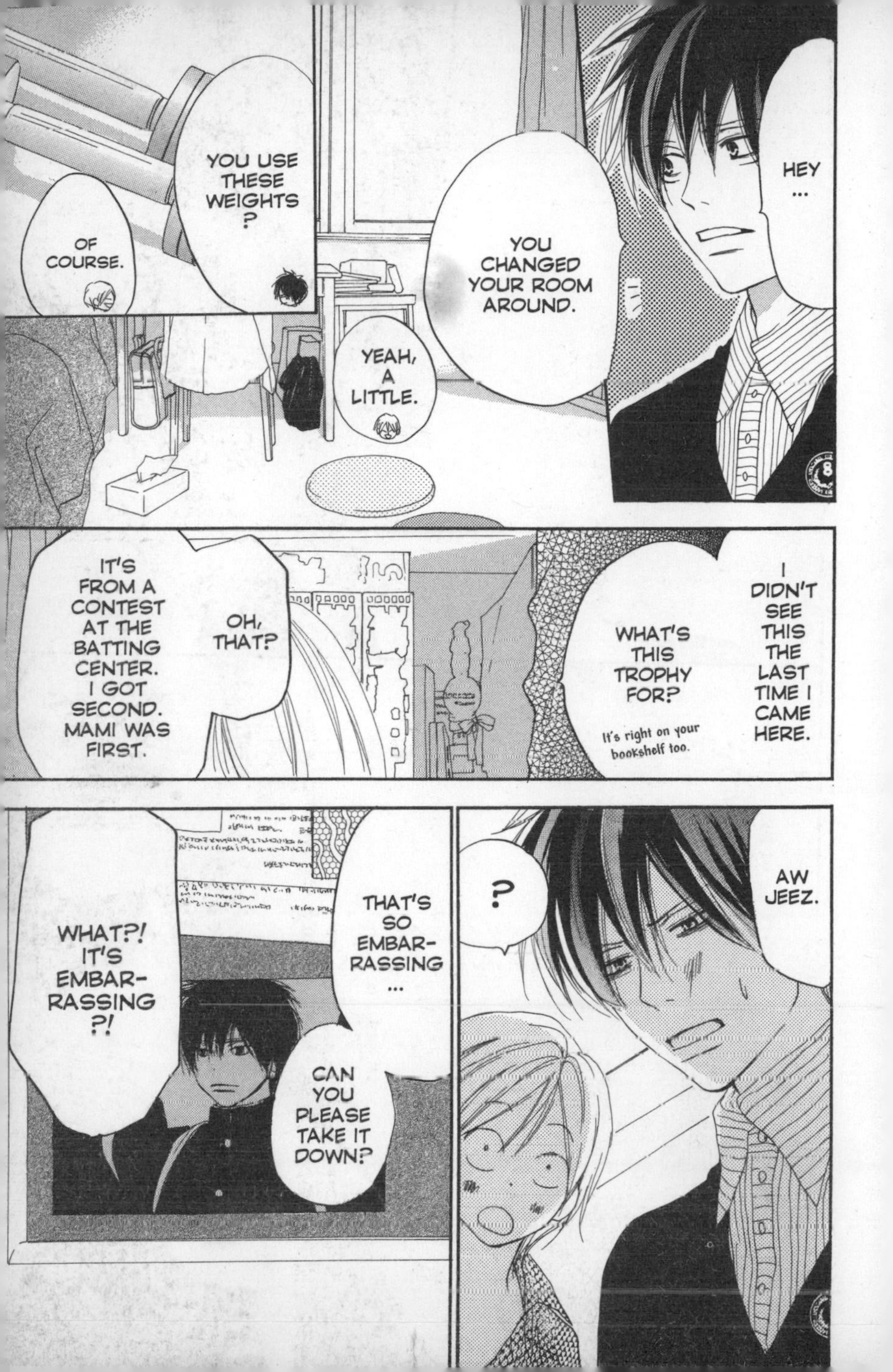

HEY ...
YOU CHANGED YOUR ROOM AROUND.
YEAH, A LITTLE.
YOU USE THESE WEIGHTS?
OF COURSE.
I DIDN'T SEE THIS THE LAST TIME I CAME HERE.
WHAT'S THIS TROPHY FOR?
It's right on your bookshelf too.
OH, THAT?
IT'S FROM A CONTEST AT THE BATTING CENTER. I GOT SECOND. MAMI WAS FIRST.
AW JEEZ.
?
THAT'S SO EMBAR-RASSING ...
WHAT?! IT'S EMBAR-RASSING?!
CAN YOU PLEASE TAKE IT DOWN?

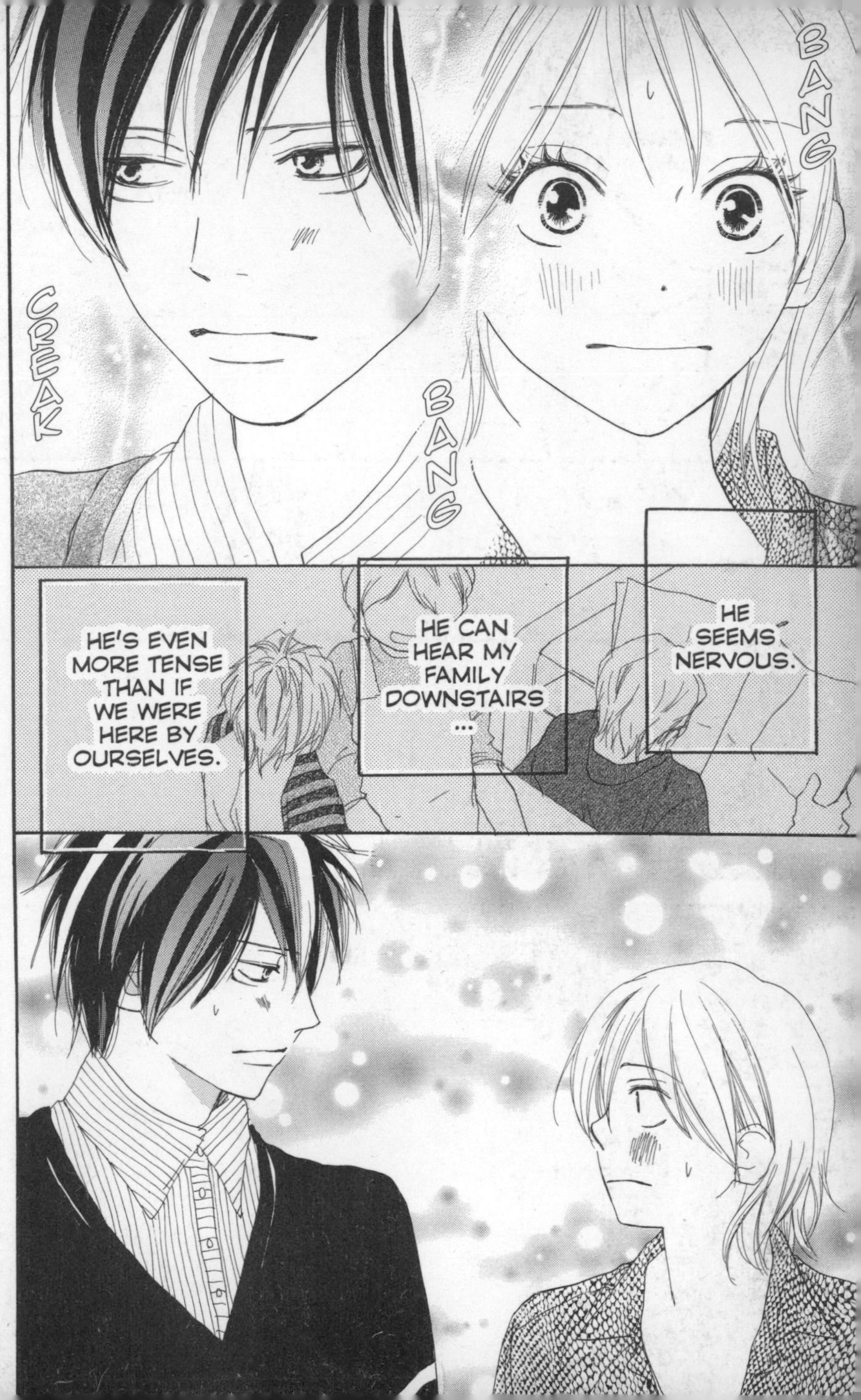
BANG
BANG
CREAK
HE SEEMS NERVOUS.
HE CAN HEAR MY FAMILY DOWNSTAIRS ...
HE'S EVEN MORE TENSE THAN IF WE WERE HERE BY OURSELVES.

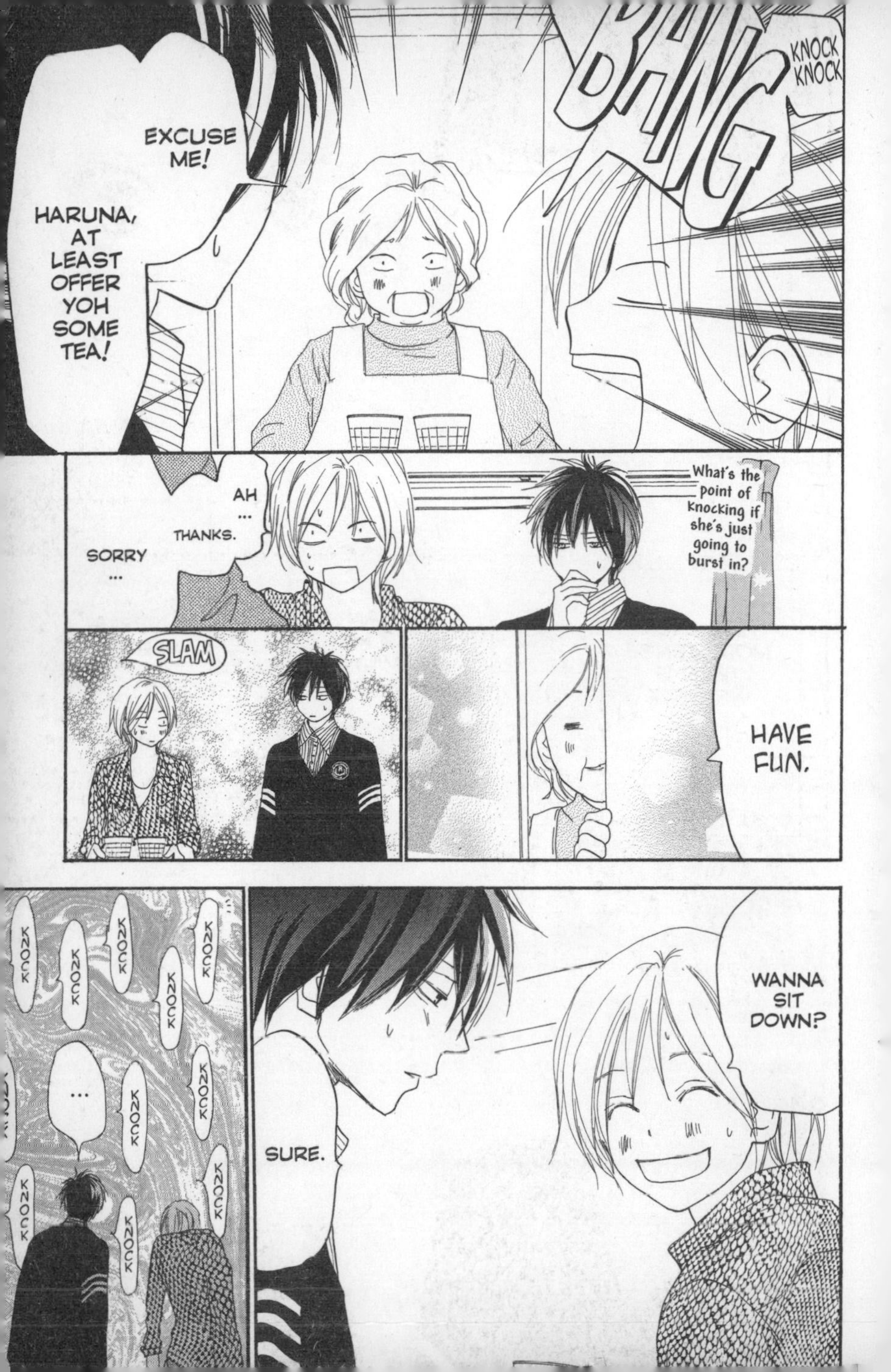
BAHNG
KNOCK KNOCK
EXCUSE ME!
HARUNA, AT LEAST OFFER YOH SOME TEA!
What's the point of knocking if she's just going to burst in?
AH ...
THANKS.
SORRY ...
HAVE FUN.
SLAM
WANNA SIT DOWN?
SURE.
KNOCK
KNOCK
KNOCK
KNOCK
KNOCK
...
KNOCK
KNOCK
KNOCK
KNOCK
KNOCK

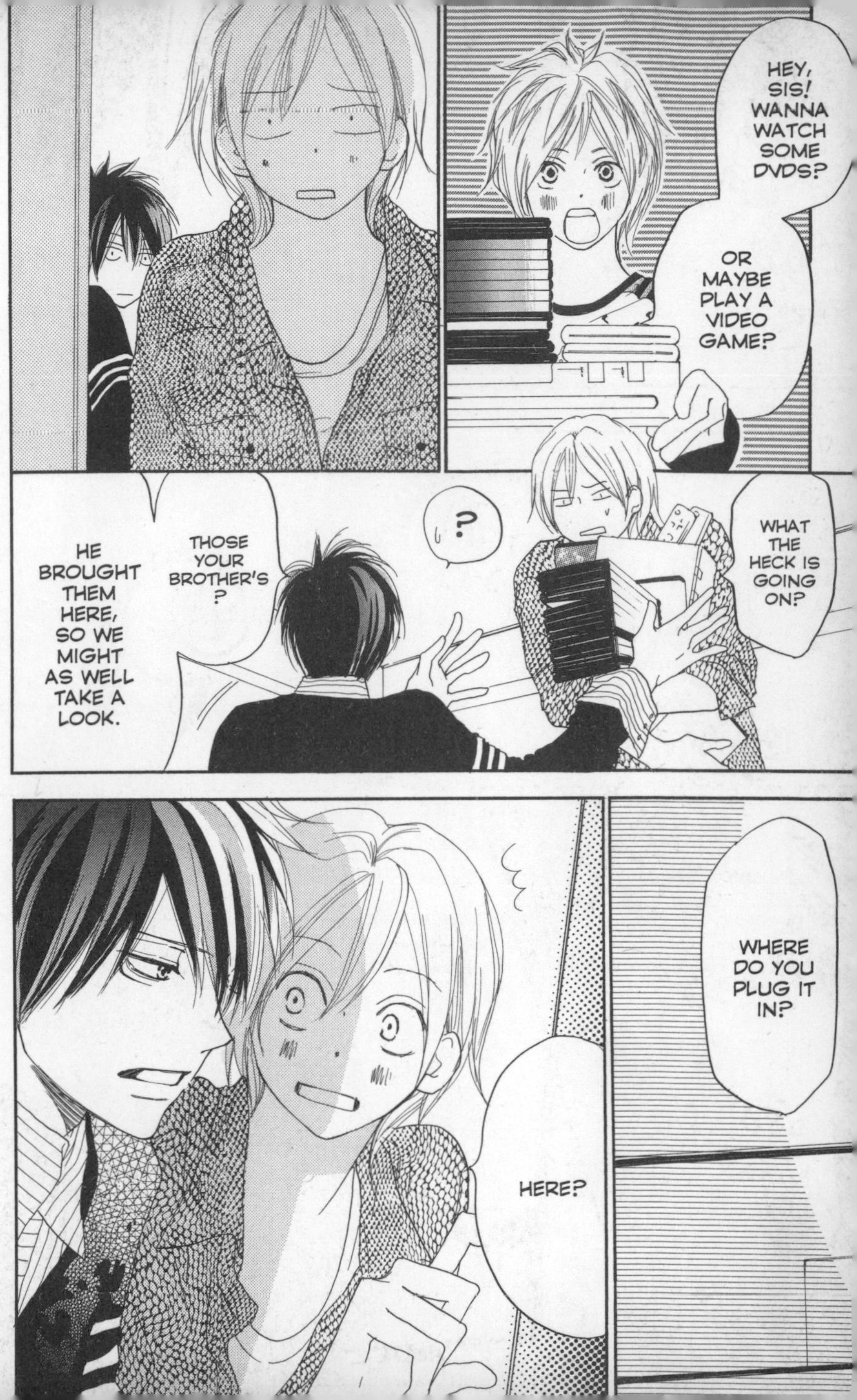
HEY, SIS! WANNA WATCH SOME DVDS?
OR MAYBE PLAY A VIDEO GAME?
WHAT THE HECK IS GOING ON?
?
THOSE YOUR BROTHER'S?
HE BROUGHT THEM HERE, SO WE MIGHT AS WELL TAKE A LOOK.
WHERE DO YOU PLUG IT IN?
HERE?

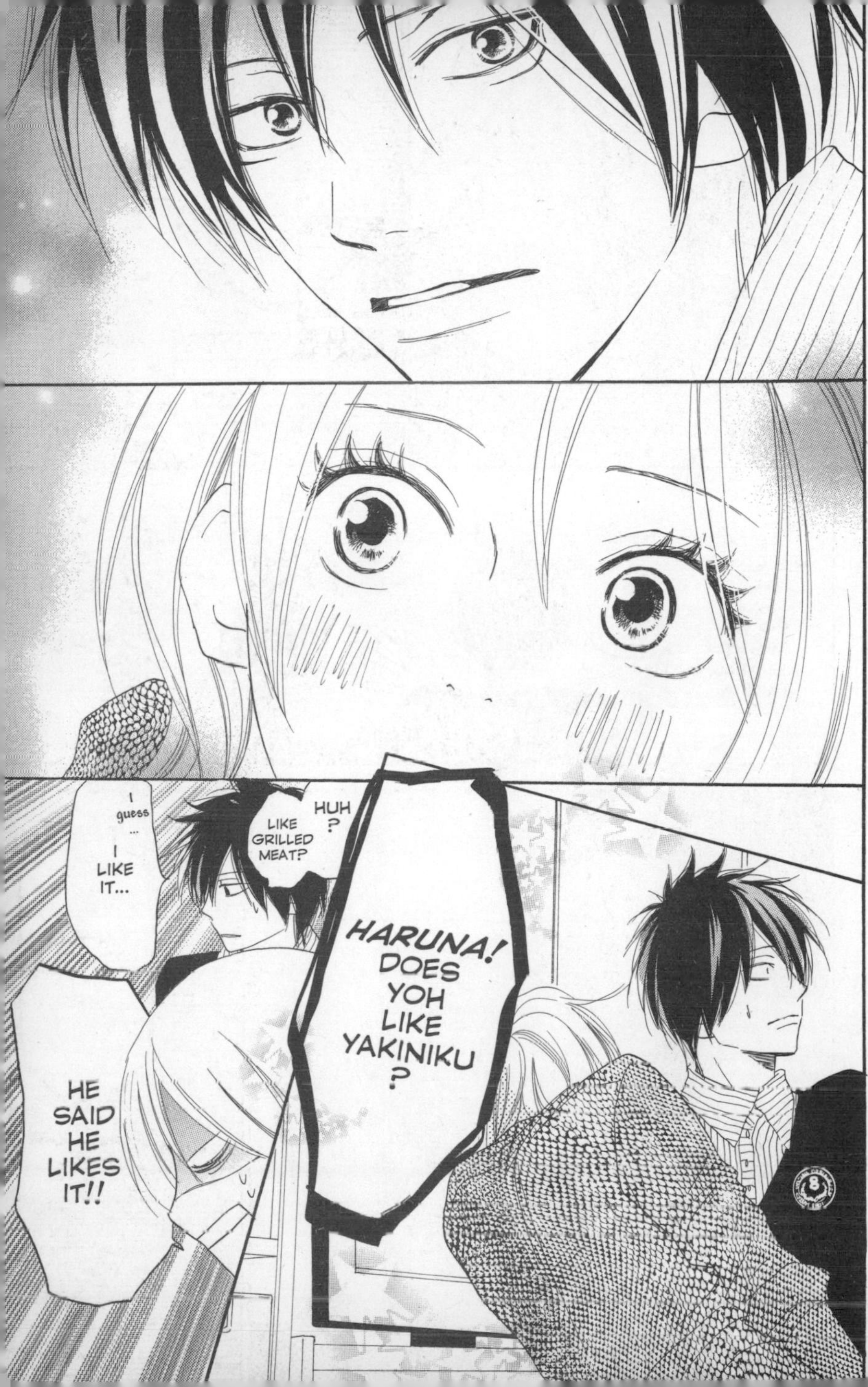
HARUNA! DOES YOH LIKE YAKINIKU?
HUH?
LIKE GRILLED MEAT?
I guess... I LIKE IT...
HE SAID HE LIKES IT!!

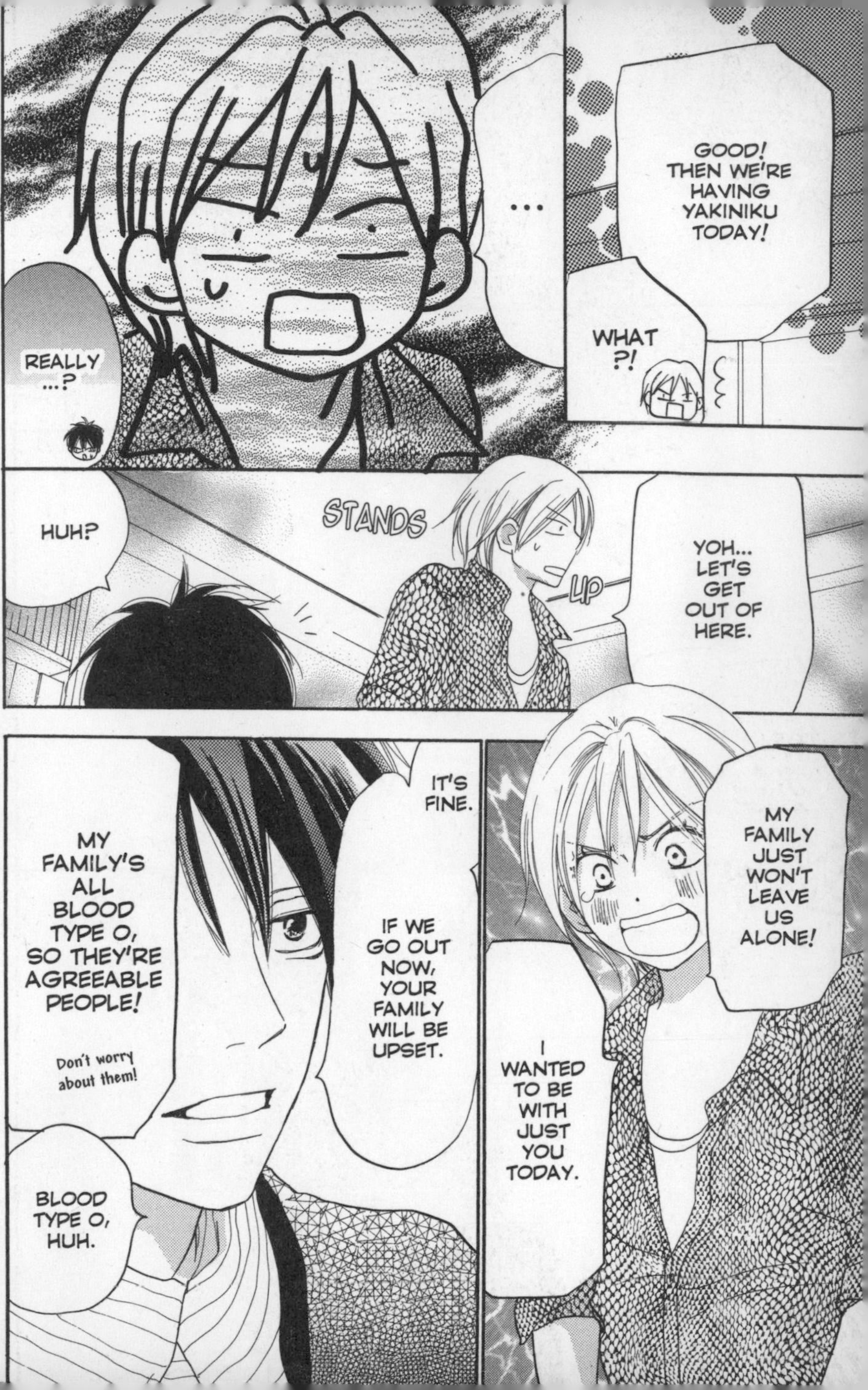
GOOD! THEN WE'RE HAVING YAKINIKU TODAY!
WHAT?!
...
REALLY ...?
YOH... LET'S GET OUT OF HERE.
STANDS UP
HUH?
MY FAMILY JUST WON'T LEAVE US ALONE!
I WANTED TO BE WITH JUST YOU TODAY.
IT'S FINE.
IF WE GO OUT NOW, YOUR FAMILY WILL BE UPSET.
MY FAMILY'S ALL BLOOD TYPE O, SO THEY'RE AGREEABLE PEOPLE!
Don't worry about them!
BLOOD TYPE O, HUH.

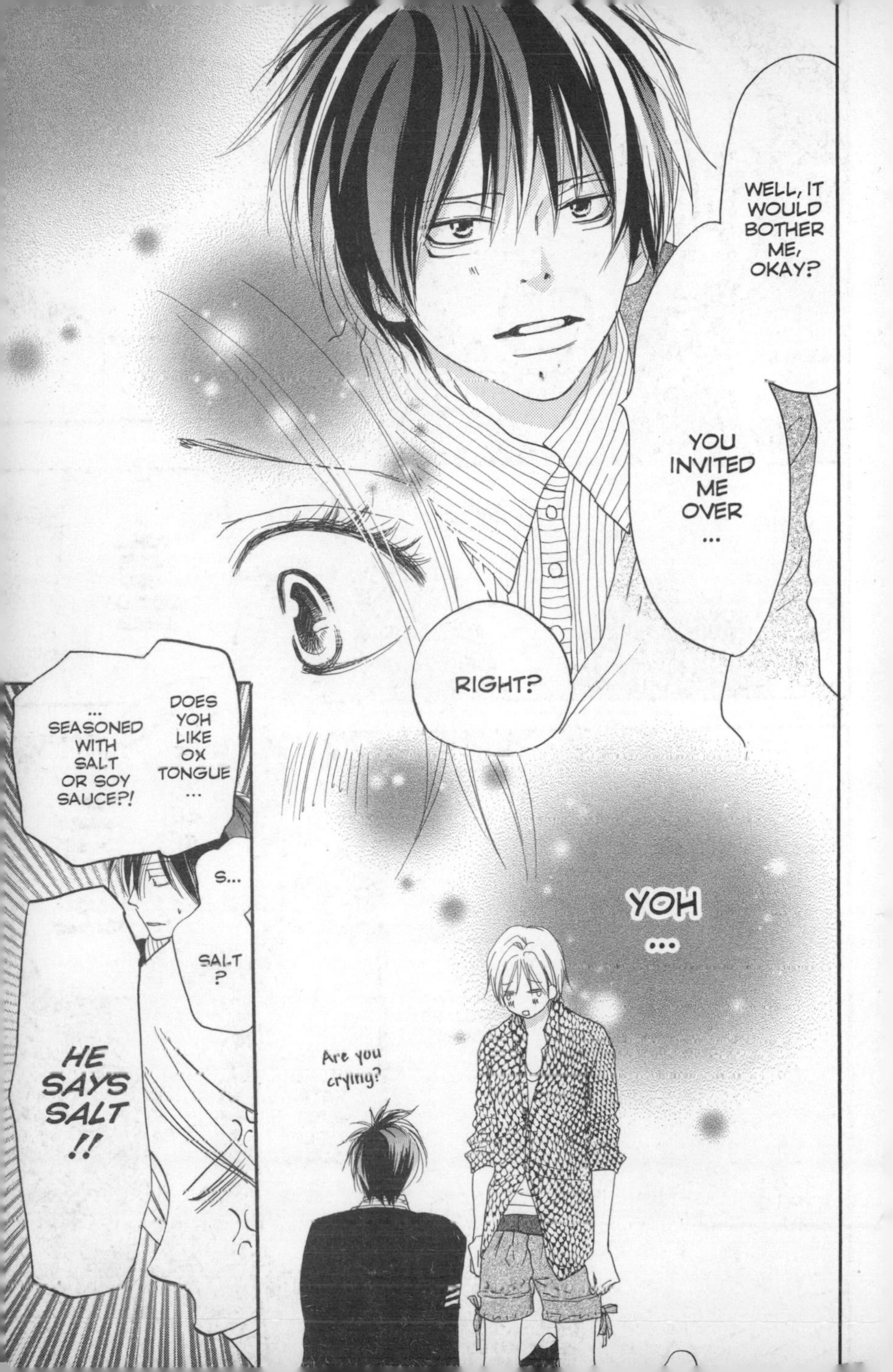
WELL, IT WOULD BOTHER ME, OKAY?
YOU INVITED ME OVER ...
RIGHT?
YOH ...
Are you crying?
DOES YOH LIKE OX TONGUE ...
... SEASONED WITH SALT OR SOY SAUCE?!
S...
SALT ?
HE SAYS SALT !!

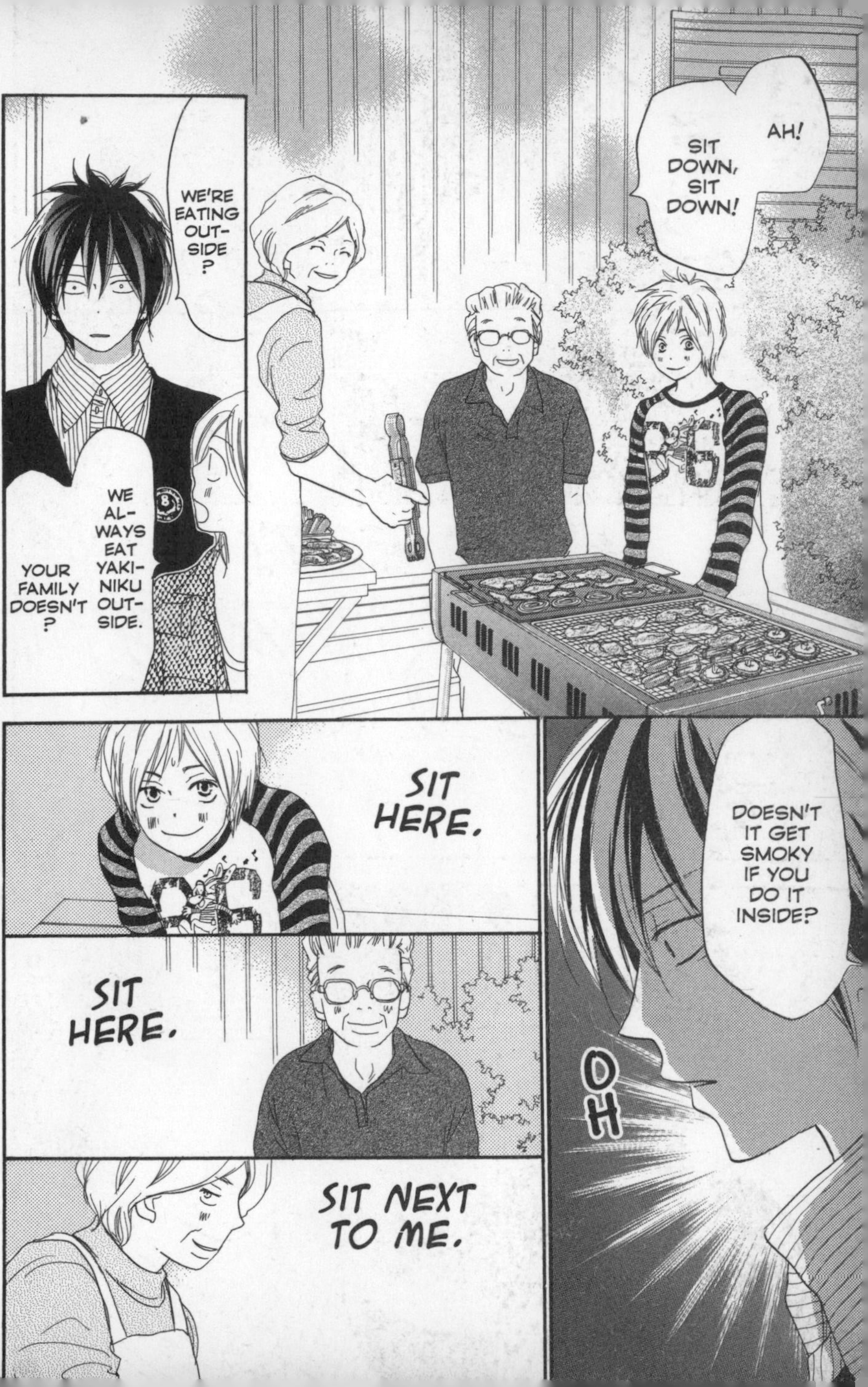
AH! SIT DOWN, SIT DOWN!
WE'RE EATING OUTSIDE?
WE ALWAYS EAT YAKINIKU OUTSIDE.
YOUR FAMILY DOESN'T?
DOESN'T IT GET SMOKY IF YOU DO IT INSIDE?
OH
SIT HERE.
SIT HERE.
SIT NEXT TO ME.

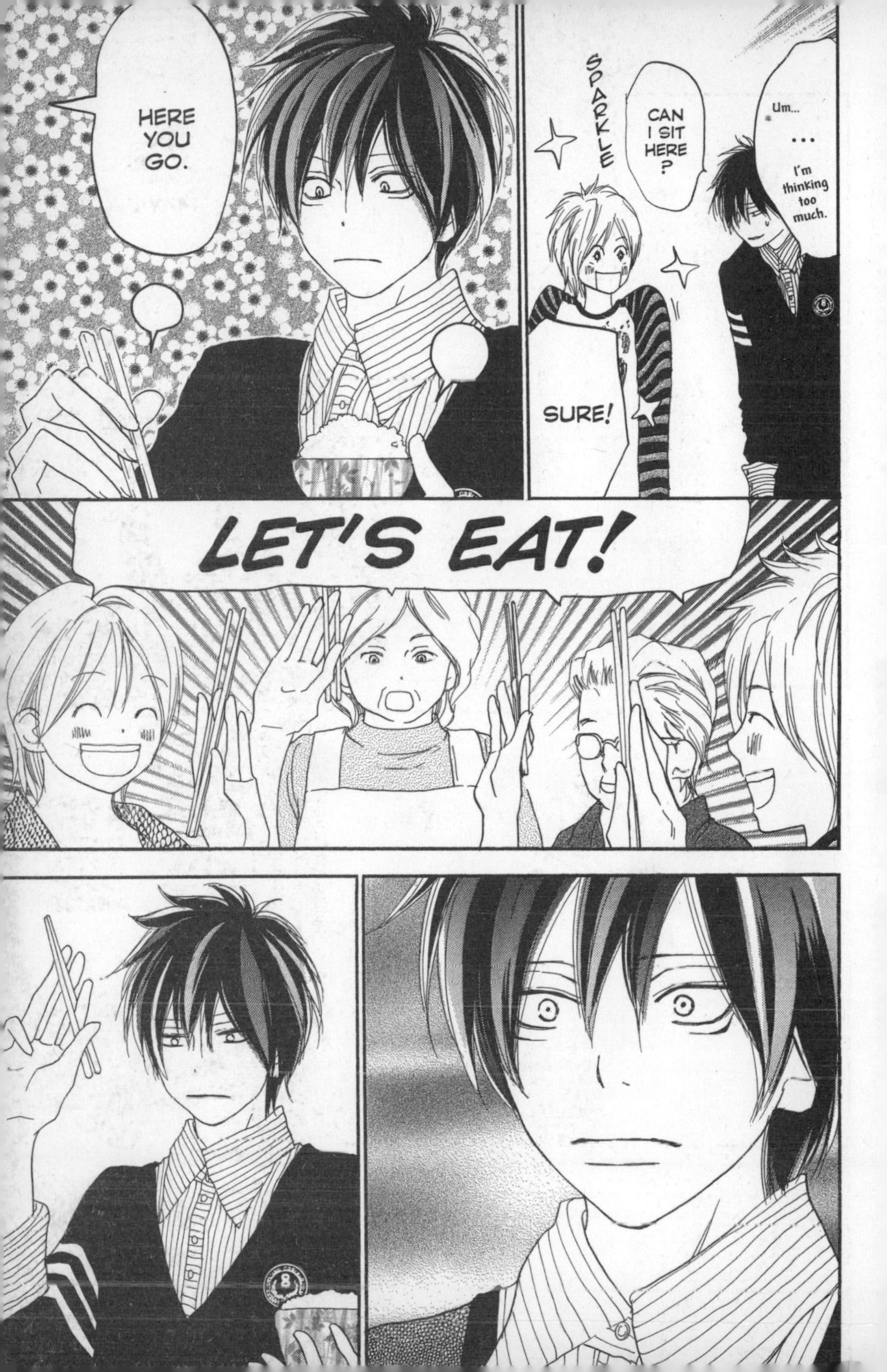
Um... ... I'm thinking too much.
CAN I SIT HERE?
SPARKLE
SURE!
HERE YOU GO.
LET'S EAT!

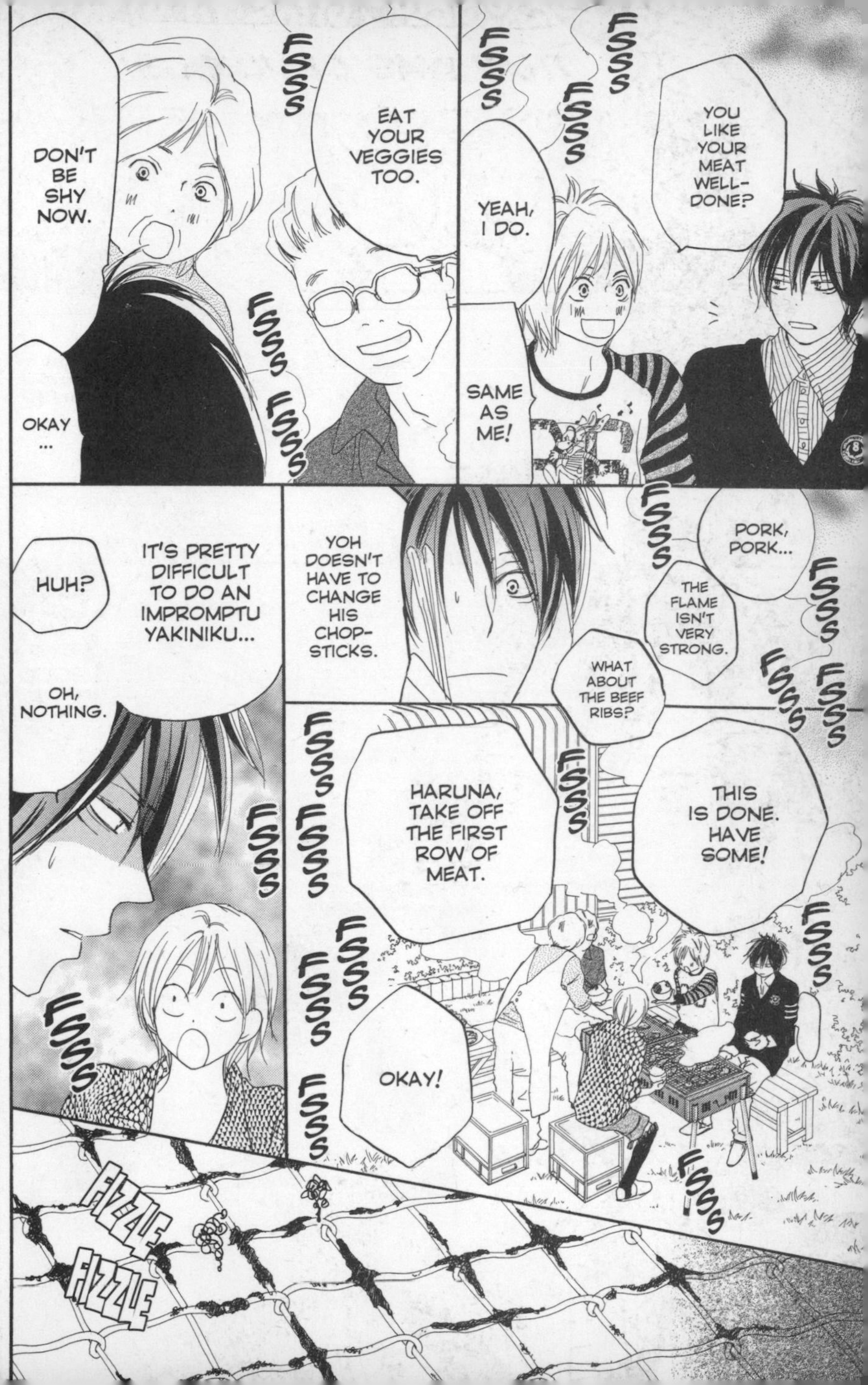
FSSS
FSSS
FSSS
YOU LIKE YOUR MEAT WELL-DONE?
YEAH, I DO.
SAME AS ME!
FSSS
EAT YOUR VEGGIES TOO.
DON'T BE SHY NOW.
FSSS
FSSS
OKAY ...
FSSS
PORK, PORK...
THE FLAME ISN'T VERY STRONG.
WHAT ABOUT THE BEEF RIBS?
YOH DOESN'T HAVE TO CHANGE HIS CHOPSTICKS.
FSSS
FSSS
FSSS
THIS IS DONE. HAVE SOME!
FSSS
HARUNA, TAKE OFF THE FIRST ROW OF MEAT.
FSSS
FSSS
FSSS
FSSS
FSSS
OKAY!
FSSS
FSSS
IT'S PRETTY DIFFICULT TO DO AN IMPROMPTU YAKINIKU...
HUH?
OH, NOTHING.
FSSS
FSSS
FIZZLE
FIZZLE

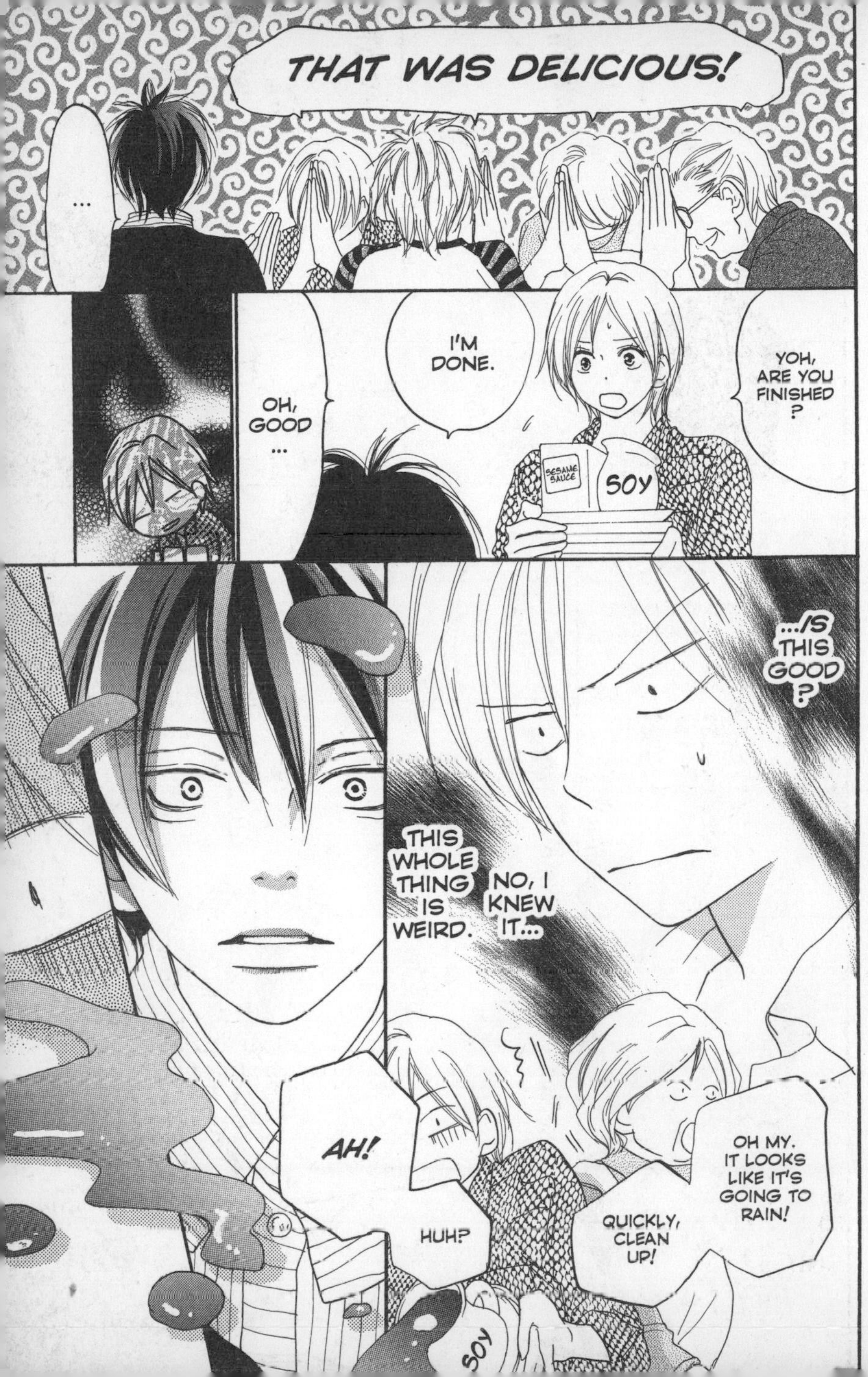
THAT WAS DELICIOUS!
...
YOH, ARE YOU FINISHED?
I'M DONE.
OH, GOOD ...
SESAME SAUCE
SOY
...IS THIS GOOD?
NO, I KNEW IT...
THIS WHOLE THING IS WEIRD.
OH MY. IT LOOKS LIKE IT'S GOING TO RAIN!
QUICKLY, CLEAN UP!
HUH?
AH!
SOY

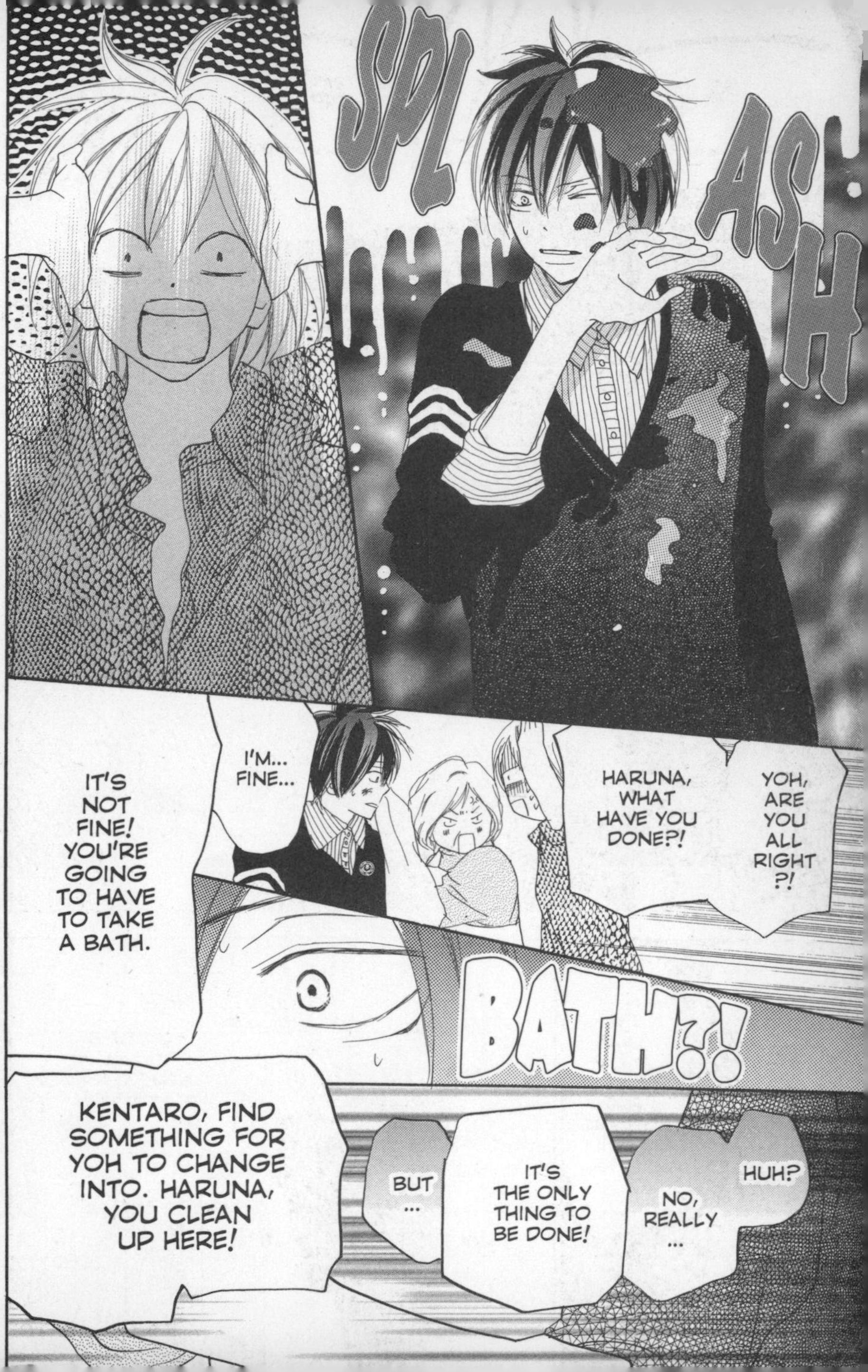
SPLASH
YOH, ARE YOU ALL RIGHT?!
HARUNA, WHAT HAVE YOU DONE?!
I'M... FINE...
IT'S NOT FINE! YOU'RE GOING TO HAVE TO TAKE A BATH.
BATH?!
HUH?
NO, REALLY...
IT'S THE ONLY THING TO BE DONE!
BUT...
KENTARO, FIND SOMETHING FOR YOH TO CHANGE INTO. HARUNA, YOU CLEAN UP HERE!

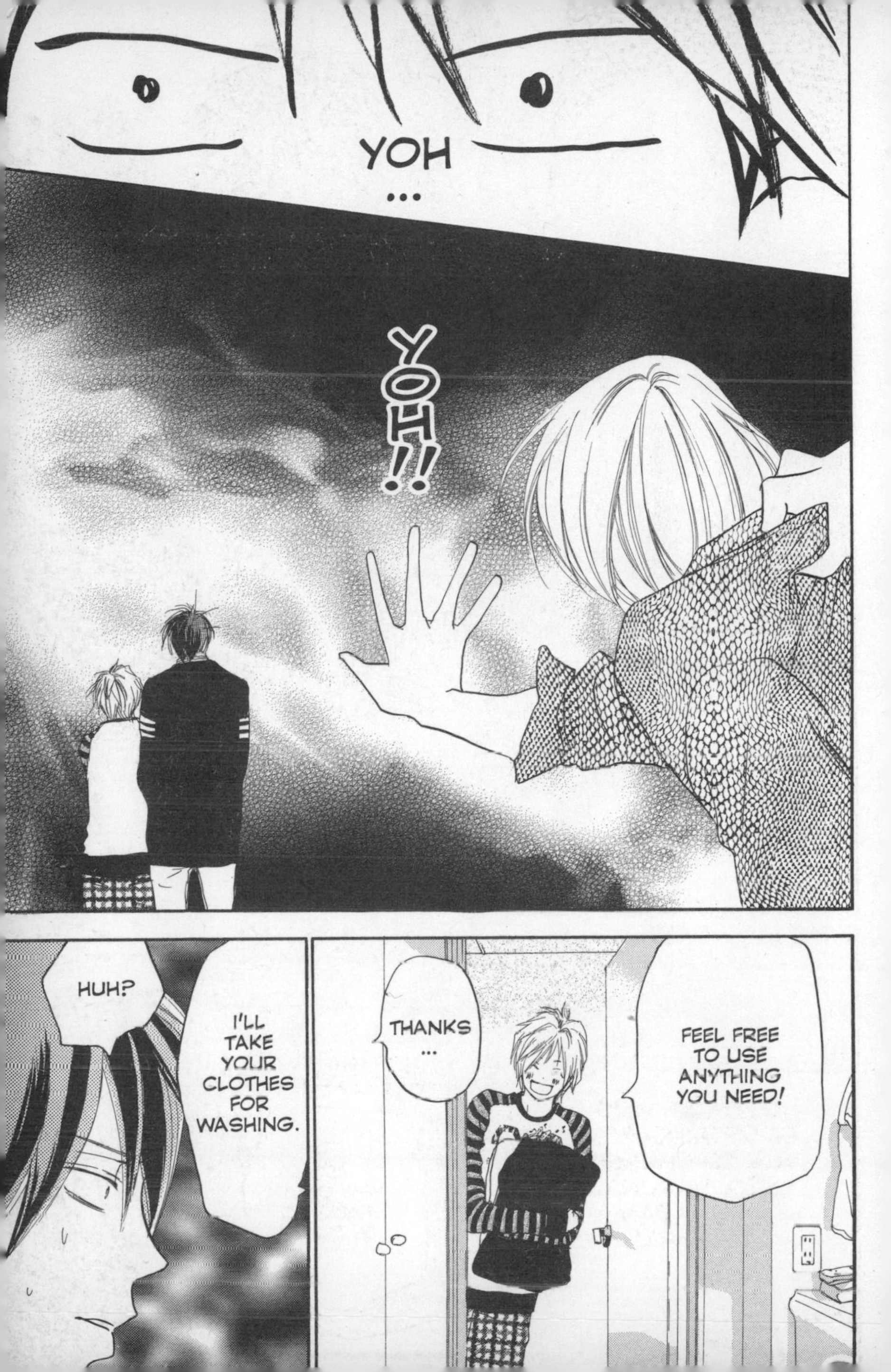
YOH ...
YOH!!
FEEL FREE TO USE ANYTHING YOU NEED!
THANKS ...
I'LL TAKE YOUR CLOTHES FOR WASHING.
HUH?

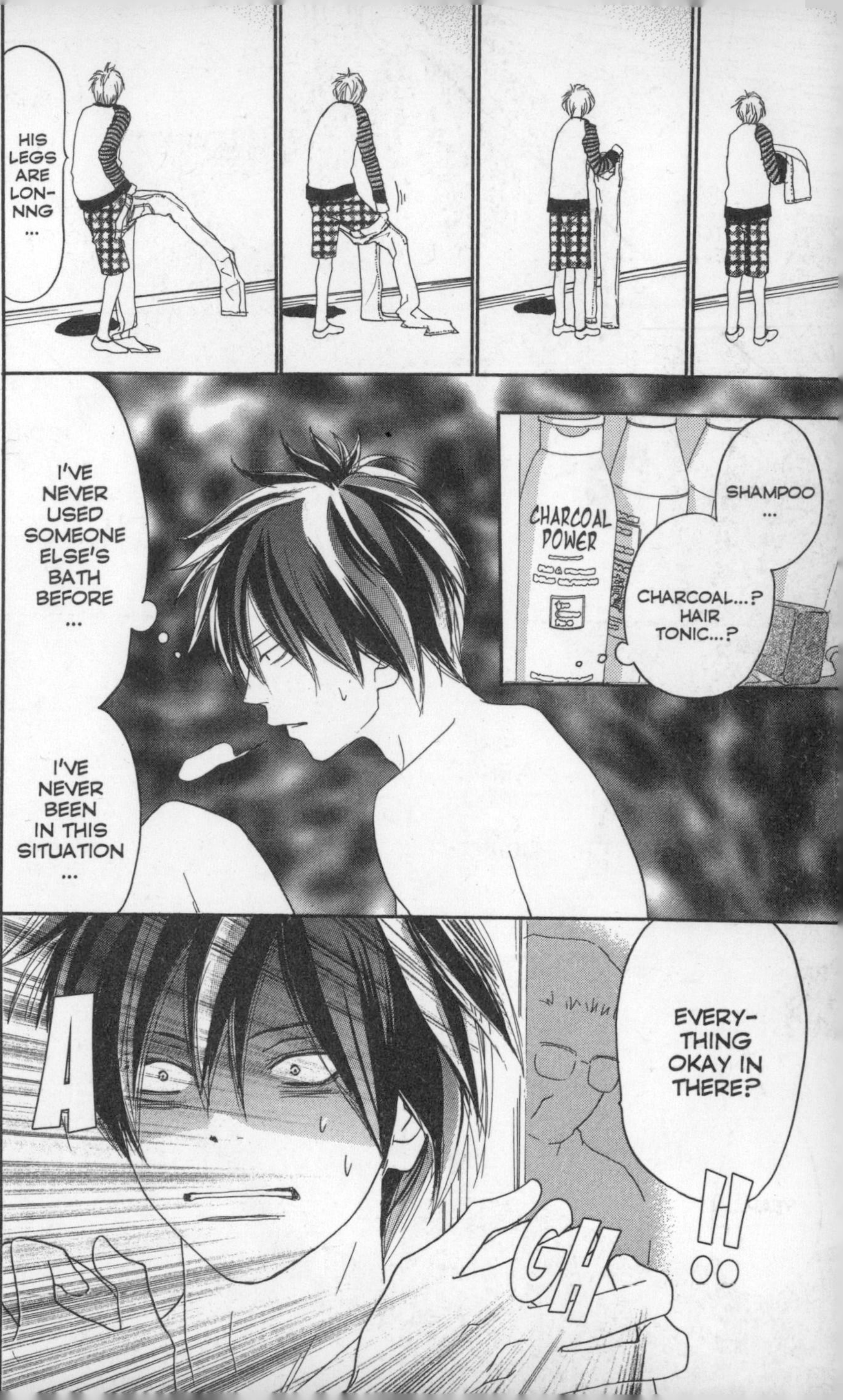
HIS LEGS ARE LONNNG ...
SHAMPOO ...
CHARCOAL POWER
CHARCOAL...? HAIR TONIC...?
I'VE NEVER USED SOMEONE ELSE'S BATH BEFORE ...
I'VE NEVER BEEN IN THIS SITUATION ...
EVERYTHING OKAY IN THERE?
!!
GH
A

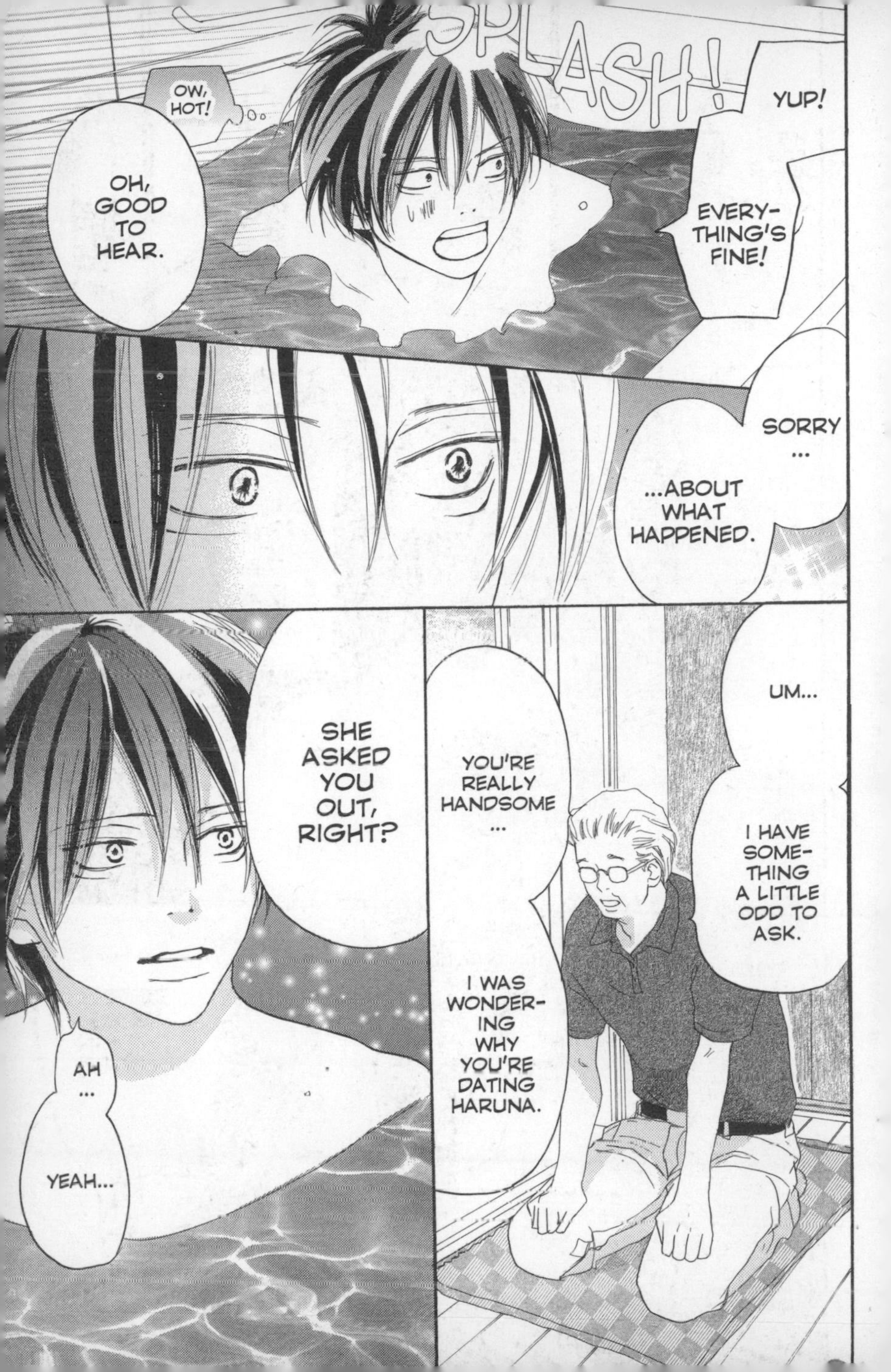
SPLASH!
YUP!
EVERY-THING'S FINE!
OW, HOT!
OH, GOOD TO HEAR.
SORRY...
...ABOUT WHAT HAPPENED.
UM...
I HAVE SOMETHING A LITTLE ODD TO ASK.
YOU'RE REALLY HANDSOME...
I WAS WONDERING WHY YOU'RE DATING HARUNA.
SHE ASKED YOU OUT, RIGHT?
AH...
YEAH...

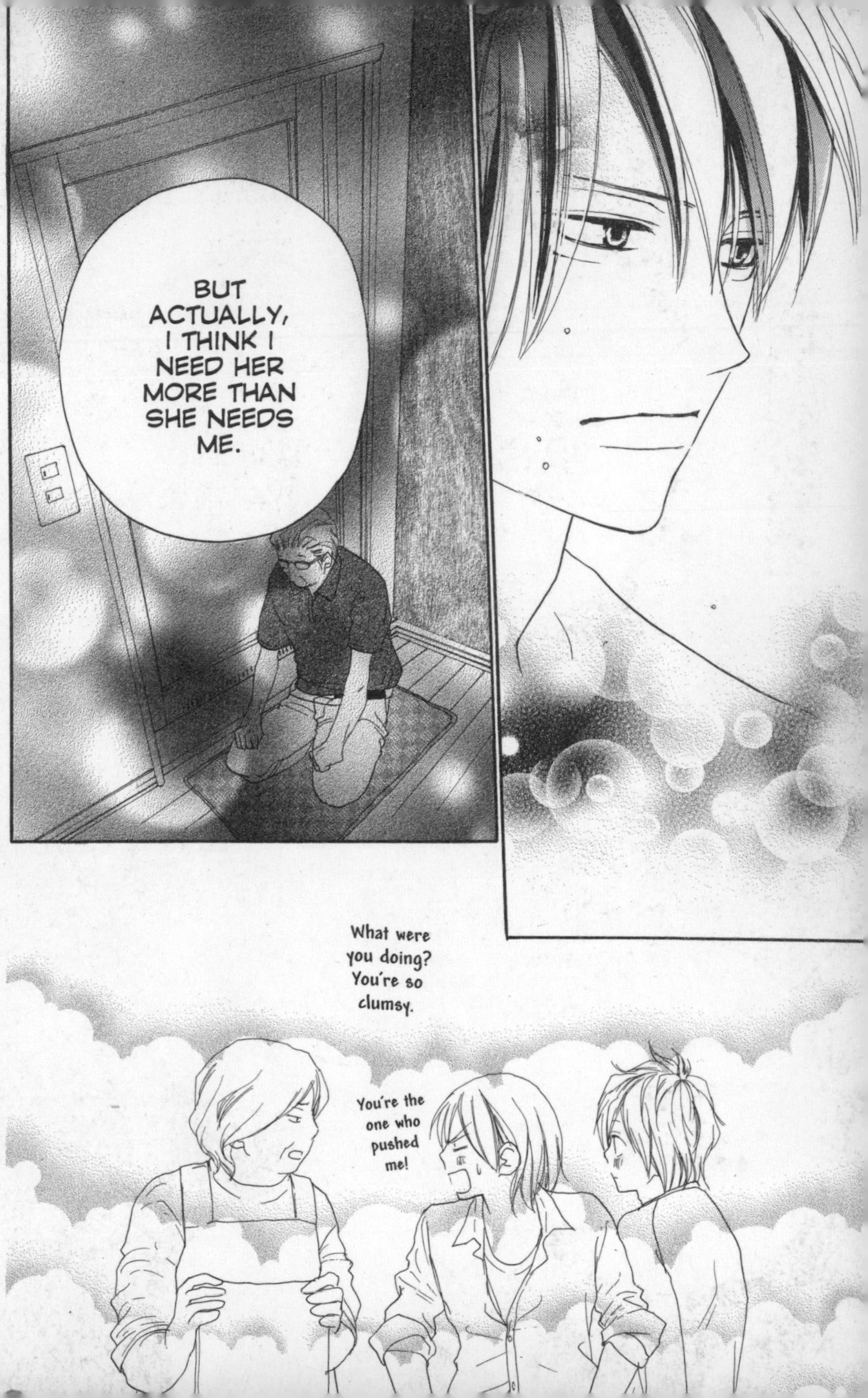
BUT ACTUALLY, I THINK I NEED HER MORE THAN SHE NEEDS ME.
What were you doing? You're so clumsy.
You're the one who pushed me!

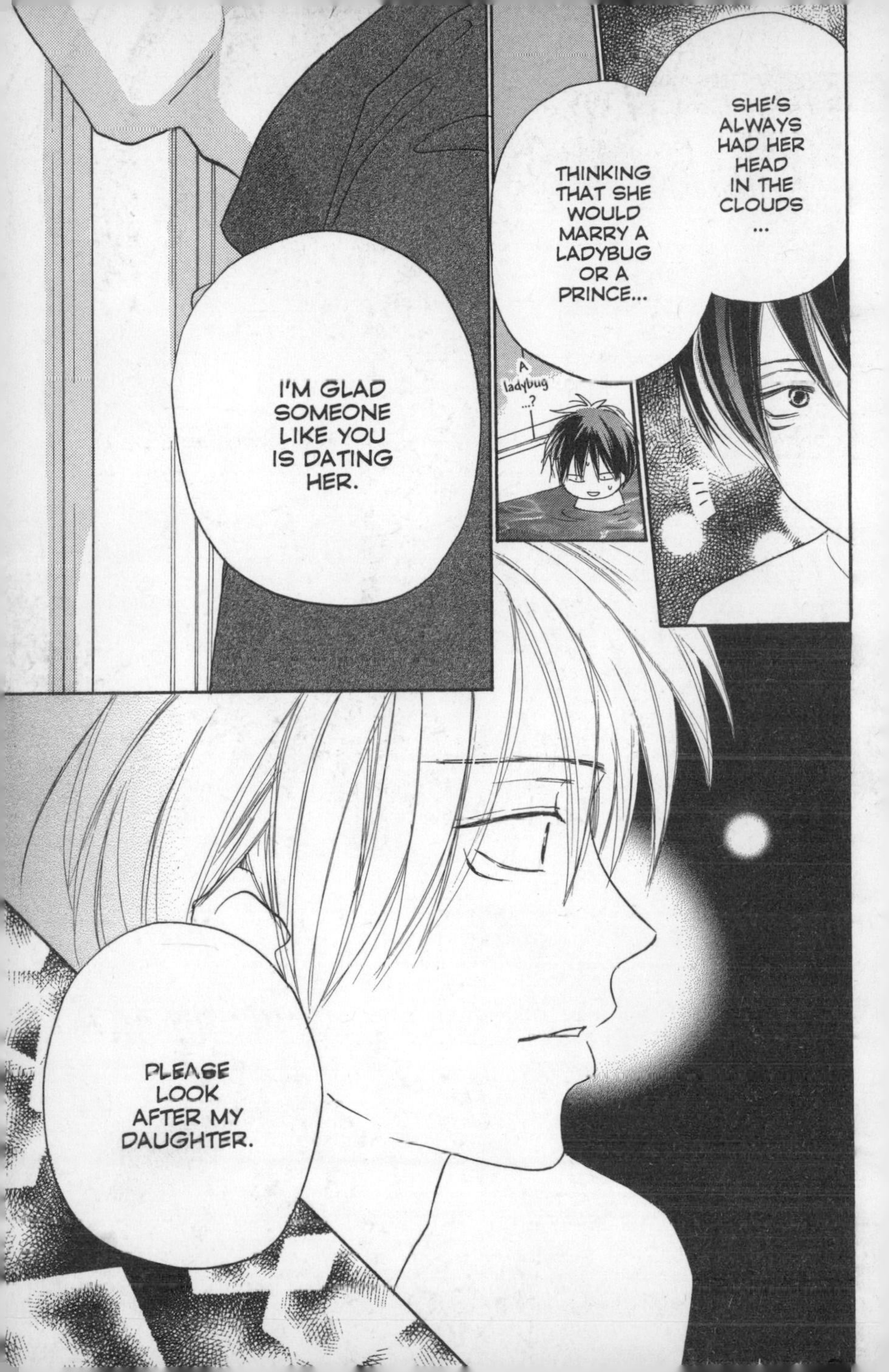
SHE'S ALWAYS HAD HER HEAD IN THE CLOUDS...
THINKING THAT SHE WOULD MARRY A LADYBUG OR A PRINCE...
A ladybug ...?
I'M GLAD SOMEONE LIKE YOU IS DATING HER.
PLEASE LOOK AFTER MY DAUGHTER.

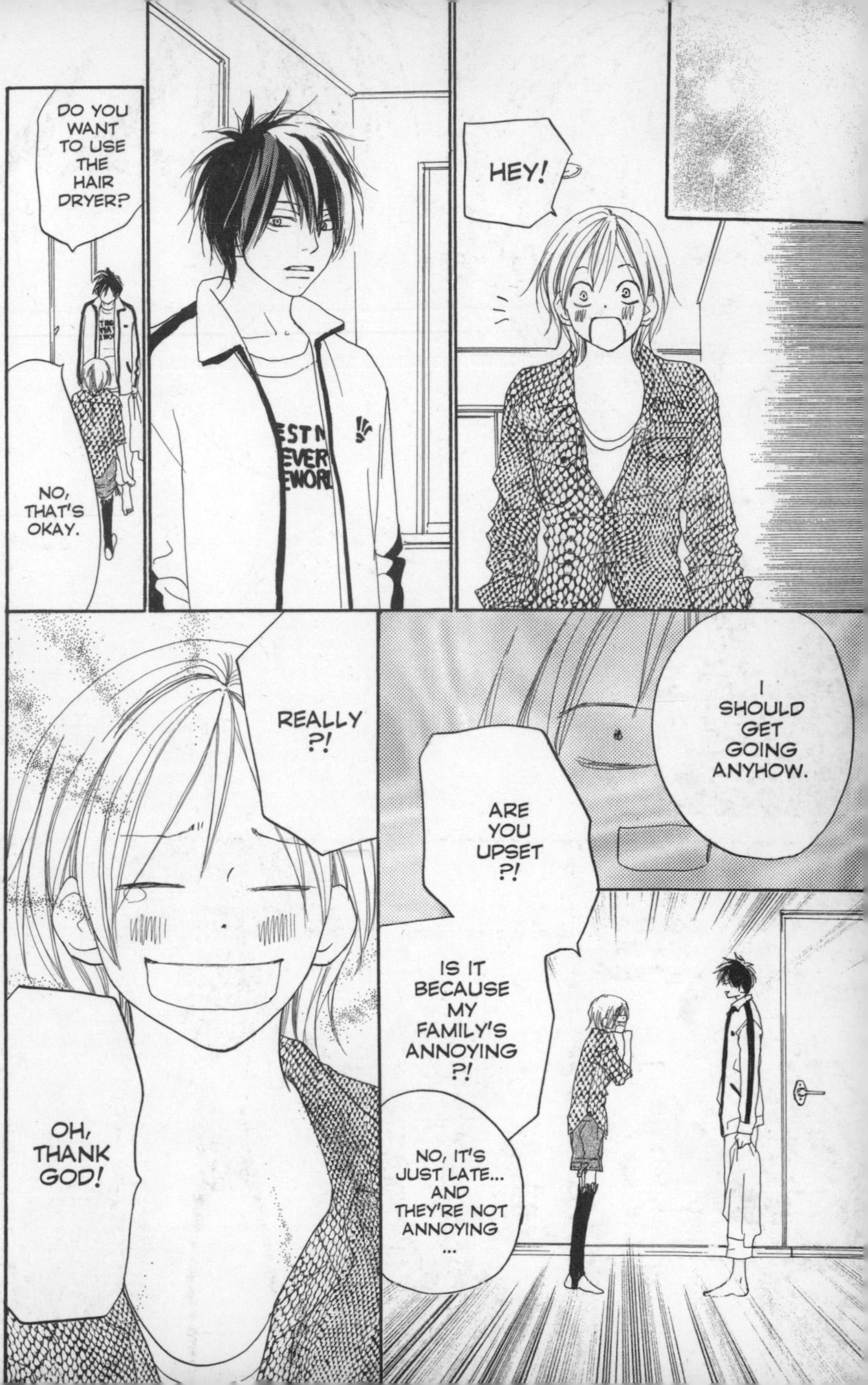
HEY!
DO YOU WANT TO USE THE HAIR DRYER?
NO, THAT'S OKAY.
I SHOULD GET GOING ANYHOW.
ARE YOU UPSET ?!
IS IT BECAUSE MY FAMILY'S ANNOYING ?!
NO, IT'S JUST LATE... AND THEY'RE NOT ANNOYING ...
REALLY ?!
OH, THANK GOD!

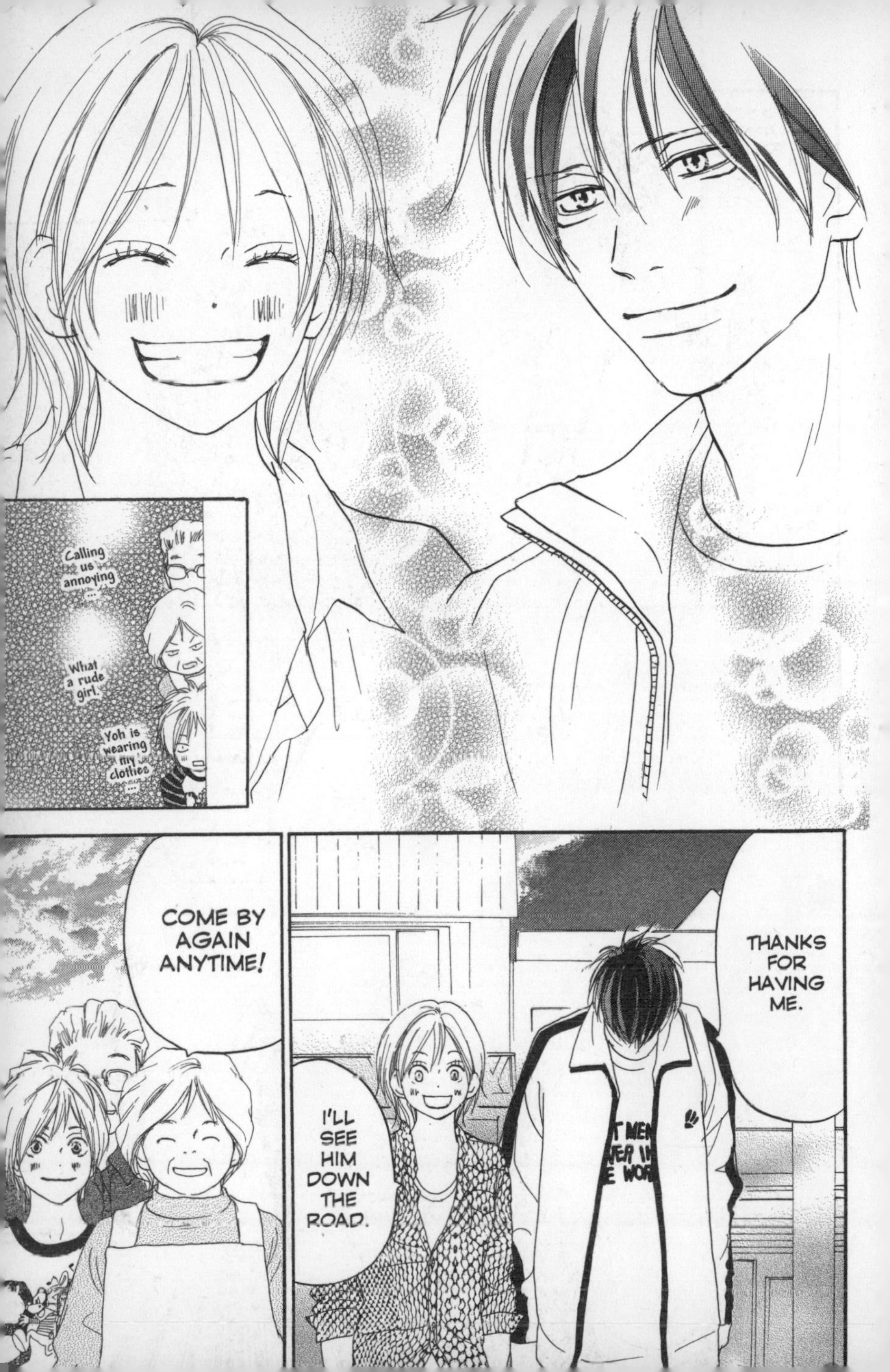
Calling us annoying ...
What a rude girl.
Yoh is wearing my clothes ...
THANKS FOR HAVING ME.
I'LL SEE HIM DOWN THE ROAD.
COME BY AGAIN ANYTIME!

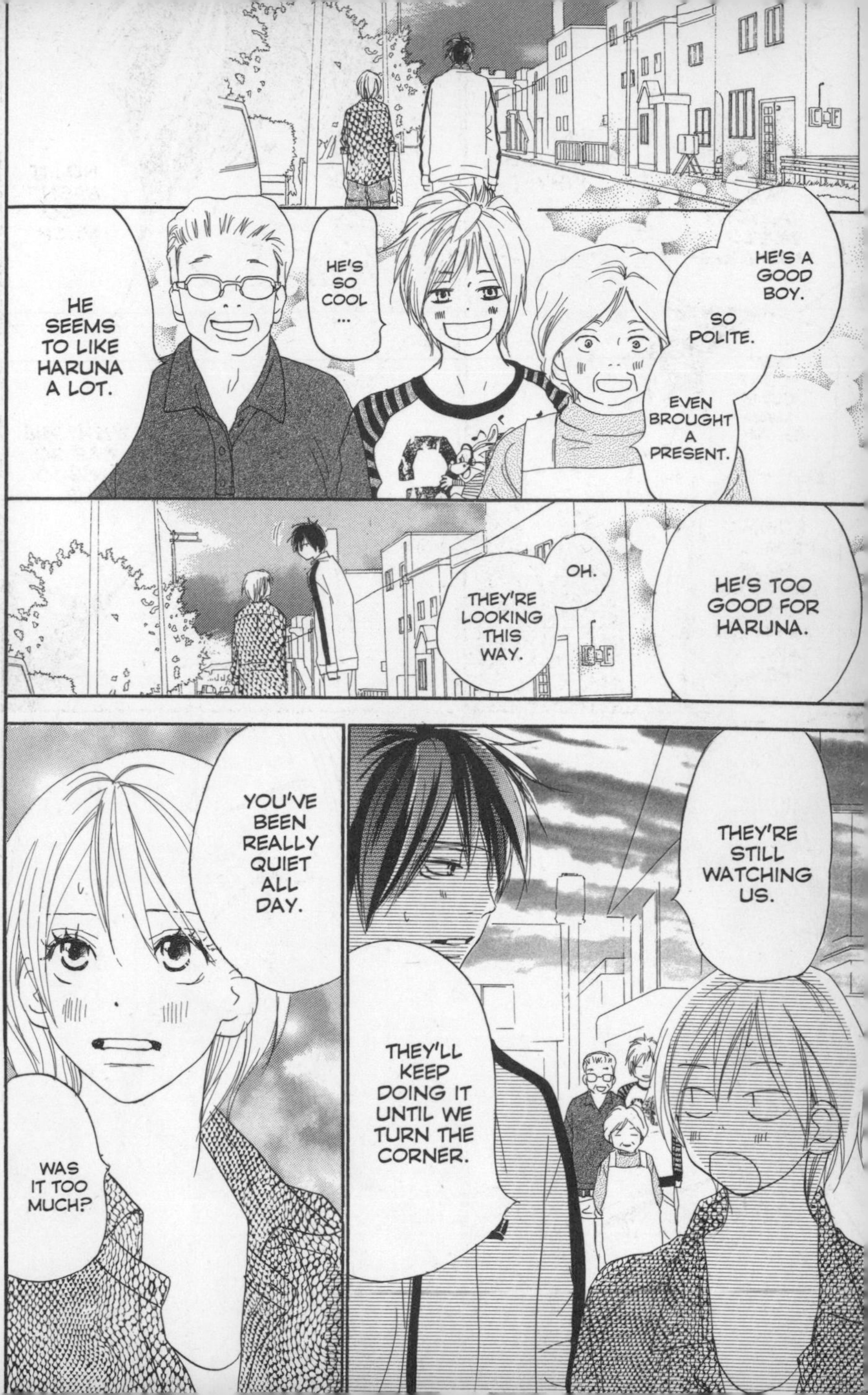
HE'S A GOOD BOY.
SO POLITE.
EVEN BROUGHT A PRESENT.
HE'S SO COOL ...
HE SEEMS TO LIKE HARUNA A LOT.
HE'S TOO GOOD FOR HARUNA.
OH.
THEY'RE LOOKING THIS WAY.
THEY'RE STILL WATCHING US.
THEY'LL KEEP DOING IT UNTIL WE TURN THE CORNER.
YOU'VE BEEN REALLY QUIET ALL DAY.
WAS IT TOO MUCH?

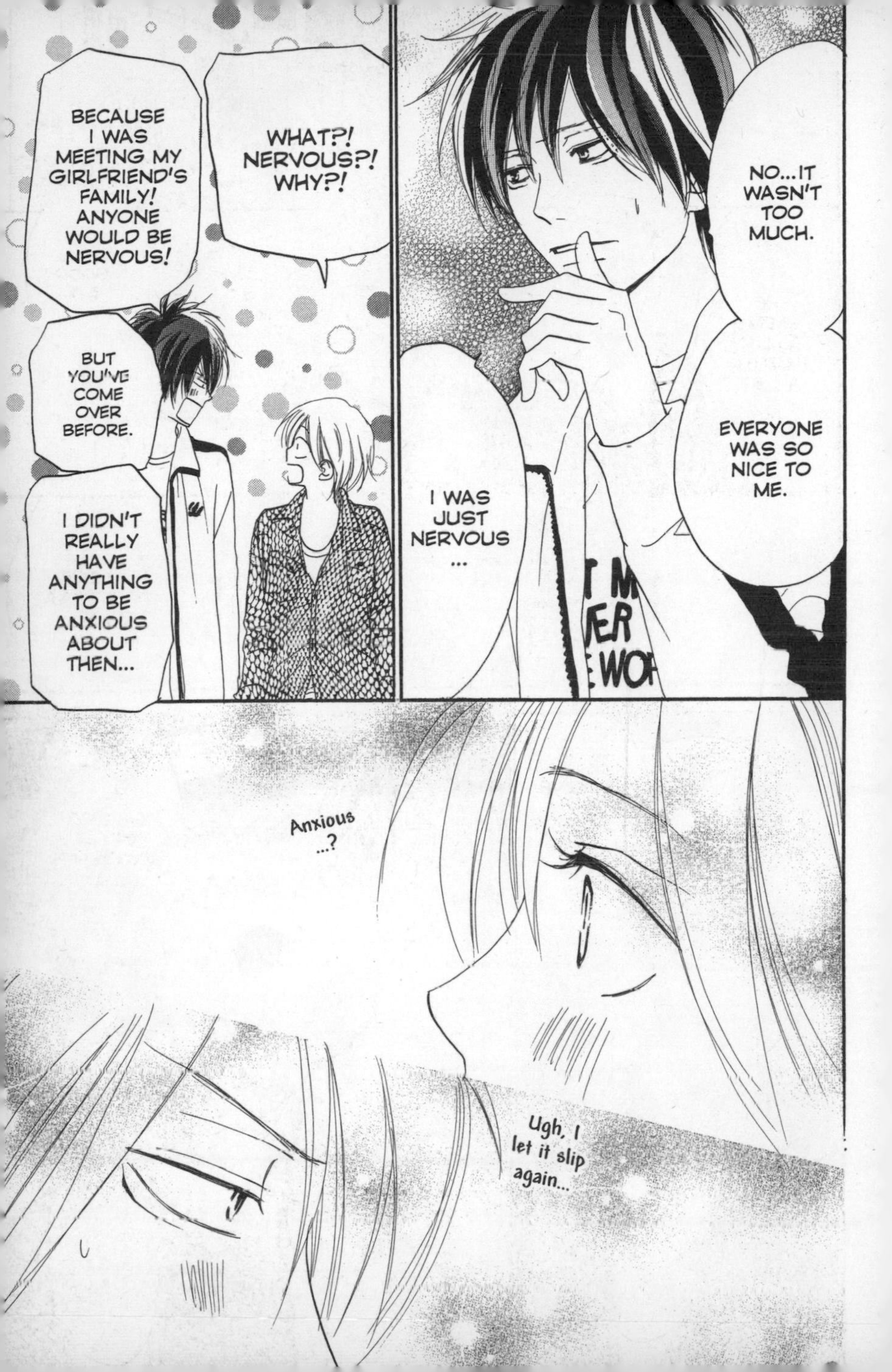
NO...IT WASN'T TOO MUCH.
EVERYONE WAS SO NICE TO ME.
I WAS JUST NERVOUS ...
WHAT?! NERVOUS?! WHY?!
BECAUSE I WAS MEETING MY GIRLFRIEND'S FAMILY! ANYONE WOULD BE NERVOUS!
BUT YOU'VE COME OVER BEFORE.
I DIDN'T REALLY HAVE ANYTHING TO BE ANXIOUS ABOUT THEN...
Anxious ...?
Ugh, I let it slip again...

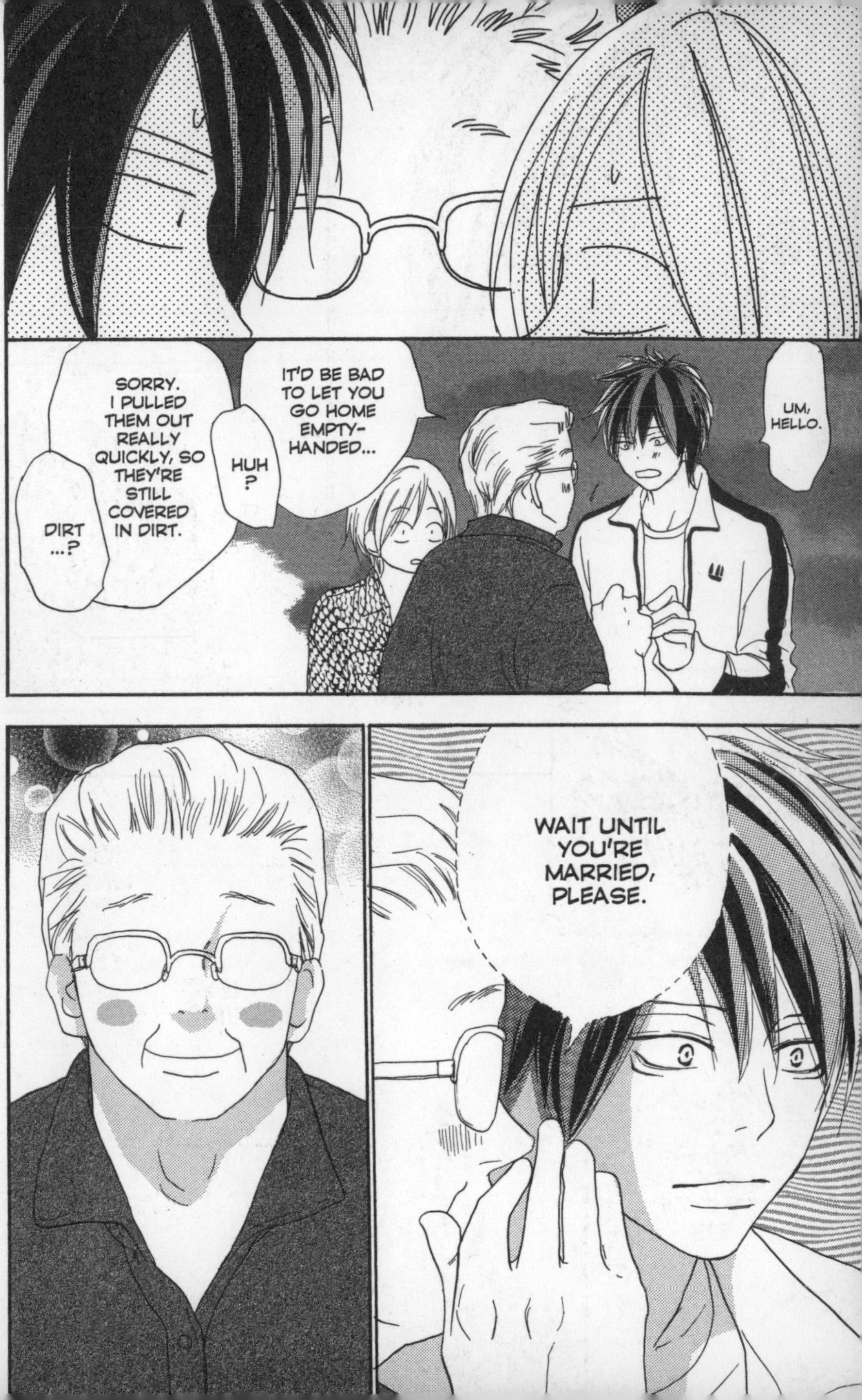
UM, HELLO.
IT'D BE BAD TO LET YOU GO HOME EMPTY-HANDED...
HUH?
SORRY. I PULLED THEM OUT REALLY QUICKLY, SO THEY'RE STILL COVERED IN DIRT.
DIRT...?
WAIT UNTIL YOU'RE MARRIED, PLEASE.

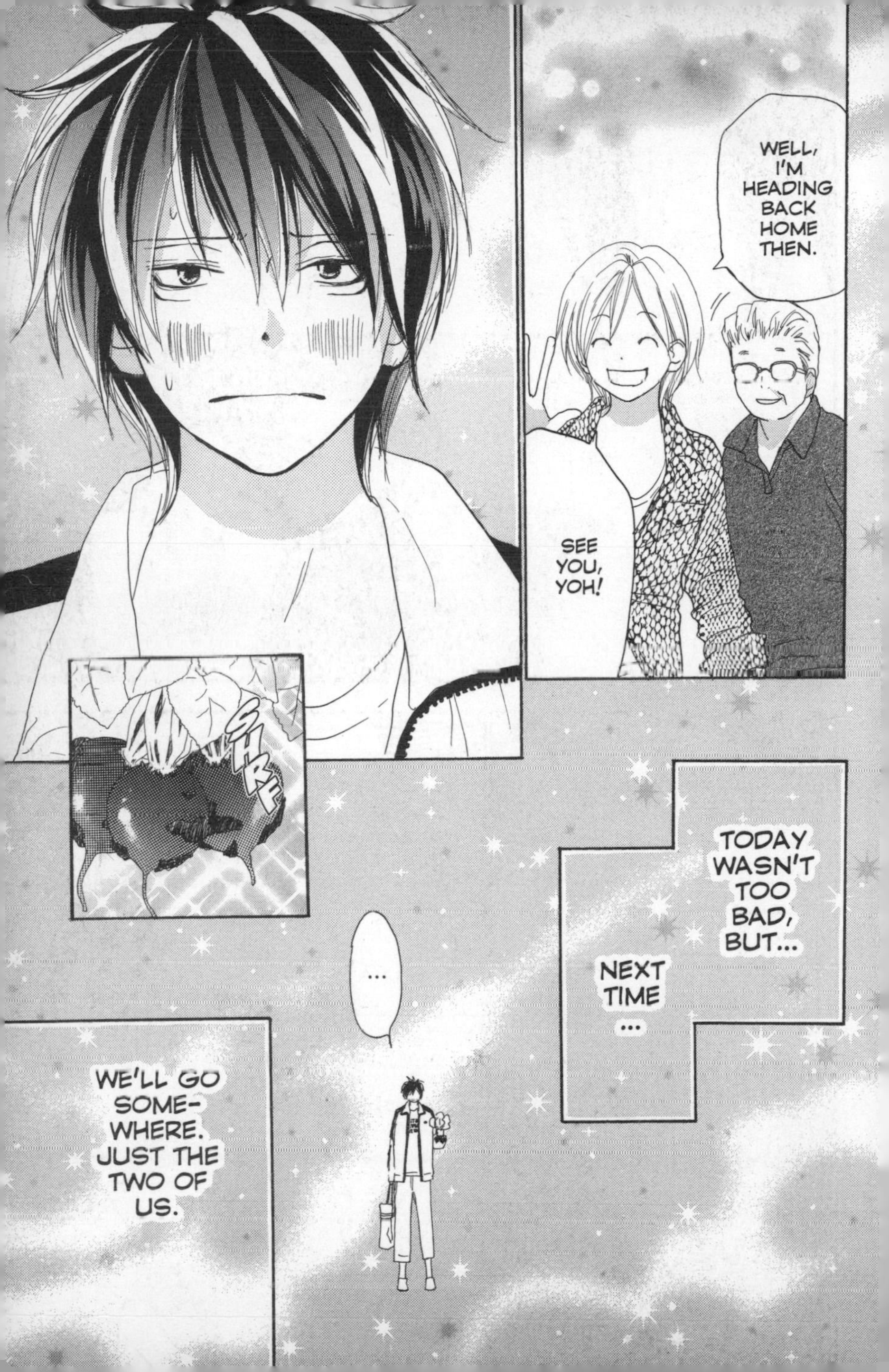
WELL, I'M HEADING BACK HOME THEN.
SEE YOU, YOH!
SHRF
TODAY WASN'T TOO BAD, BUT...
NEXT TIME ...
...
WE'LL GO SOME-WHERE. JUST THE TWO OF US.

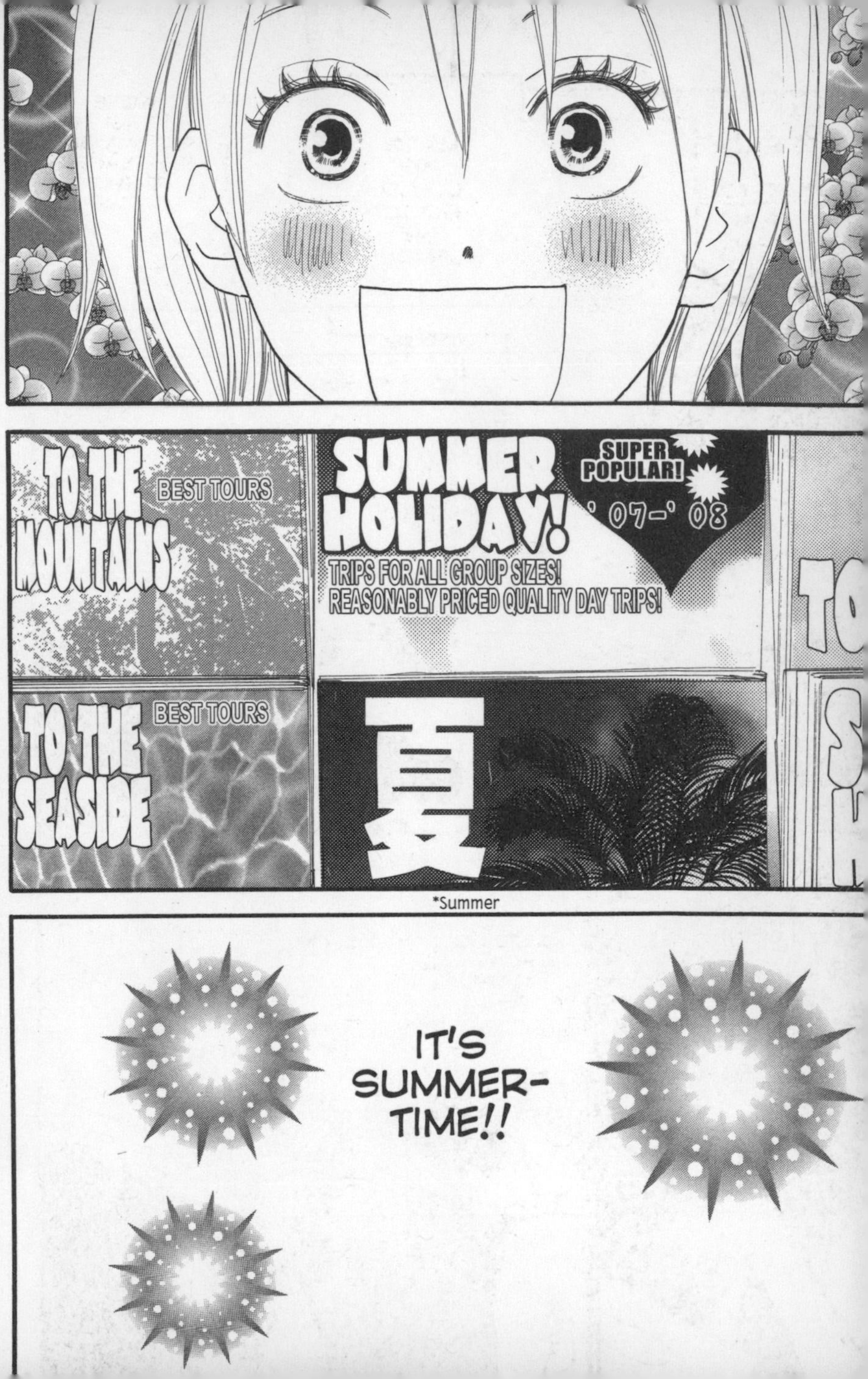
TO
SUPER POPULAR!
'07-'08
SUMMER HOLIDAY!
TRIPS FOR ALL GROUP SIZES!
REASONABLY PRICED QUALITY DAY TRIPS!
夏
BEST TOURS
TO THE MOUNTAINS
BEST TOURS
TO THE SEASIDE
*Summer
IT'S SUMMER-TIME!!

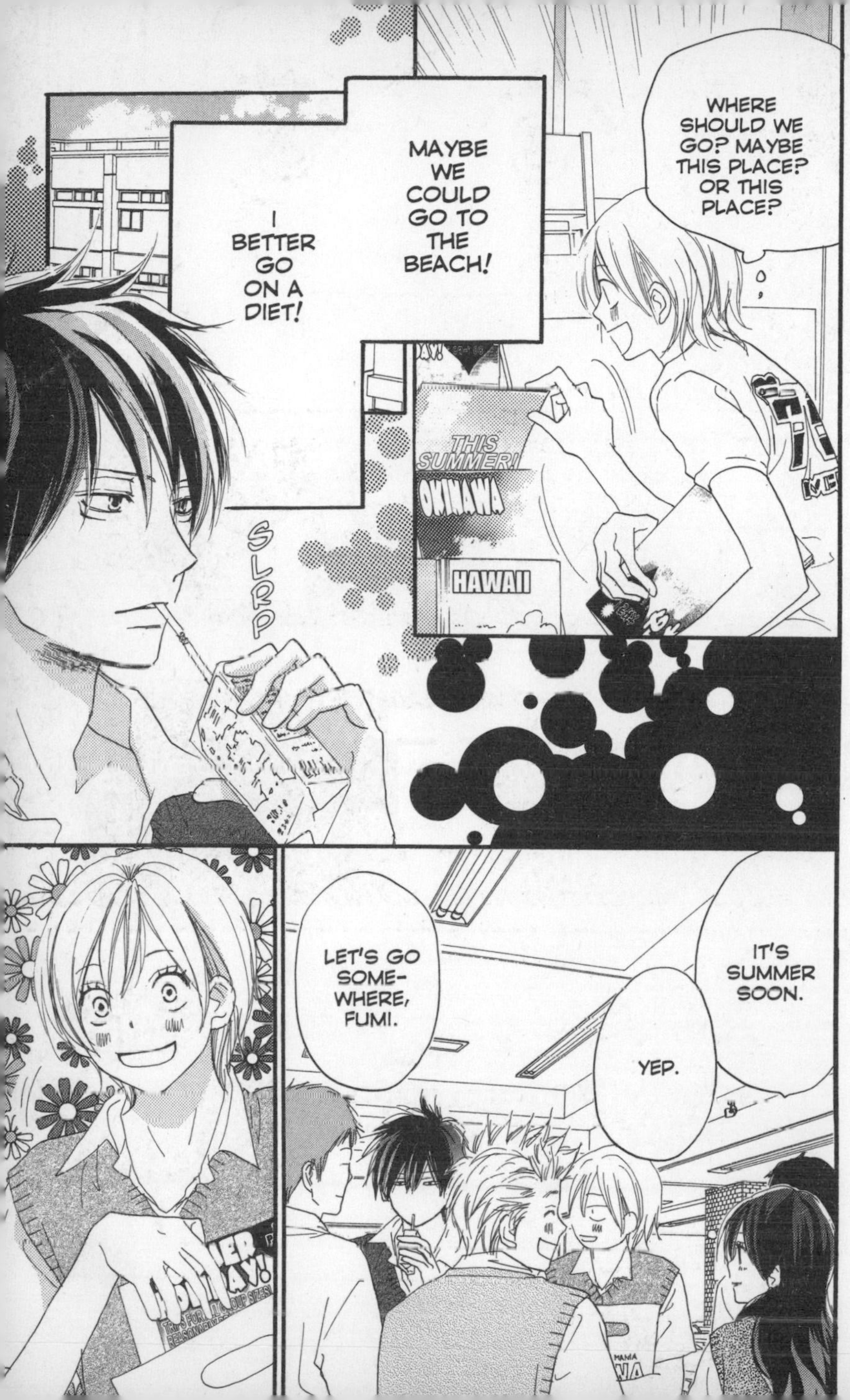
WHERE SHOULD WE GO? MAYBE THIS PLACE? OR THIS PLACE?
THIS SUMMER!
OKINAWA
HAWAII
MAYBE WE COULD GO TO THE BEACH!
I BETTER GO ON A DIET!
SLRP
IT'S SUMMER SOON.
YEP.
LET'S GO SOME-WHERE, FUMI.

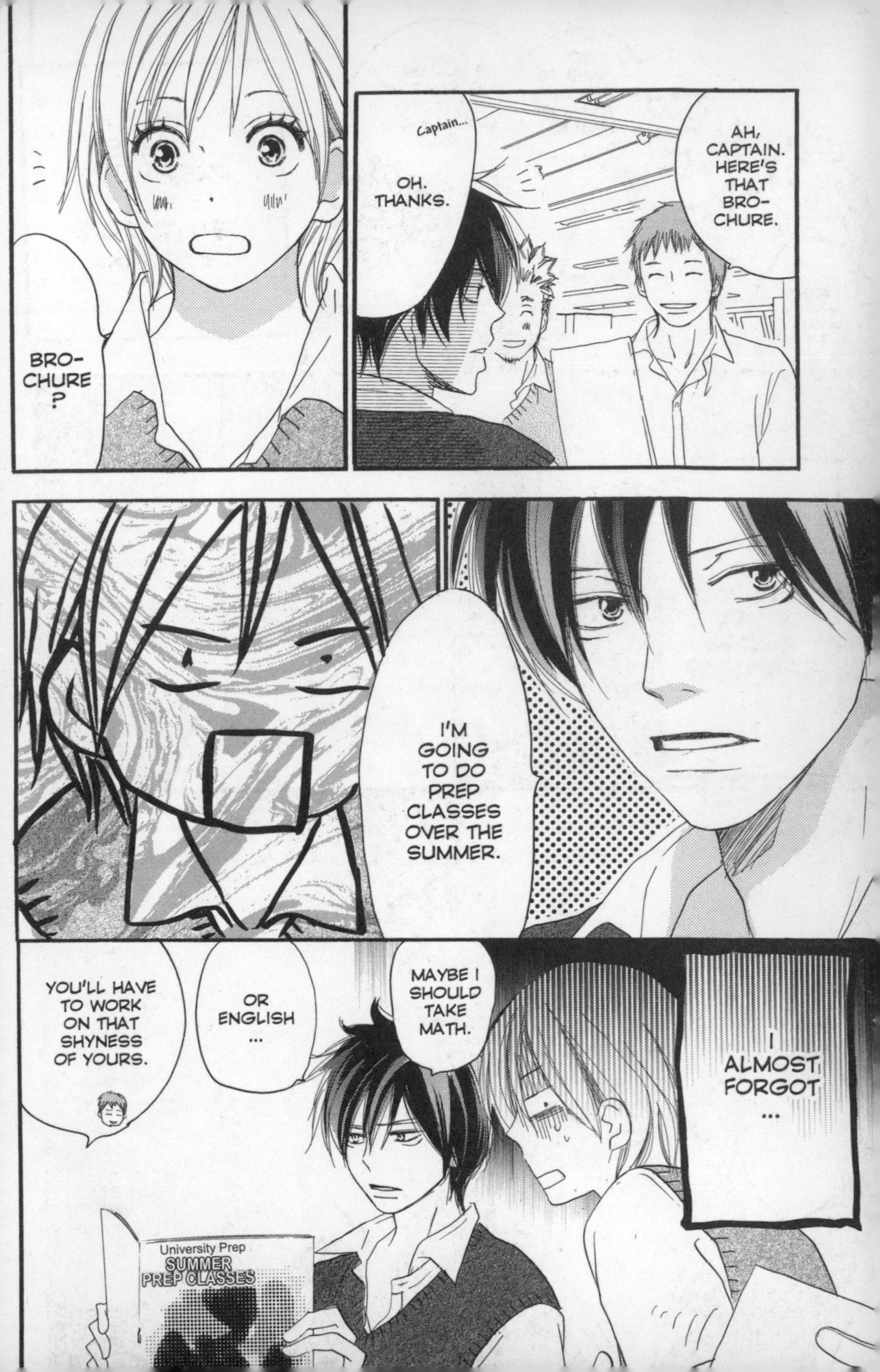
AH, CAPTAIN. HERE'S THAT BRO-CHURE.
Captain...
OH. THANKS.
BRO-CHURE?
I'M GOING TO DO PREP CLASSES OVER THE SUMMER.
I ALMOST FORGOT...
MAYBE I SHOULD TAKE MATH.
OR ENGLISH...
YOU'LL HAVE TO WORK ON THAT SHYNESS OF YOURS.
University Prep
SUMMER PREP CLASSES

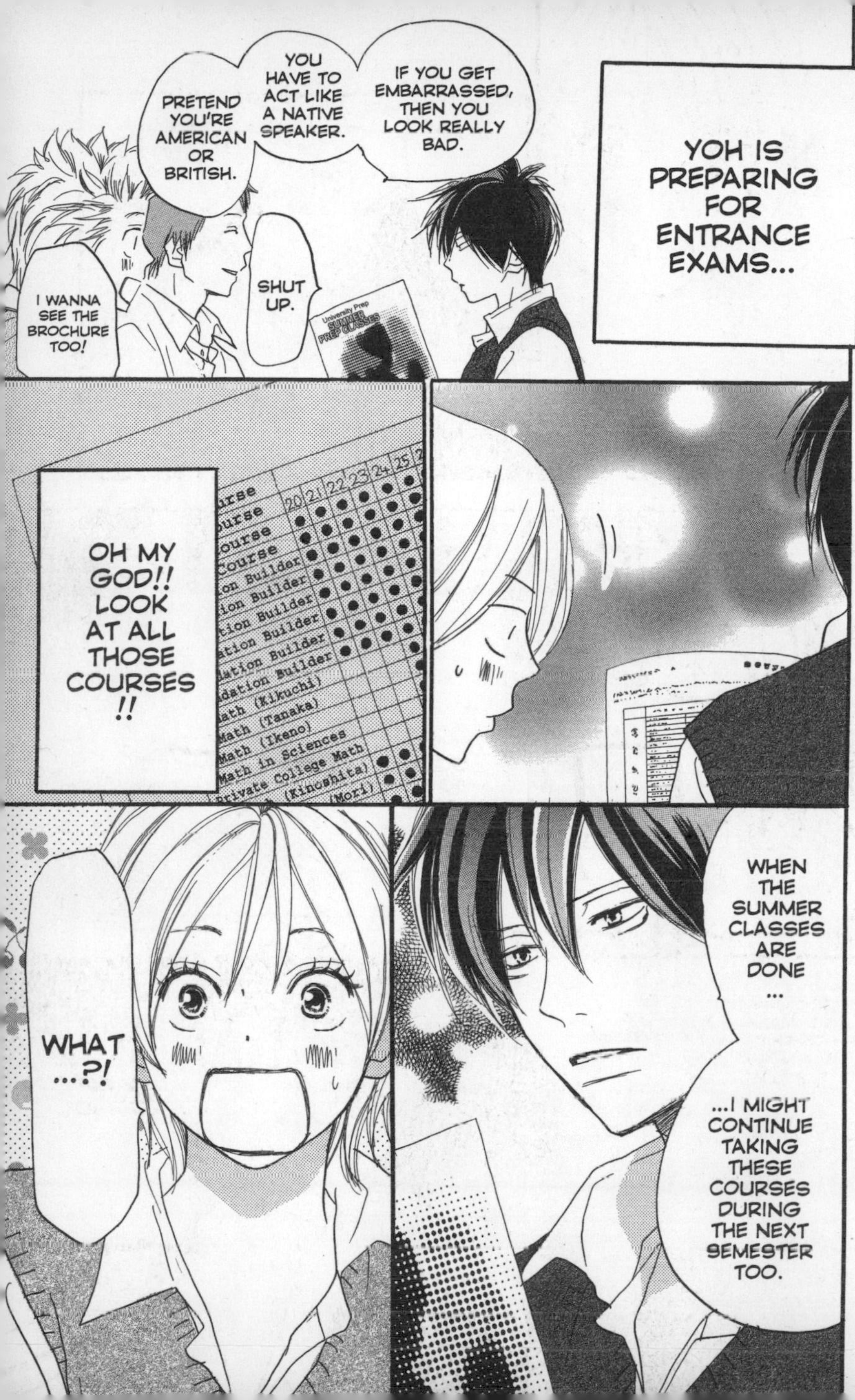
YOH IS PREPARING FOR ENTRANCE EXAMS...
IF YOU GET EMBARRASSED, THEN YOU LOOK REALLY BAD.
YOU HAVE TO ACT LIKE A NATIVE SPEAKER.
PRETEND YOU'RE AMERICAN OR BRITISH.
University Prep SUMMER PREP CLASSES
SHUT UP.
I WANNA SEE THE BROCHURE TOO!
OH MY GOD!! LOOK AT ALL THOSE COURSES !!
WHEN THE SUMMER CLASSES ARE DONE ...
...I MIGHT CONTINUE TAKING THESE COURSES DURING THE NEXT SEMESTER TOO.
WHAT ...?!

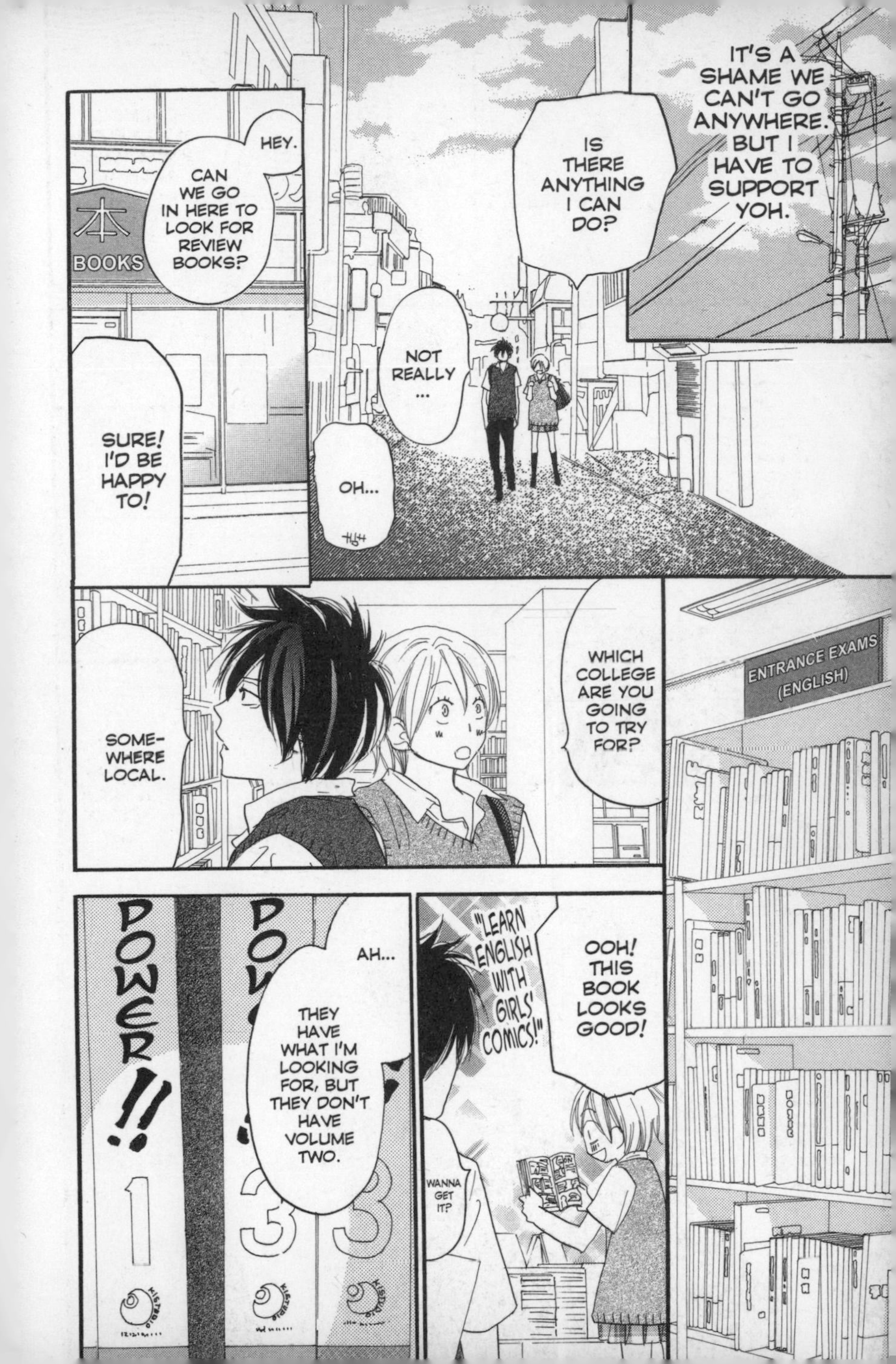
IT'S A SHAME WE CAN'T GO ANYWHERE. BUT I HAVE TO SUPPORT YOH.
IS THERE ANYTHING I CAN DO?
NOT REALLY ...
OH...
HEY.
CAN WE GO IN HERE TO LOOK FOR REVIEW BOOKS?
本
BOOKS
SURE! I'D BE HAPPY TO!
ENTRANCE EXAMS (ENGLISH)
WHICH COLLEGE ARE YOU GOING TO TRY FOR?
SOME-WHERE LOCAL.
OOH! THIS BOOK LOOKS GOOD!
"LEARN ENGLISH WITH GIRLS' COMICS!"
WANNA GET IT?
AH...
THEY HAVE WHAT I'M LOOKING FOR, BUT THEY DON'T HAVE VOLUME TWO.
POWER!!
1
3
3

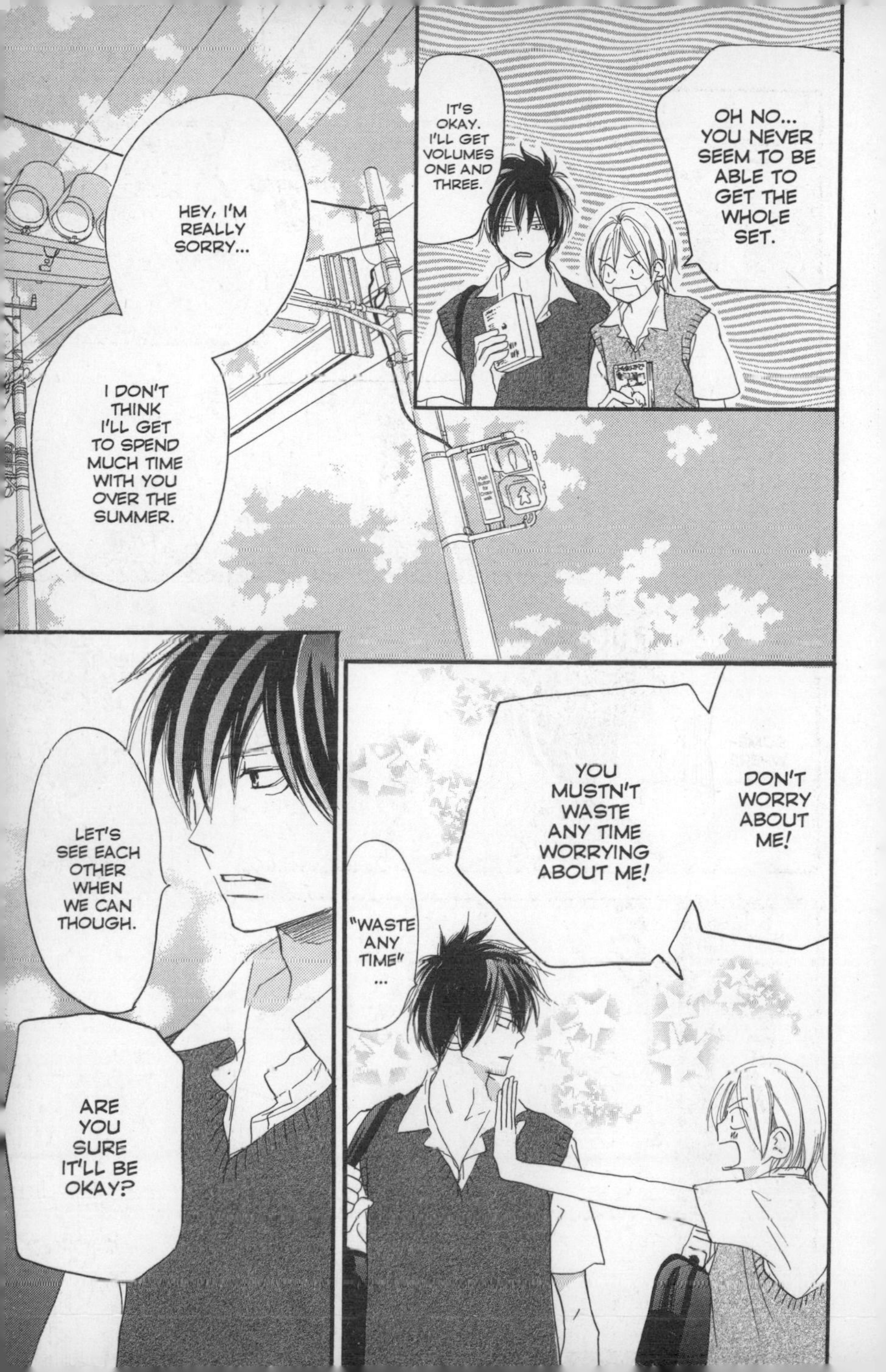

OH NO... YOU NEVER SEEM TO BE ABLE TO GET THE WHOLE SET.
IT'S OKAY. I'LL GET VOLUMES ONE AND THREE.
HEY, I'M REALLY SORRY...
I DON'T THINK I'LL GET TO SPEND MUCH TIME WITH YOU OVER THE SUMMER.
DON'T WORRY ABOUT ME!
YOU MUSTN'T WASTE ANY TIME WORRYING ABOUT ME!
"WASTE ANY TIME"...
LET'S SEE EACH OTHER WHEN WE CAN THOUGH.
ARE YOU SURE IT'LL BE OKAY?

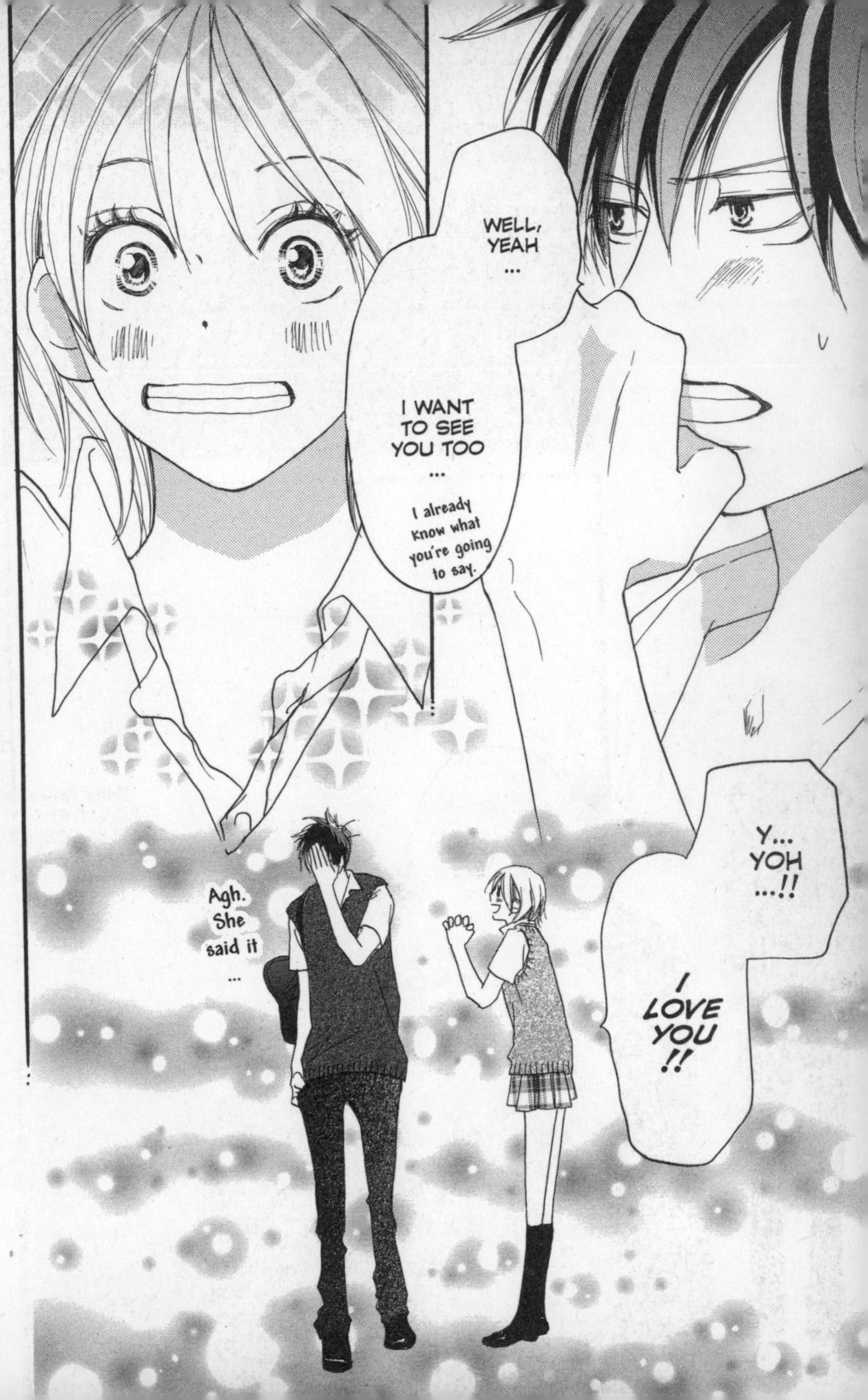
WELL, YEAH ...
I WANT TO SEE YOU TOO ...
I already know what you're going to say.
Y... YOH ...!!
I LOVE YOU!!
Agh. She said it ...

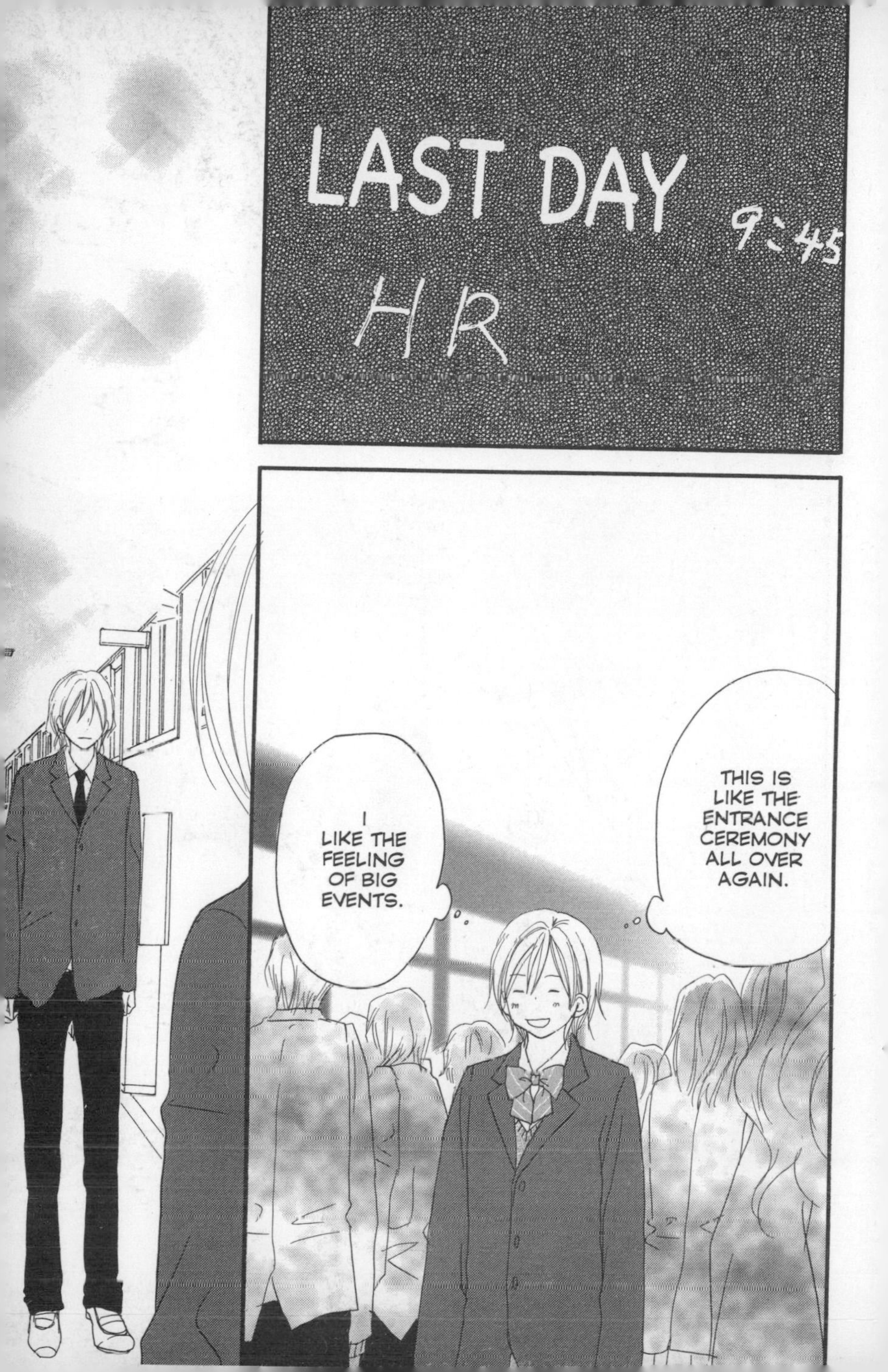
LAST DAY HR 9:45
THIS IS LIKE THE ENTRANCE CEREMONY ALL OVER AGAIN.
I LIKE THE FEELING OF BIG EVENTS.

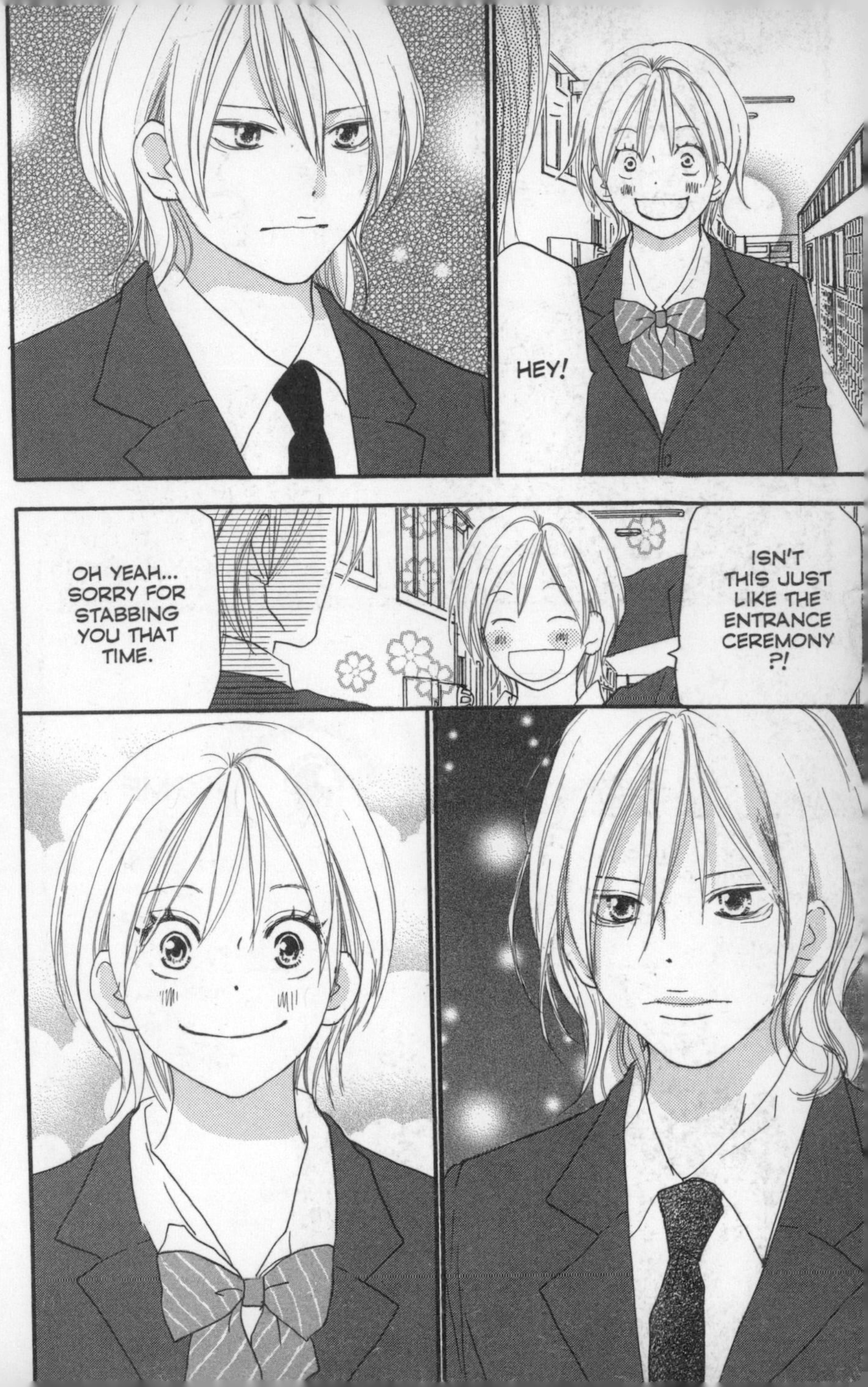
HEY!
ISN'T THIS JUST LIKE THE ENTRANCE CEREMONY?!
OH YEAH... SORRY FOR STABBING YOU THAT TIME.

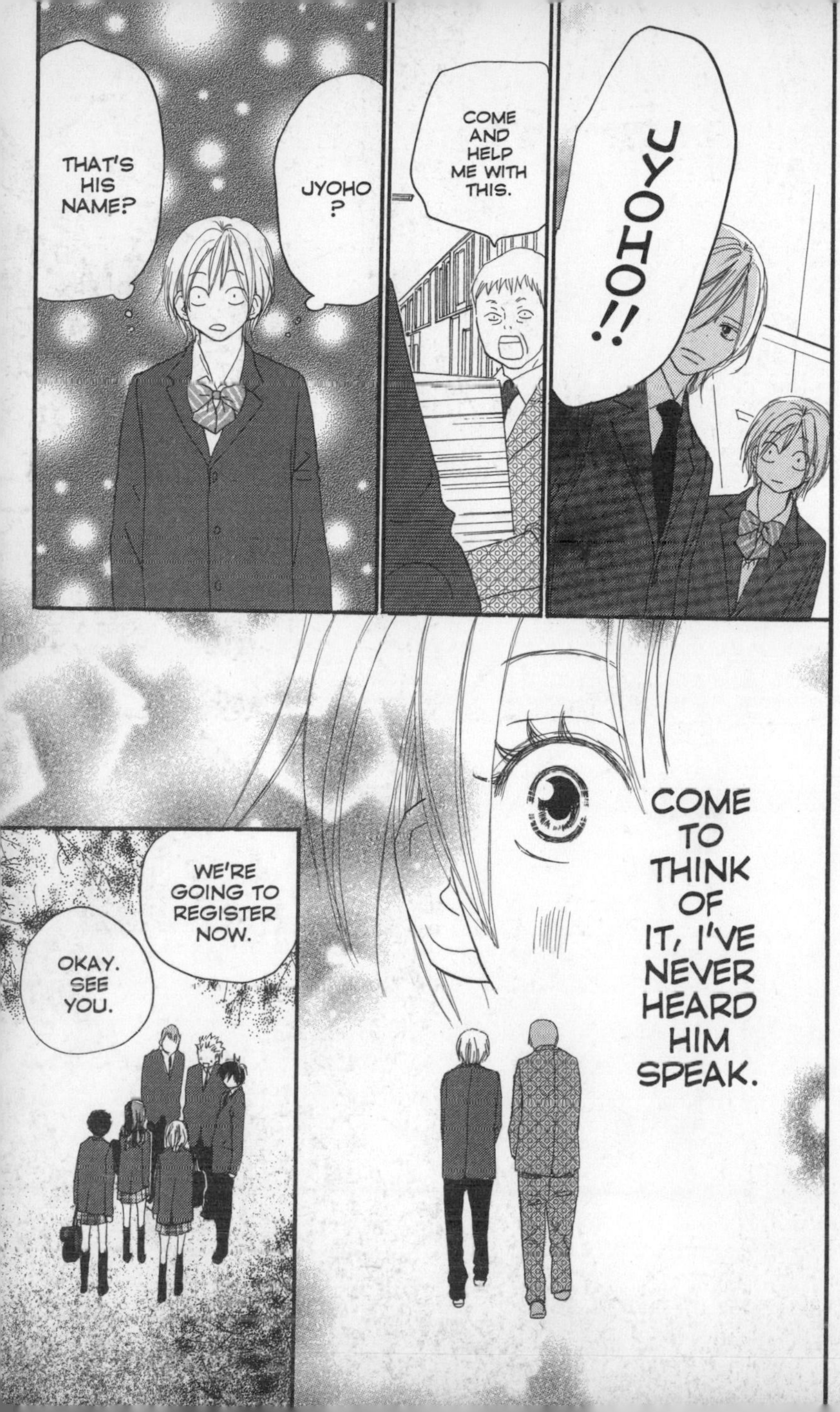
JYOHO!!
COME AND HELP ME WITH THIS.
JYOHO ?
THAT'S HIS NAME?
COME TO THINK OF IT, I'VE NEVER HEARD HIM SPEAK.
WE'RE GOING TO REGISTER NOW.
OKAY. SEE YOU.

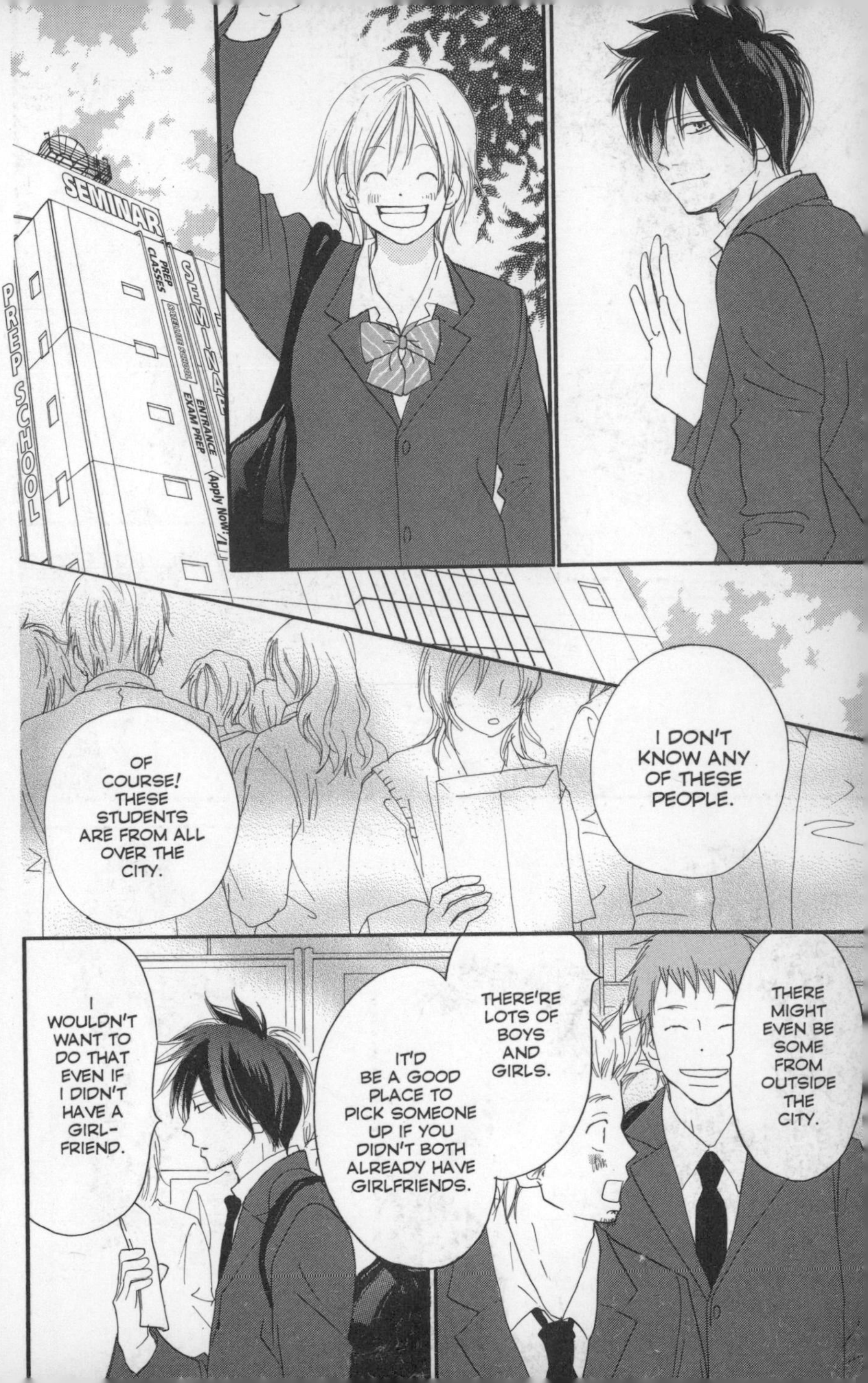
SEMINAR
PREP CLASSES
SEMINAR
ENTRANCE EXAM PREP
Apply Now!
PREP SCHOOL
I DON'T KNOW ANY OF THESE PEOPLE.
OF COURSE! THESE STUDENTS ARE FROM ALL OVER THE CITY.
THERE MIGHT EVEN BE SOME FROM OUTSIDE THE CITY.
THERE'RE LOTS OF BOYS AND GIRLS.
IT'D BE A GOOD PLACE TO PICK SOMEONE UP IF YOU DIDN'T BOTH ALREADY HAVE GIRLFRIENDS.
I WOULDN'T WANT TO DO THAT EVEN IF I DIDN'T HAVE A GIRL-FRIEND.

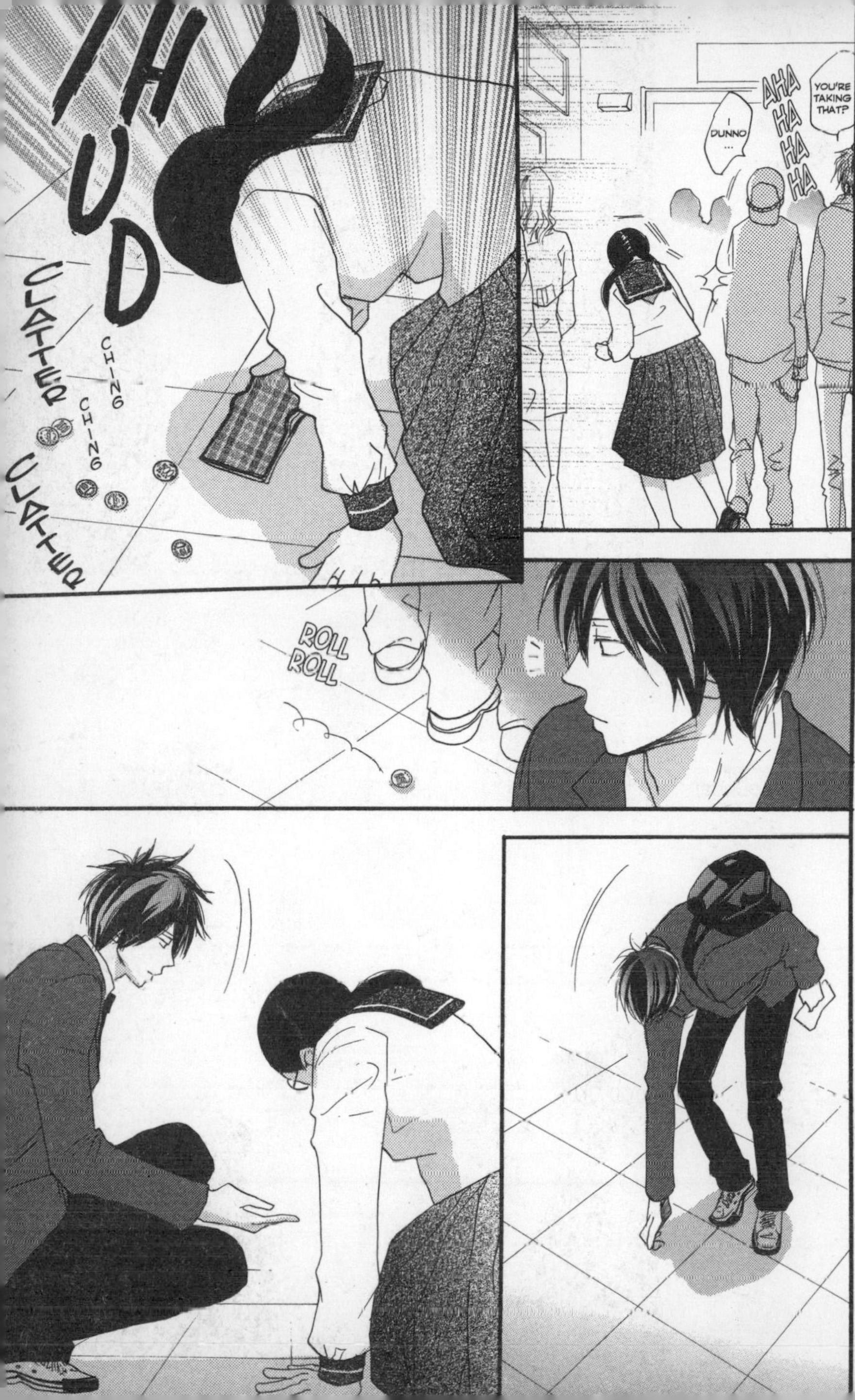
YOU'RE TAKING THAT?
AHAHAHAHAHA
I DUNNO...
THUD
CLATTER
CHING CHING
CLATTER
ROLL ROLL

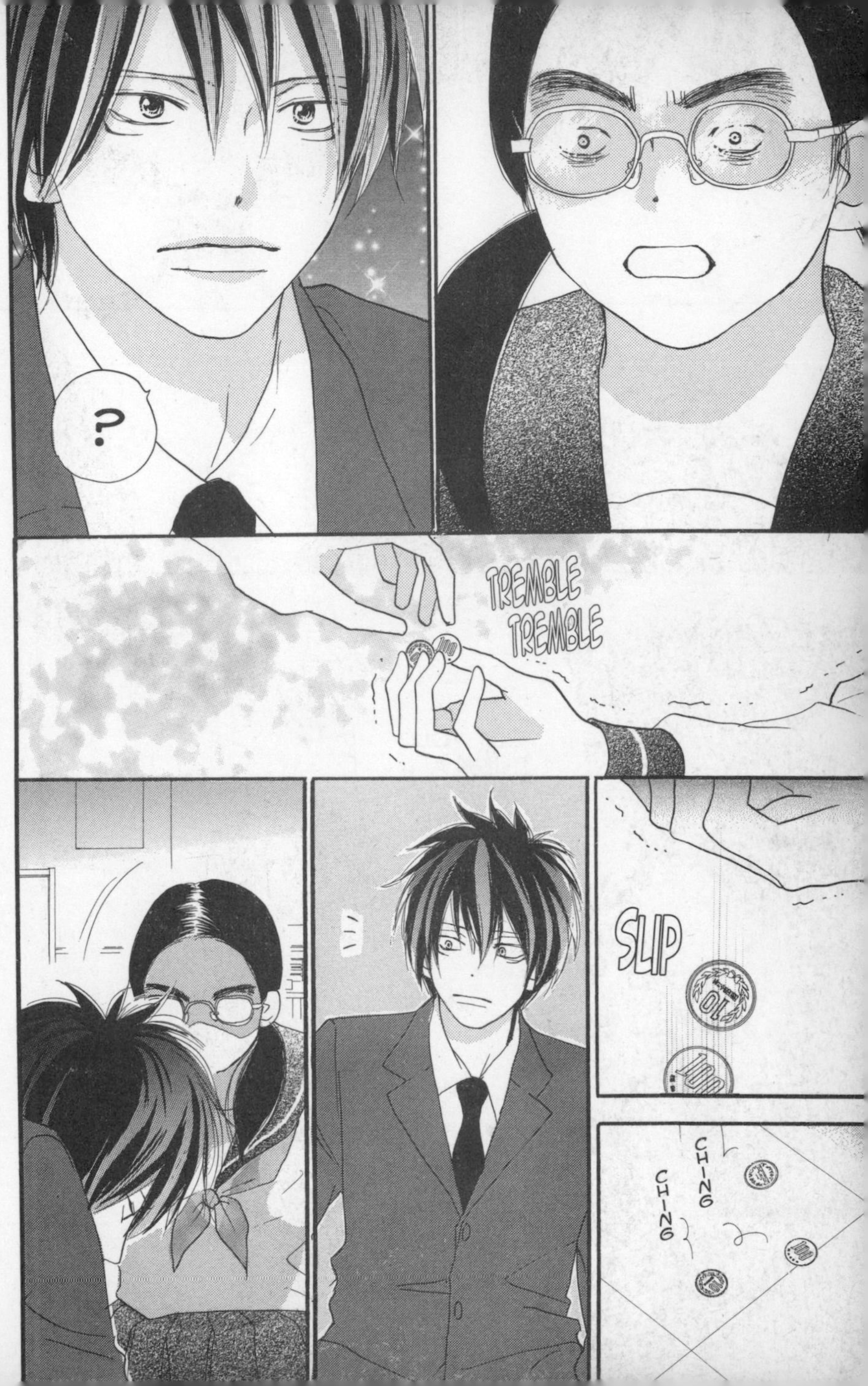
?
TREMBLE TREMBLE
SLIP
CHING CHING

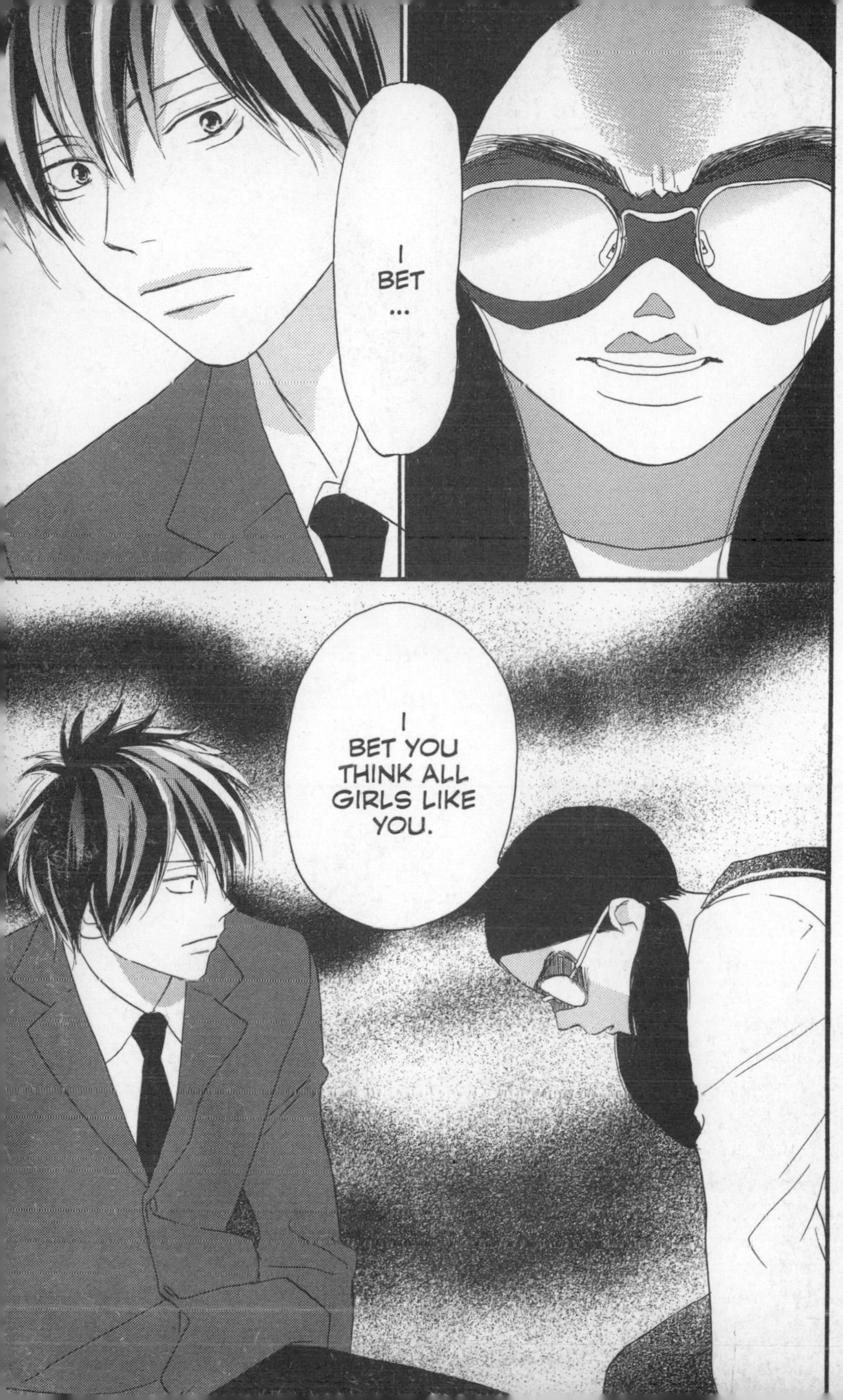
I BET ...
I BET YOU THINK ALL GIRLS LIKE YOU.

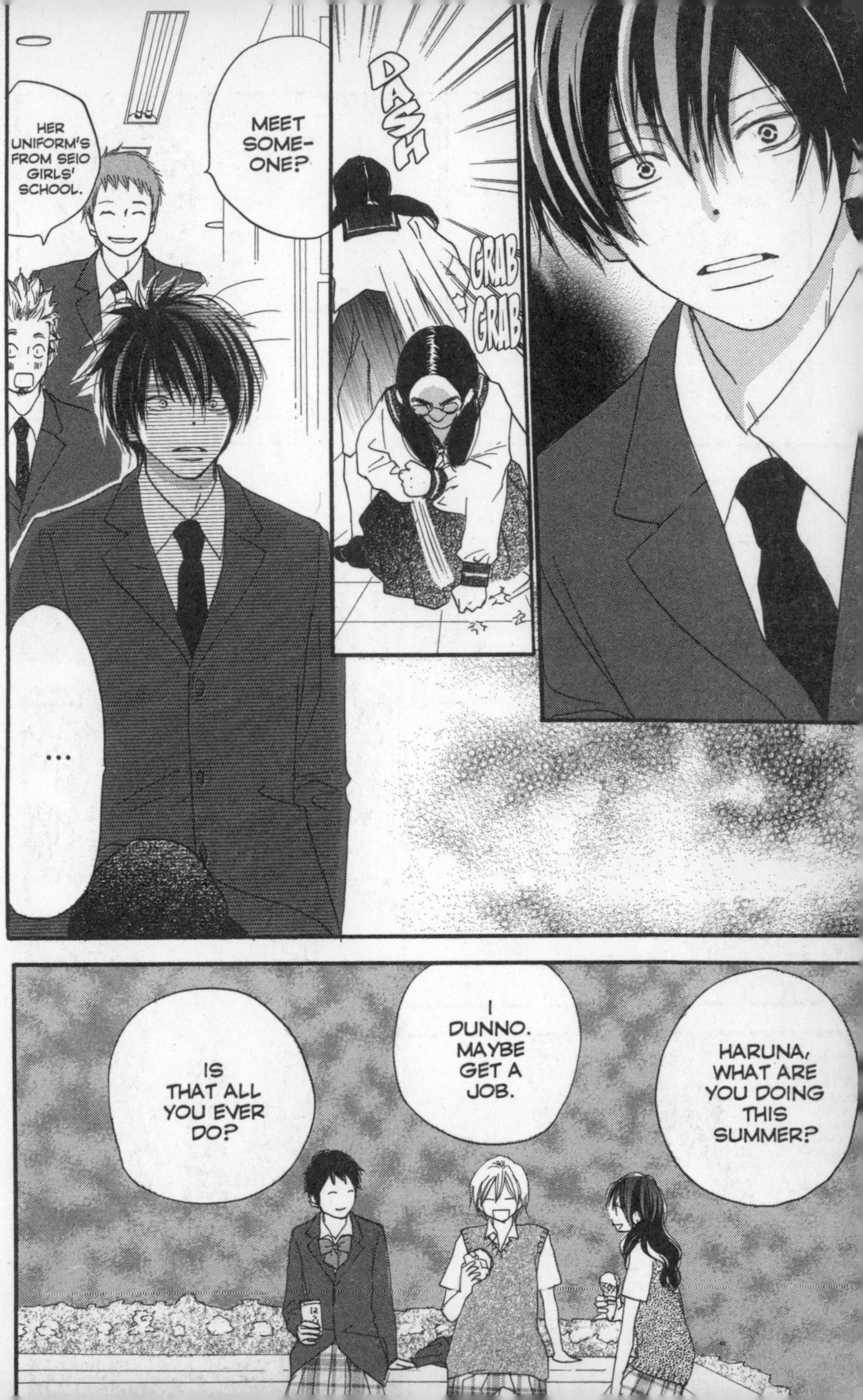
DASH
GRAB
GRAB
MEET SOME-ONE?
HER UNIFORM'S FROM SEIO GIRLS' SCHOOL.
...
HARUNA, WHAT ARE YOU DOING THIS SUMMER?
I DUNNO. MAYBE GET A JOB.
IS THAT ALL YOU EVER DO?

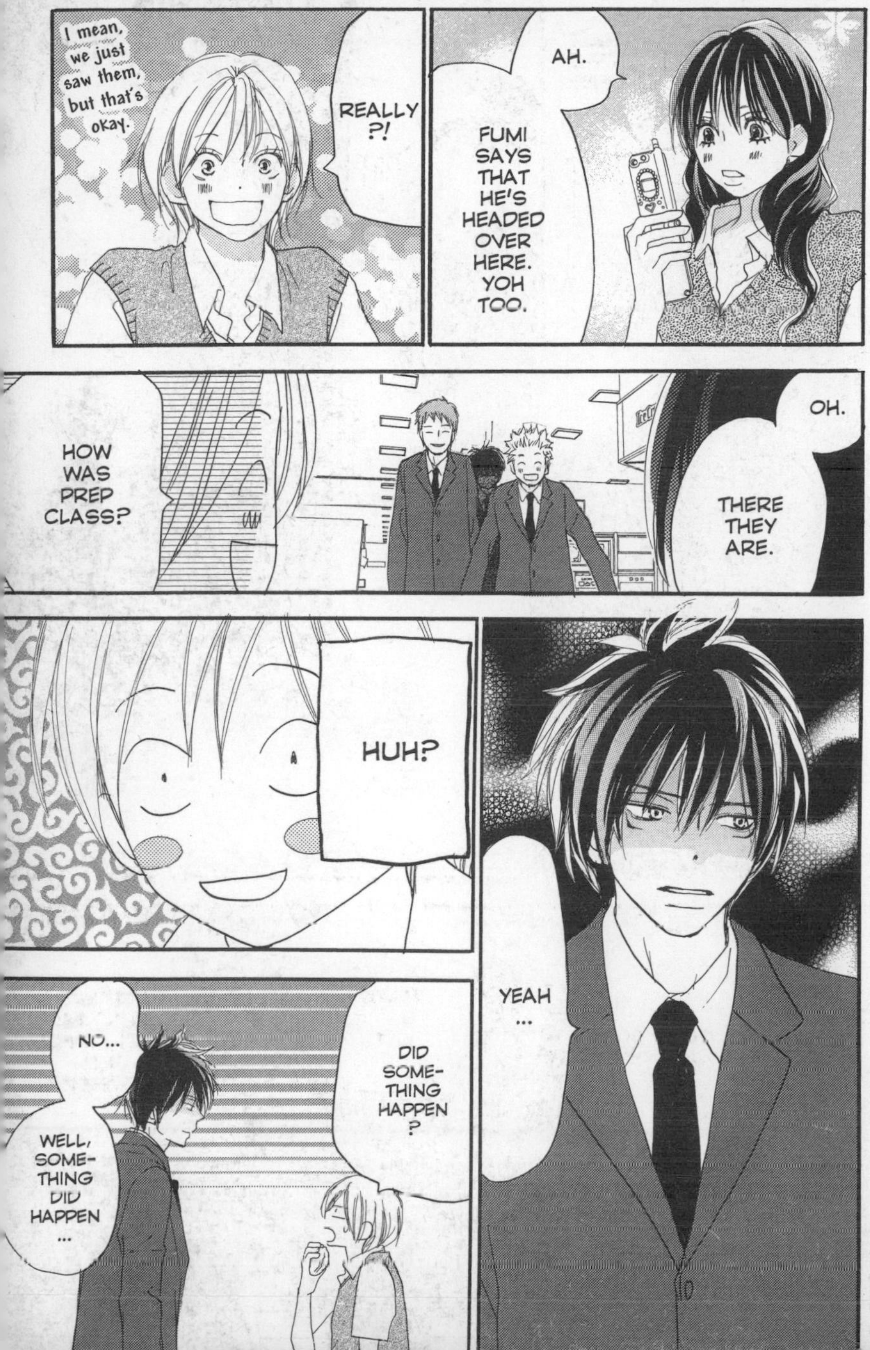
AH.
FUMI SAYS THAT HE'S HEADED OVER HERE. YOH TOO.
REALLY ?!
I mean, we just saw them, but that's okay.
OH.
THERE THEY ARE.
HOW WAS PREP CLASS?
YEAH ...
HUH?
DID SOME-THING HAPPEN ?
NO...
WELL, SOME-THING DID HAPPEN ...

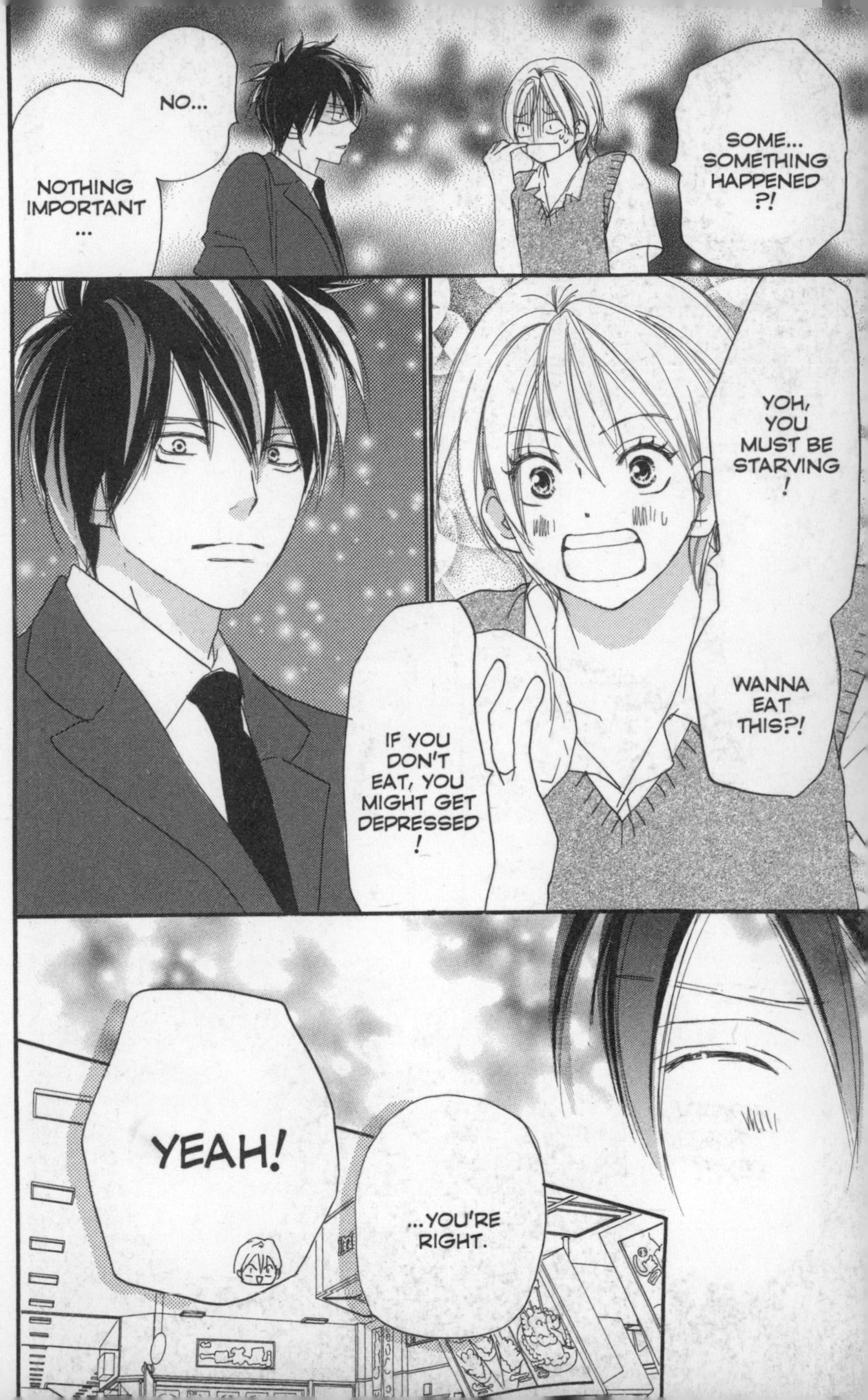
SOME... SOMETHING HAPPENED?!
NO... NOTHING IMPORTANT...
YOH, YOU MUST BE STARVING!
WANNA EAT THIS?!
IF YOU DON'T EAT, YOU MIGHT GET DEPRESSED!
...YOU'RE RIGHT.
YEAH!

SEE YOU!
BYE BYE!
IT WAS UNEXPECTED, BUT I'M REALLY HAPPY I GOT TO SEE YOH!
BEEP BEEP
Incoming Mail
From: Yoh
Subject: Thanks
I'm glad we got to hang out. You really cheered me up. I'll text you later. See you.
I'M...
...SAVING THIS TEXT!!

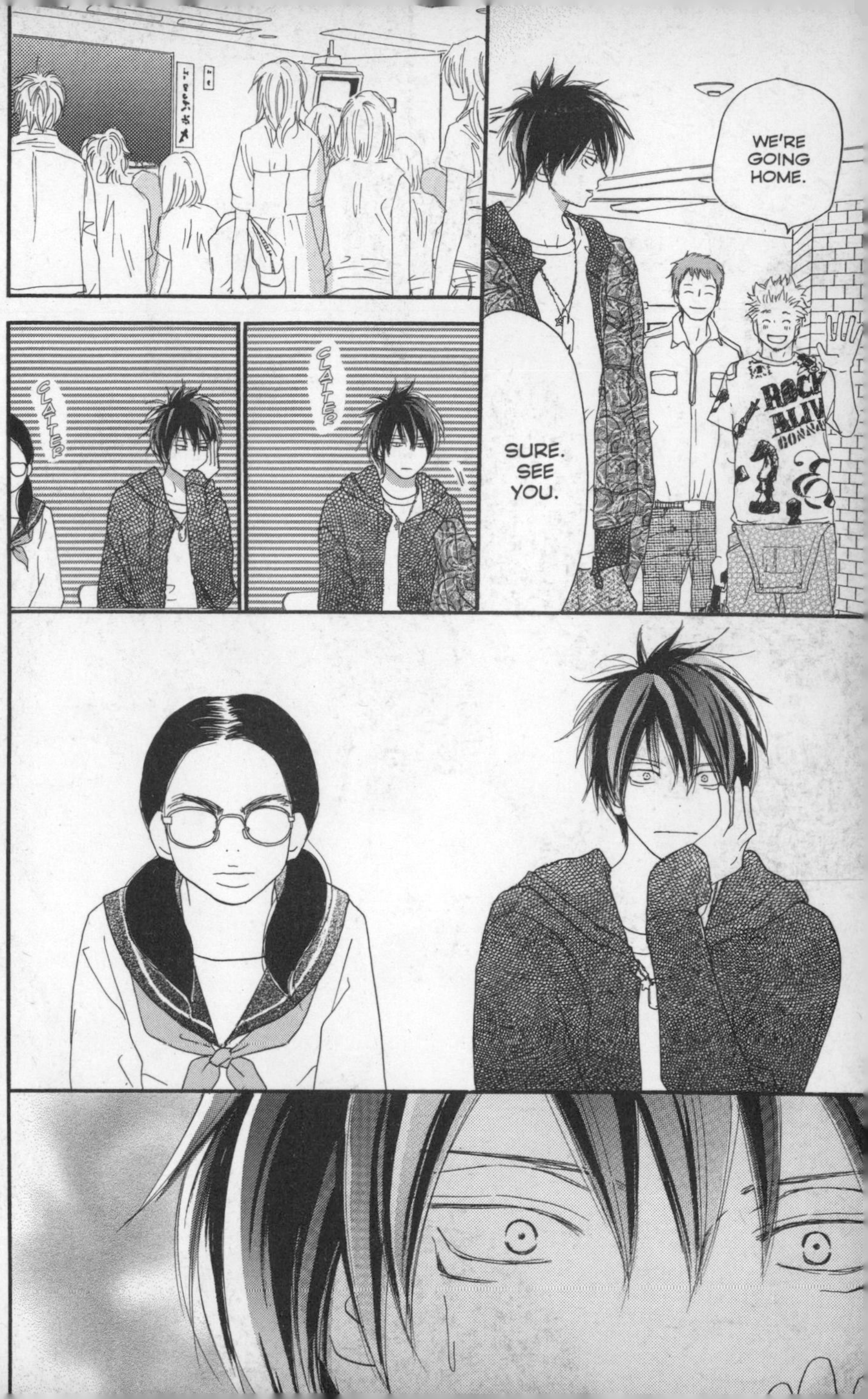
WE'RE GOING HOME.
SURE. SEE YOU.
CLATTER
CLATTER

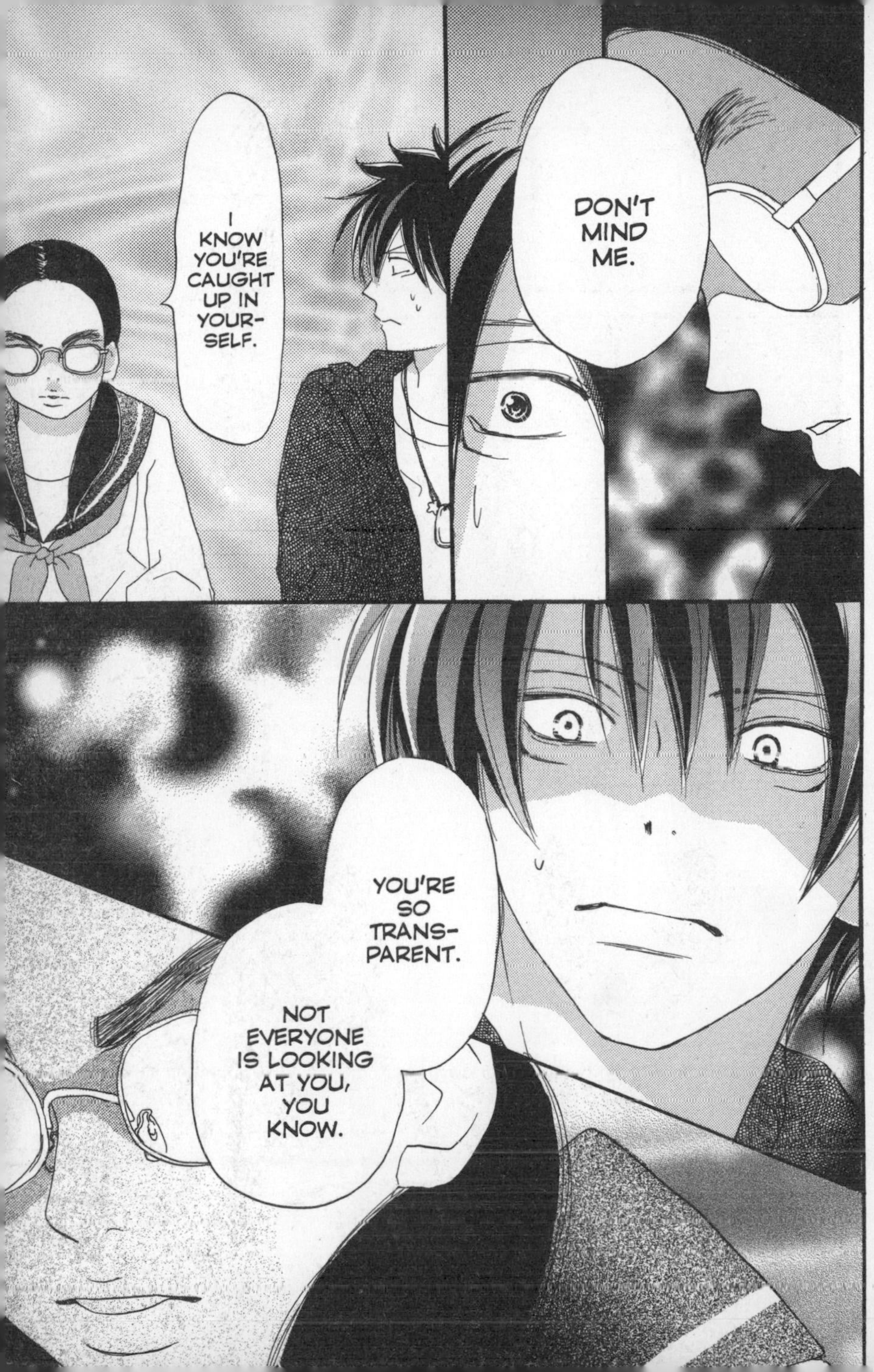
DON'T MIND ME.
I KNOW YOU'RE CAUGHT UP IN YOUR-SELF.
YOU'RE SO TRANS-PARENT.
NOT EVERYONE IS LOOKING AT YOU, YOU KNOW.

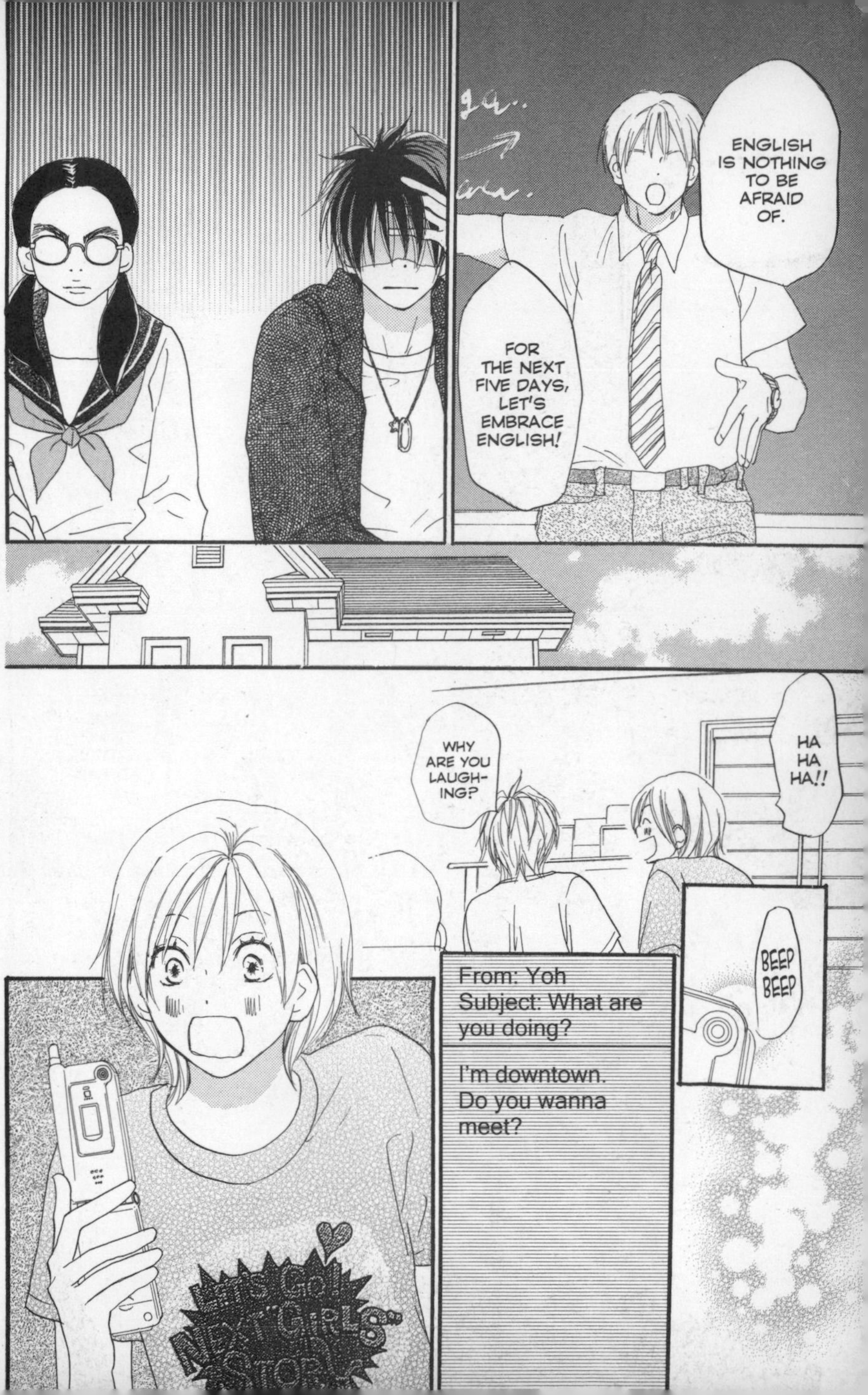
ENGLISH IS NOTHING TO BE AFRAID OF.
FOR THE NEXT FIVE DAYS, LET'S EMBRACE ENGLISH!
HA HA HA!!
WHY ARE YOU LAUGHING?
BEEP BEEP
From: Yoh
Subject: What are you doing?
I'm downtown. Do you wanna meet?

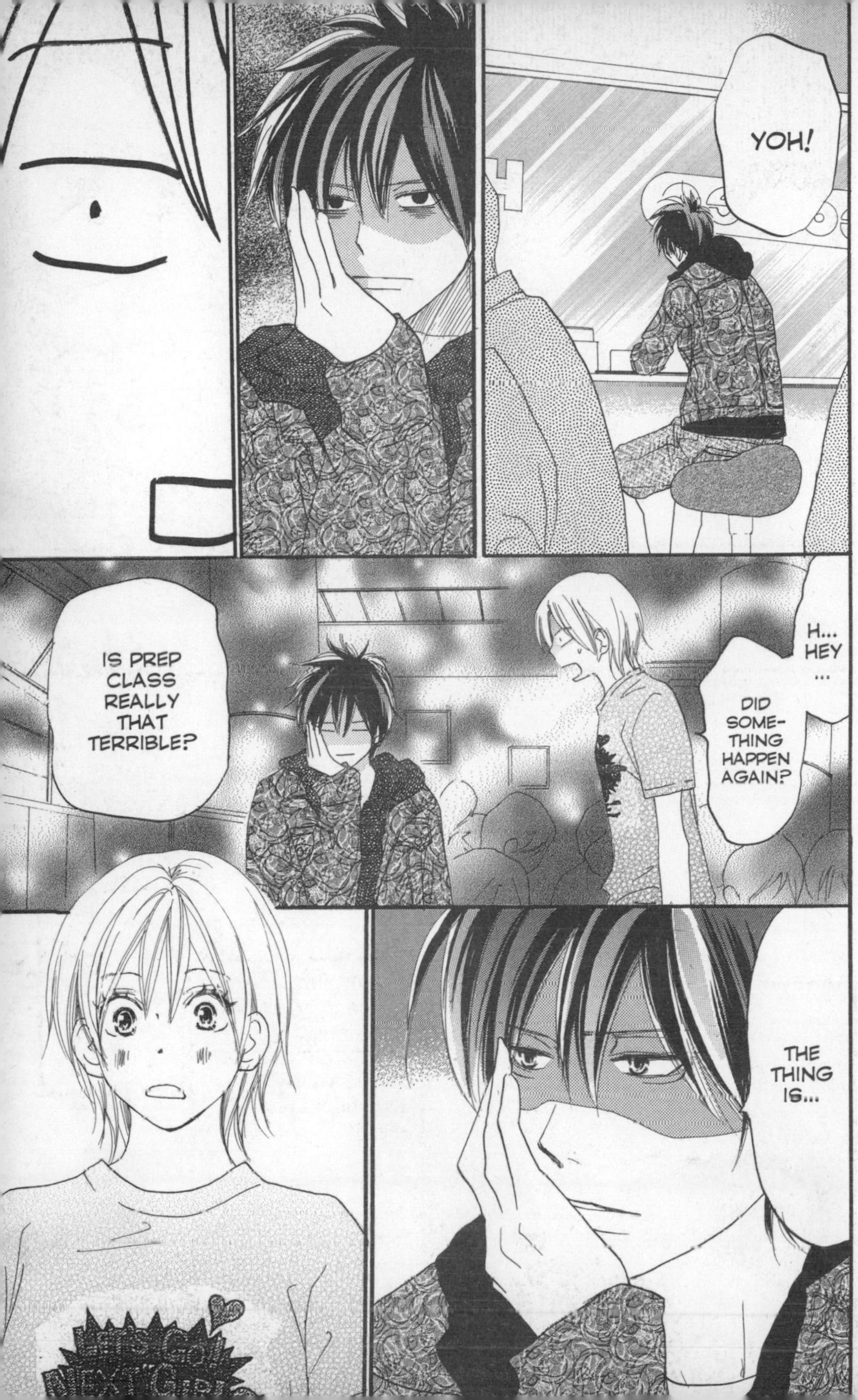
YOH!
H... HEY ...
DID SOME-THING HAPPEN AGAIN?
IS PREP CLASS REALLY THAT TERRIBLE?
THE THING IS...

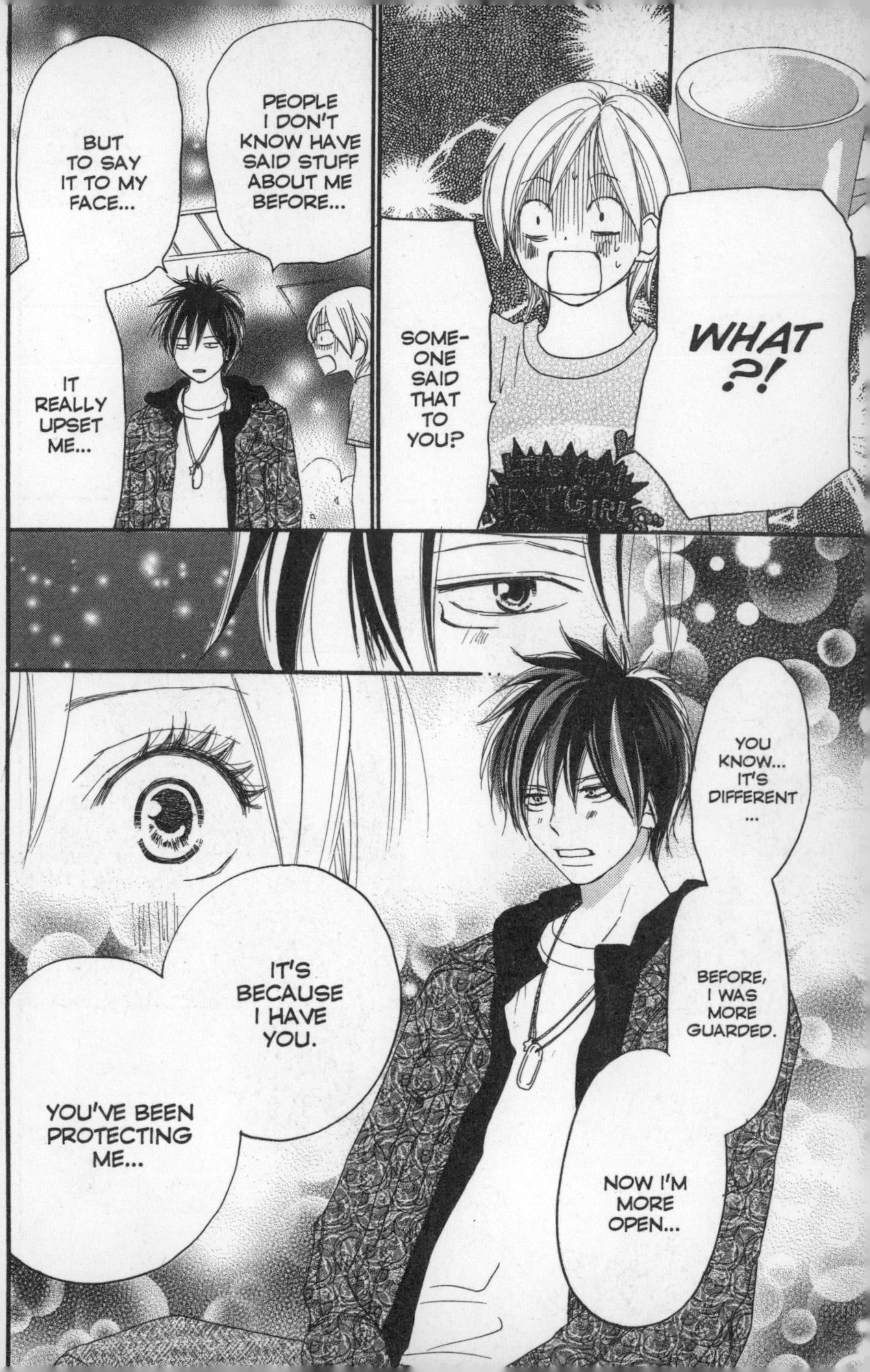
WHAT?!
SOME-ONE SAID THAT TO YOU?
PEOPLE I DON'T KNOW HAVE SAID STUFF ABOUT ME BEFORE...
BUT TO SAY IT TO MY FACE...
IT REALLY UPSET ME...
YOU KNOW... IT'S DIFFERENT ...
BEFORE, I WAS MORE GUARDED.
NOW I'M MORE OPEN...
IT'S BECAUSE I HAVE YOU.
YOU'VE BEEN PROTECTING ME...

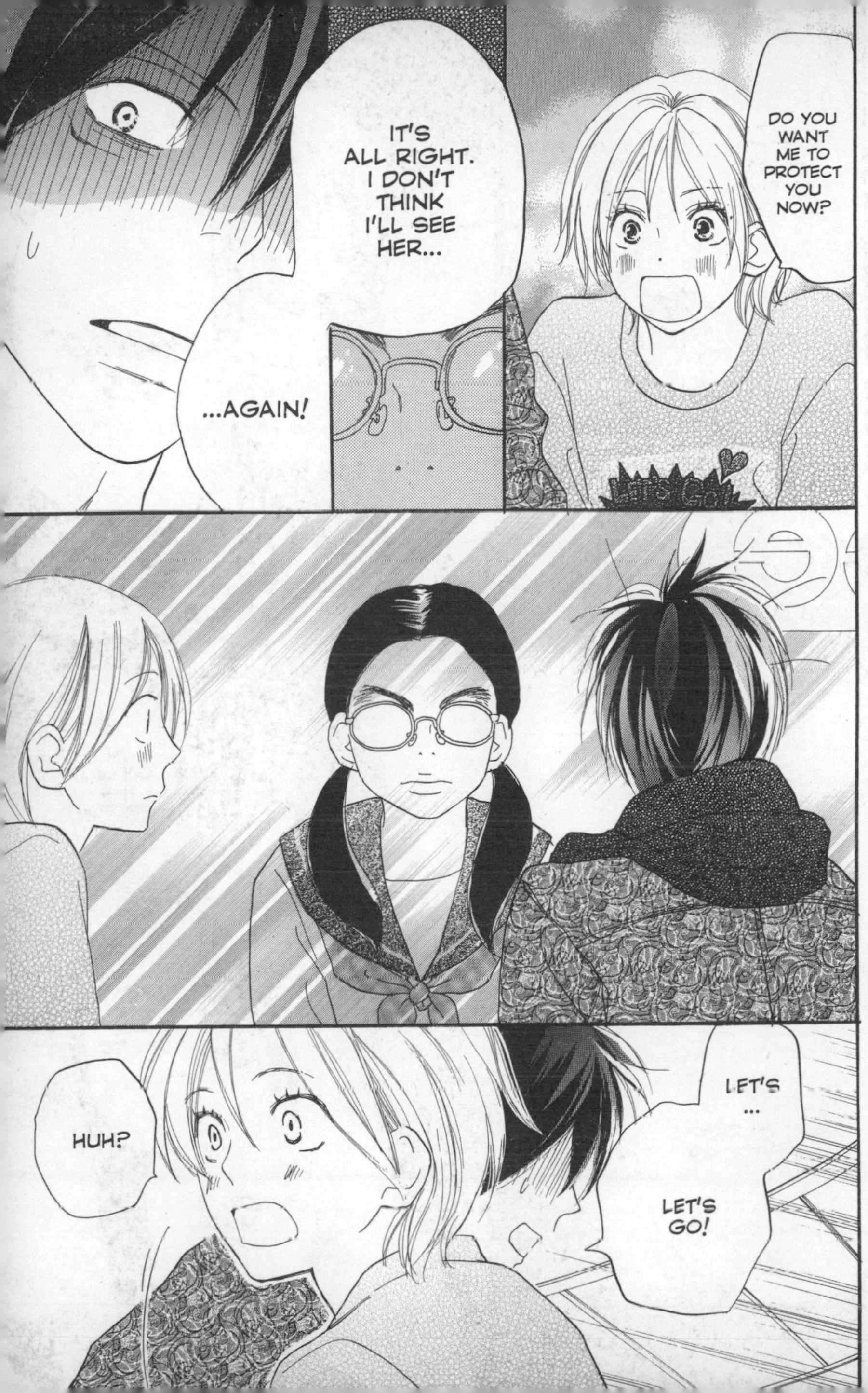
DO YOU WANT ME TO PROTECT YOU NOW?
IT'S ALL RIGHT. I DON'T THINK I'LL SEE HER...
...AGAIN!
LET'S ...
LET'S GO!
HUH?

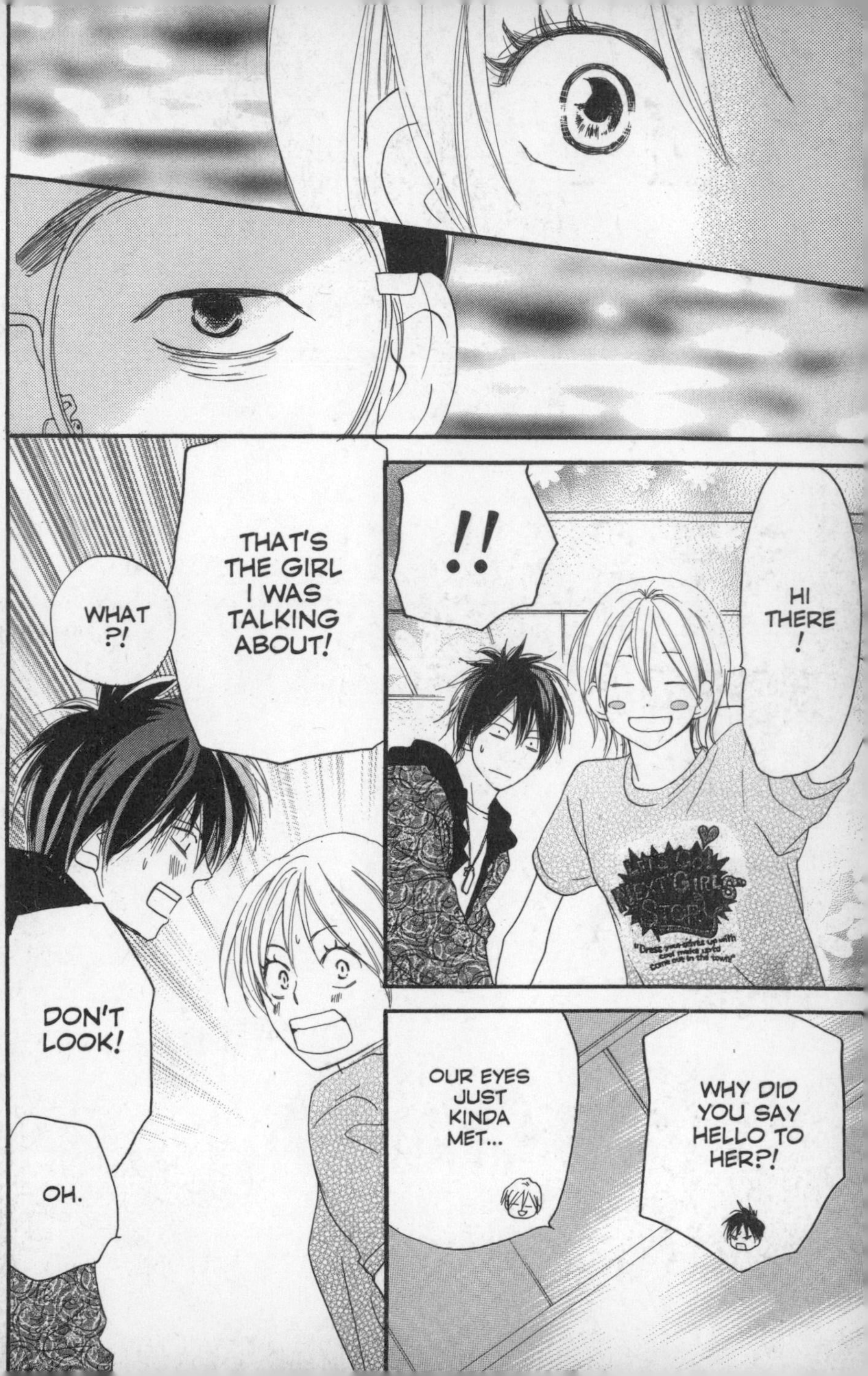
HI THERE!
!!
WHY DID YOU SAY HELLO TO HER?!
OUR EYES JUST KINDA MET...
THAT'S THE GIRL I WAS TALKING ABOUT!
WHAT?!
DON'T LOOK!
OH.

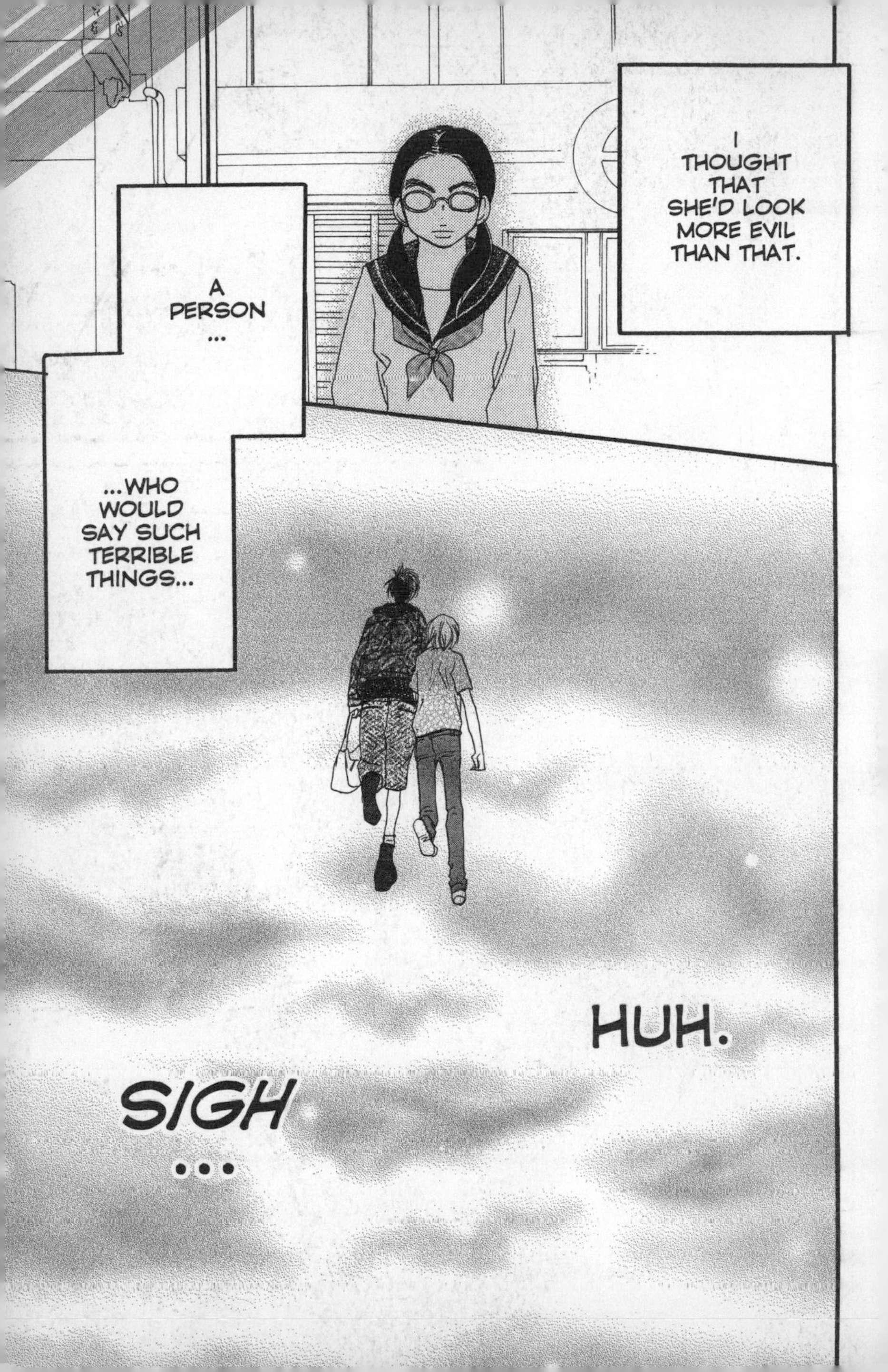
I THOUGHT THAT SHE'D LOOK MORE EVIL THAN THAT.
A PERSON ...
...WHO WOULD SAY SUCH TERRIBLE THINGS...
HUH.
SIGH ...

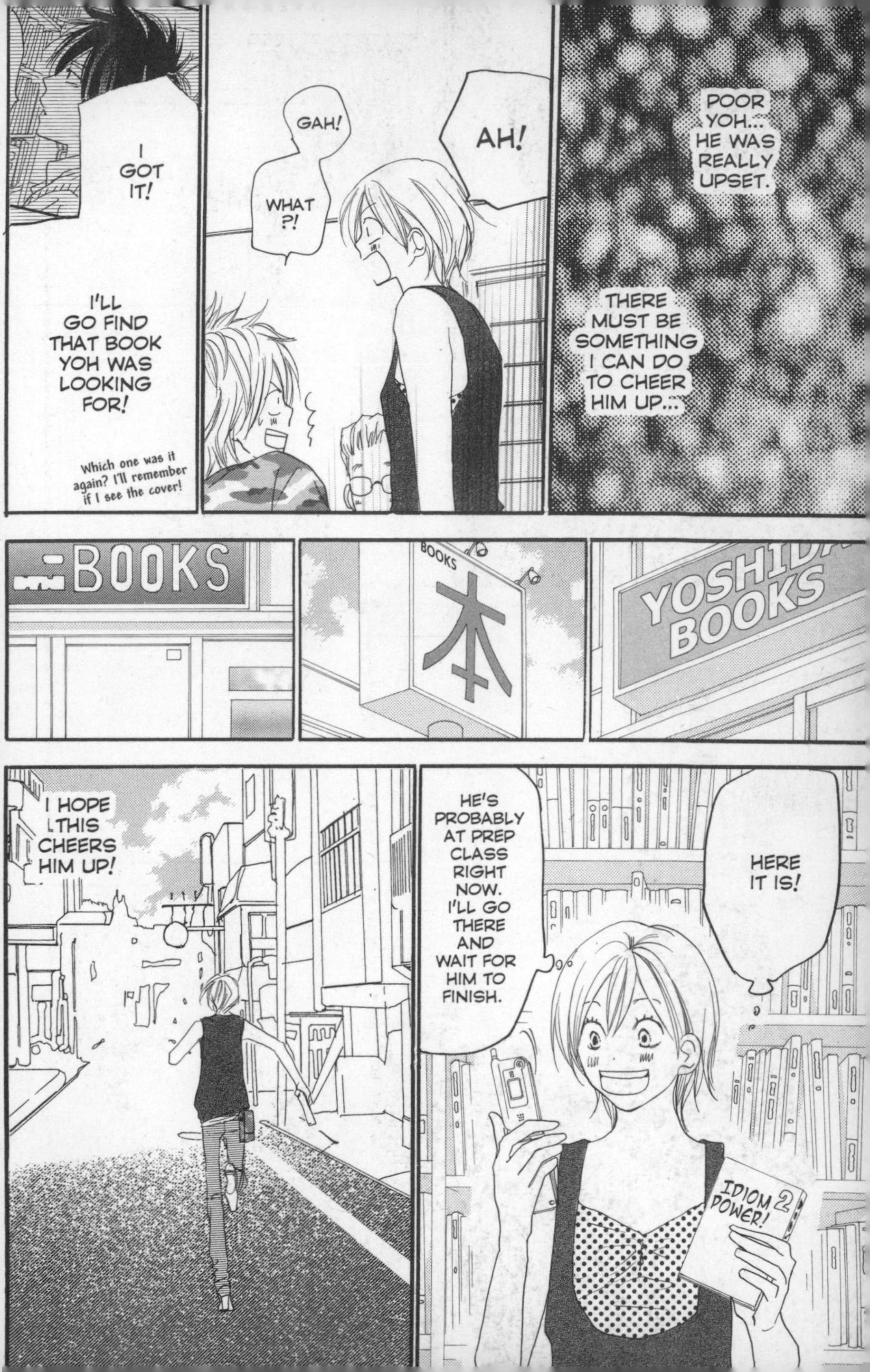
POOR YOH... HE WAS REALLY UPSET.
THERE MUST BE SOMETHING I CAN DO TO CHEER HIM UP...
AH!
GAH!
WHAT?!
I GOT IT!
I'LL GO FIND THAT BOOK YOH WAS LOOKING FOR!
Which one was it again? I'll remember if I see the cover!
YOSHIDA BOOKS
BOOKS
本
BOOKS
HERE IT IS!
HE'S PROBABLY AT PREP CLASS RIGHT NOW. I'LL GO THERE AND WAIT FOR HIM TO FINISH.
IDIOM POWER! 2
I HOPE THIS CHEERS HIM UP!

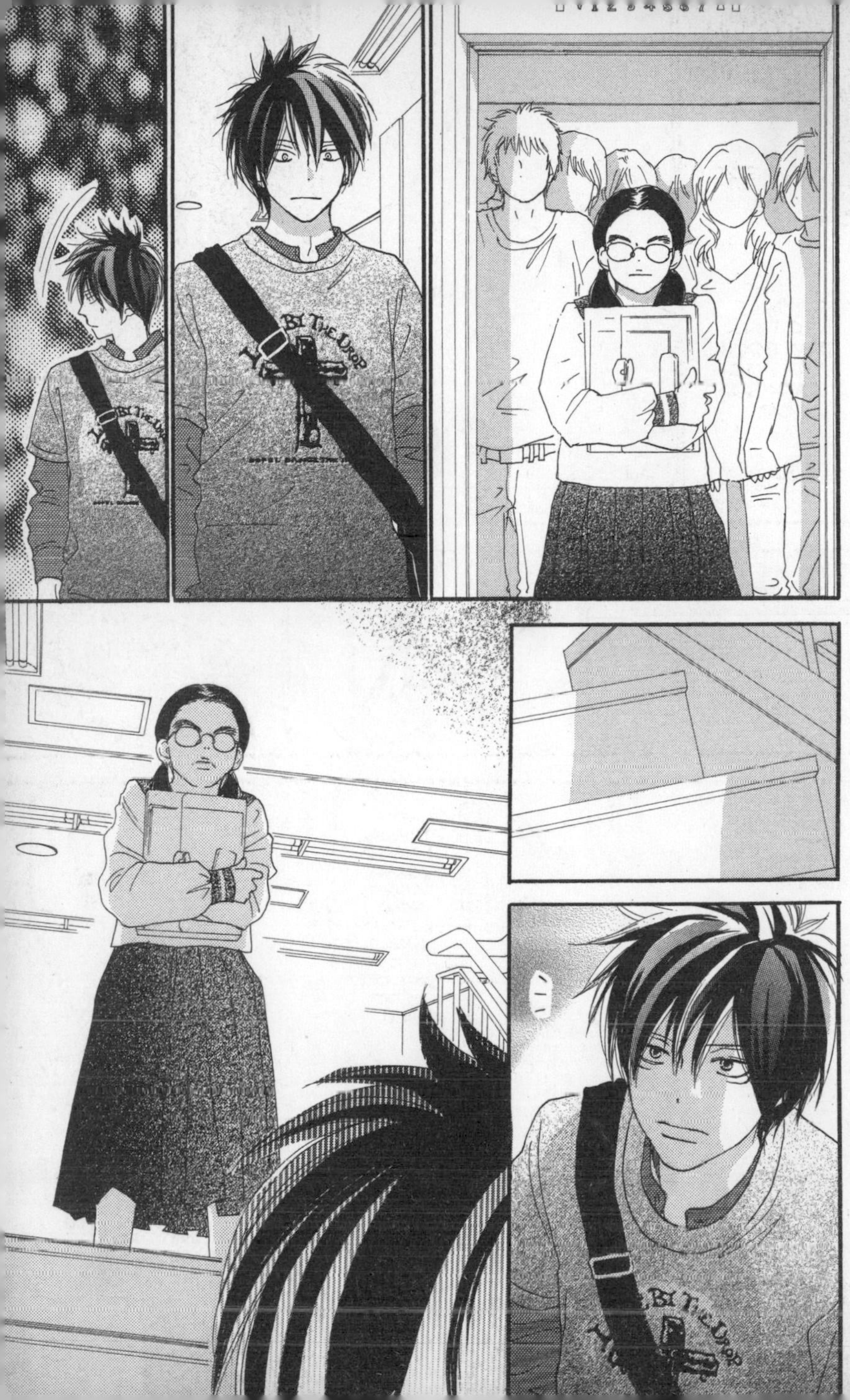
…

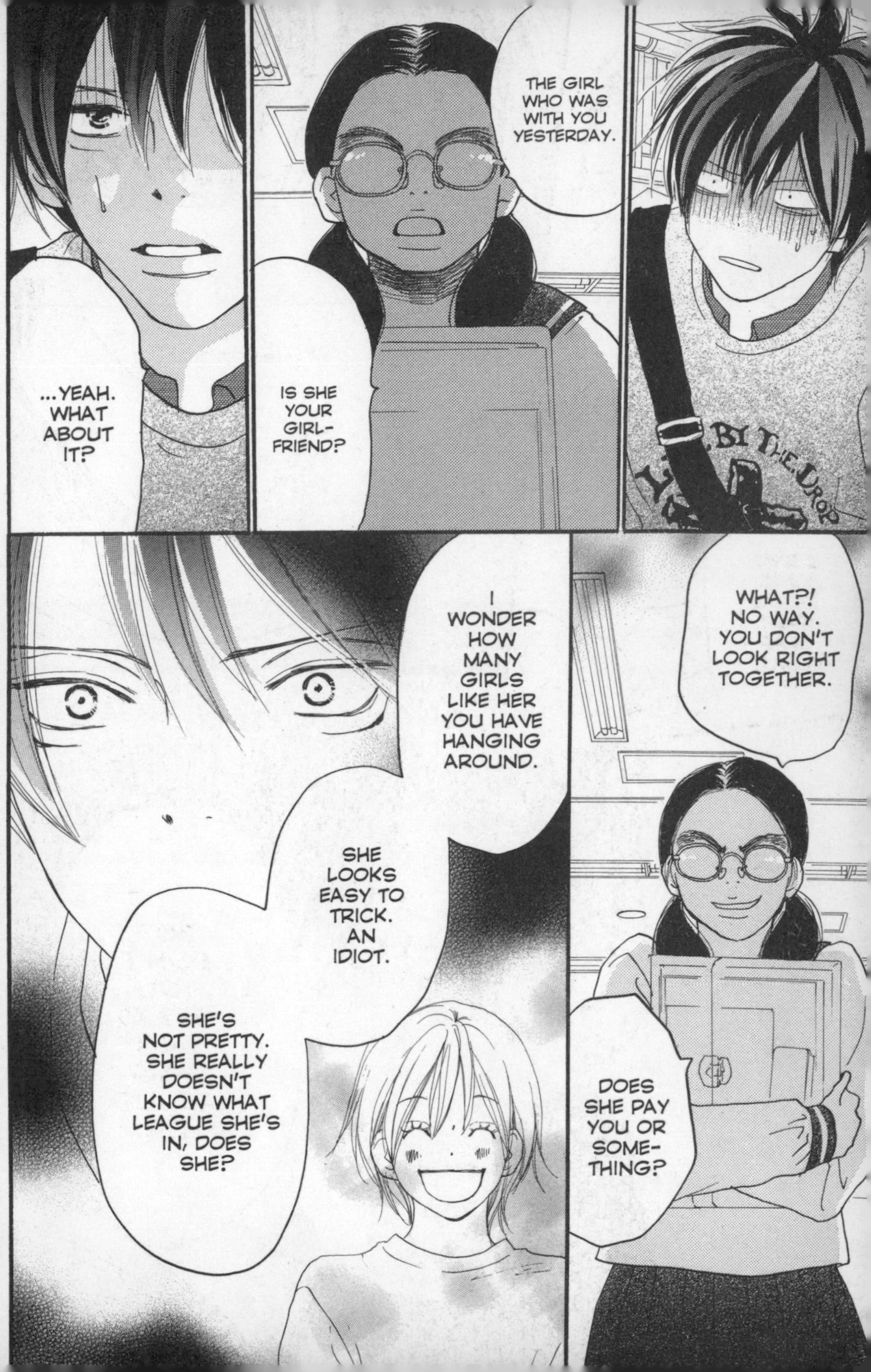

BY THE DROP
THE GIRL WHO WAS WITH YOU YESTERDAY.
IS SHE YOUR GIRL-FRIEND?
...YEAH. WHAT ABOUT IT?
WHAT?! NO WAY. YOU DON'T LOOK RIGHT TOGETHER.
DOES SHE PAY YOU OR SOME-THING?
I WONDER HOW MANY GIRLS LIKE HER YOU HAVE HANGING AROUND.
SHE LOOKS EASY TO TRICK. AN IDIOT.
SHE'S NOT PRETTY. SHE REALLY DOESN'T KNOW WHAT LEAGUE SHE'S IN, DOES SHE?

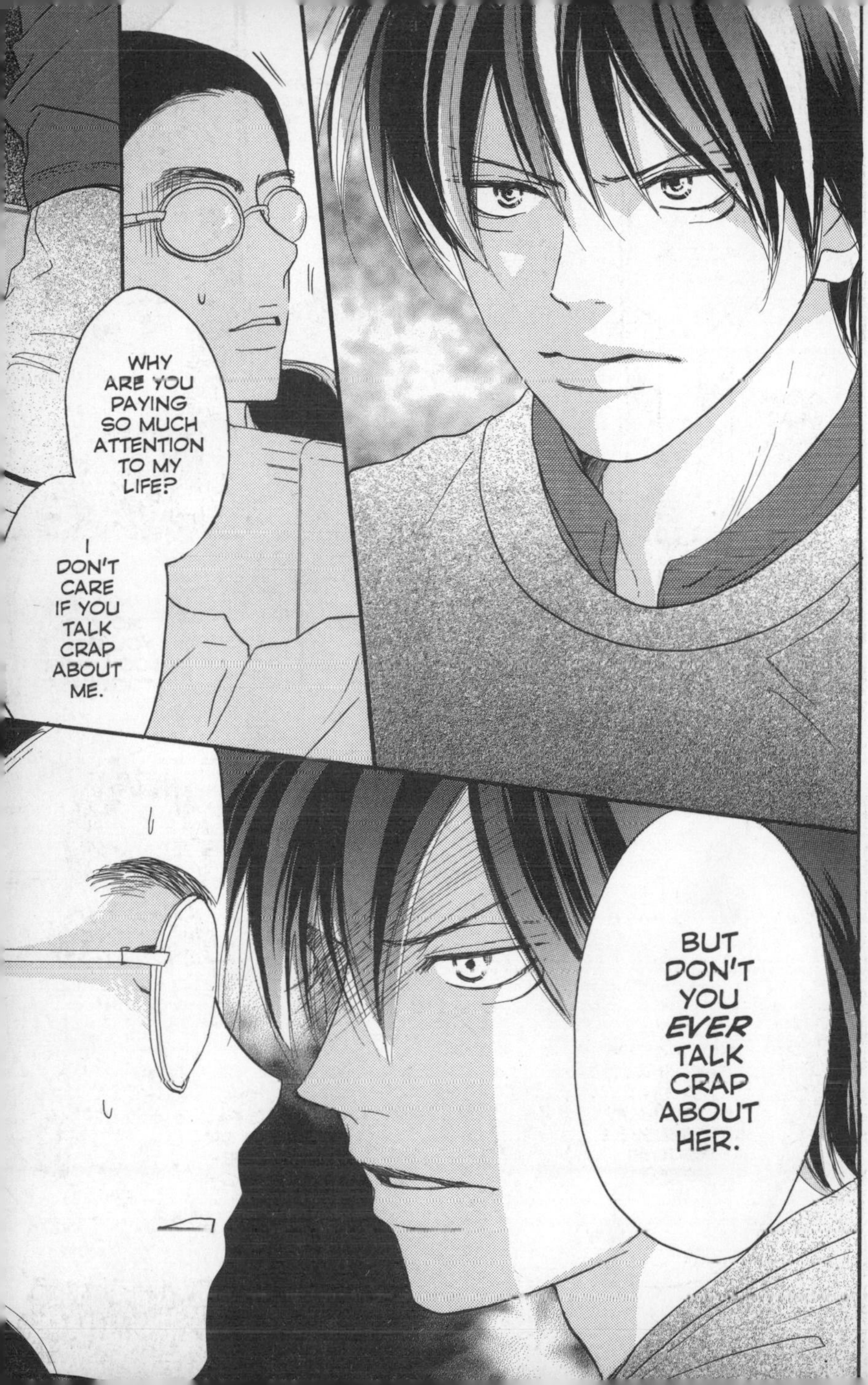
WHY ARE YOU PAYING SO MUCH ATTENTION TO MY LIFE?
I DON'T CARE IF YOU TALK CRAP ABOUT ME.
BUT DON'T YOU *EVER* TALK CRAP ABOUT HER.

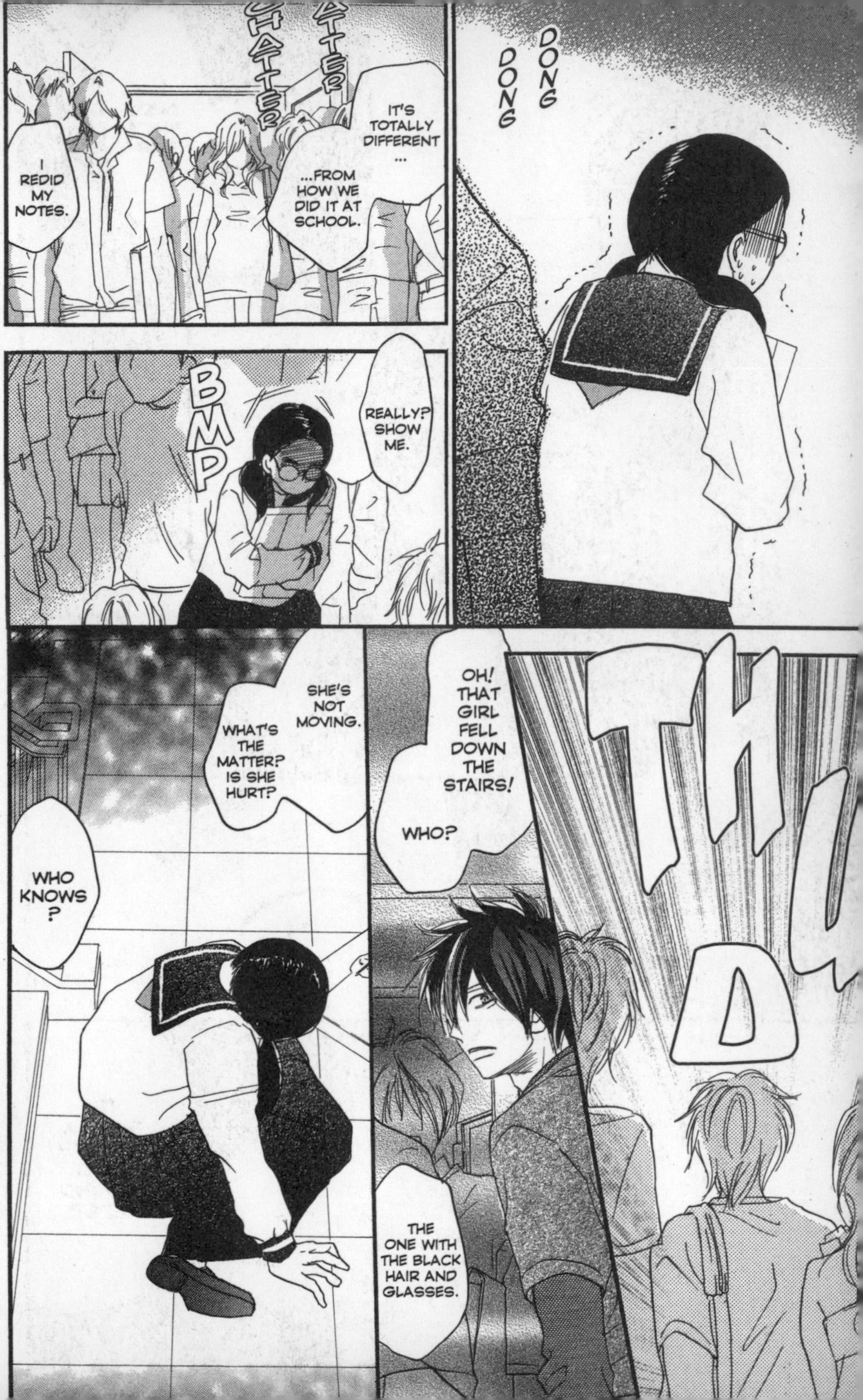
DONG DONG
CHATTER CHATTER
IT'S TOTALLY DIFFERENT ...
...FROM HOW WE DID IT AT SCHOOL.
I REDID MY NOTES.
BMP
REALLY? SHOW ME.
THUD
OH! THAT GIRL FELL DOWN THE STAIRS!
WHO?
THE ONE WITH THE BLACK HAIR AND GLASSES.
SHE'S NOT MOVING.
WHAT'S THE MATTER? IS SHE HURT?
WHO KNOWS?

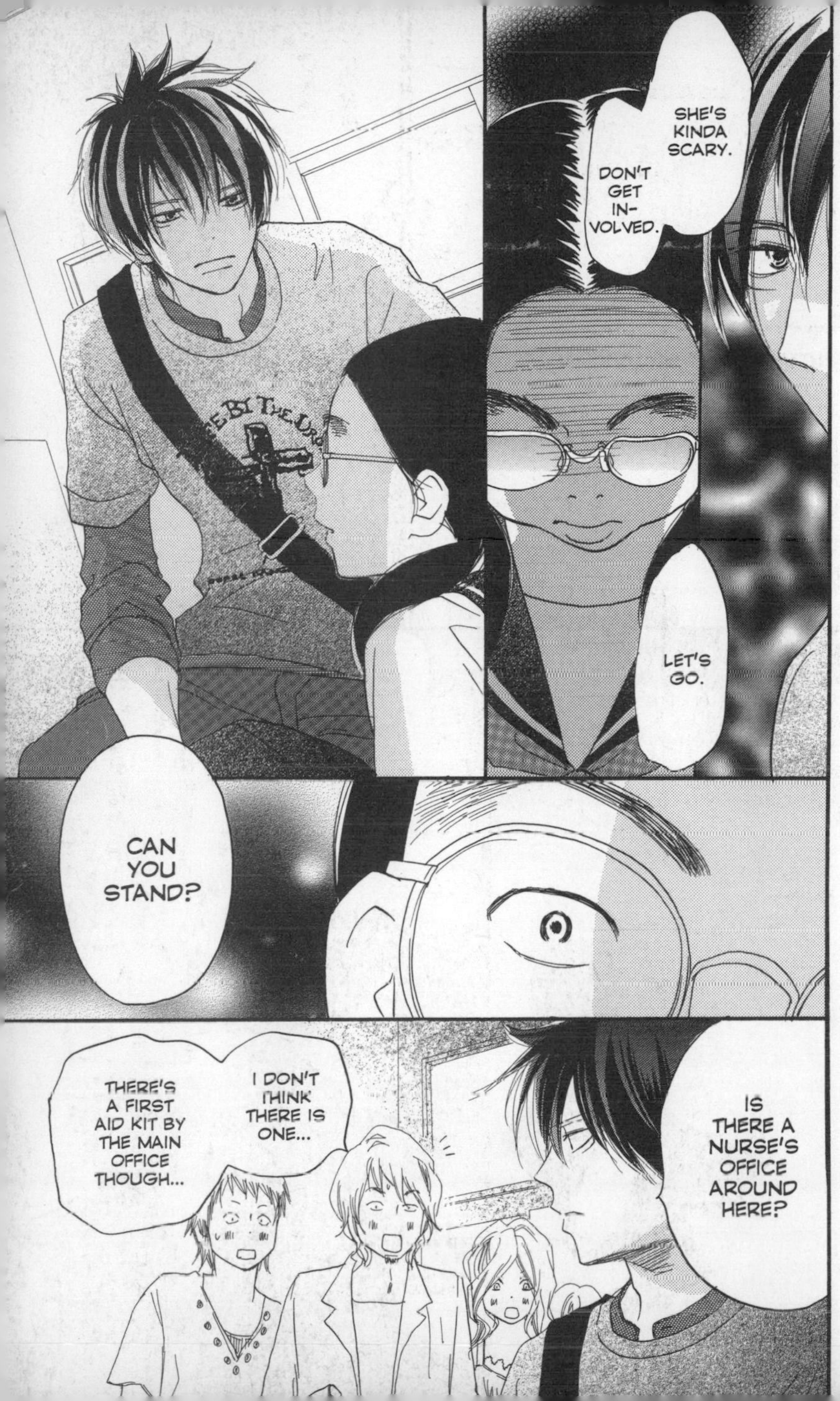
SHE'S KINDA SCARY.
DON'T GET IN-VOLVED.
LET'S GO.
CAN YOU STAND?
IS THERE A NURSE'S OFFICE AROUND HERE?
I DON'T THINK THERE IS ONE...
THERE'S A FIRST AID KIT BY THE MAIN OFFICE THOUGH...

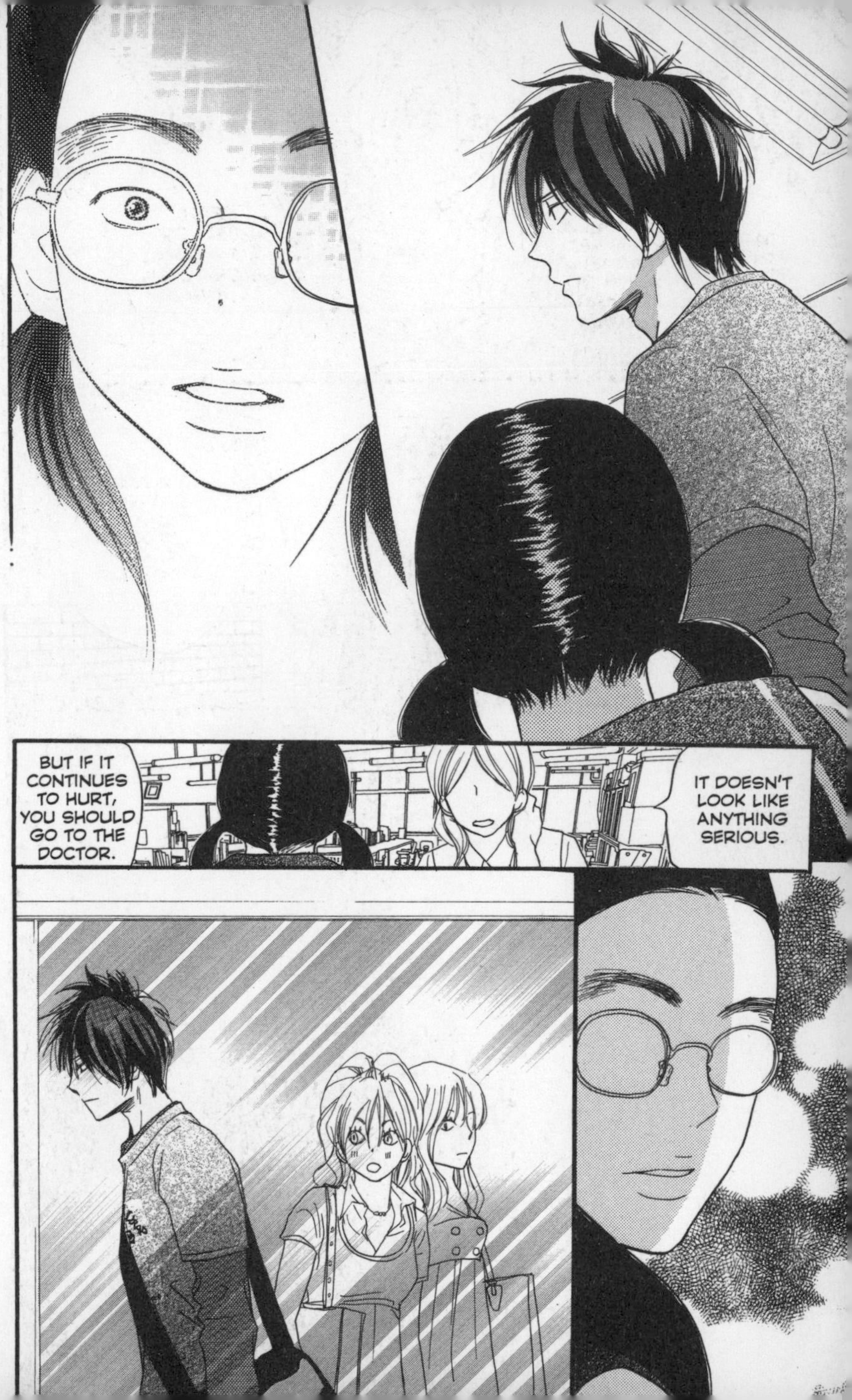
IT DOESN'T LOOK LIKE ANYTHING SERIOUS.
BUT IF IT CONTINUES TO HURT, YOU SHOULD GO TO THE DOCTOR.

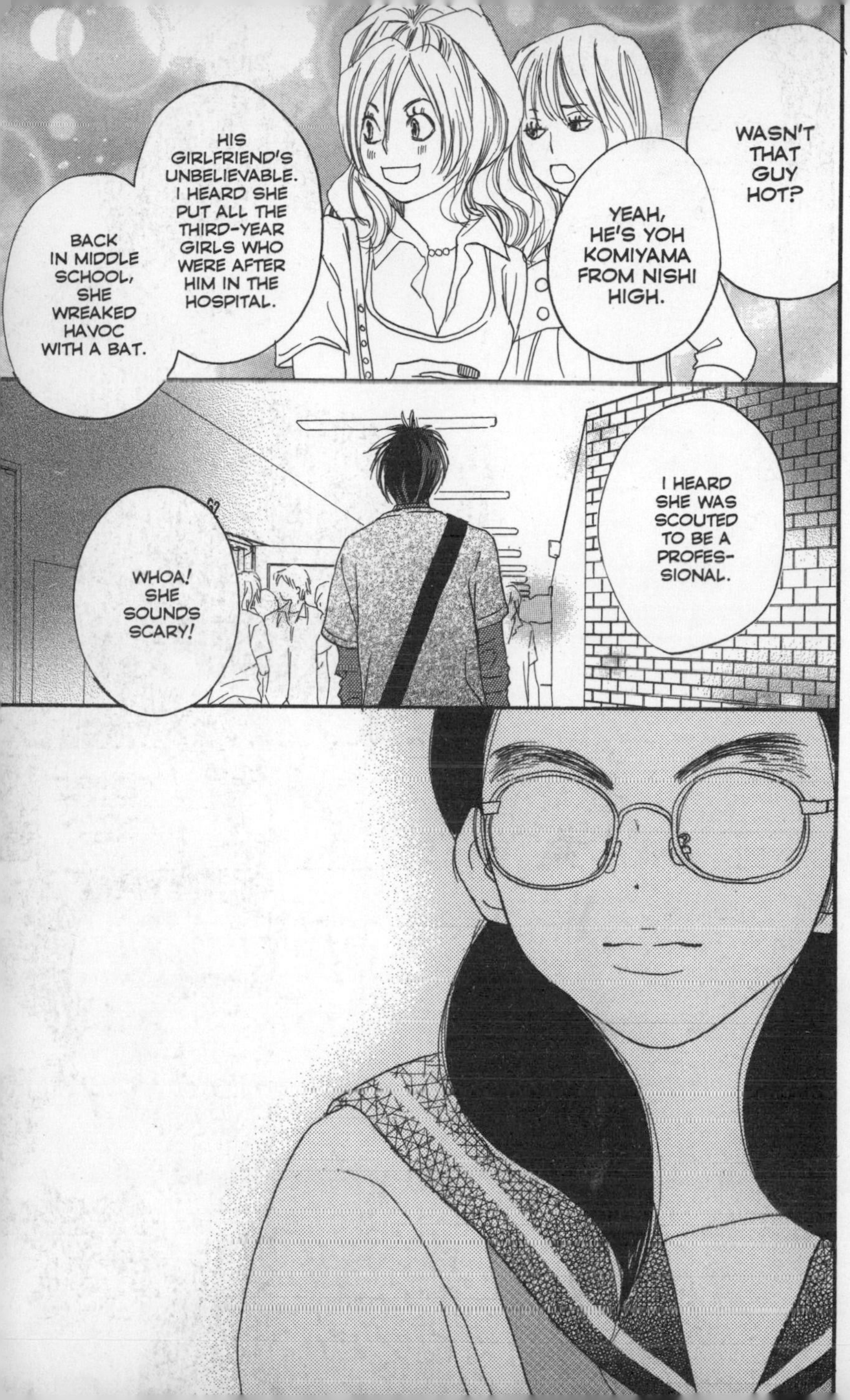
WASN'T THAT GUY HOT?
YEAH, HE'S YOH KOMIYAMA FROM NISHI HIGH.
HIS GIRLFRIEND'S UNBELIEVABLE. I HEARD SHE PUT ALL THE THIRD-YEAR GIRLS WHO WERE AFTER HIM IN THE HOSPITAL.
BACK IN MIDDLE SCHOOL, SHE WREAKED HAVOC WITH A BAT.
I HEARD SHE WAS SCOUTED TO BE A PROFES- SIONAL.
WHOA! SHE SOUNDS SCARY!

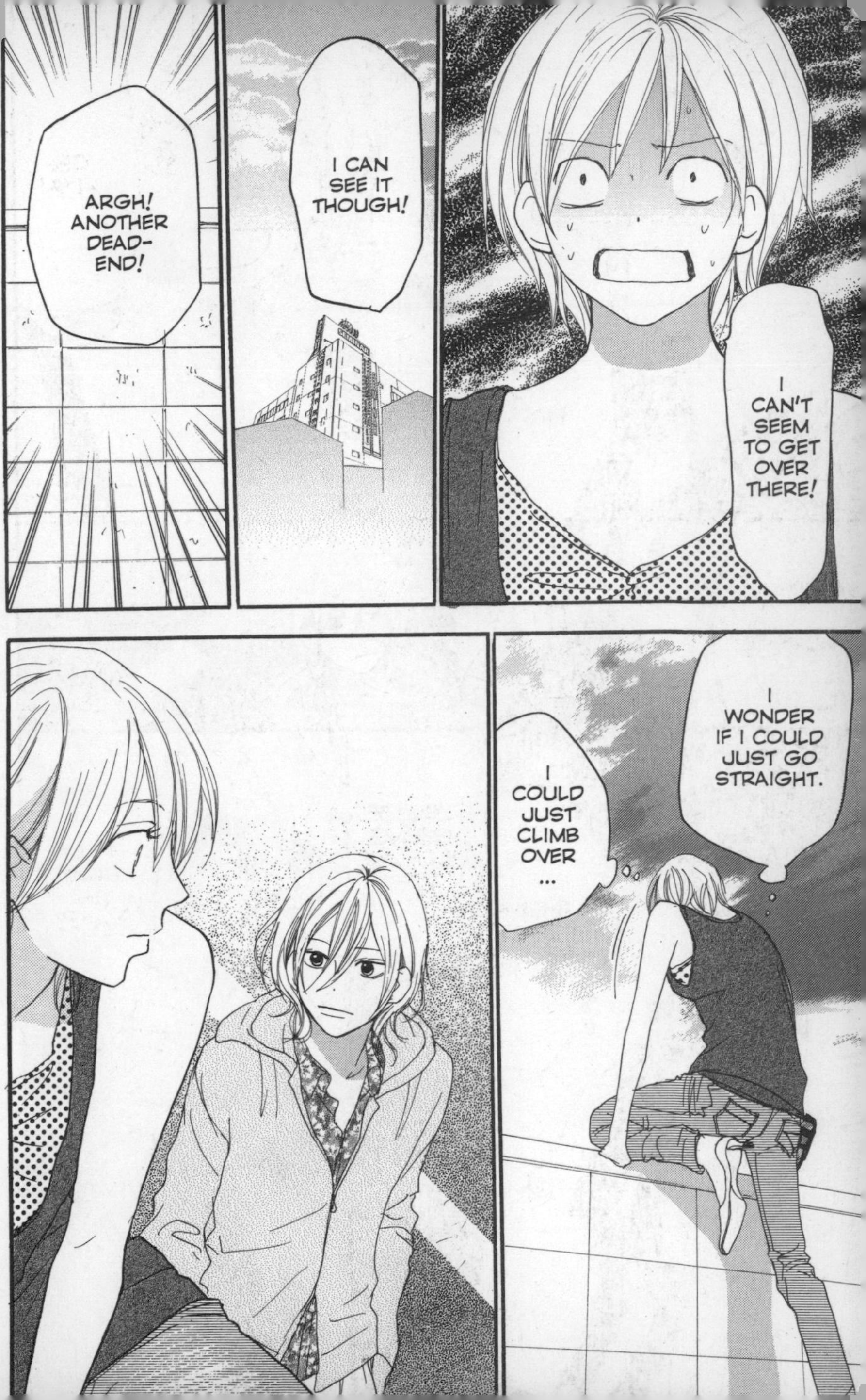
I CAN'T SEEM TO GET OVER THERE!
I CAN SEE IT THOUGH!
ARGH! ANOTHER DEAD-END!
I WONDER IF I COULD JUST GO STRAIGHT.
I COULD JUST CLIMB OVER ...

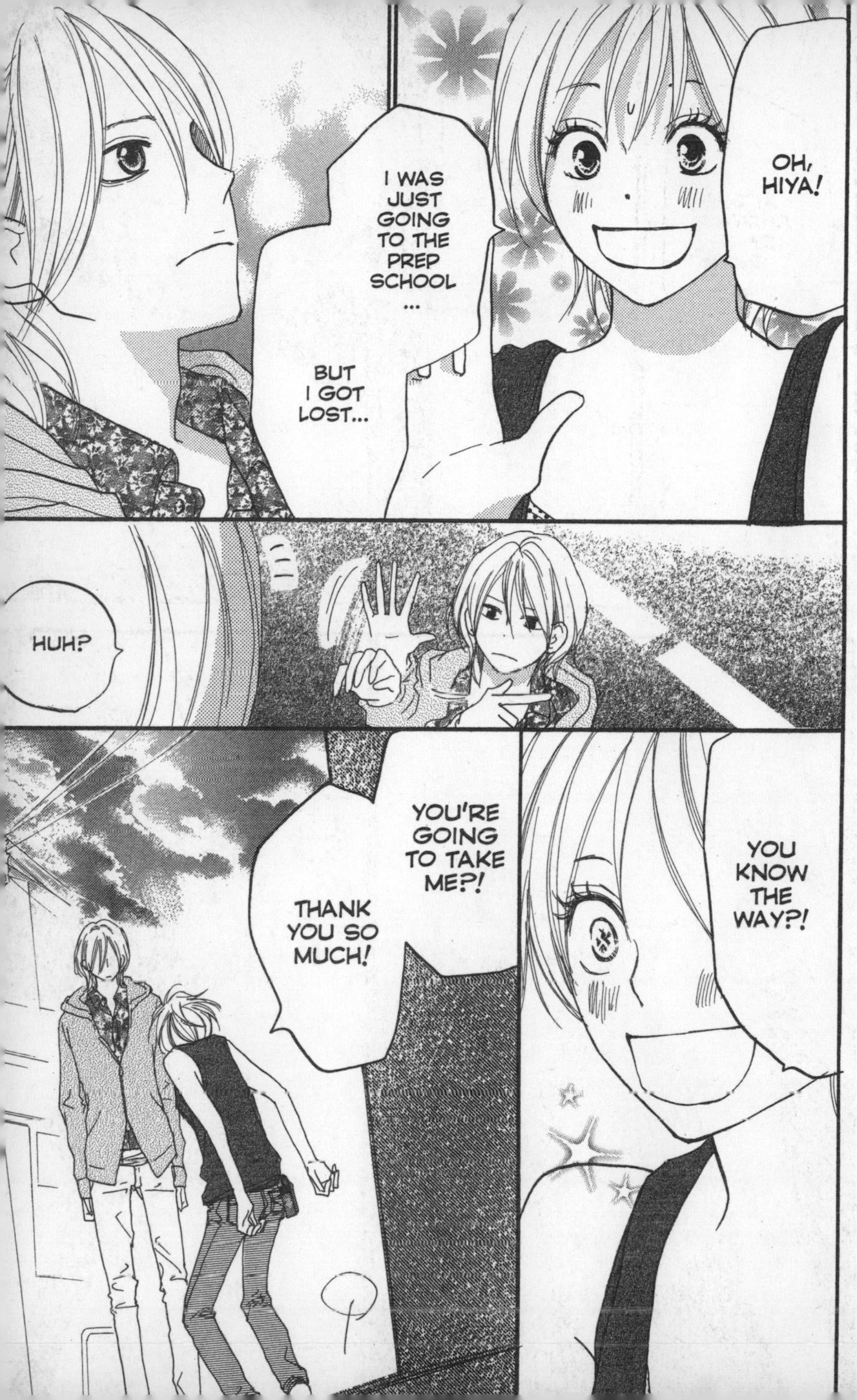
OH, HIYA!
I WAS JUST GOING TO THE PREP SCHOOL ...
BUT I GOT LOST...
HUH?
YOU KNOW THE WAY?!
YOU'RE GOING TO TAKE ME?!
THANK YOU SO MUCH!

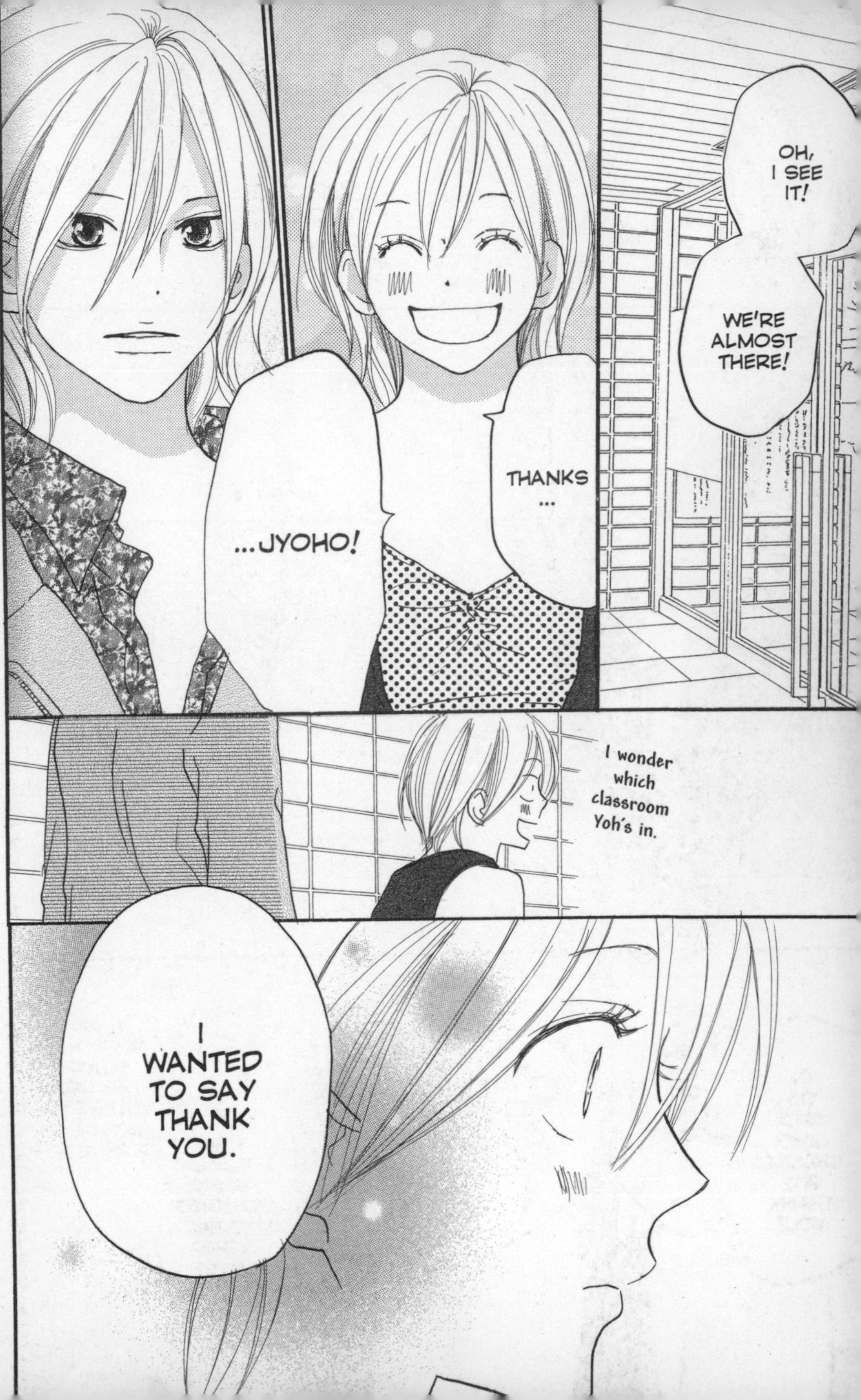
OH, I SEE IT!
WE'RE ALMOST THERE!
THANKS ...
...JYOHO!
I wonder which classroom Yoh's in.
I WANTED TO SAY THANK YOU.

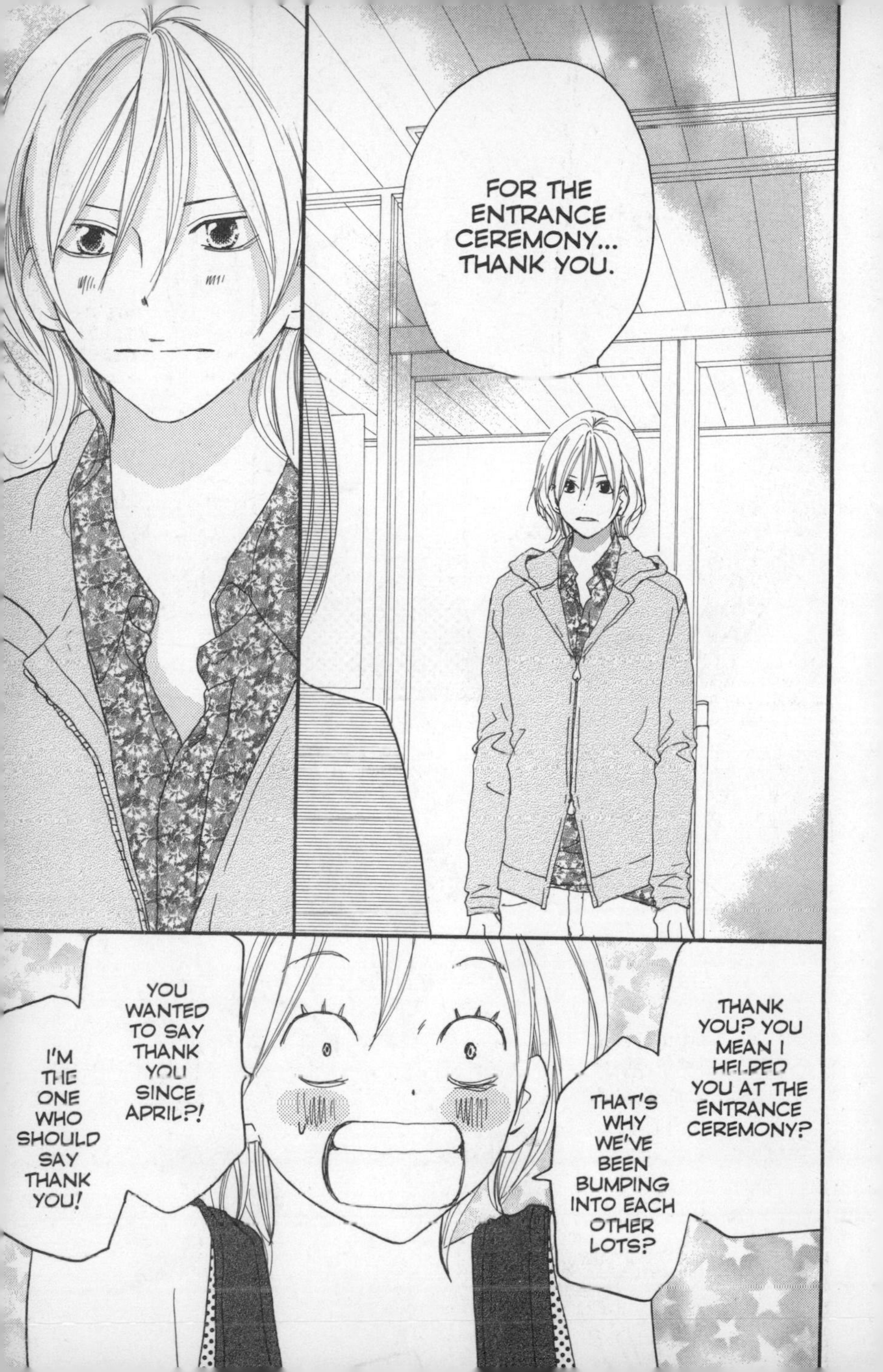
FOR THE ENTRANCE CEREMONY... THANK YOU.
THANK YOU? YOU MEAN I HELPED YOU AT THE ENTRANCE CEREMONY?
THAT'S WHY WE'VE BEEN BUMPING INTO EACH OTHER LOTS?
YOU WANTED TO SAY THANK YOU SINCE APRIL?!
I'M THE ONE WHO SHOULD SAY THANK YOU!

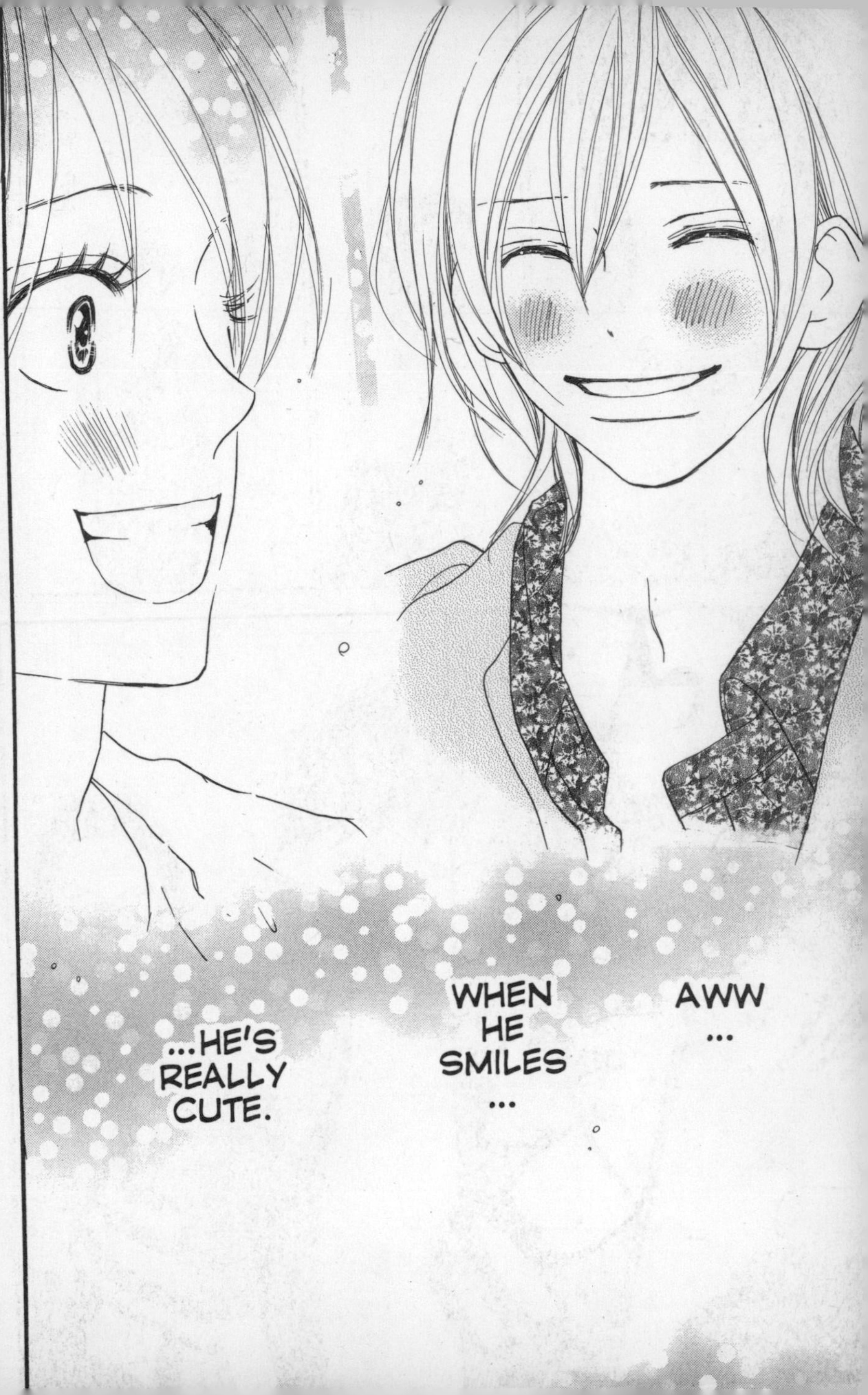
AWW ...
WHEN HE SMILES ...
...HE'S REALLY CUTE.

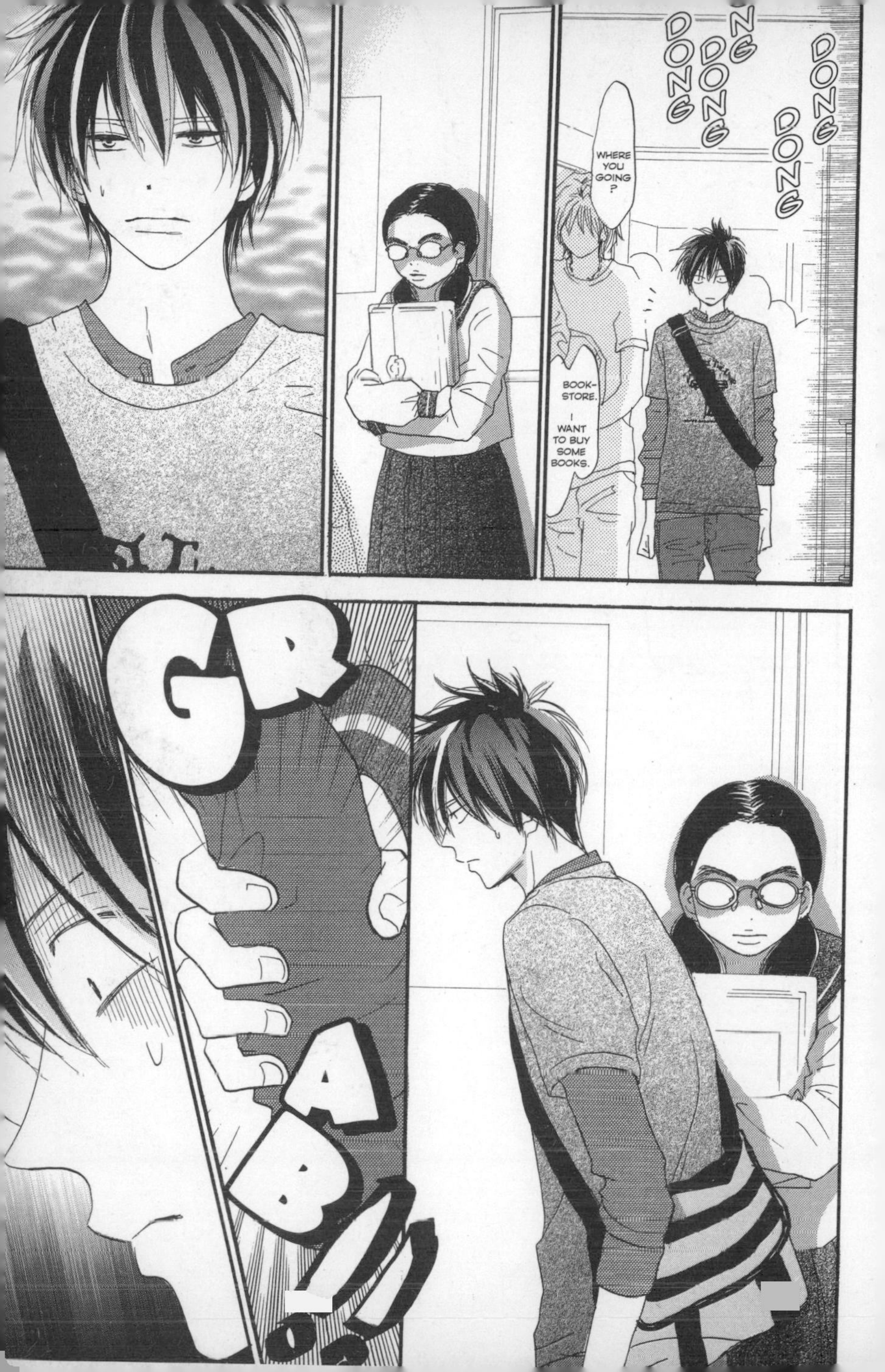
DONG
DONG
NG
DONG
DONG
WHERE YOU GOING?
BOOK-STORE.
I WANT TO BUY SOME BOOKS.
GRAB

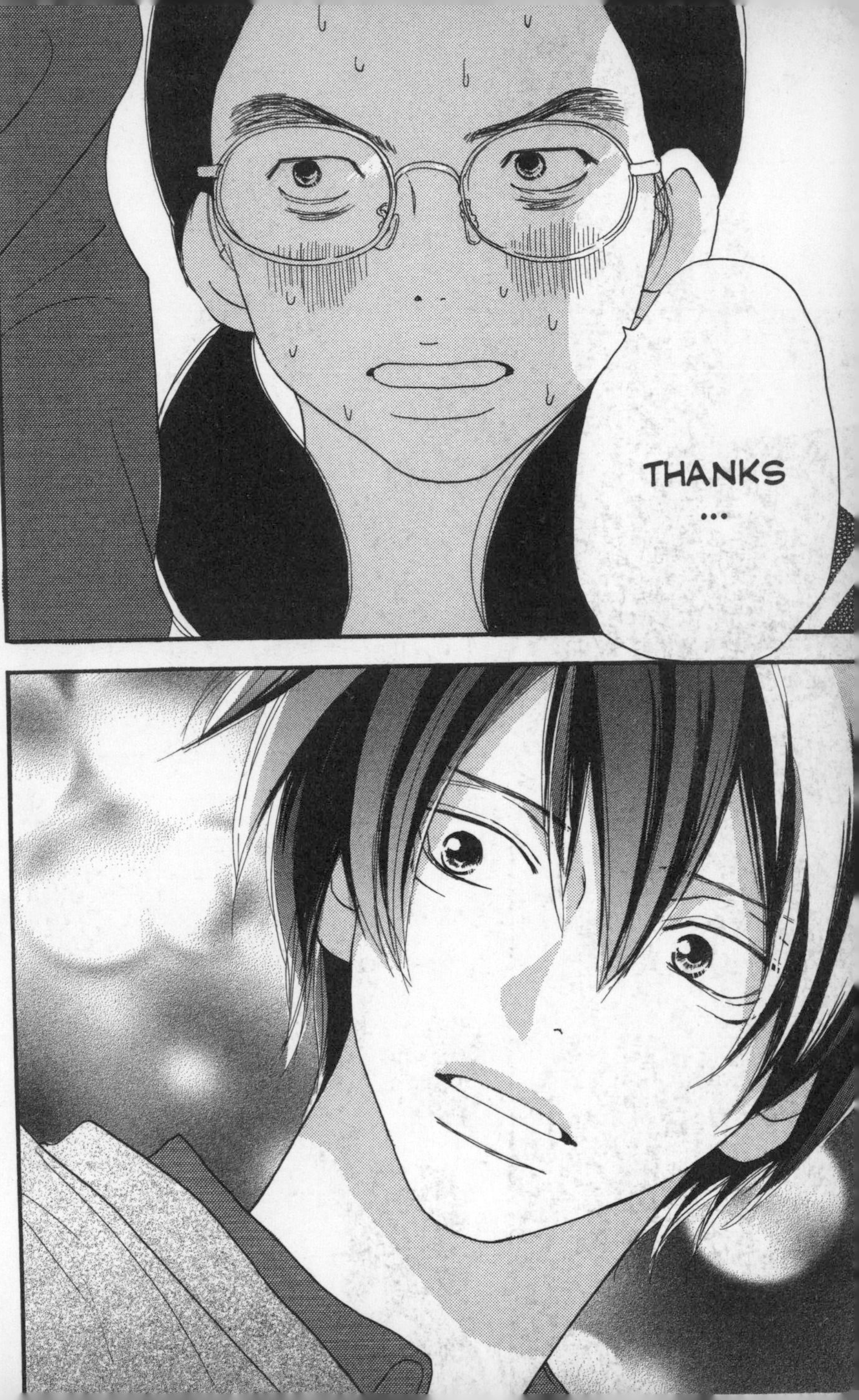
THANKS ...

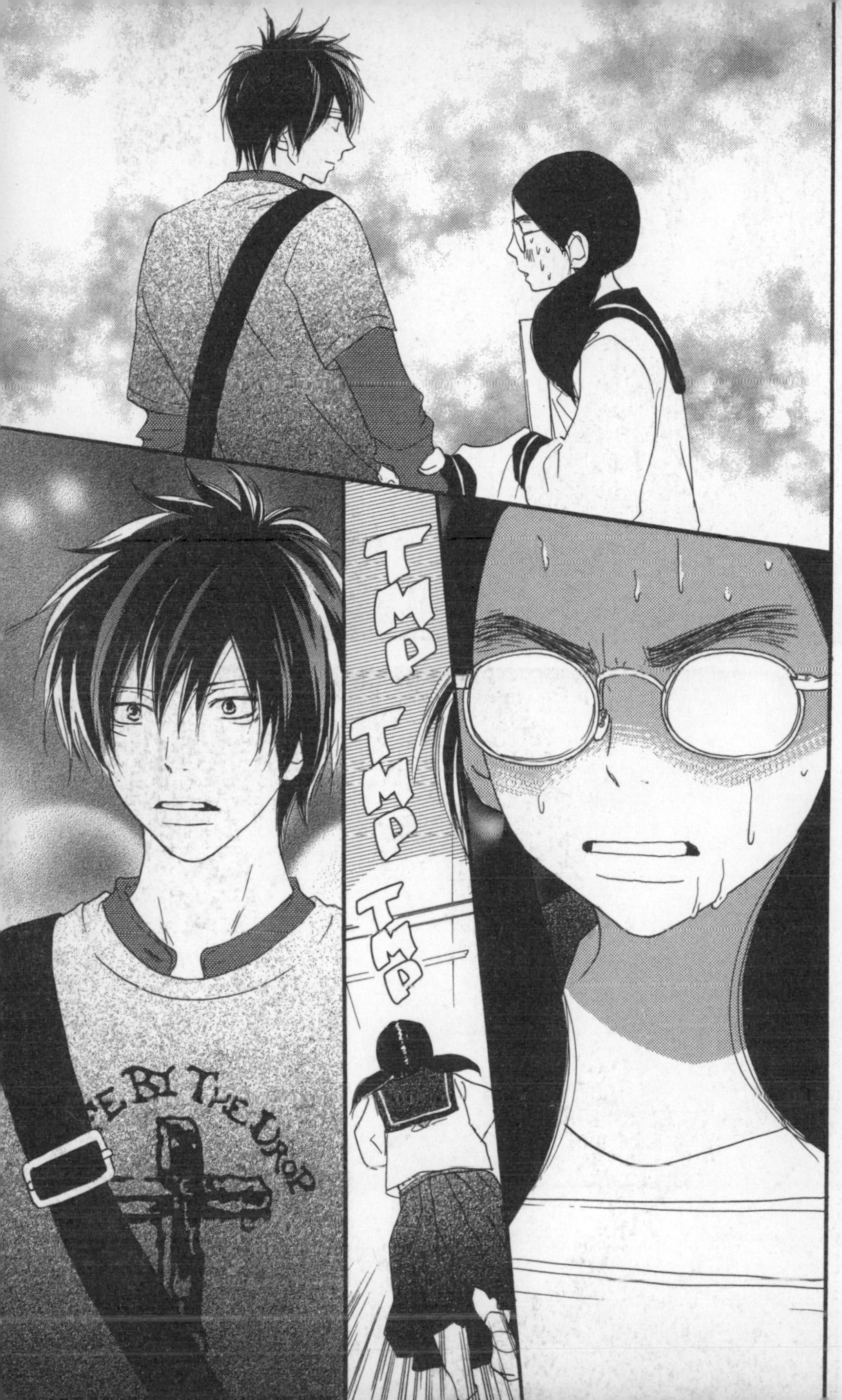
TMP TMP TMP TMP
BY THE DROP

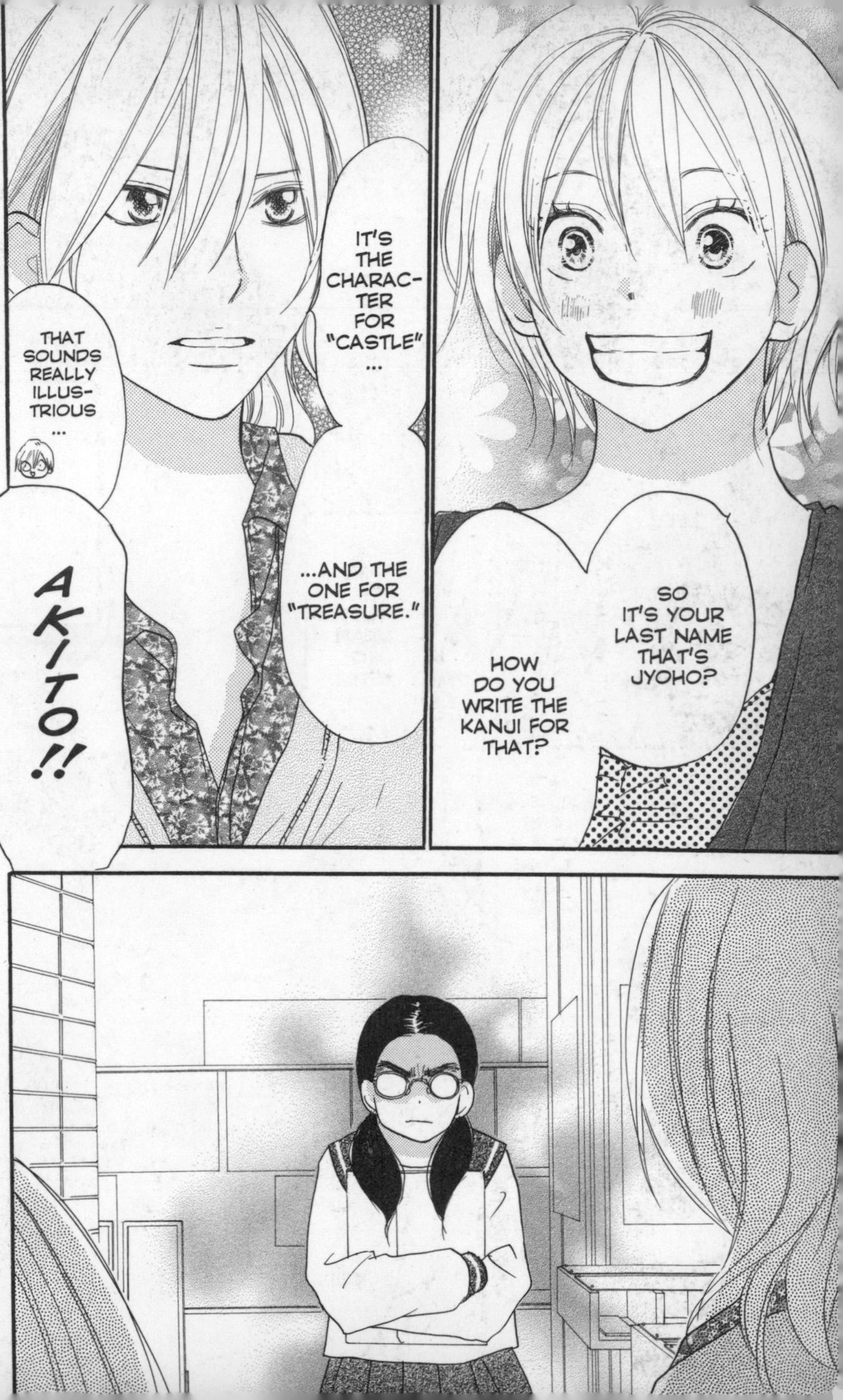
SO IT'S YOUR LAST NAME THAT'S JYOHO?
HOW DO YOU WRITE THE KANJI FOR THAT?
IT'S THE CHARACTER FOR "CASTLE"...
...AND THE ONE FOR "TREASURE."
THAT SOUNDS REALLY ILLUSTRIOUS...
AKITO!!

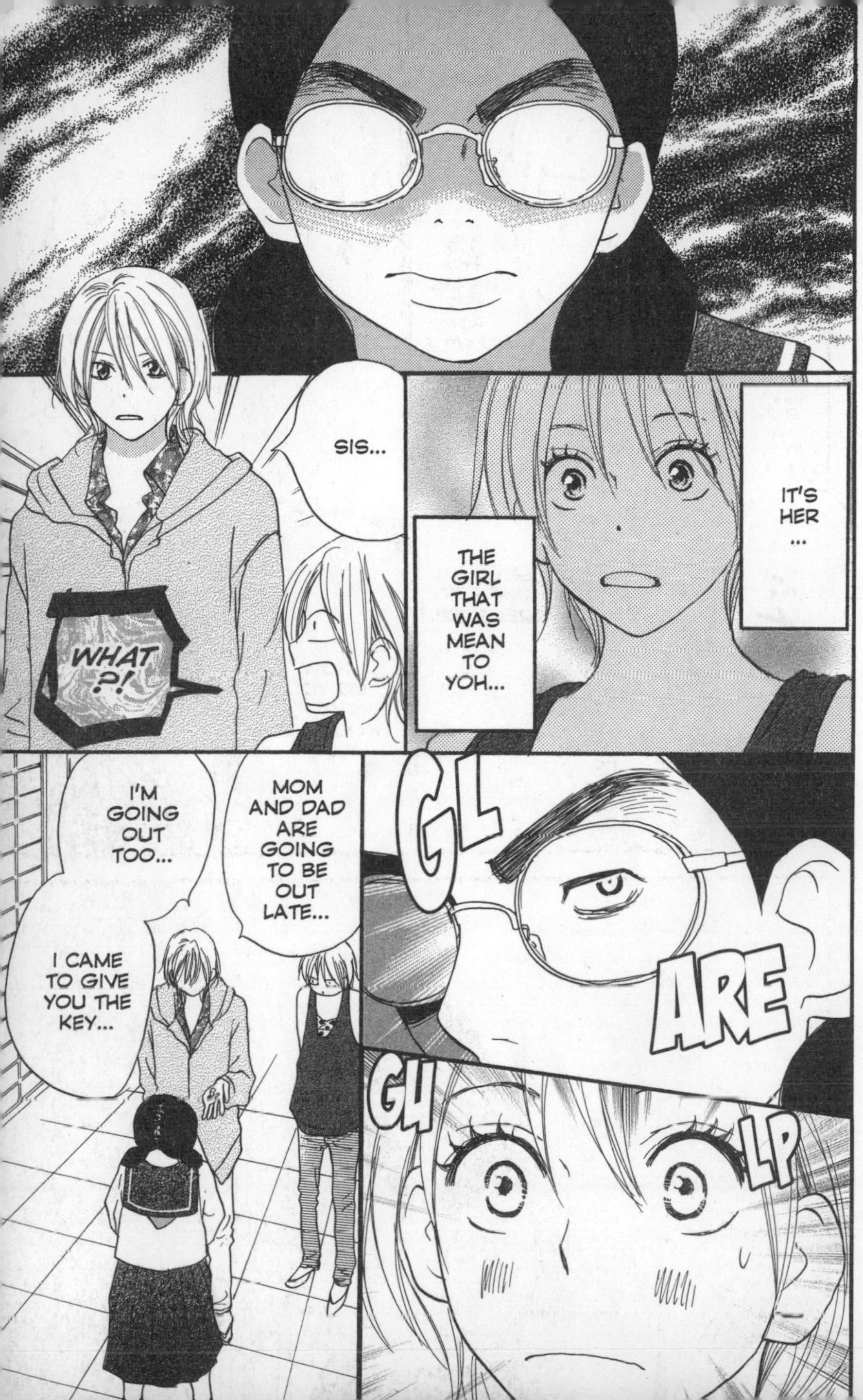
IT'S HER...
THE GIRL THAT WAS MEAN TO YOH...
SIS...
WHAT?!
GLARE
GULP
MOM AND DAD ARE GOING TO BE OUT LATE...
I'M GOING OUT TOO...
I CAME TO GIVE YOU THE KEY...

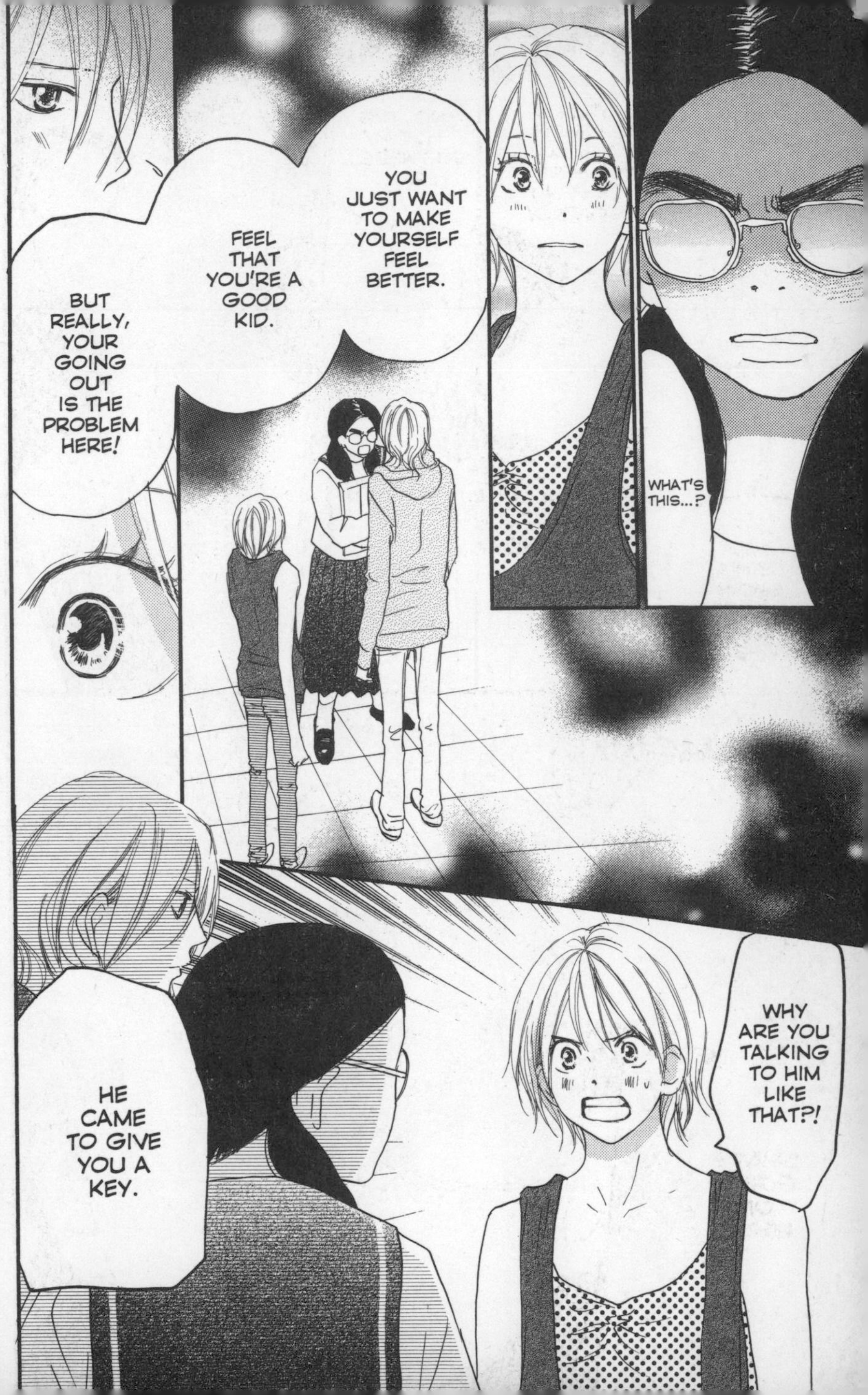
WHAT'S THIS...?
YOU JUST WANT TO MAKE YOURSELF FEEL BETTER.
FEEL THAT YOU'RE A GOOD KID.
BUT REALLY, YOUR GOING OUT IS THE PROBLEM HERE!
WHY ARE YOU TALKING TO HIM LIKE THAT?!
HE CAME TO GIVE YOU A KEY.

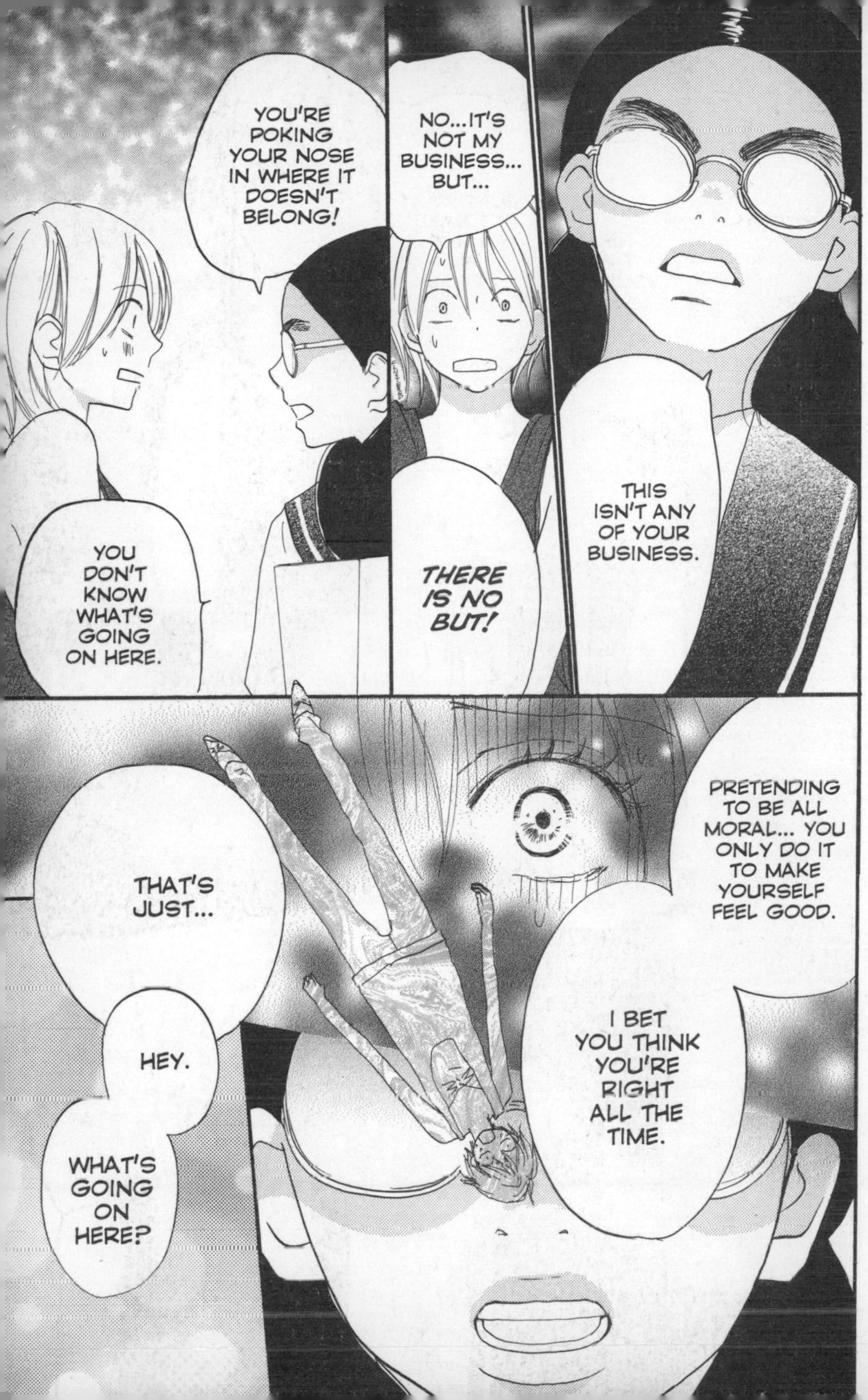
THIS ISN'T ANY OF YOUR BUSINESS.
NO...IT'S NOT MY BUSINESS... BUT...
THERE IS NO BUT!
YOU'RE POKING YOUR NOSE IN WHERE IT DOESN'T BELONG!
YOU DON'T KNOW WHAT'S GOING ON HERE.
PRETENDING TO BE ALL MORAL... YOU ONLY DO IT TO MAKE YOURSELF FEEL GOOD.
I BET YOU THINK YOU'RE RIGHT ALL THE TIME.
THAT'S JUST...
HEY.
WHAT'S GOING ON HERE?

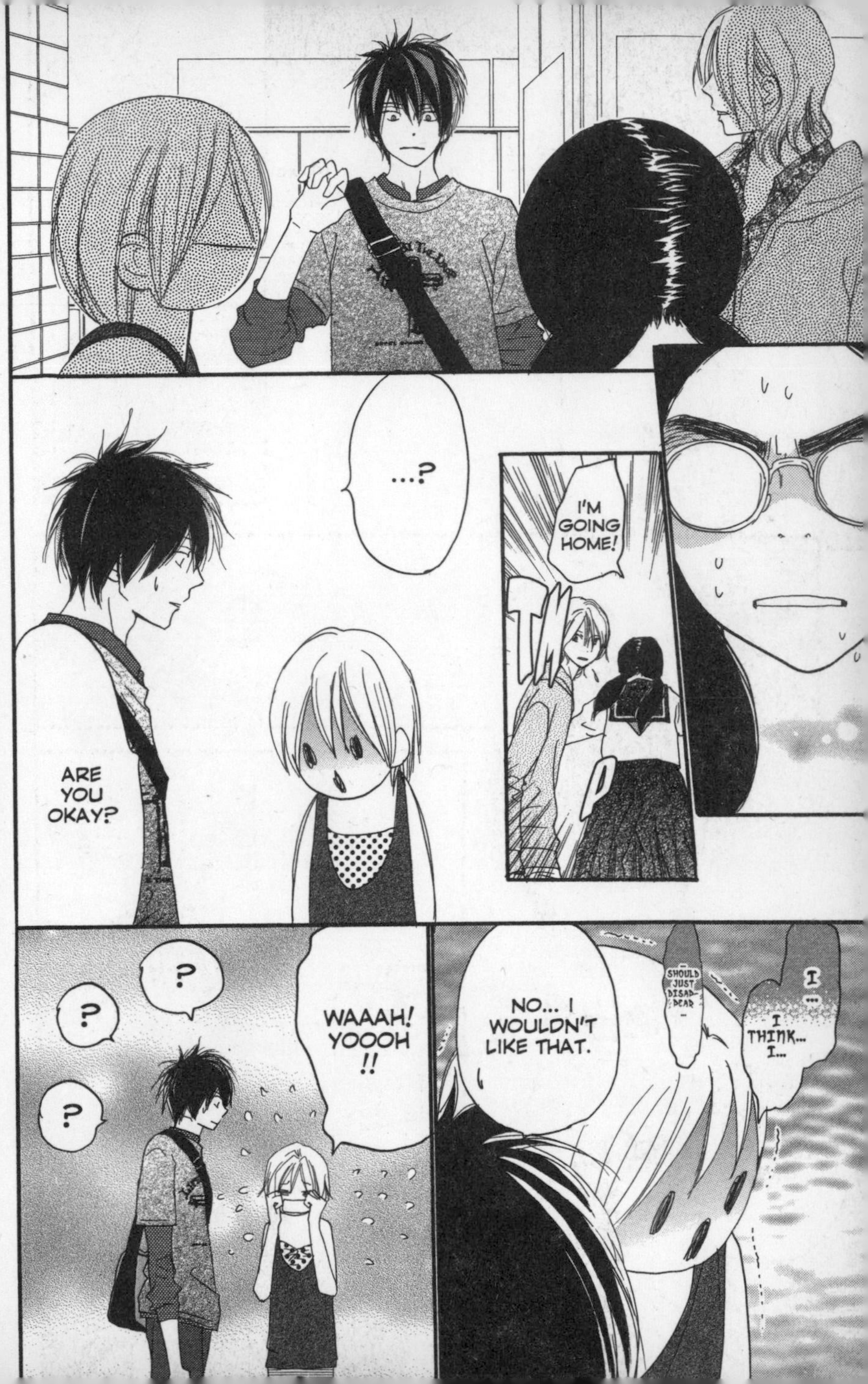
I'M GOING HOME!
...?
ARE YOU OKAY?
I... I THINK... I...
SHOULD JUST DISAPPEAR...
NO... I WOULDN'T LIKE THAT.
WAAAH! YOOOH!!
?
?
?

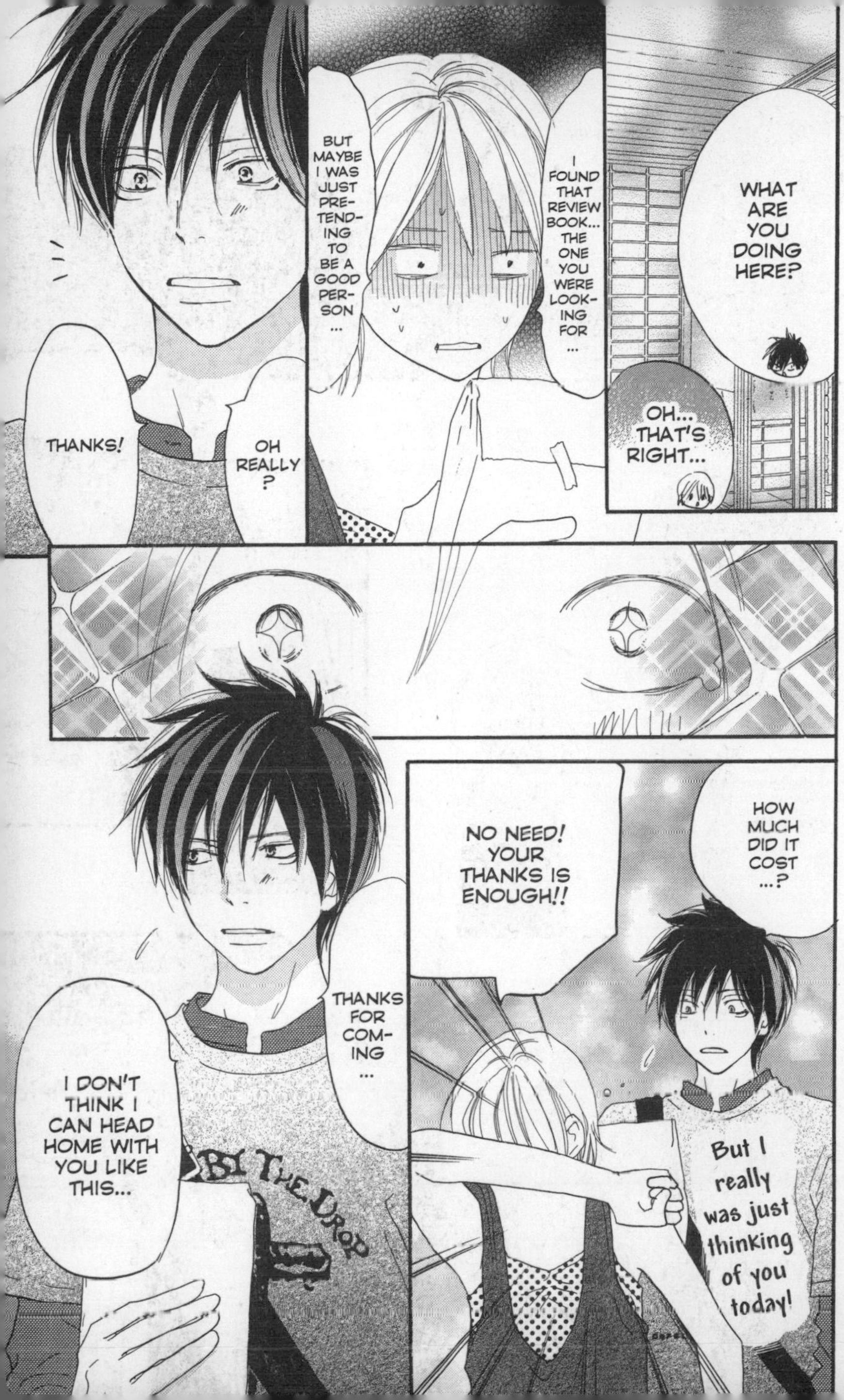
WHAT ARE YOU DOING HERE?
OH... THAT'S RIGHT...
I FOUND THAT REVIEW BOOK... THE ONE YOU WERE LOOKING FOR ...
BUT MAYBE I WAS JUST PRE-TENDING TO BE A GOOD PER-SON ...
OH REALLY ?
THANKS!
HOW MUCH DID IT COST ...?
NO NEED! YOUR THANKS IS ENOUGH!!
But I really was just thinking of you today!
THANKS FOR COM-ING ...
I DON'T THINK I CAN HEAD HOME WITH YOU LIKE THIS...
BY THE DROP

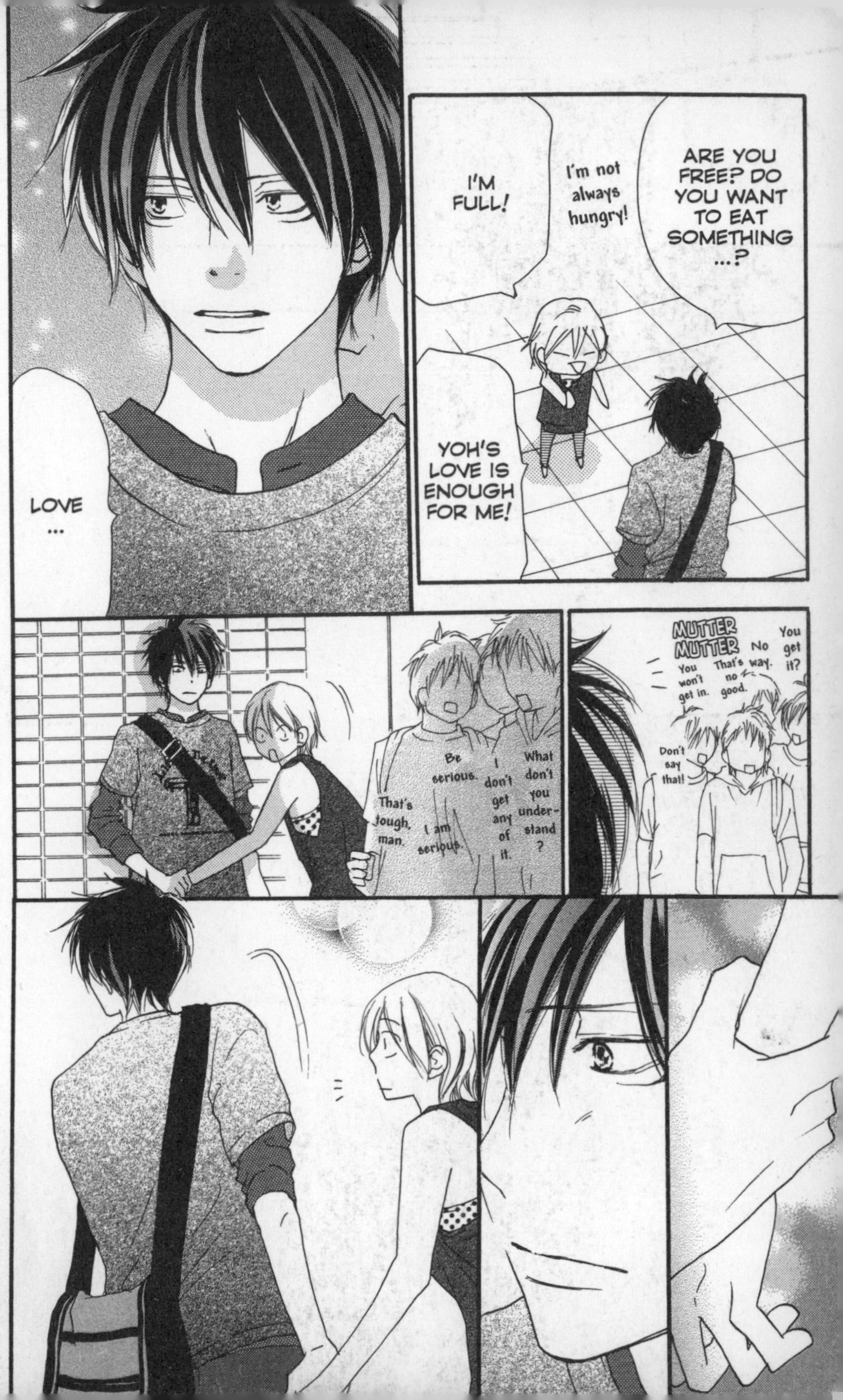
ARE YOU FREE? DO YOU WANT TO EAT SOMETHING ...?
I'm not always hungry!
I'M FULL!
YOH'S LOVE IS ENOUGH FOR ME!
LOVE ...
MUTTER MUTTER
You get it?
No way.
That's no good.
You won't get in.
Don't say that!
What don't you understand?
I don't get any of it.
Be serious.
I am serious.
That's tough, man.

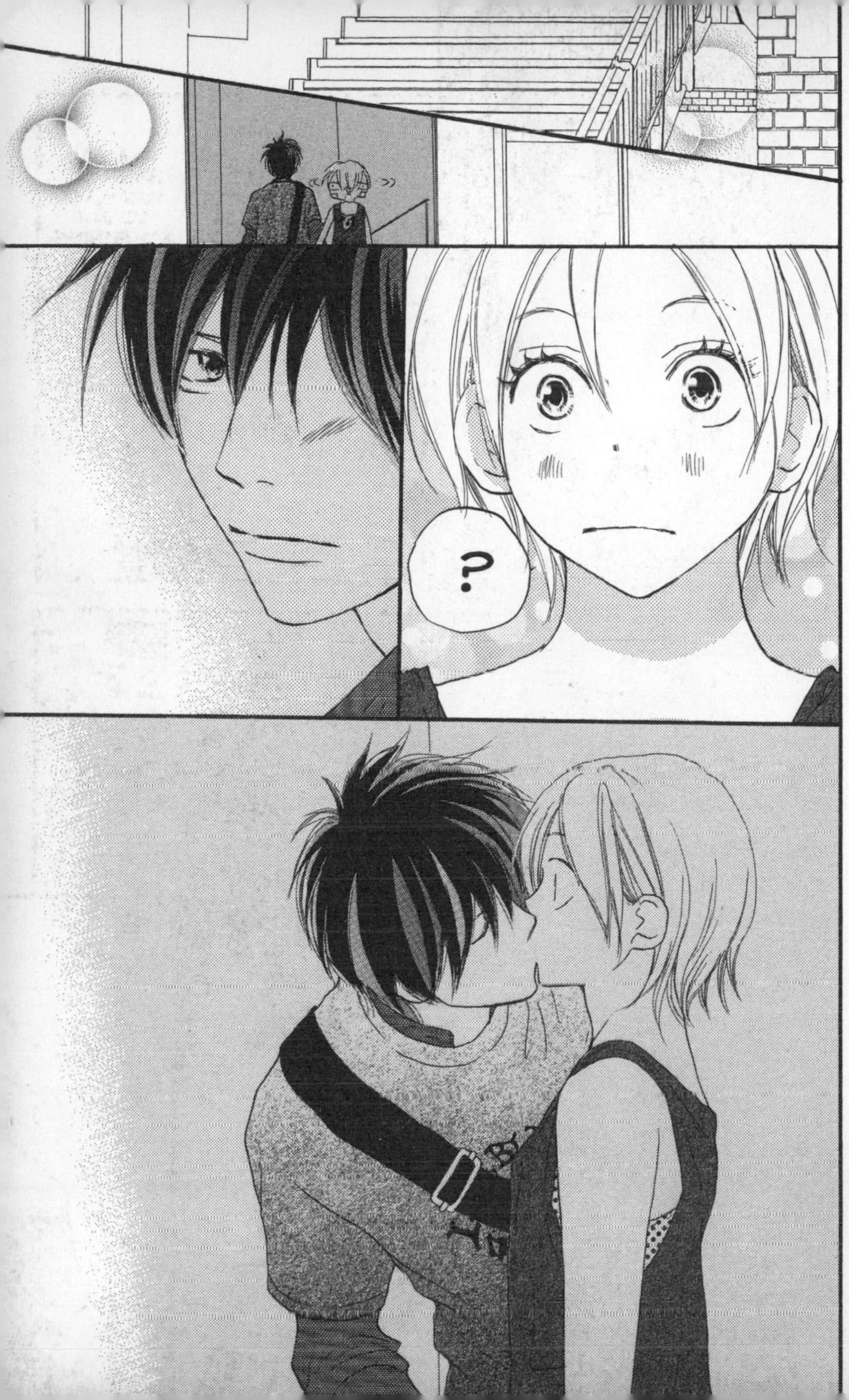
?

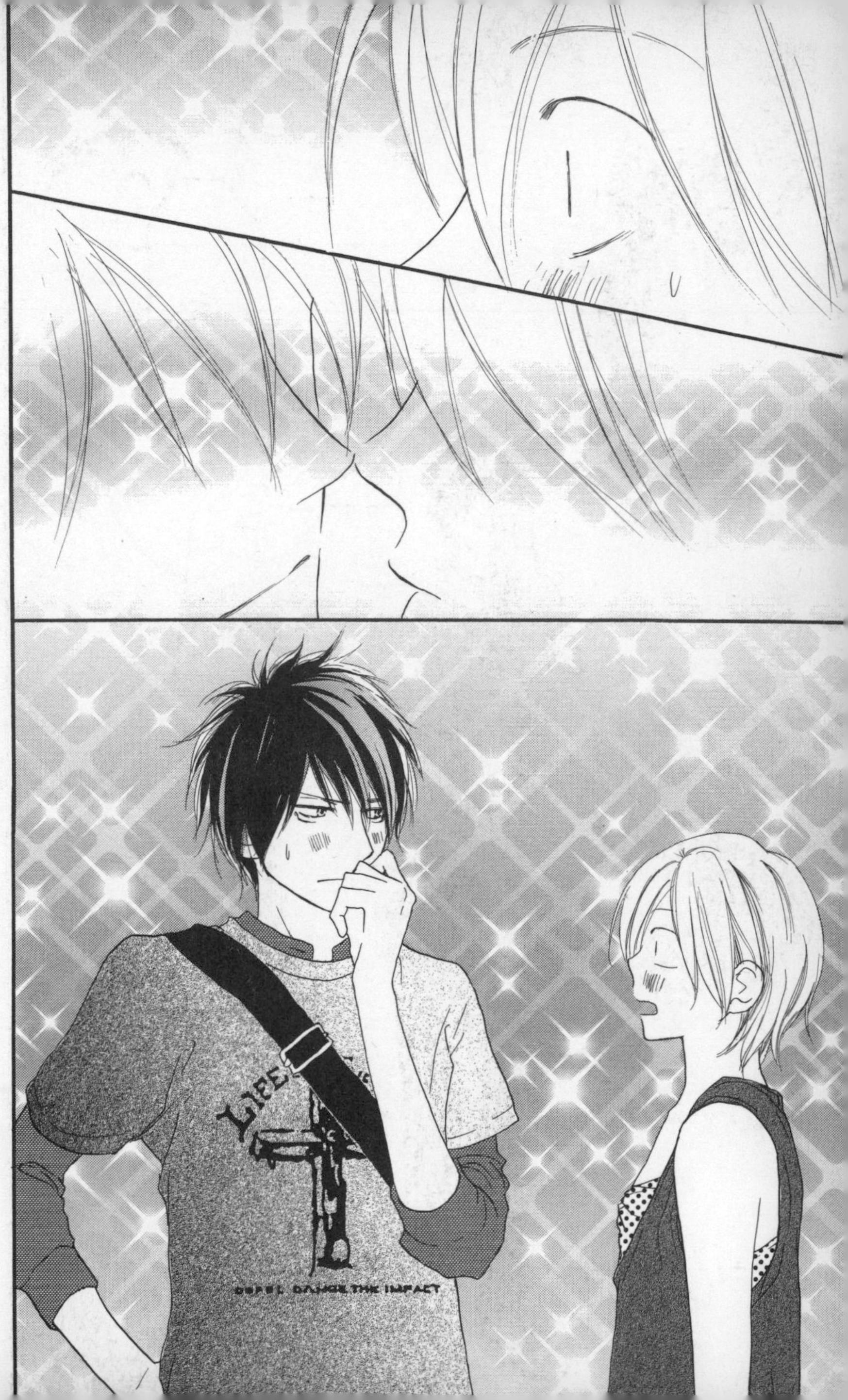

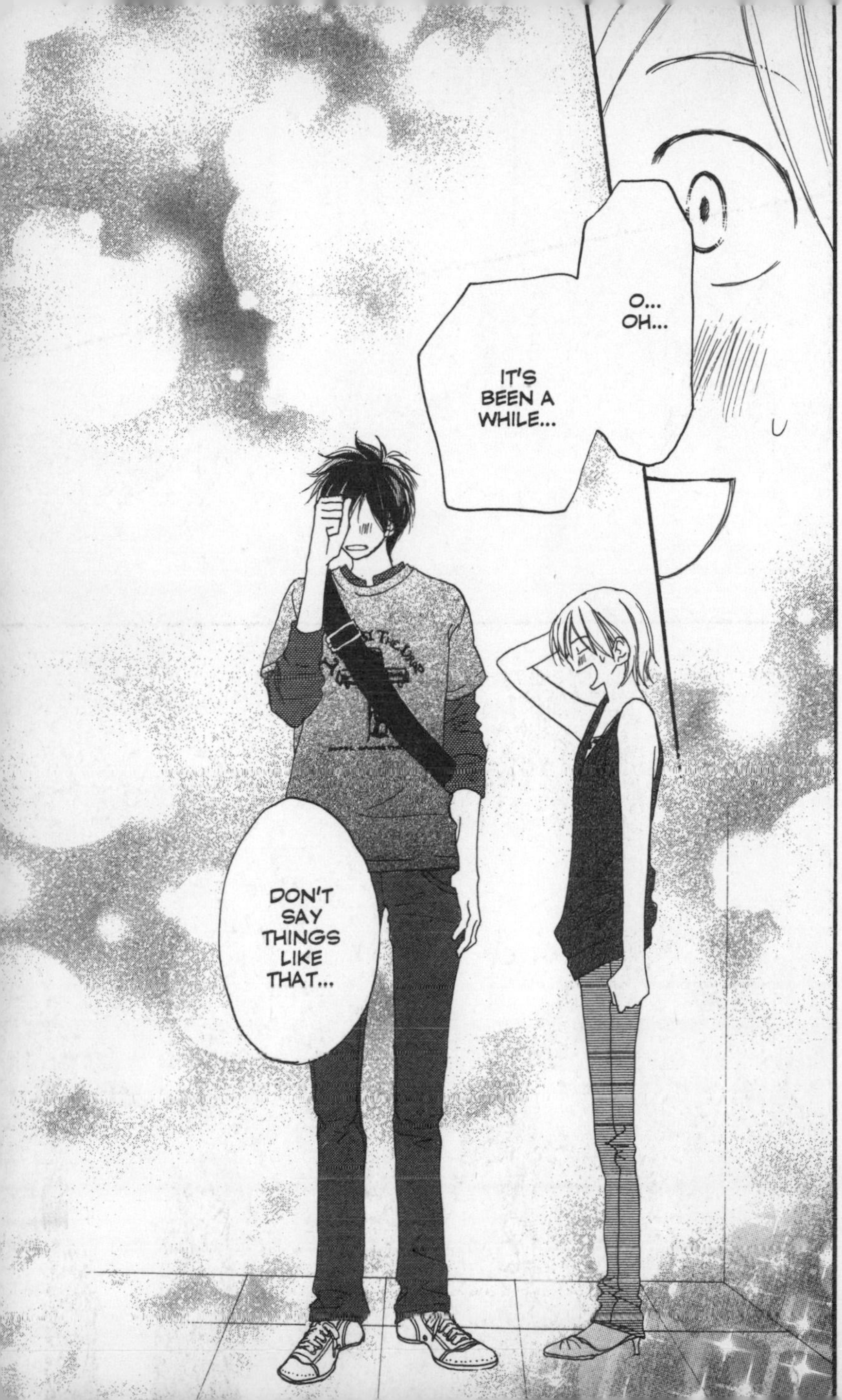
O... OH...
IT'S BEEN A WHILE...
DON'T SAY THINGS LIKE THAT...

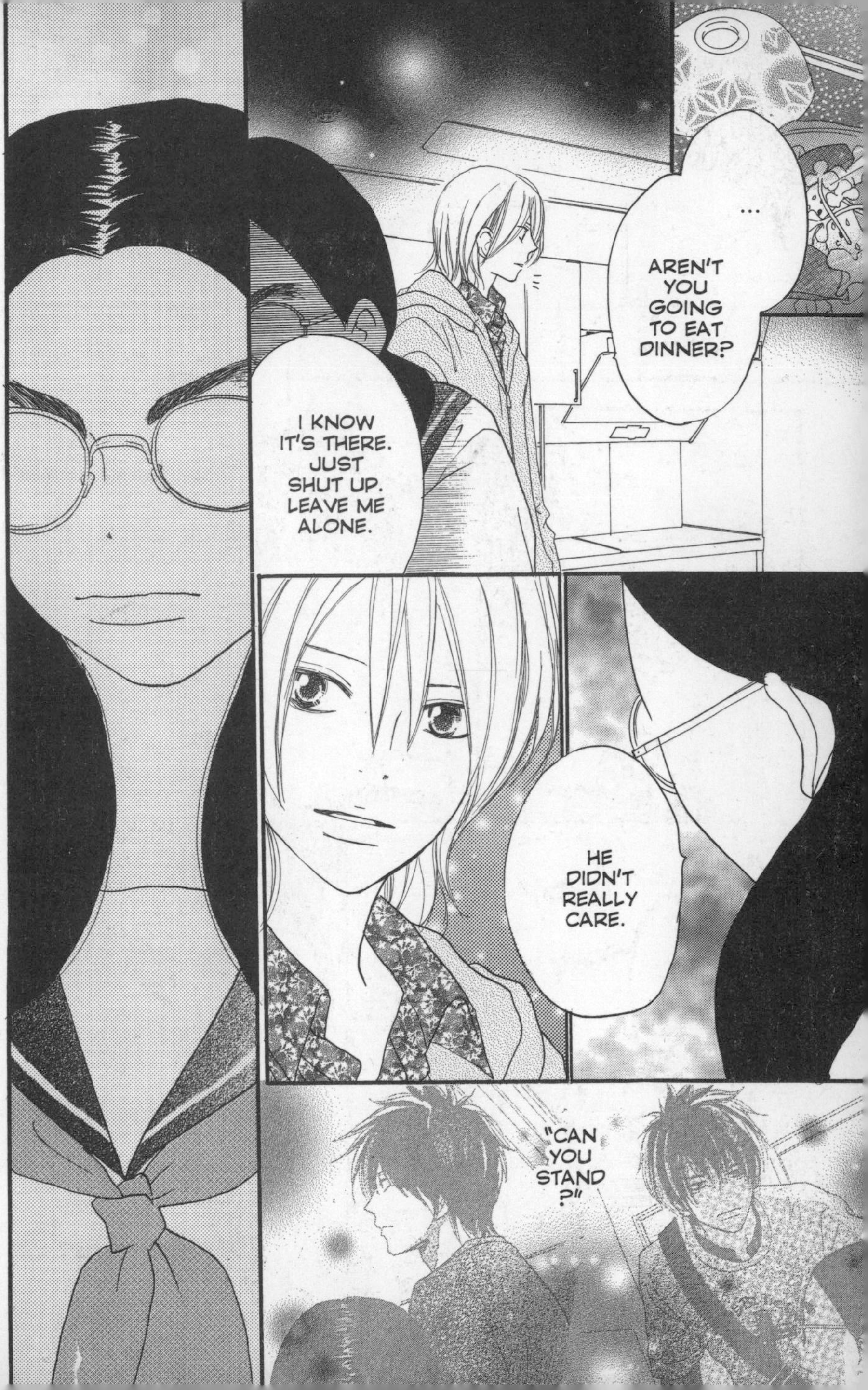
...
AREN'T YOU GOING TO EAT DINNER?
I KNOW IT'S THERE. JUST SHUT UP. LEAVE ME ALONE.
HE DIDN'T REALLY CARE.
"CAN YOU STAND?"

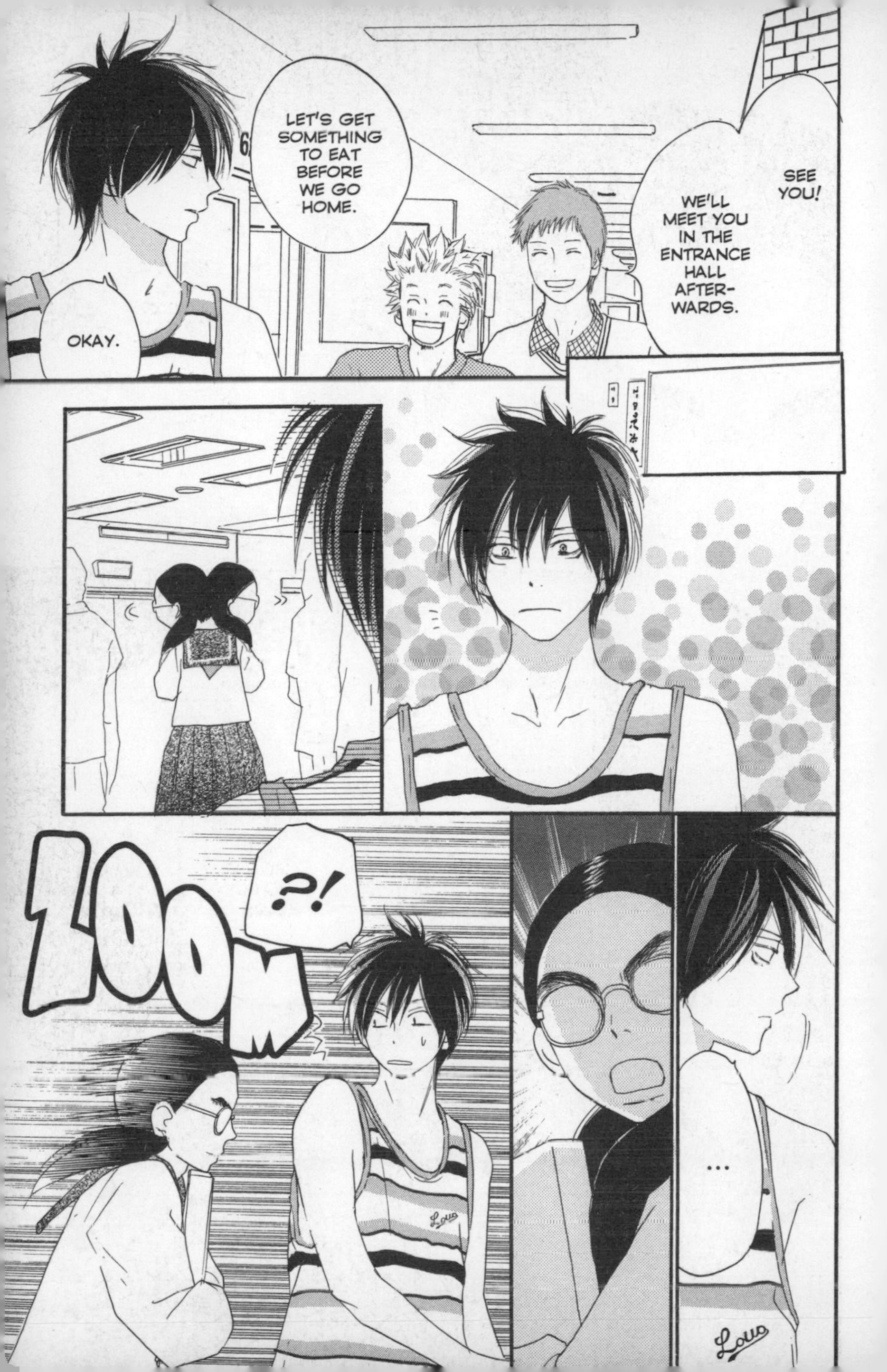
SEE YOU!
WE'LL MEET YOU IN THE ENTRANCE HALL AFTER-WARDS.
LET'S GET SOMETHING TO EAT BEFORE WE GO HOME.
OKAY.
...
?!
ZOOM

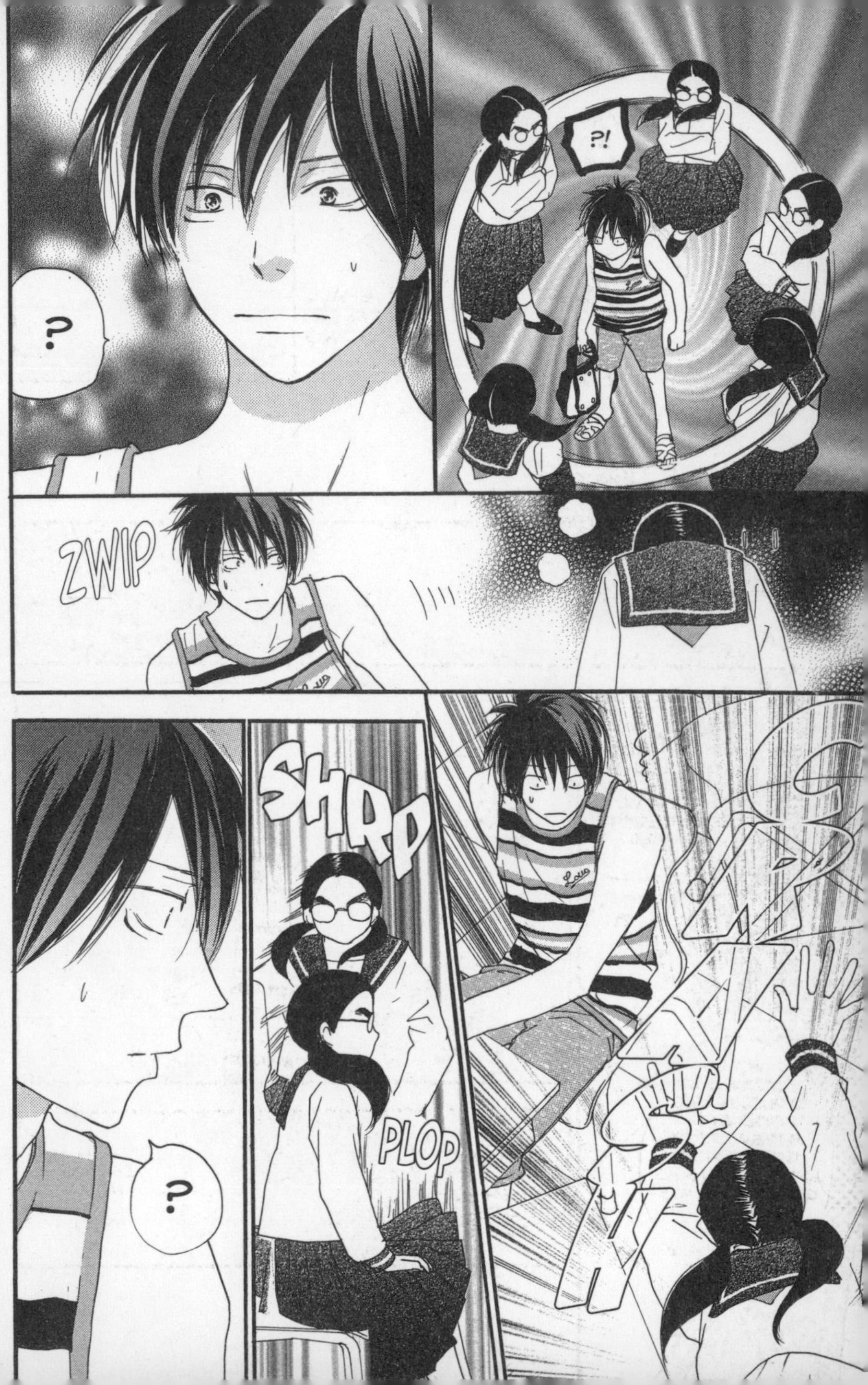
?!
?
ZWIP
SHRP
PLOP
?

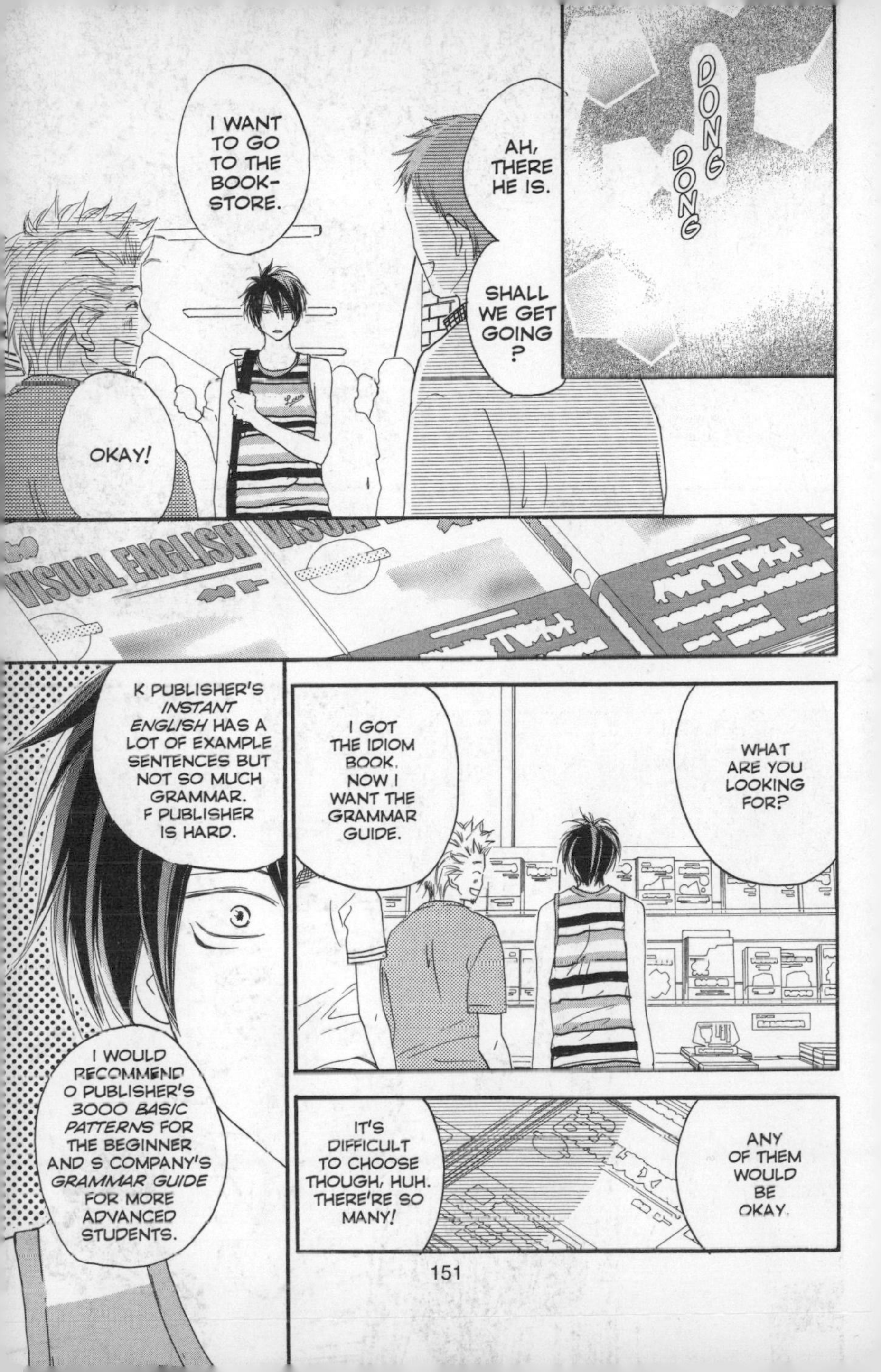
DONG DONG
AH, THERE HE IS.
SHALL WE GET GOING?
I WANT TO GO TO THE BOOK-STORE.
OKAY!
VISUAL ENGLISH
WHAT ARE YOU LOOKING FOR?
I GOT THE IDIOM BOOK. NOW I WANT THE GRAMMAR GUIDE.
ANY OF THEM WOULD BE OKAY.
IT'S DIFFICULT TO CHOOSE THOUGH, HUH. THERE'RE SO MANY!
K PUBLISHER'S *INSTANT ENGLISH* HAS A LOT OF EXAMPLE SENTENCES BUT NOT SO MUCH GRAMMAR. F PUBLISHER IS HARD.
I WOULD RECOMMEND O PUBLISHER'S *3000 BASIC PATTERNS* FOR THE BEGINNER AND S COMPANY'S *GRAMMAR GUIDE* FOR MORE ADVANCED STUDENTS.

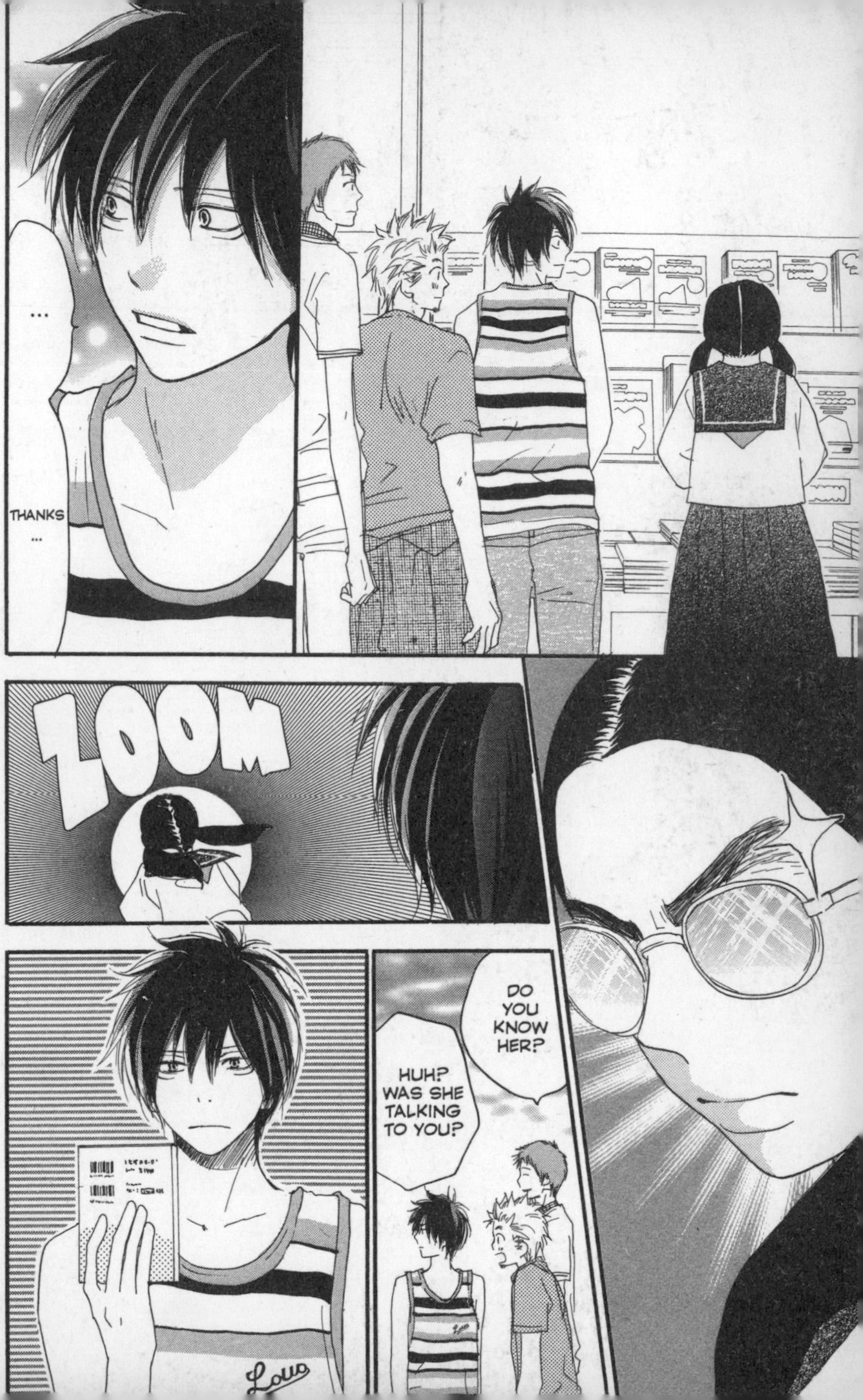
...
THANKS ...
ZOOM
DO YOU KNOW HER?
HUH? WAS SHE TALKING TO YOU?

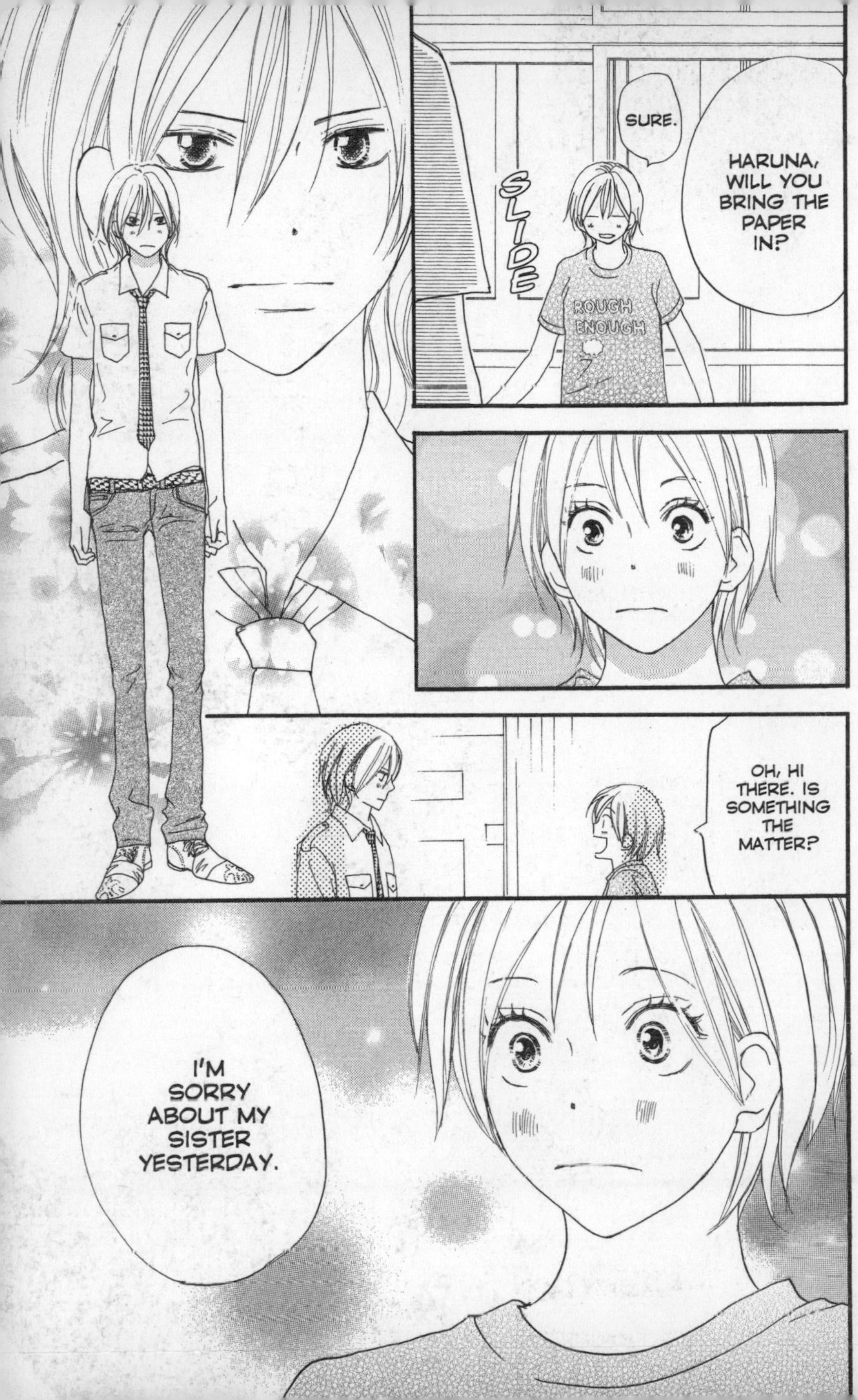
HARUNA, WILL YOU BRING THE PAPER IN?
SURE.
SLIDE
ROUGH ENOUGH
OH, HI THERE. IS SOMETHING THE MATTER?
I'M SORRY ABOUT MY SISTER YESTERDAY.

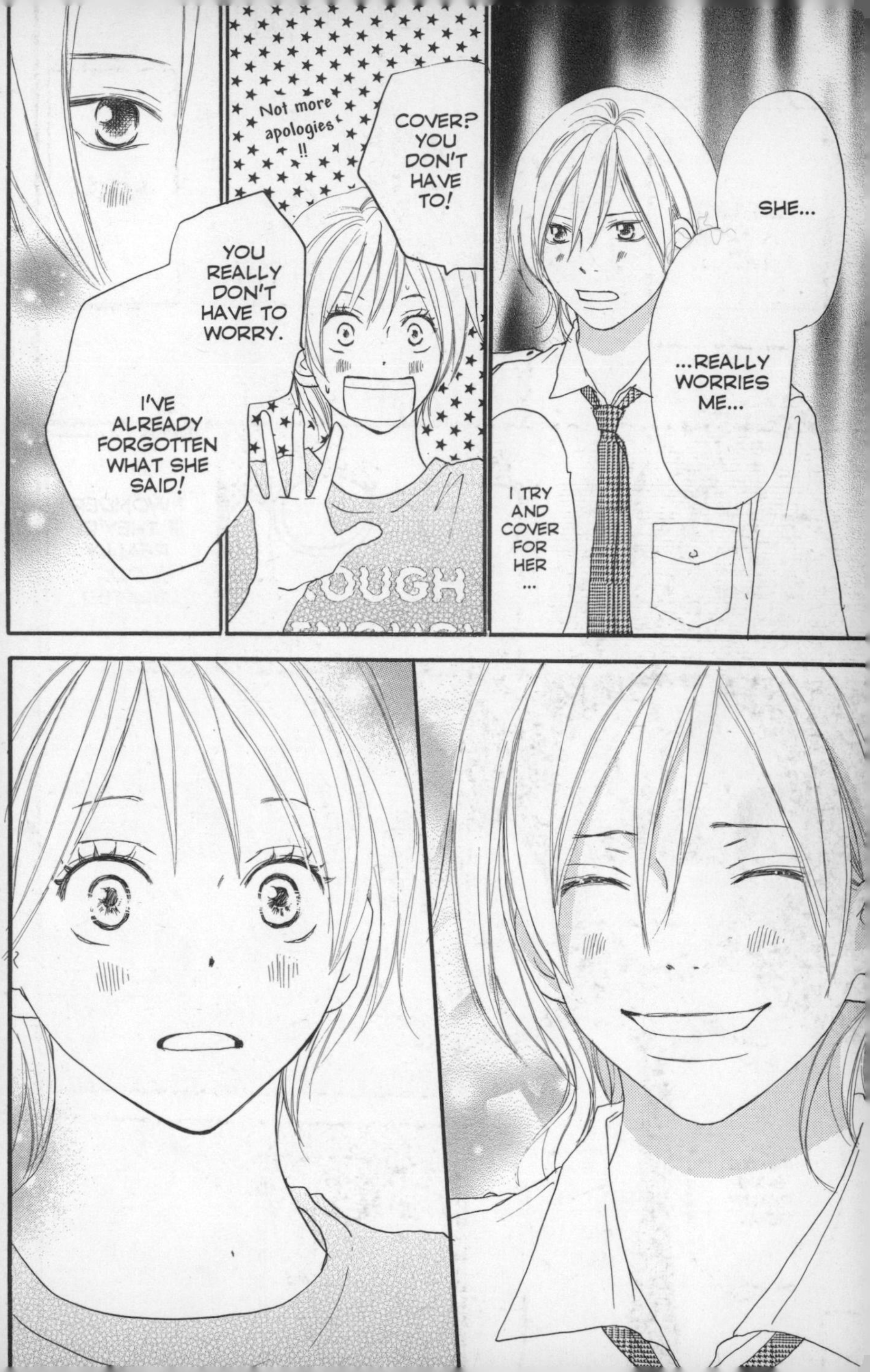
SHE...
...REALLY WORRIES ME...
I TRY AND COVER FOR HER ...
COVER? YOU DON'T HAVE TO!
Not more apologies!!
YOU REALLY DON'T HAVE TO WORRY.
I'VE ALREADY FORGOTTEN WHAT SHE SAID!

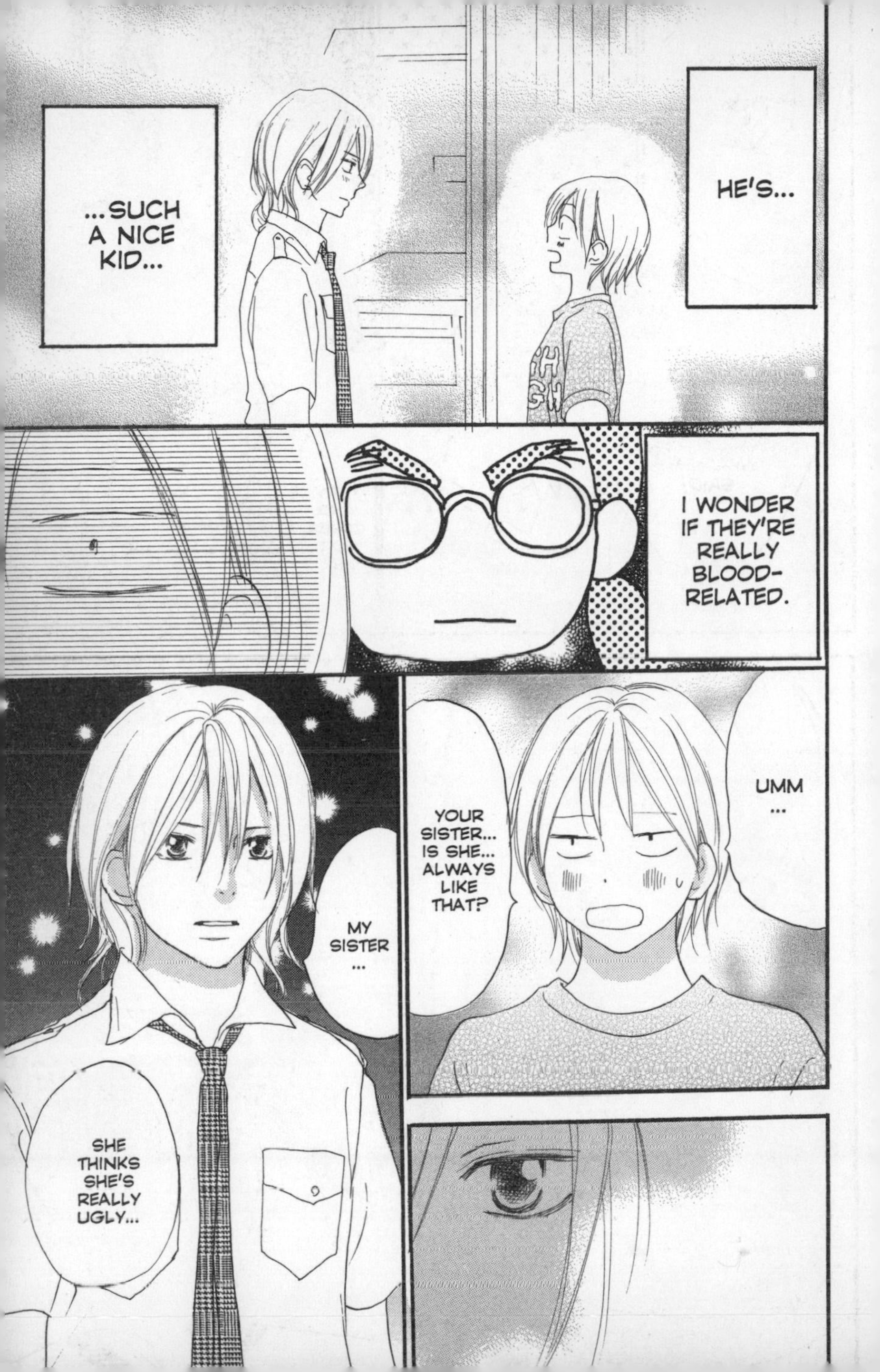
HE'S...
...SUCH A NICE KID...
I WONDER IF THEY'RE REALLY BLOOD-RELATED.
UMM ...
YOUR SISTER... IS SHE... ALWAYS LIKE THAT?
MY SISTER ...
SHE THINKS SHE'S REALLY UGLY...

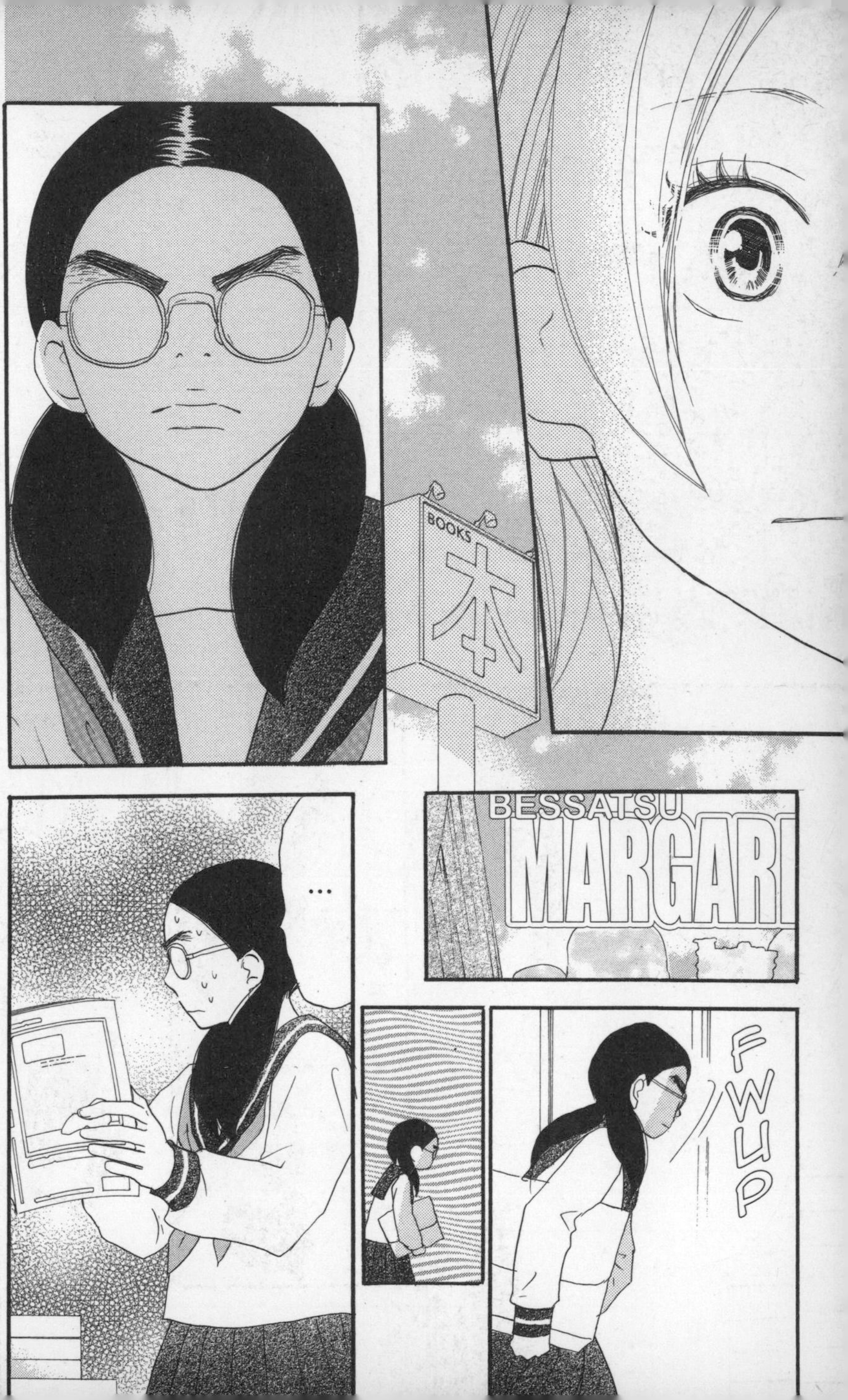
BOOKS
本
BESSATSU
MARGARE
...
FWUP

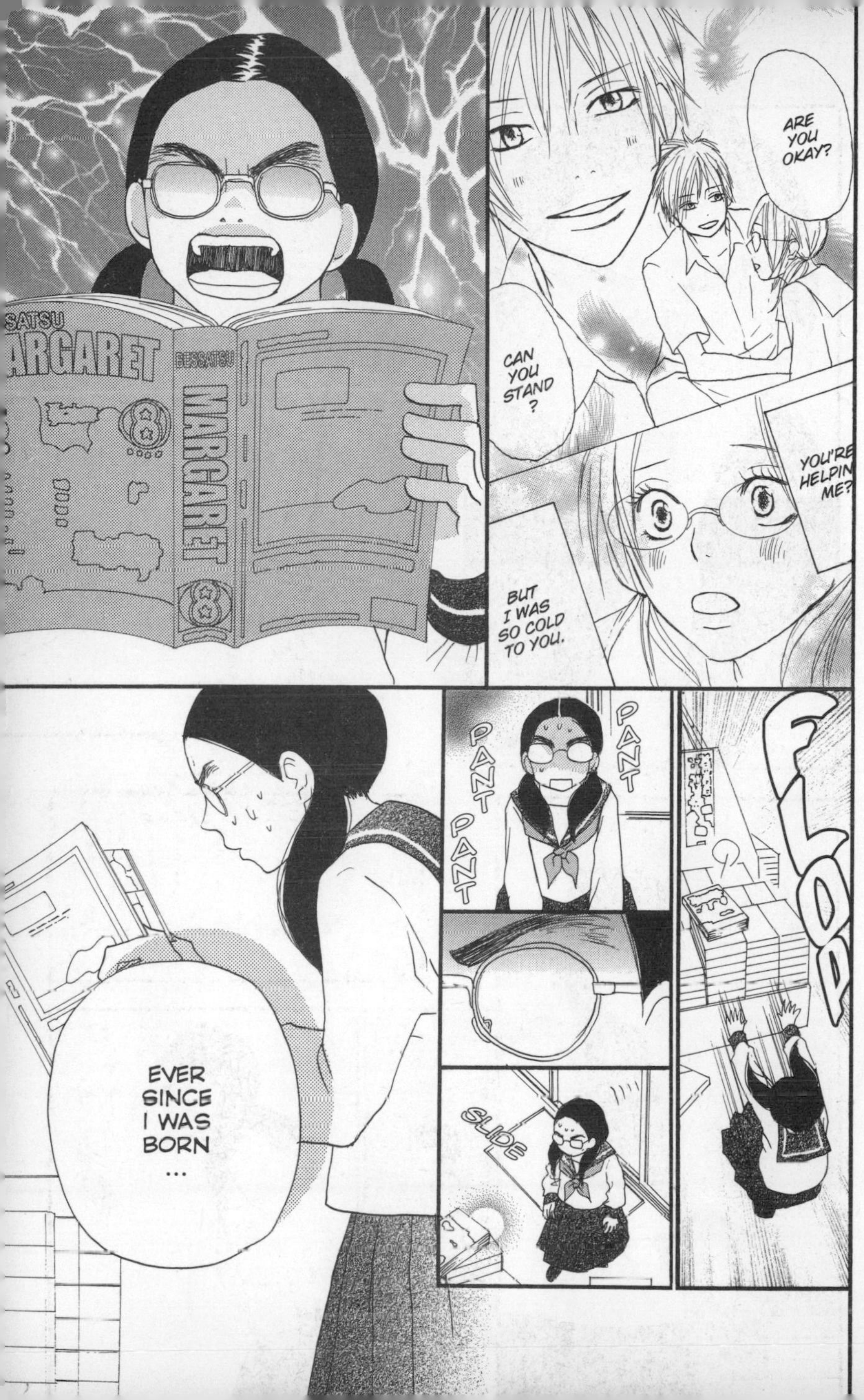
ARE YOU OKAY?
CAN YOU STAND?
YOU'RE HELPING ME?
BUT I WAS SO COLD TO YOU.
BESSATSU MARGARET
FLOP
PANT PANT
PANT PANT
SLIDE
EVER SINCE I WAS BORN ...

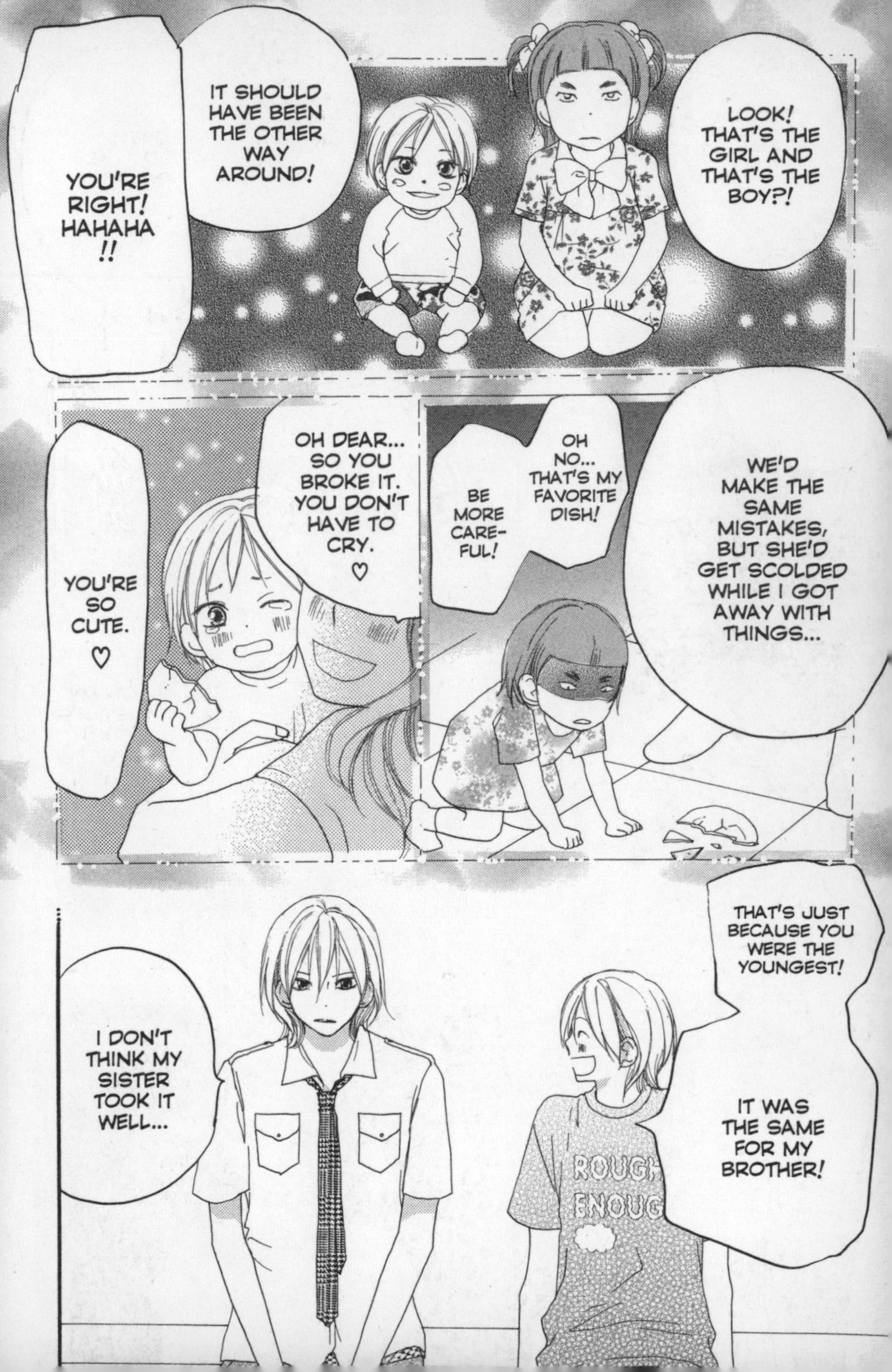
LOOK! THAT'S THE GIRL AND THAT'S THE BOY?!
IT SHOULD HAVE BEEN THE OTHER WAY AROUND!
YOU'RE RIGHT! HAHAHA!!
WE'D MAKE THE SAME MISTAKES, BUT SHE'D GET SCOLDED WHILE I GOT AWAY WITH THINGS...
OH NO... THAT'S MY FAVORITE DISH!
BE MORE CARE-FUL!
OH DEAR... SO YOU BROKE IT. YOU DON'T HAVE TO CRY. ♡
YOU'RE SO CUTE. ♡
THAT'S JUST BECAUSE YOU WERE THE YOUNGEST!
IT WAS THE SAME FOR MY BROTHER!
I DON'T THINK MY SISTER TOOK IT WELL...

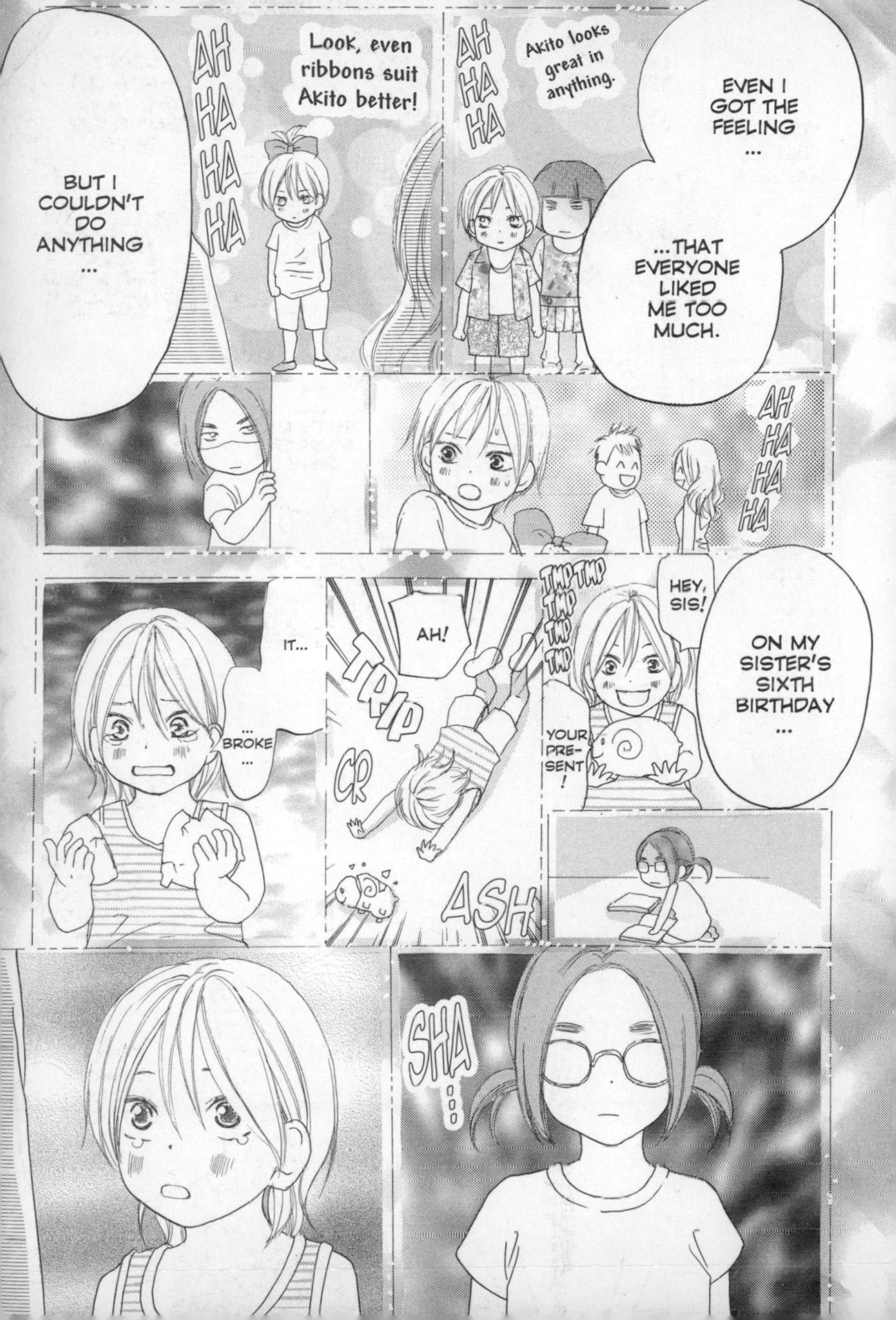
EVEN I GOT THE FEELING ...
...THAT EVERYONE LIKED ME TOO MUCH.
Akito looks great in anything.
AH HA HA
Look, even ribbons suit Akito better!
AH HA HA HA HA
BUT I COULDN'T DO ANYTHING ...
AH HA HA HA
ON MY SISTER'S SIXTH BIRTHDAY ...
HEY, SIS!
TMP TMP TMP TMP TMP
YOUR PRE-SENT!
AH!
TRIP
CR
ASH
IT...
... BROKE ...
SHA ...

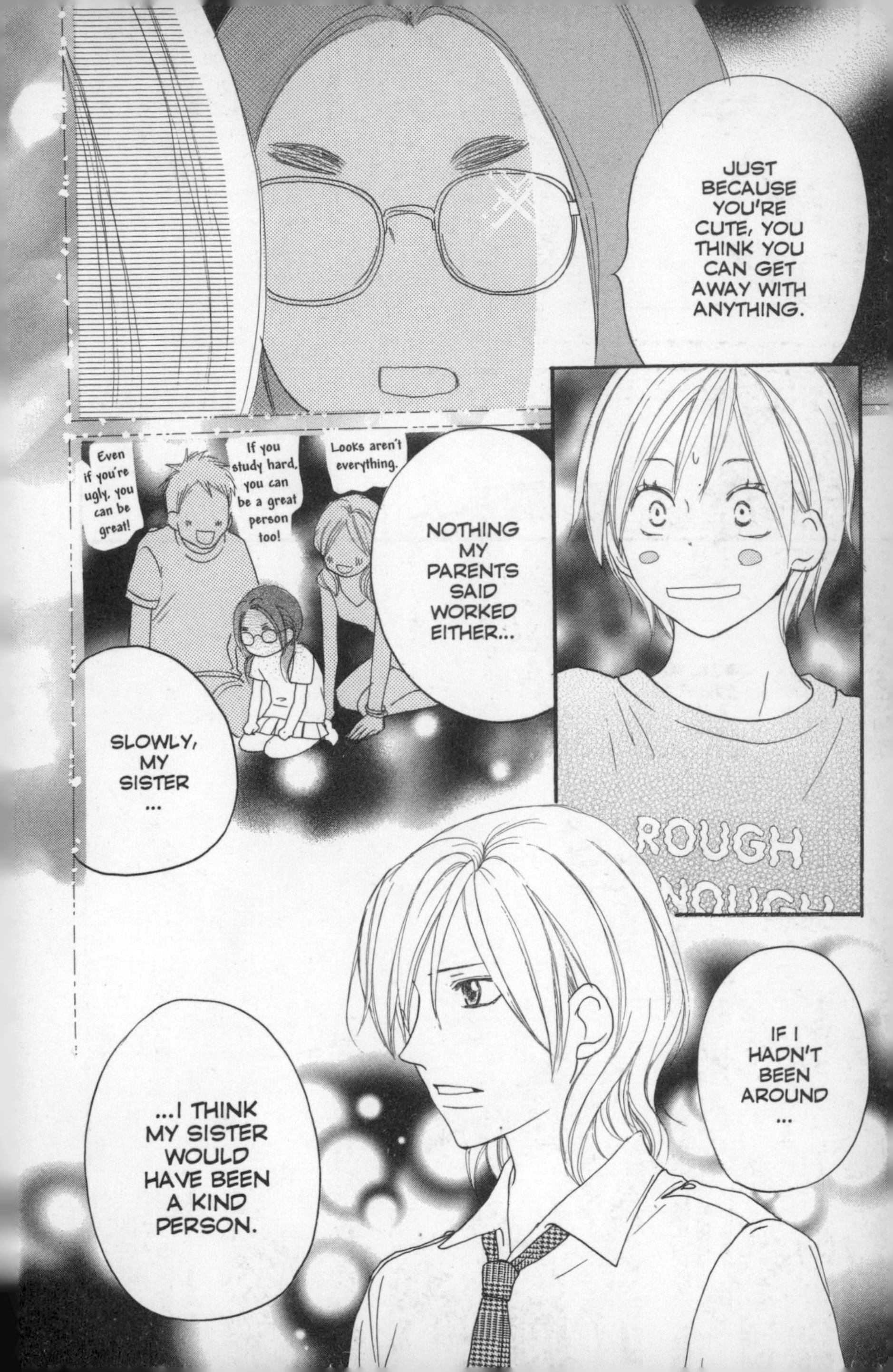
JUST BECAUSE YOU'RE CUTE, YOU THINK YOU CAN GET AWAY WITH ANYTHING.
ROUGH
NOTHING MY PARENTS SAID WORKED EITHER...
Looks aren't everything.
If you study hard, you can be a great person too!
Even if you're ugly, you can be great!
SLOWLY, MY SISTER ...
IF I HADN'T BEEN AROUND ...
...I THINK MY SISTER WOULD HAVE BEEN A KIND PERSON.

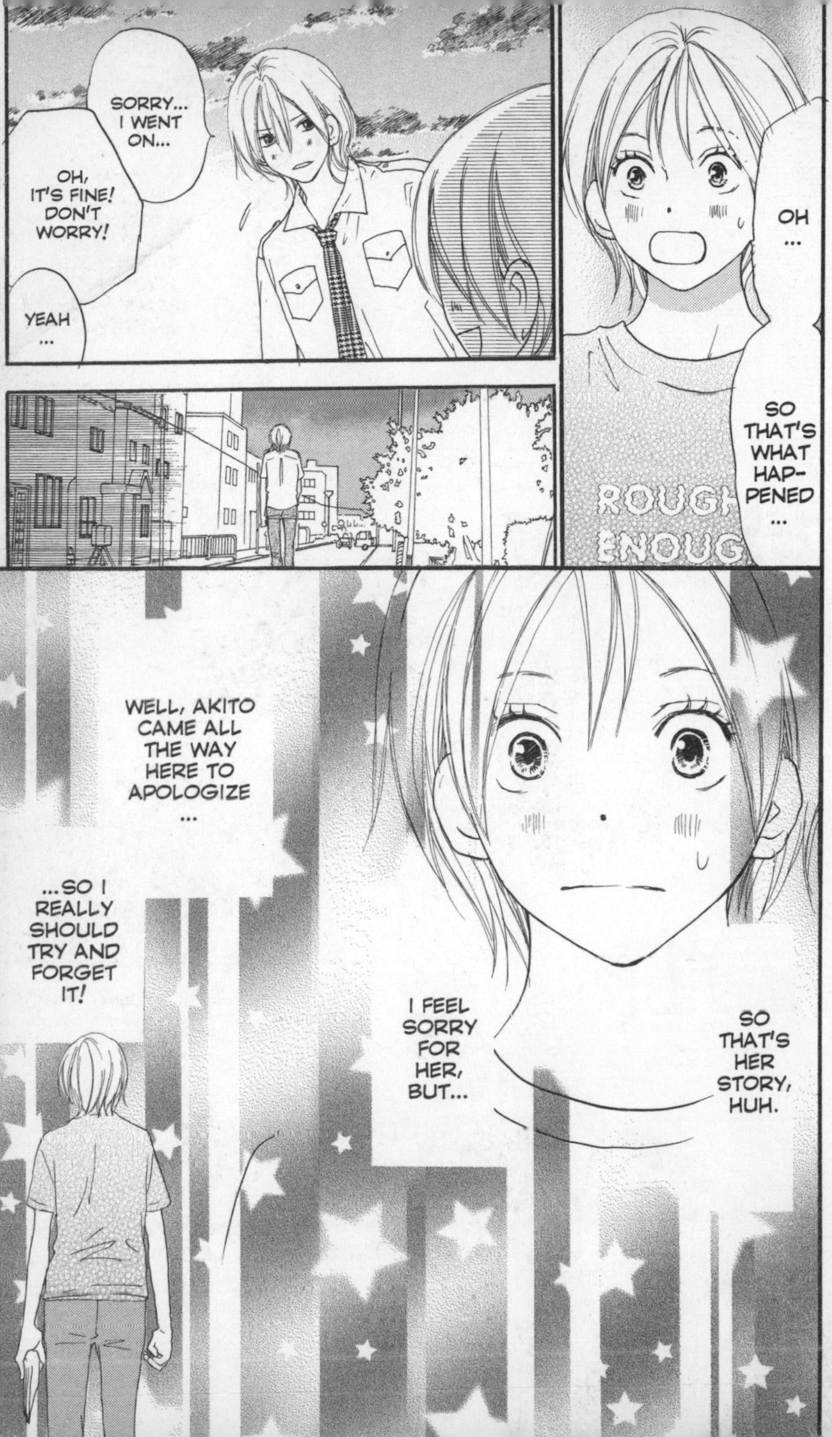
OH ...
SO THAT'S WHAT HAP-PENED ...
SORRY... I WENT ON...
OH, IT'S FINE! DON'T WORRY!
YEAH ...
SO THAT'S HER STORY, HUH.
I FEEL SORRY FOR HER, BUT...
WELL, AKITO CAME ALL THE WAY HERE TO APOLOGIZE ...
...SO I REALLY SHOULD TRY AND FORGET IT!

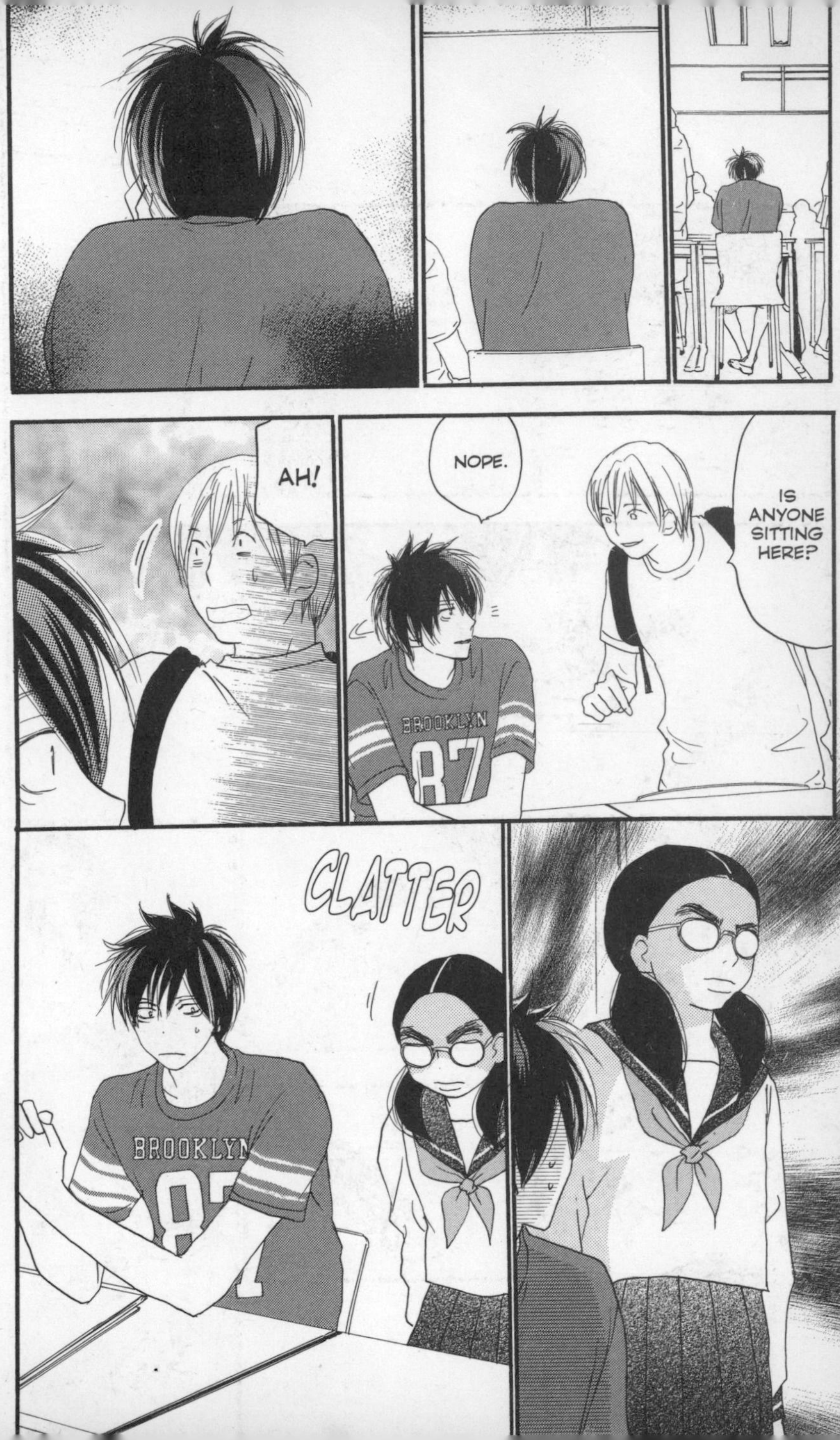
IS ANYONE SITTING HERE?
NOPE.
AH!
CLATTER

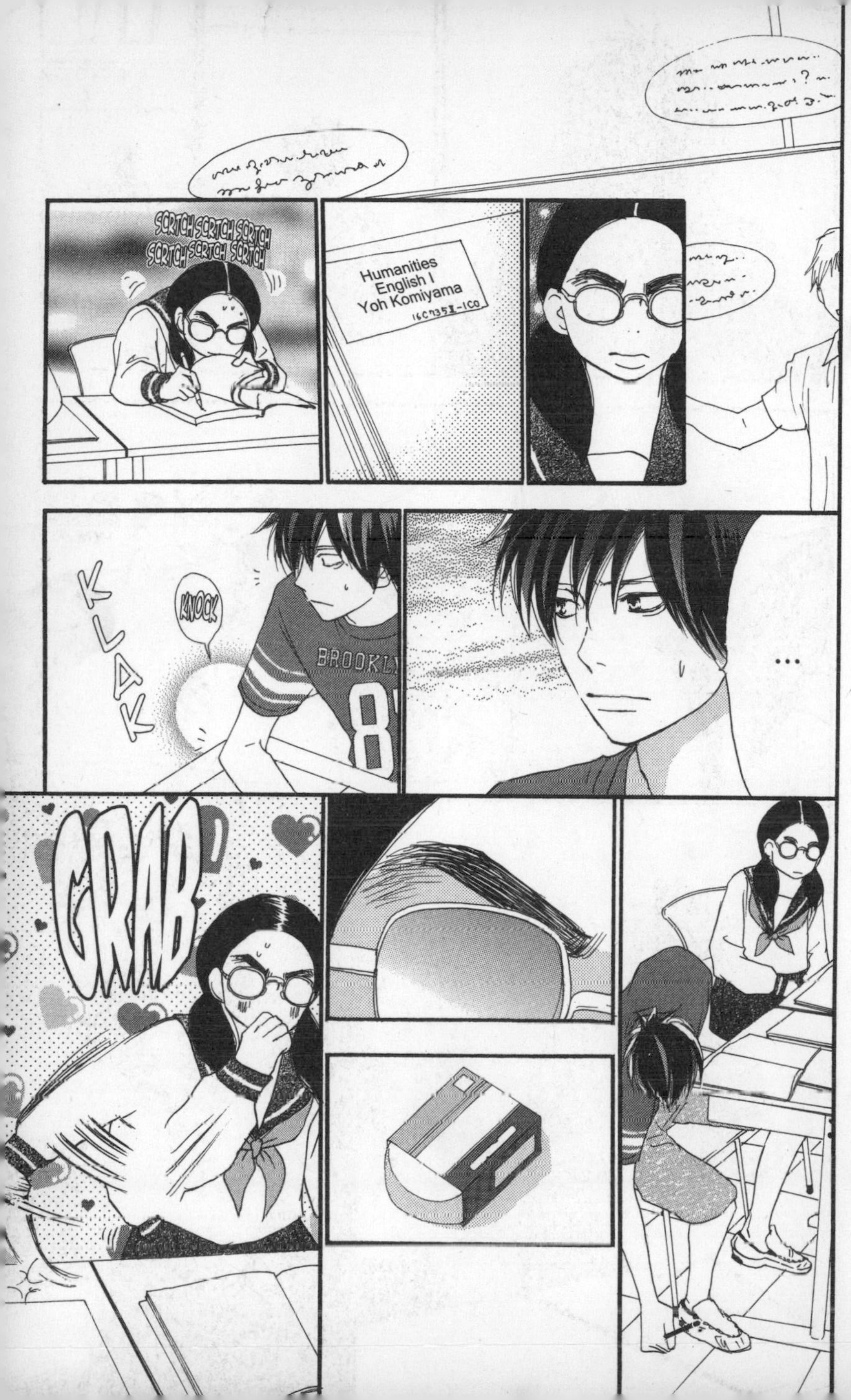
Humanities
English I
Yoh Komiyama
SCRITCH SCRITCH SCRITCH
SCRITCH SCRITCH SCRITCH
...
KNOCK
KLAK
GRAB

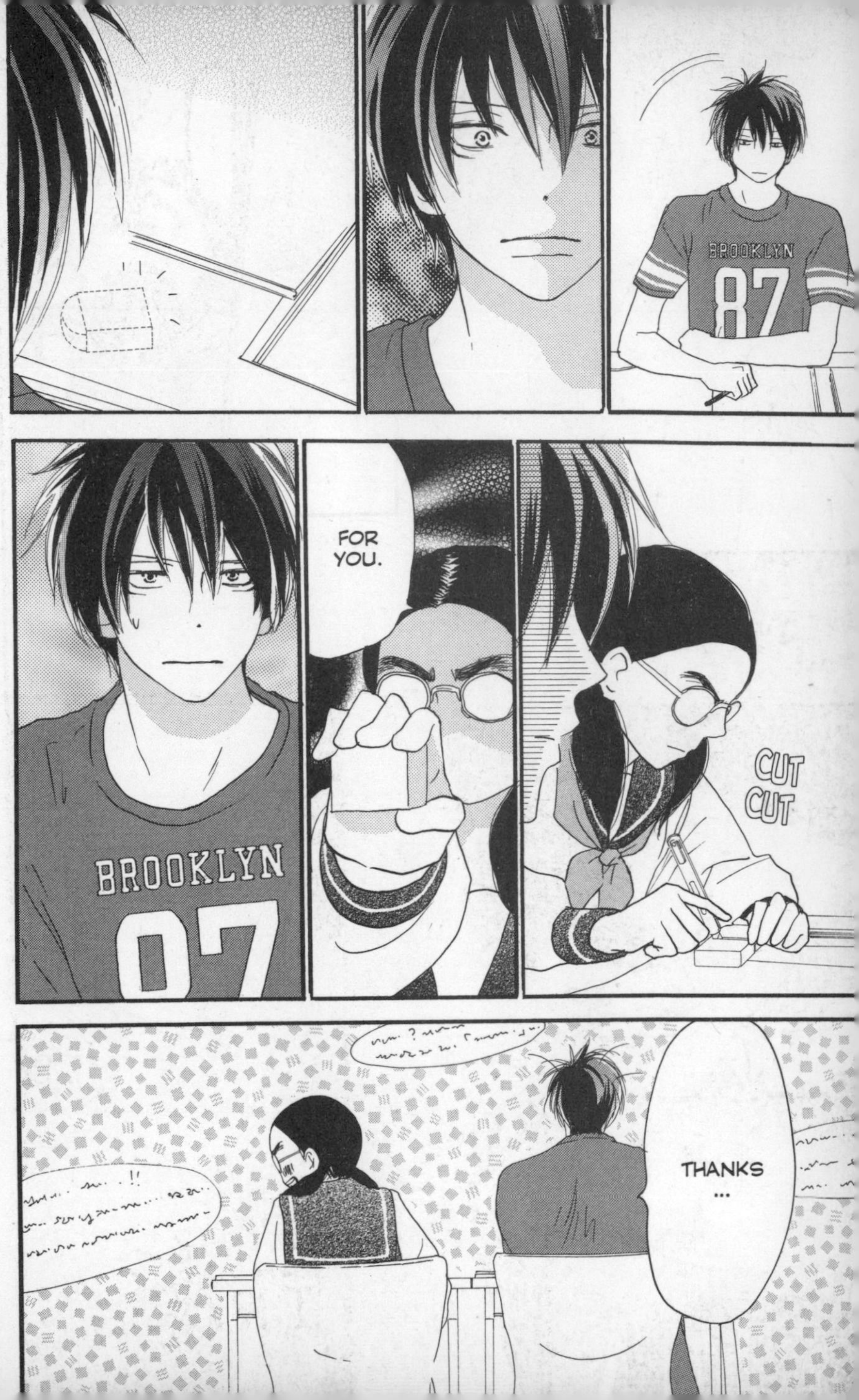
BROOKLYN
87
CUT CUT
FOR YOU.
BROOKLYN
87
THANKS ...

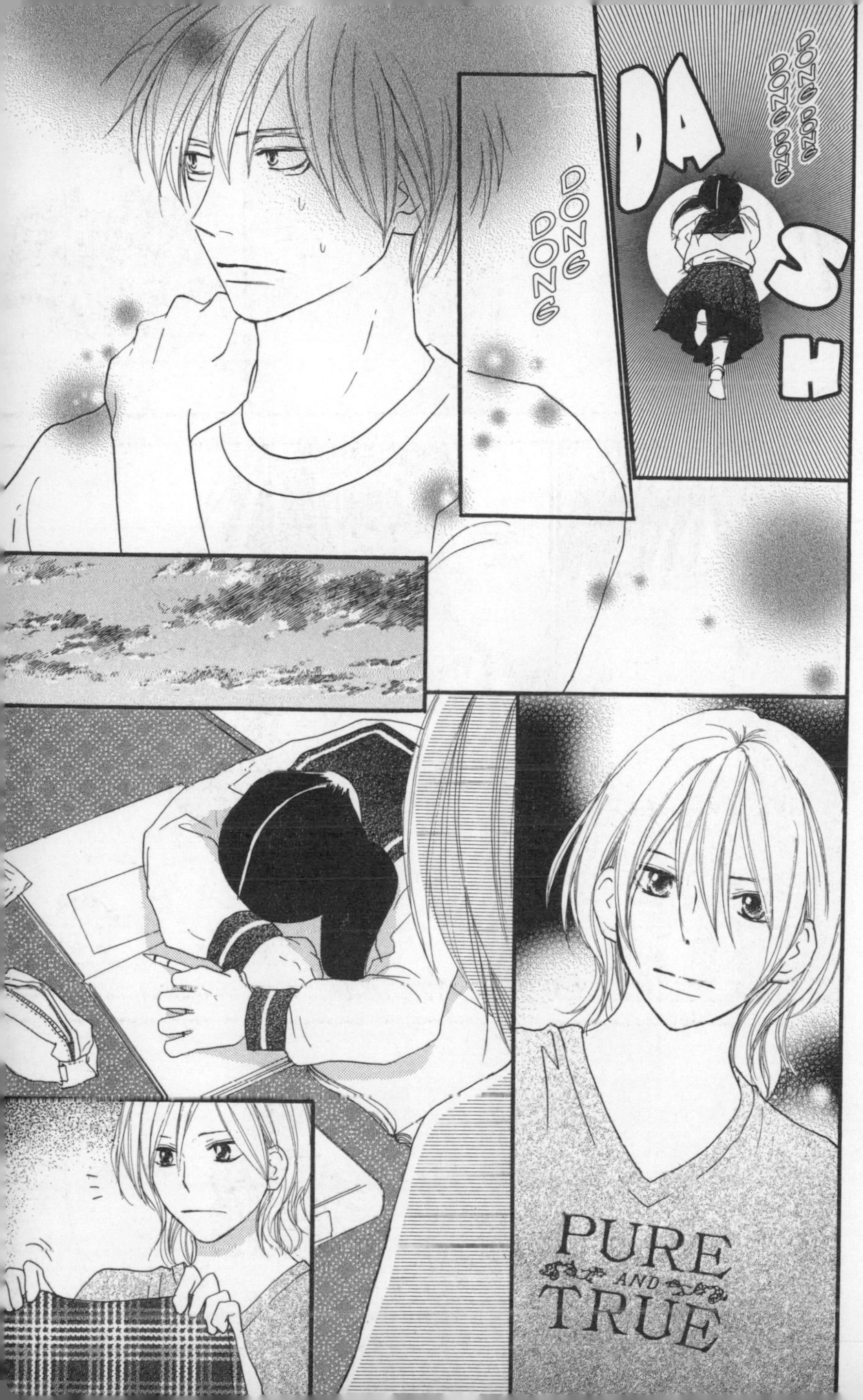
DONG DONG DONG DONG
DASH
DONG DONG DONG
PURE AND TRUE

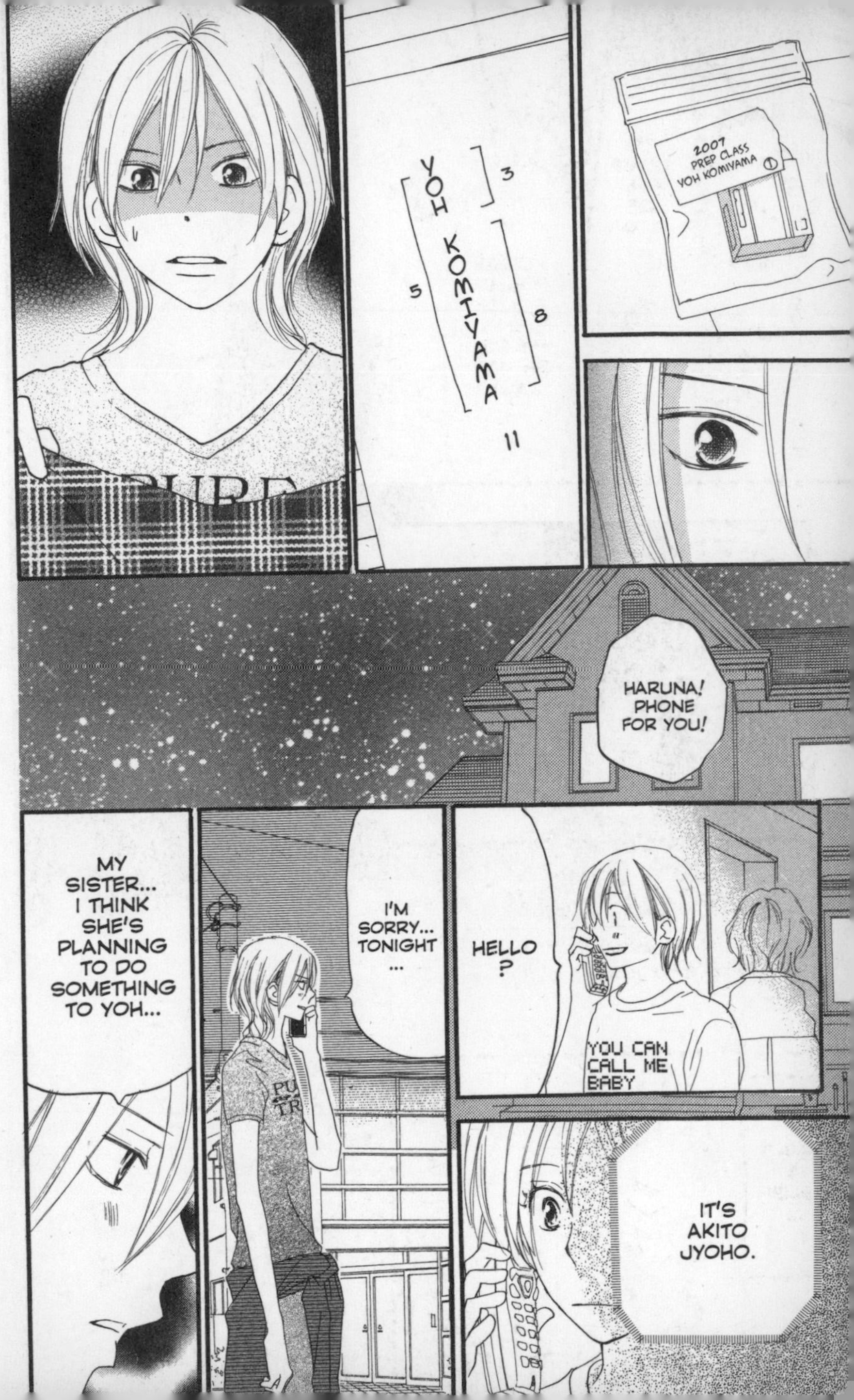
2007
PREP CLASS
YOH KOMIYAMA ①
YOH KOMIYAMA
3 5 8 11
HARUNA! PHONE FOR YOU!
HELLO?
YOU CAN CALL ME BABY
IT'S AKITO JYOHO.
I'M SORRY... TONIGHT ...
MY SISTER... I THINK SHE'S PLANNING TO DO SOMETHING TO YOH...

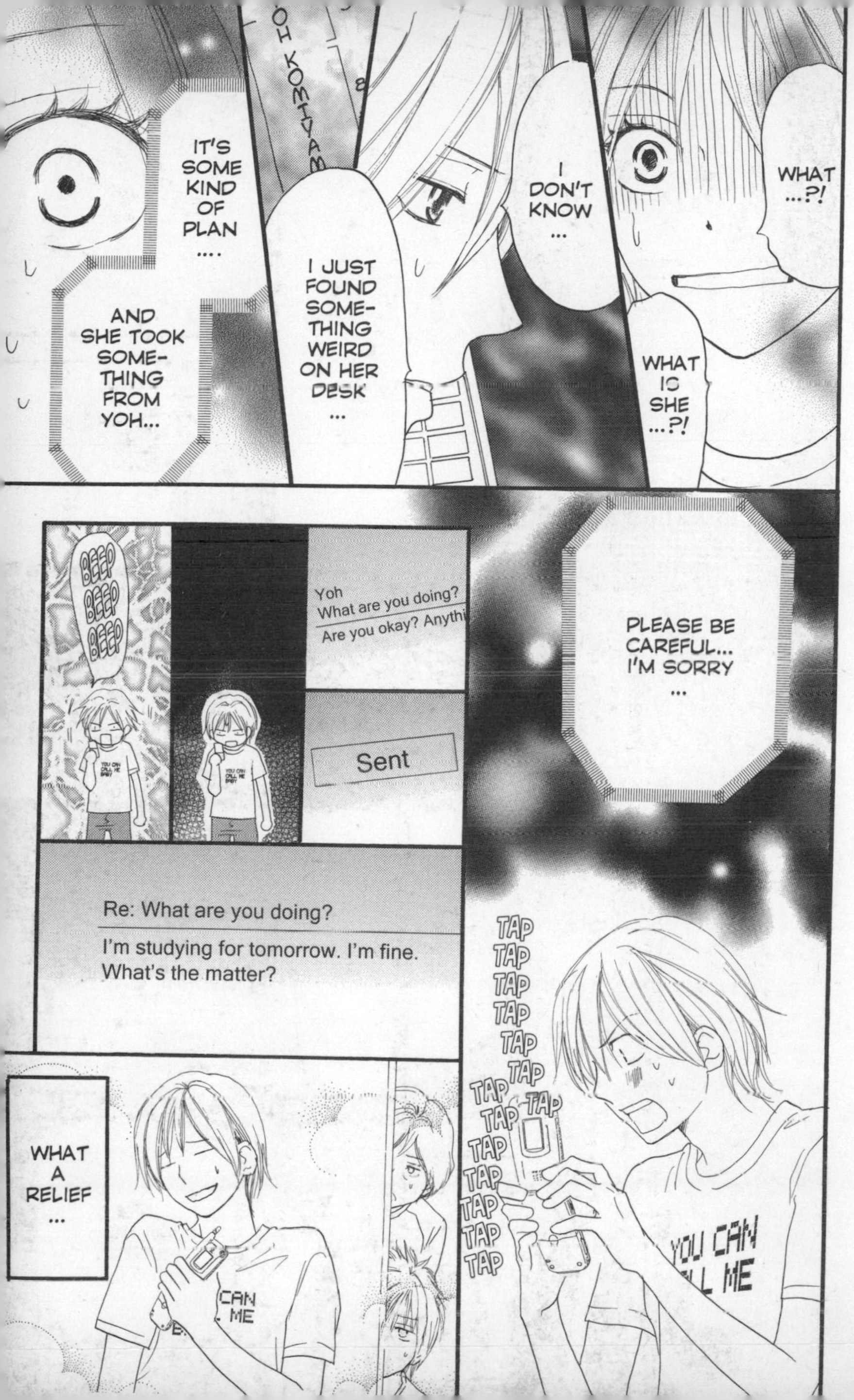
WHAT ...?!
WHAT IS SHE ...?!
I DON'T KNOW ...
I JUST FOUND SOMETHING WEIRD ON HER DESK ...
IT'S SOME KIND OF PLAN ....
AND SHE TOOK SOMETHING FROM YOH...
PLEASE BE CAREFUL... I'M SORRY ...
TAP TAP TAP TAP TAP TAP TAP TAP TAP TAP TAP TAP TAP TAP
Yoh
What are you doing?
Are you okay? Anythi
Sent
BEEP BEEP BEEP
Re: What are you doing?
I'm studying for tomorrow. I'm fine. What's the matter?
WHAT A RELIEF ...

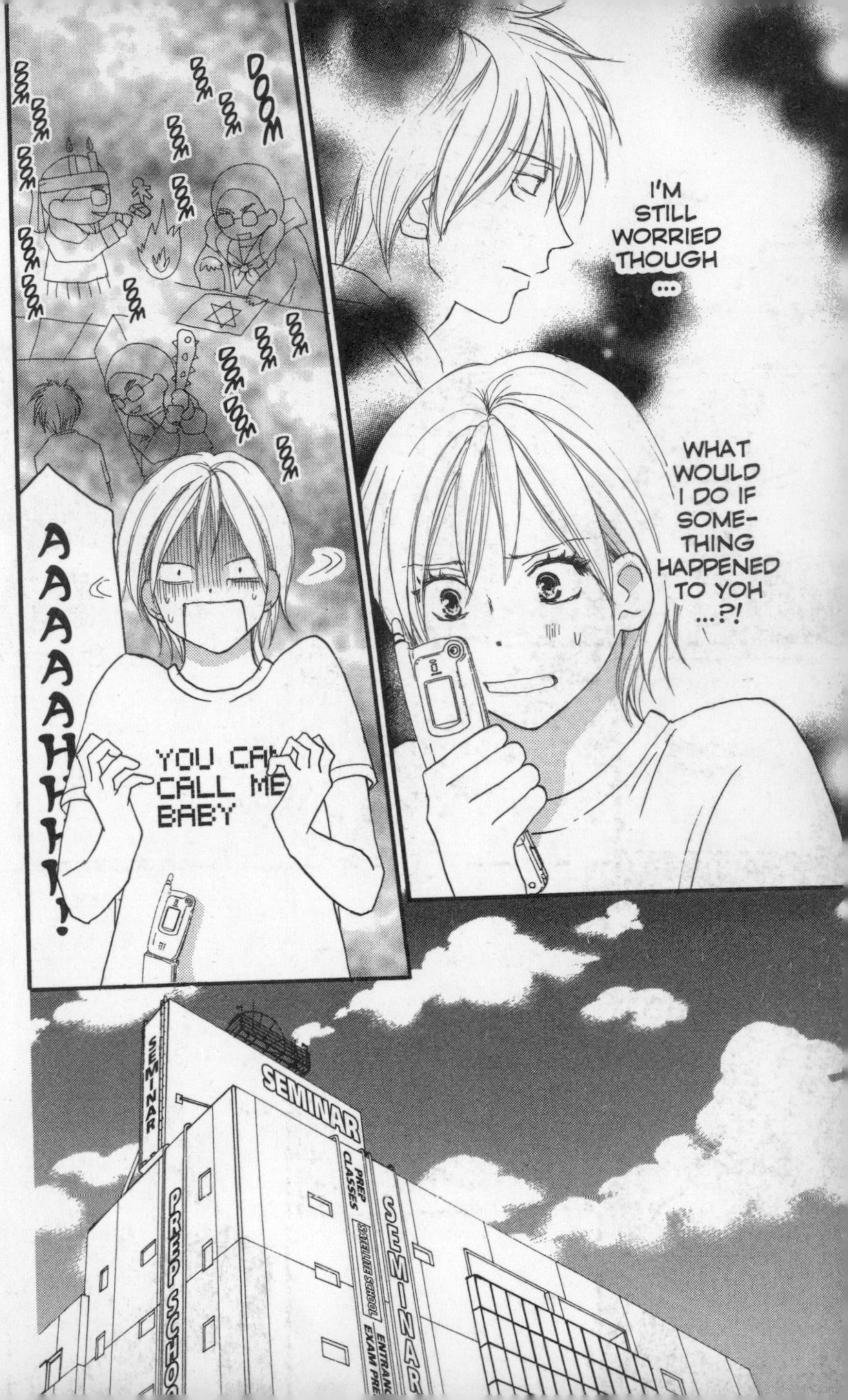
I'M STILL WORRIED THOUGH ...
WHAT WOULD I DO IF SOME-THING HAPPENED TO YOH ...?!
DOOM
AAAAAAHHHH!
CALL ME BABY
SEMINAR
SEMINAR
PREP CLASSES
SATELLITE SCHOOL
SEMINAR

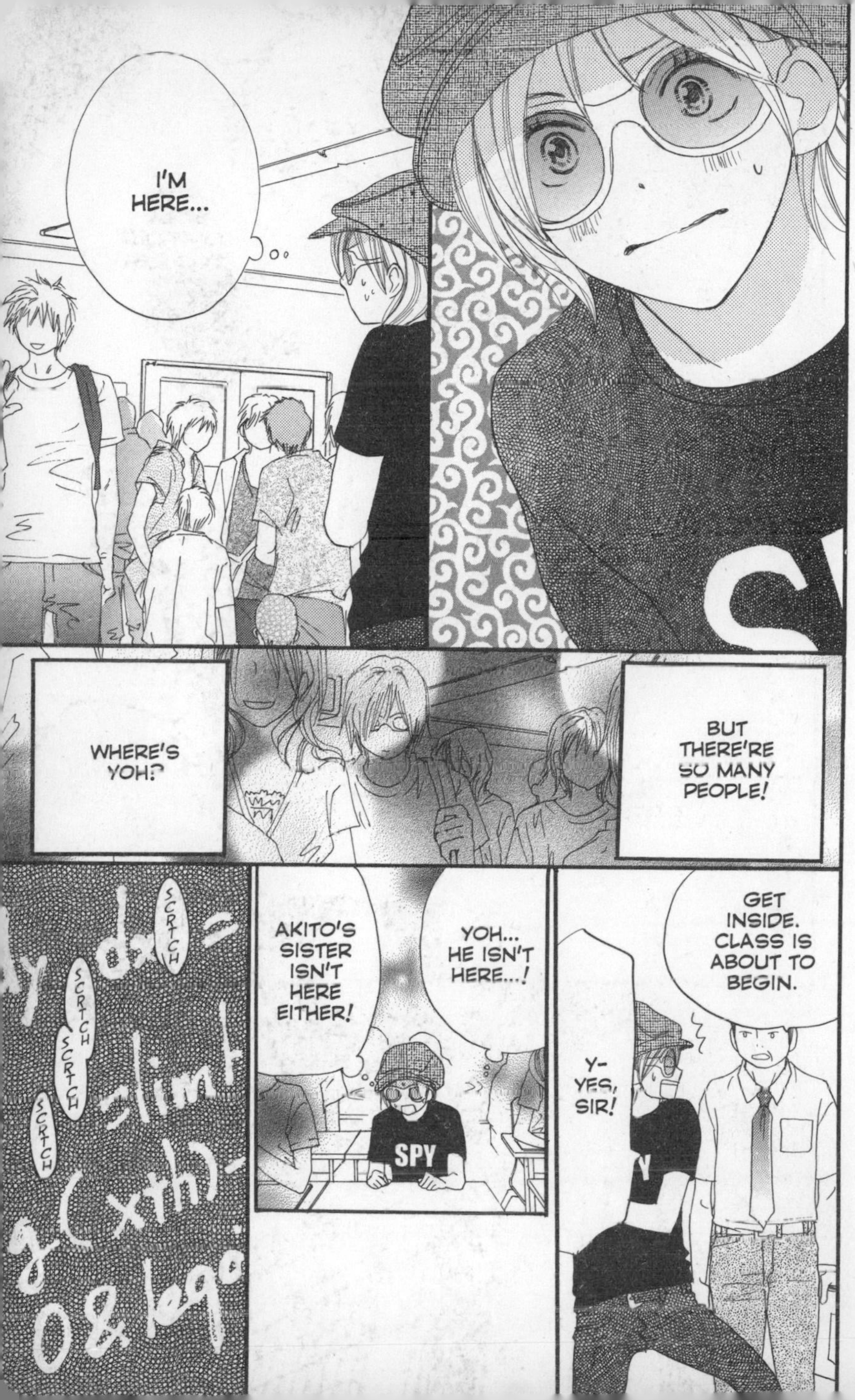
I'M HERE...
BUT THERE'RE SO MANY PEOPLE!
WHERE'S YOH?
GET INSIDE. CLASS IS ABOUT TO BEGIN.
Y-YES, SIR!
YOH... HE ISN'T HERE...!
AKITO'S SISTER ISN'T HERE EITHER!
SPY
SCRTCH
SCRTCH
SCRTCH
SCRTCH

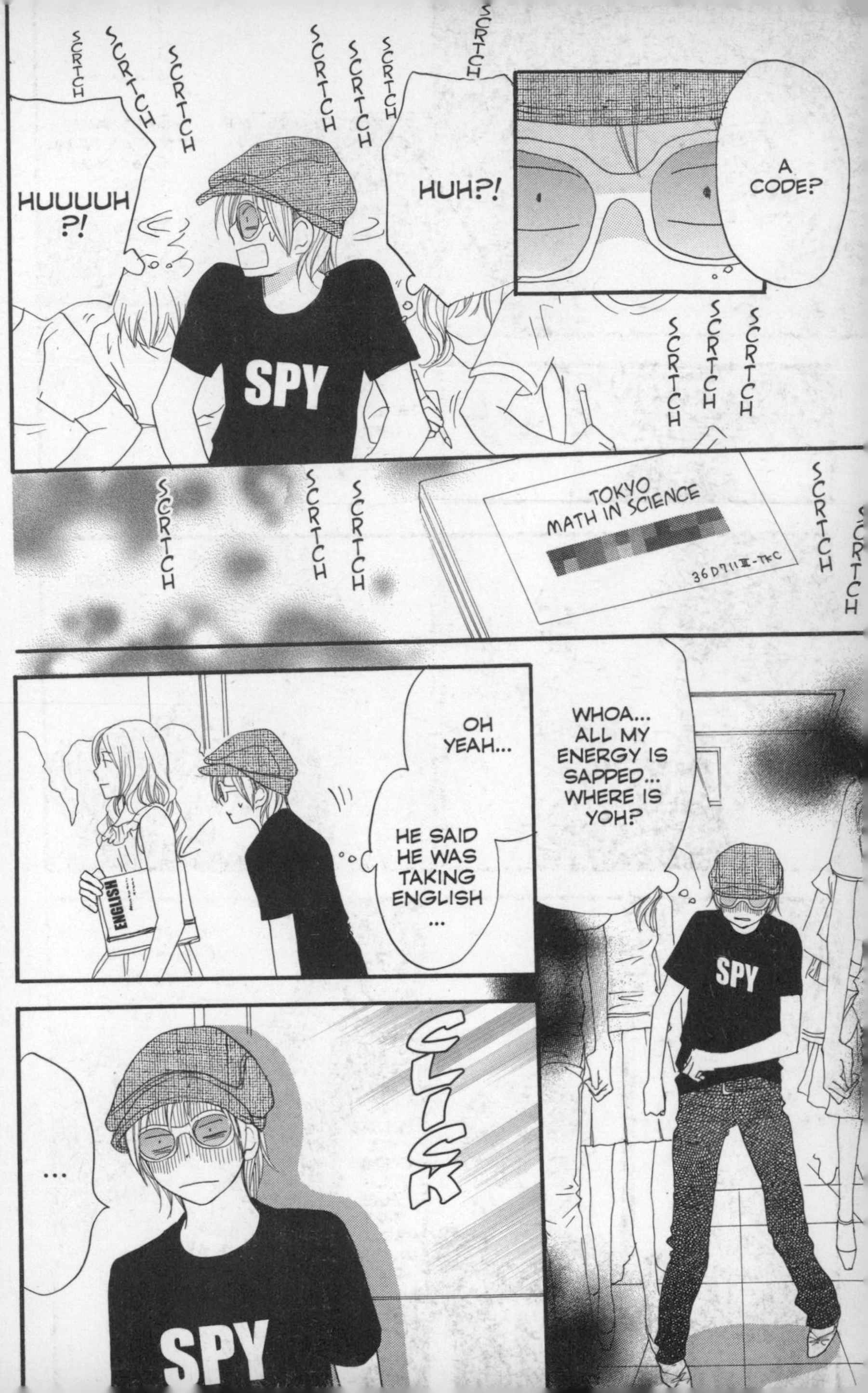
A CODE?
SCRTCH
SCRTCH
SCRTCH
SCRTCH
SCRTCH
SCRTCH
SCRTCH
HUH?!
SPY
SCRTCH
SCRTCH
SCRTCH
HUUUUH ?!
SCRTCH
SCRTCH
TOKYO MATH IN SCIENCE
36D711Ⅲ-TFC
SCRTCH
SCRTCH
SCRTCH
WHOA... ALL MY ENERGY IS SAPPED... WHERE IS YOH?
SPY
OH YEAH...
HE SAID HE WAS TAKING ENGLISH ...
ENGLISH
CLICK
...
SPY

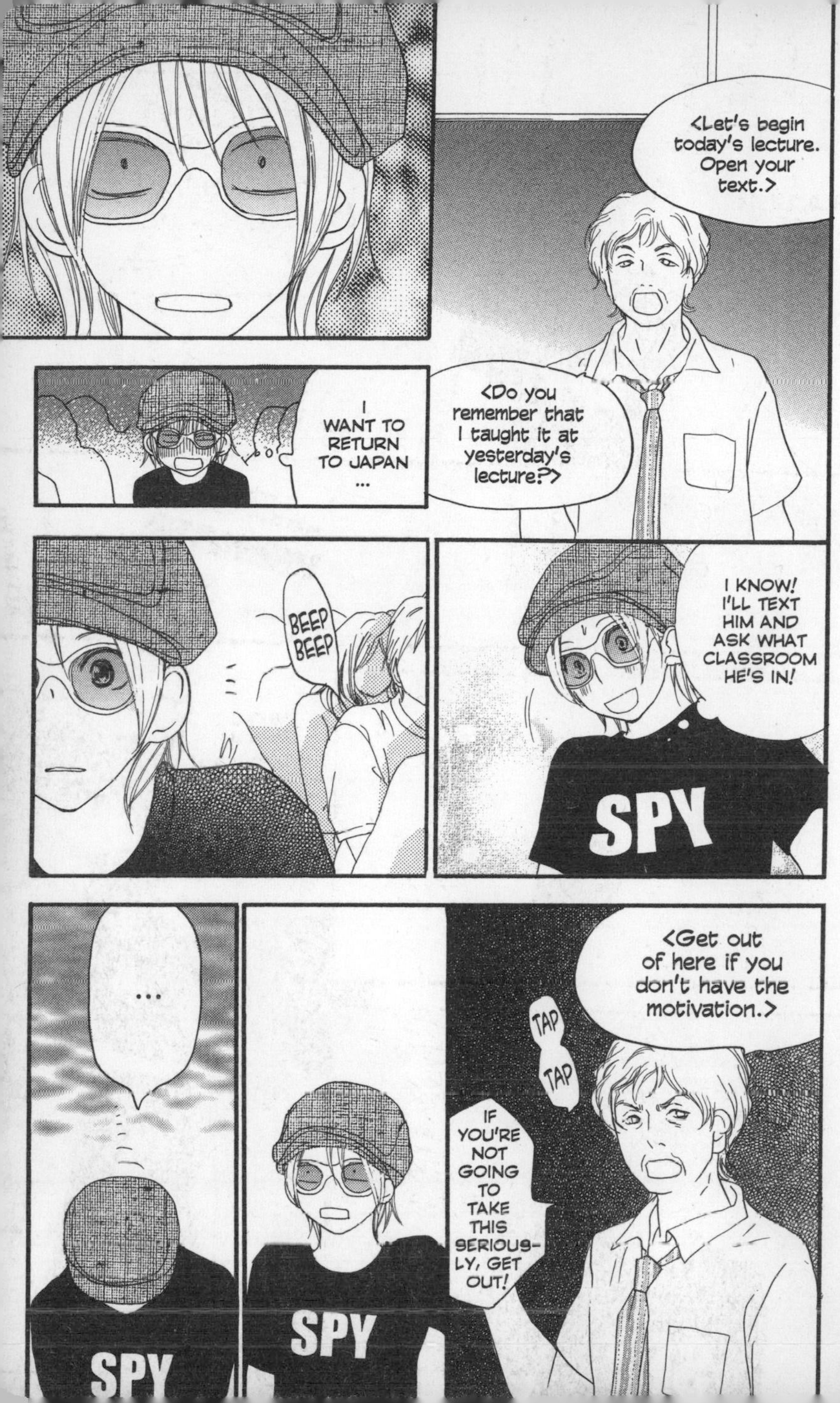
<Let's begin today's lecture. Open your text.>
<Do you remember that I taught it at yesterday's lecture?>
I WANT TO RETURN TO JAPAN ...
I KNOW! I'LL TEXT HIM AND ASK WHAT CLASSROOM HE'S IN!
SPY
BEEP BEEP
<Get out of here if you don't have the motivation.>
TAP
TAP
IF YOU'RE NOT GOING TO TAKE THIS SERIOUS-LY, GET OUT!
SPY
...
SPY

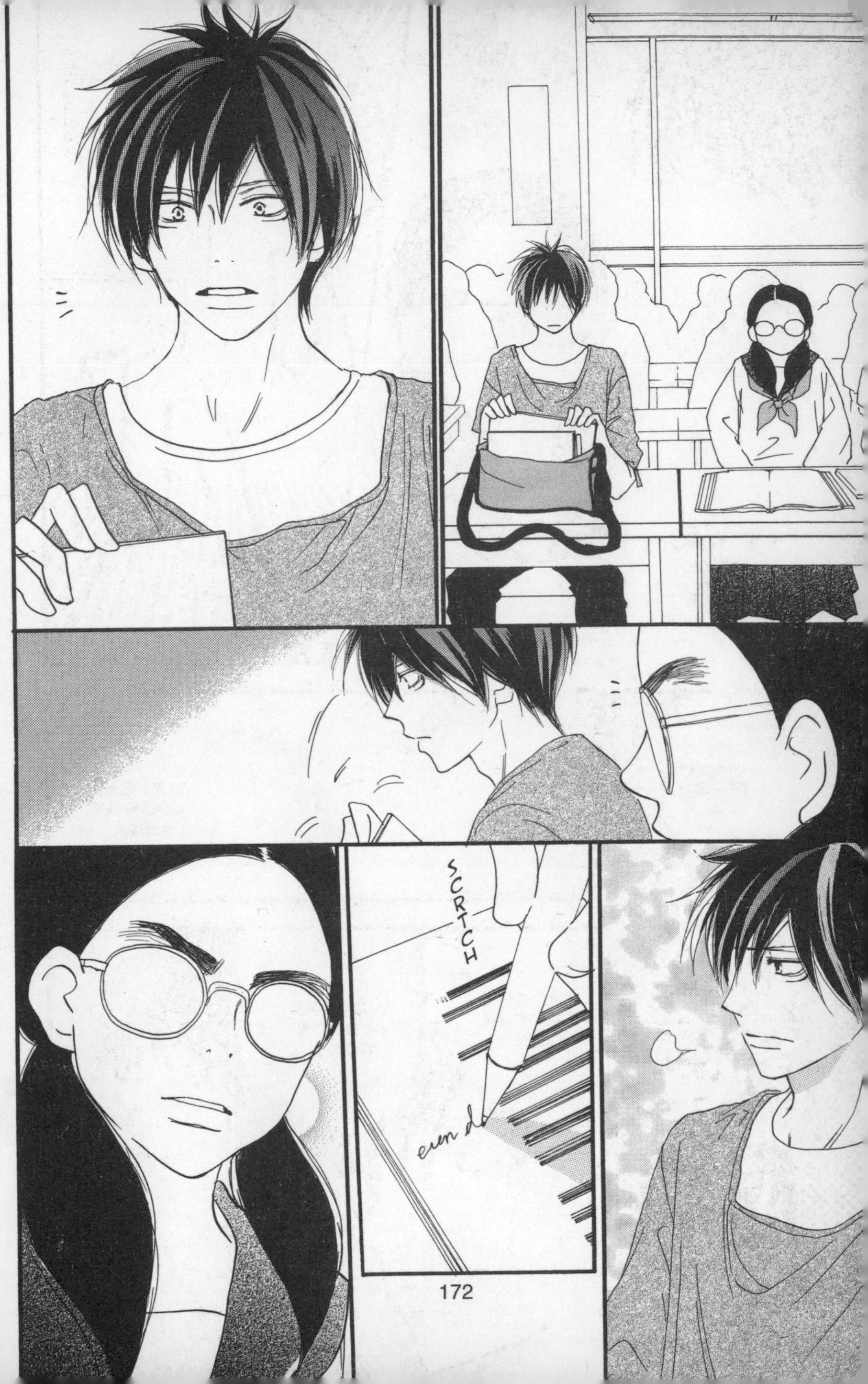
SCRTCH

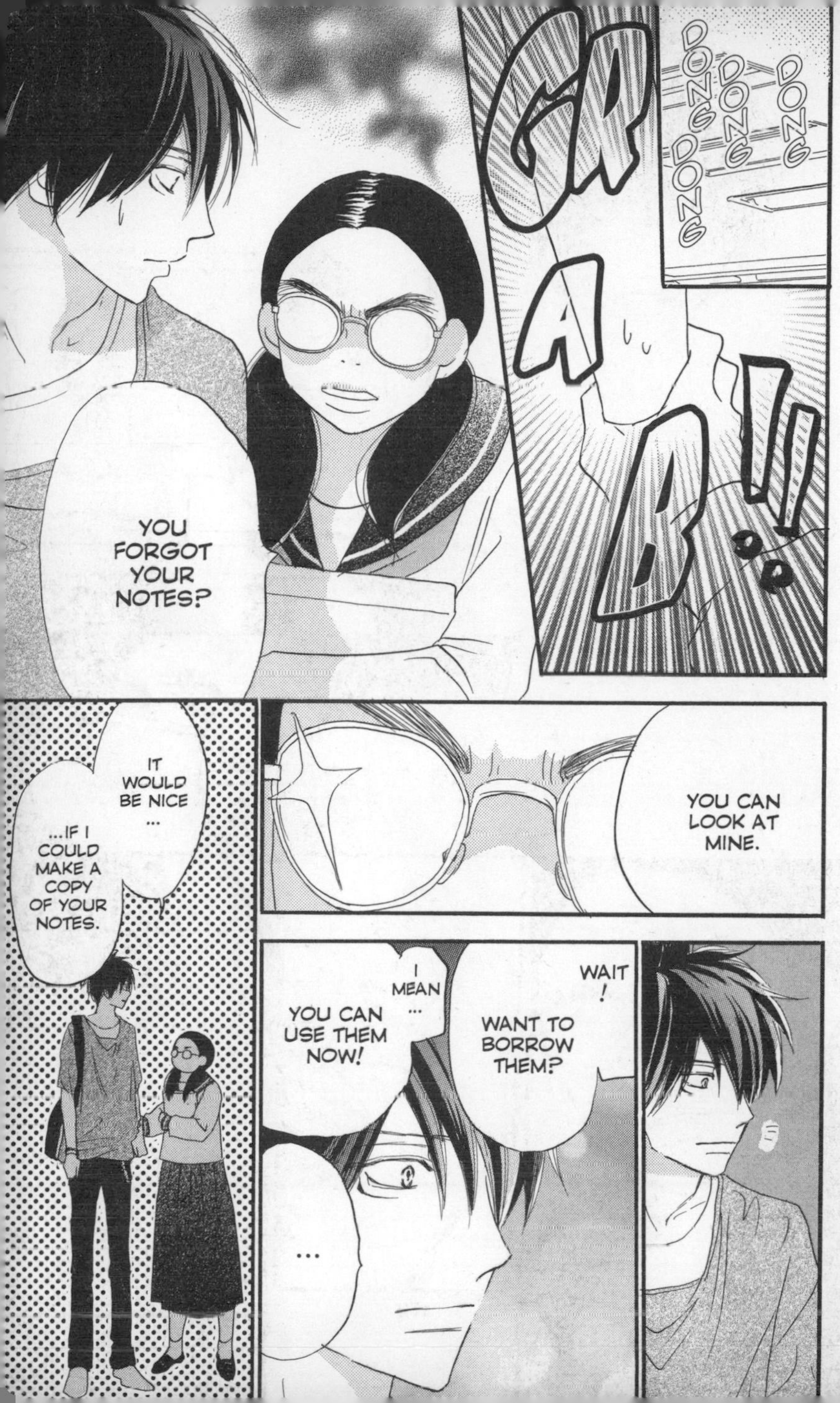
DONG DONG
DONG DONG
DONG DONG
GRAB!!
YOU FORGOT YOUR NOTES?
YOU CAN LOOK AT MINE.
WAIT!
WANT TO BORROW THEM?
I MEAN...
YOU CAN USE THEM NOW!
...
IT WOULD BE NICE...
...IF I COULD MAKE A COPY OF YOUR NOTES.

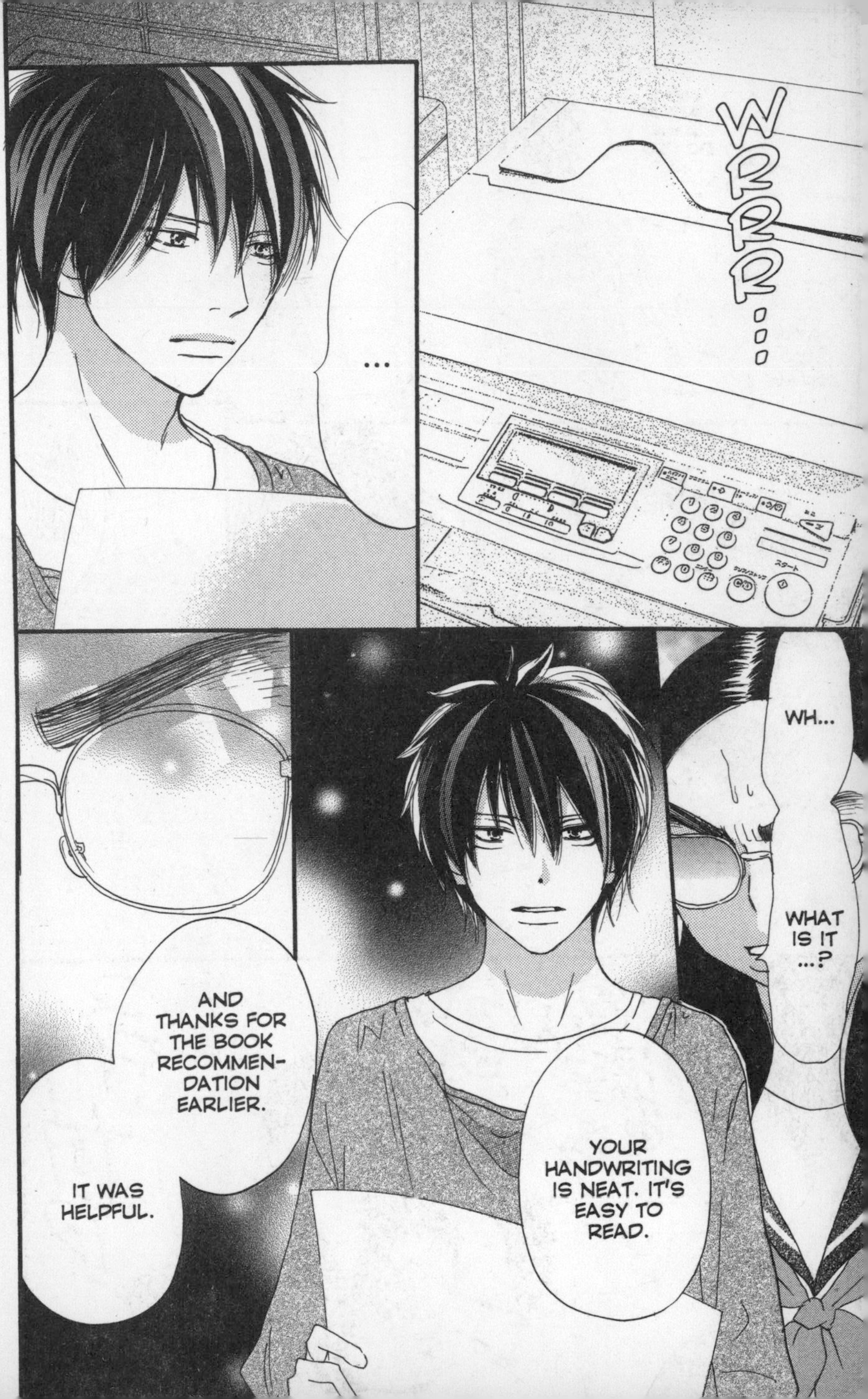
WRRR...
...
WH...
WHAT IS IT ...?
YOUR HANDWRITING IS NEAT. IT'S EASY TO READ.
AND THANKS FOR THE BOOK RECOMMEN-DATION EARLIER.
IT WAS HELPFUL.

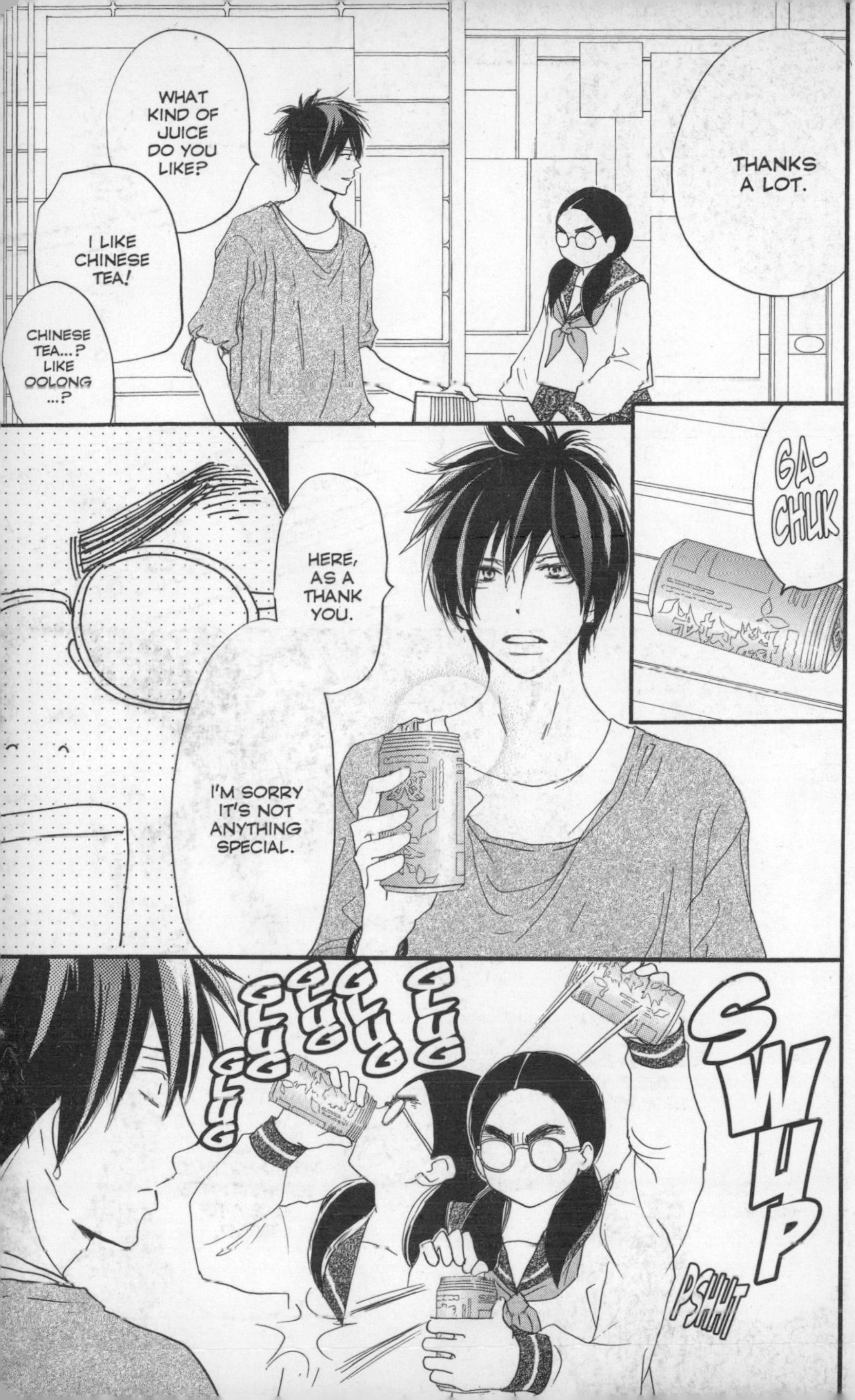
THANKS A LOT.
WHAT KIND OF JUICE DO YOU LIKE?
I LIKE CHINESE TEA!
CHINESE TEA...? LIKE OOLONG ...?
GA-CHUK
HERE, AS A THANK YOU.
I'M SORRY IT'S NOT ANYTHING SPECIAL.
SWUP
PSHHT
GLUG
GLUG
GLUG
GLUG

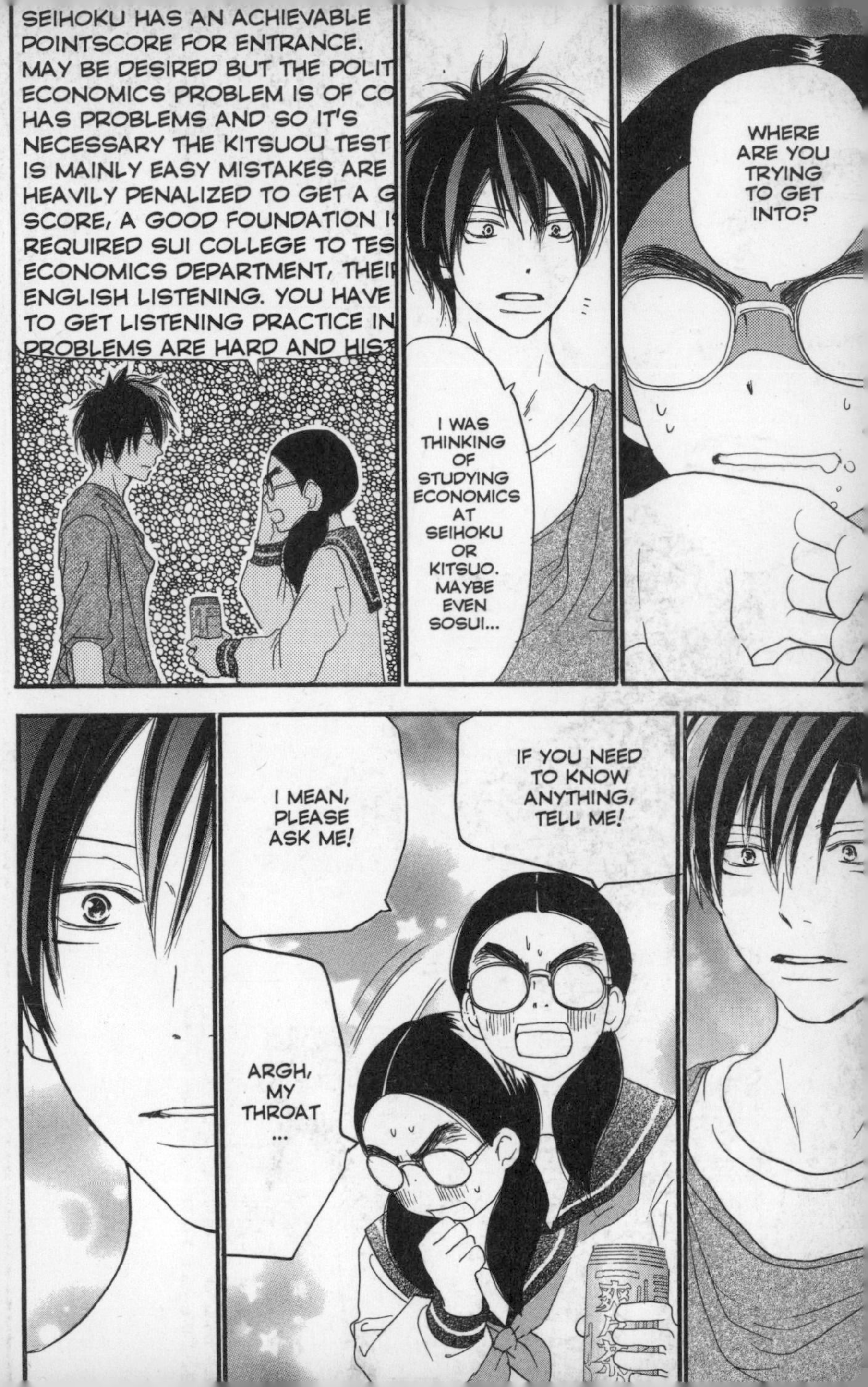
WHERE ARE YOU TRYING TO GET INTO?
I WAS THINKING OF STUDYING ECONOMICS AT SEIHOKU OR KITSUO. MAYBE EVEN SOSUI...
SEIHOKU HAS AN ACHIEVABLE POINTSCORE FOR ENTRANCE. MAY BE DESIRED BUT THE POLIT ECONOMICS PROBLEM IS OF CO HAS PROBLEMS AND SO IT'S NECESSARY THE KITSUOU TEST IS MAINLY EASY MISTAKES ARE HEAVILY PENALIZED TO GET A G SCORE, A GOOD FOUNDATION I REQUIRED SUI COLLEGE TO TES ECONOMICS DEPARTMENT, THEI ENGLISH LISTENING. YOU HAVE TO GET LISTENING PRACTICE IN PROBLEMS ARE HARD AND HIS
IF YOU NEED TO KNOW ANYTHING, TELL ME!
I MEAN, PLEASE ASK ME!
ARGH, MY THROAT ...

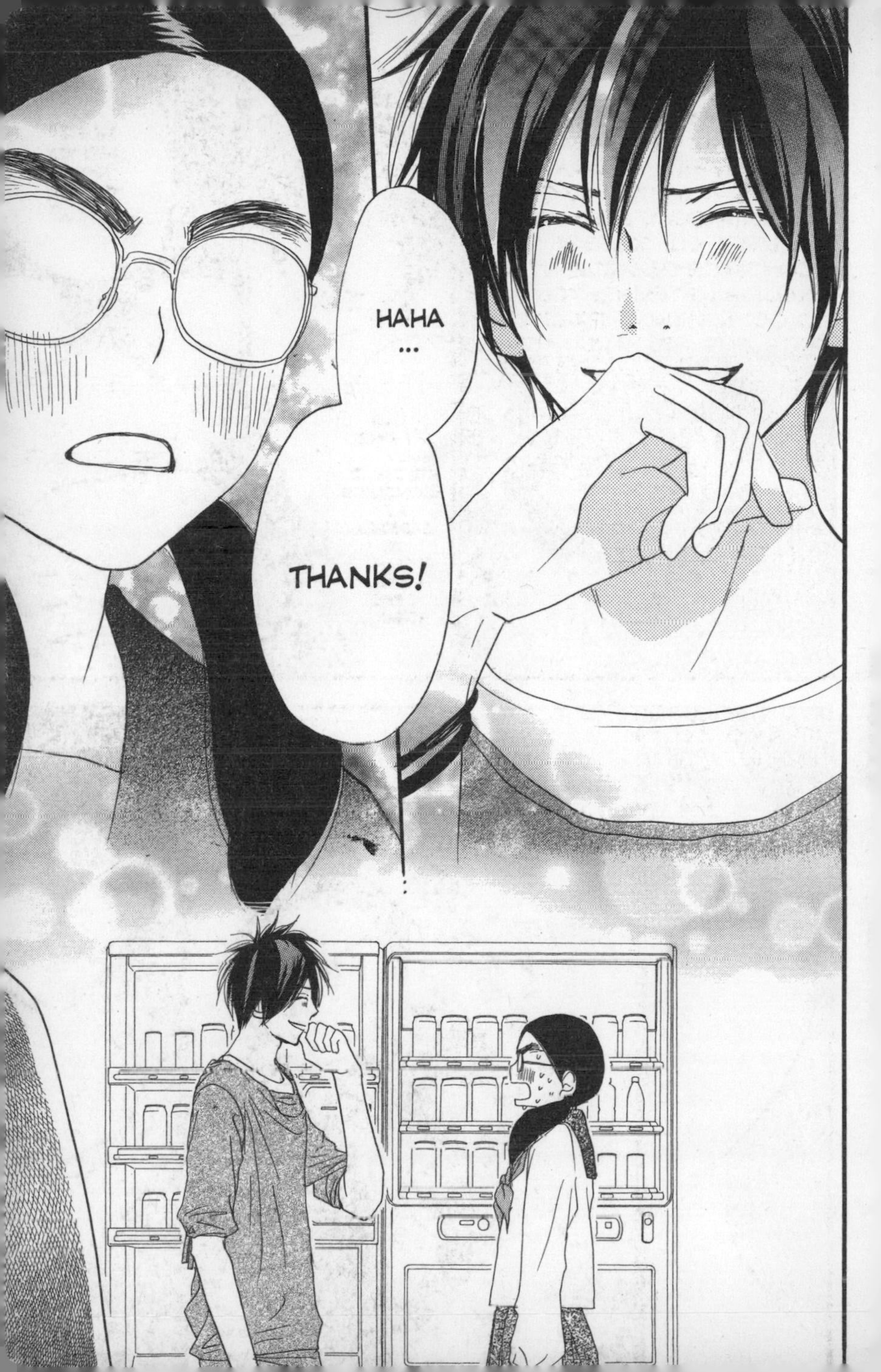
HAHA ... THANKS!

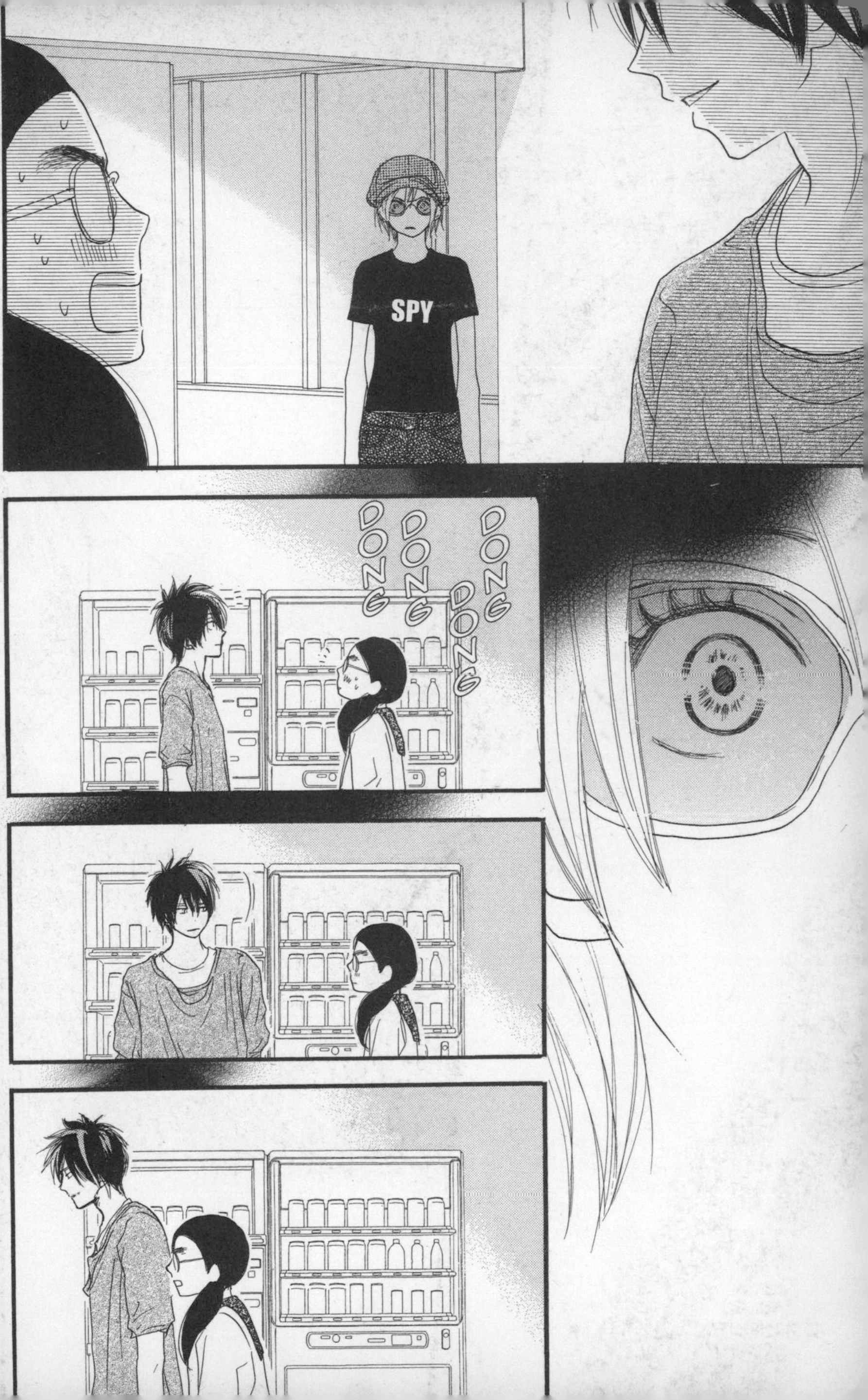
SPY
DONG
DONG
DONG
DONG

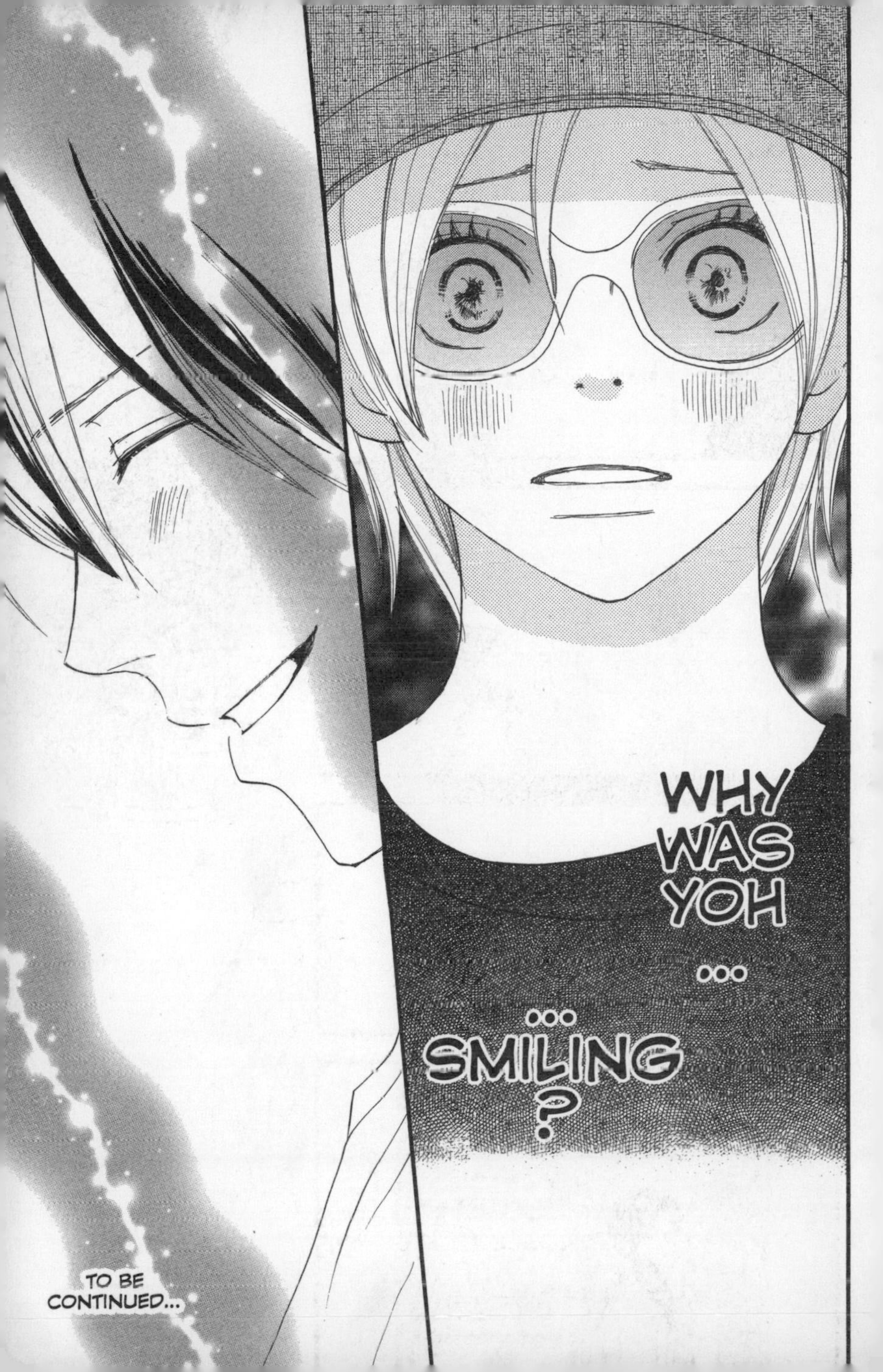
WHY WAS YOH ...
... SMILING ?
TO BE CONTINUED...

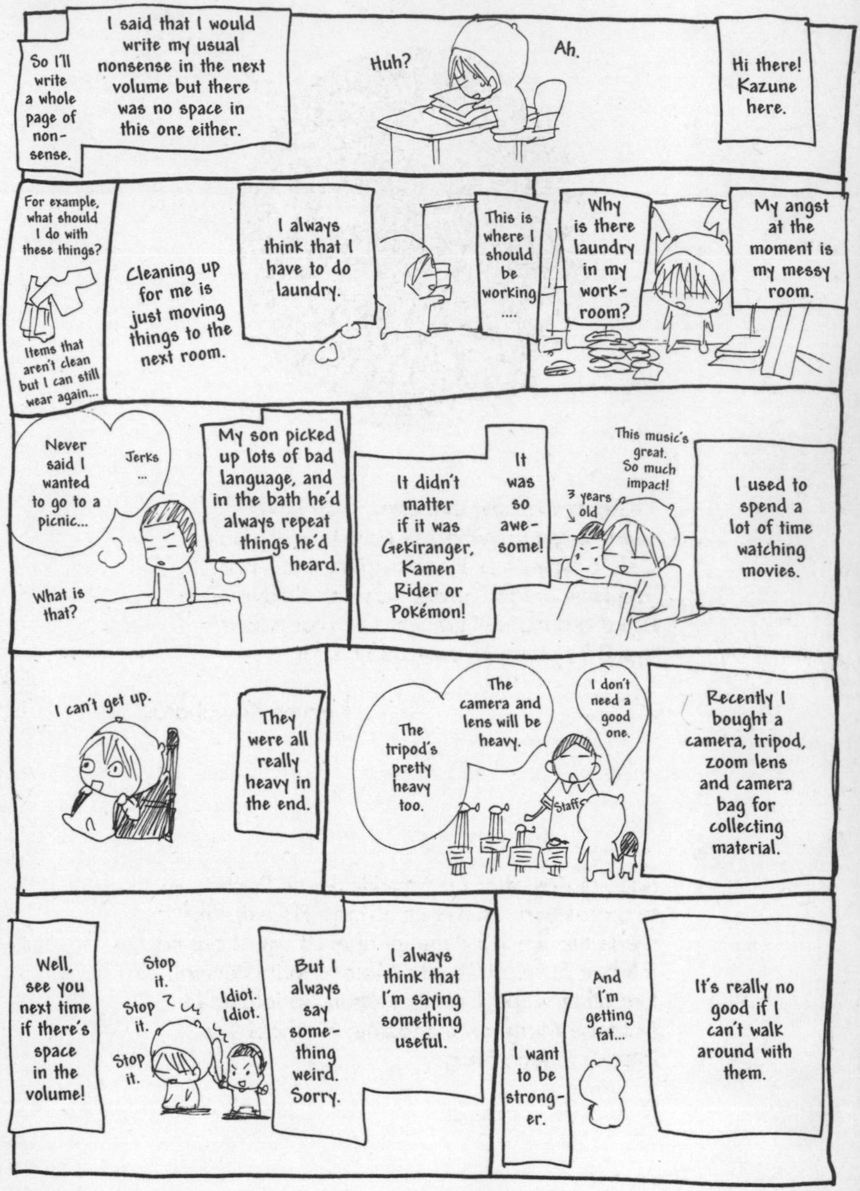
Hi there! Kazune here.
Ah.
Huh?
I said that I would write my usual nonsense in the next volume but there was no space in this one either.
So I'll write a whole page of nonsense.
My angst at the moment is my messy room.
Why is there laundry in my work-room?
This is where I should be working ....
I always think that I have to do laundry.
Cleaning up for me is just moving things to the next room.
For example, what should I do with these things?
Items that aren't clean but I can still wear again...
I used to spend a lot of time watching movies.
This music's great. So much impact!
3 years old
It was so awe-some!
It didn't matter if it was Gekiranger, Kamen Rider or Pokémon!
My son picked up lots of bad language, and in the bath he'd always repeat things he'd heard.
Jerks ...
Never said I wanted to go to a picnic...
What is that?
Recently I bought a camera, tripod, zoom lens and camera bag for collecting material.
I don't need a good one.
Staff
The camera and lens will be heavy.
The tripod's pretty heavy too.
They were all really heavy in the end.
I can't get up.
It's really no good if I can't walk around with them.
And I'm getting fat...
I want to be stronger.
I always think that I'm saying something useful.
But I always say something weird. Sorry.
Idiot. Idiot.
Stop it.
Stop it.
Stop it.
Well, see you next time if there's space in the volume!

I keep trying new exercises, but I never seem to get anywhere. I want to try Turbo Cell [a type of exercise legging that helps you lose weight] next. I was appalled when I realized that 30 percent body fat means that 30 percent of your body is fat.

– Kazune Kawahara

Kazune Kawahara is from Hokkaido Prefecture and was born on March 11th (a Pisces!). She made her manga debut at age 18 with *Kare no Ichiban Sukina Hito* (His Most Favorite Person). Her other works include *Sensei!*, serialized in *Bessatsu Margaret* magazine. Her hobby is interior redecorating.

HIGH SCHOOL DEBUT
VOL. 10
The Shojo Beat Manga Edition

STORY & ART BY
KAZUNE KAWAHARA

Translation & Adaptation/Gemma Collinge
Touch-up Art & Lettering/Rina Mapa
Design/Courtney Utt
Editor/Amy Yu

Editor in Chief, Books/Alvin Lu
Editor in Chief, Magazines/Marc Weidenbaum
VP, Publishing Licensing/Rika Inouye
VP, Sales & Product Marketing/Gonzalo Ferreyra
VP, Creative/Linda Espinosa
Publisher/Hyoe Narita

First published in Japan in 2003 by SHUEISHA Inc., Tokyo.
English translation rights arranged by SHUEISHA Inc.

Printed in Canada

Published by VIZ Media, LLC
P.O. Box 77010
San Francisco, CA 94107

Shojo Beat Manga Edition
10 9 8 7 6 5 4 3 2 1
First printing, July 2009

www.viz.com
store.viz.com